Teaching Elementary Language Arts

Teaching Elementary Language Arts:
A Literature Approach

Betty Coody

Lamar University

David Nelson

Saginaw Valley State University

WAVELAND
PRESS, INC.

Prospect Heights, Illinois

For information about this book, write or call:

Waveland Press, Inc.
P.O. Box 400
Prospect Heights, Illinois 60070
(312) 634-0081

Also by the same authors and available from Waveland Press, Inc.:

SUCCESSFUL ACTIVITIES TO ENRICH THE LANGUAGE ARTS

a guidebook that provides elementary teachers with engaging, cognitively
oriented activities that strengthen and improve language skills

Chapter Opening Credits

To Andrea and Amy

Contents

Preface

WE HAVE WRITTEN THIS BOOK because of our firm belief that books for children can and must become an integral part of the language arts curriculum. The idea is not new. It has been generally supported by language arts and reading teachers for years. As a matter of fact, it would be difficult to find a person who disagrees with the fundamental notion of using children's books to improve language arts skills. To find the theory being practiced in the classroom, however, is not so common, and to locate a textbook outlining the procedure is next to impossible. The purpose of our text is to meet an obvious need in the teaching of communication skills.

We believe that *Teaching Elementary Language Arts: A Literature Approach* will appeal to college instructors concerned about the pressure being exerted on teachers in public and private schools to improve the teaching of language arts skills, to supplement traditional materials, and to individualize instruction. The fundamental concepts in our text are based on the newest information to be found in hundreds of books, journals, and scholarly papers; they reflect the current national trend toward an emphasis on skills.

Instructors who teach language arts methods courses use a variety of strategies, ranging from formally organized plans to field-centered approaches. Our text is flexible enough to be useful with most strategies. We offer structured college classroom activities and present a means of relating to children and understanding them through their literature. Our aim is to enable beginning or experienced teachers to enter any type of classroom (multicultural, bilingual, accelerated) and begin a rich program of language and literature.

In *Teaching Elementary Language Arts* we present a carefully developed theoretical framework for a pragmatic approach to the language arts. The book contains step-by-step procedures for beginning teachers to use in the elementary classroom, but it avoids the "bag of tricks" syndrome. Each activity is based on sound theory, which is fully explained. The book is unique because it features children's literature; nevertheless, it is a complete language arts text. We cover the aspects of listening, speaking, reading, and writing that are featured in more traditional textbooks. Moreover, we emphasize the interrelatedness of the language arts and their natural bond with children's literature.

This textbook is intended to be a teaching aid and reference that will be useful to college students as well as to teachers in the elementary school classroom. We have written simply and clearly for maximum comprehension by students who have had little or no experience with children in the classroom. Concepts are clarified by means of drawings and photographs with explanatory captions. At the end of each chapter, children's books are listed and reviewed and a bibliography is provided to encourage further reading.

A unique feature of each chapter of our text is a profile of a popular children's author. Each profile contains biographical information pre-sented in a format suitable for use with children. We feel that prospective teachers should become familiar not only with children's literature but also with the creators of that literature. In turn, they may lead children to appreciate fine books and to care about the art and skill of writing.

Acknowledgments

We are deeply and forever grateful to the many kind people who helped us in the preparation of this book. Our spouses, H. L. Coody and Carol Nelson, have given unselfish support to our writing project over the past three years, and to them go our sincere thanks. Karen Sanders did an excellent job of typing the manuscript, and Barbara Ellis proved to be a genius in turning our stick figures into beautiful line drawings.

We appreciate the work of Mike Coody and E. R. McIntosh, who took just the right pictures for the book. John Somerfield helped prepare the illustrations for reproduction.

Peggy Flynn and Dan Coody created many of the beautiful bulletin boards used to illustrate certain points in the book, and Kathy Yoder Coody made helpful suggestions for revision as she proofread the first draft.

We wish to express our gratitude for the expertise of Les Sternberg in the development of Chapter 15. His understanding of children with special problems was an inspiration to us, and we tried to reflect it in our writing.

Several people reviewed the text at various stages, and we would especially like to thank them: Mary H. Appleberry, Stephen F. Austin State University; Robin L. Carr, Illinois State University; Margaret L. Hiatt, Western Oregon State College; James E. Kerber, Ohio State University; Dorris Lee, Portland State University; Dianne L. Monson, University of Washington; June DeBode Oxstein, California State University; Leo M. Schell, Kansas State University; Darryl J. Strickler, Indiana University; LaVisa C. Wilson, Auburn University; and Wanna M. Zinsmaster, California State University.

Roger Peterson and Joan Garbutt of Wadsworth Publishing Company were always prompt and professional in giving us the editorial assistance we needed; it was invaluable in helping us meet our deadlines.

Finally, we wish to express our gratitude to the graduate and undergraduate students at Lamar University. They have been encouraging and supportive in every way, and their excellent ideas have been incorporated into each chapter. ¡Gracias!

Teaching Elementary Language Arts

Chapter 1

The Midas Touch: The Language Arts and Children's Literature—An Introduction

The barn was very large. It was very old. It smelled of hay and it smelled of manure. It smelled of the perspiration of tired horses and the wonderful sweet breath of patient cows. It often had a sort of peaceful smell—as though nothing bad could happen ever again in the world. It smelled of grain and of harness dressing and of axle grease and of rubber boots and of new rope. And whenever the cat was given a fish-head to eat, the barn would smell of fish. But mostly it smelled of hay.[1]

ALMOST ANY LANGUAGE ARTS teacher in the elementary school will recognize this image. It was created by E. B. White for *Charlotte's Web,* a book held in affection by every child who has had the good fortune to become acquainted with it. On reading the passage, a rural child, an inner-city child, or a child of the suburbs is able to open the wide doors of a barn and look inside. Imagery of this kind makes a child want to read and want to know *how* to read. Fine library books, both classical and contemporary, are the hidden gold that lightens the task.

Children's literature abounds with characters that readers never forget, plots that help them make some order out of the chaotic events around them, language that stirs the imagination, and themes that are as real as life itself. No resource for teaching the language arts—listening, speaking, reading, and writing—can compare with a collection of excellent library books.

The Language Arts Skills

Listening, speaking, reading, and writing are the heart of the elementary school curriculum. They form the basis for practically all classroom learning activities, both planned and spontaneous. Consequently, the language arts program has a great impact on a school's success in achieving its instructional goals. To communicate with someone is to better understand that person, and

[1]E. B. White, *Charlotte's Web* (New York: Harper & Row, 1952), p. 13.

to help children express their thoughts and feelings effectively is the central goal of learning. It is in this context that the modern elementary school should perceive its role in sequential language arts instruction.

Unlike other subject areas, language arts does not have an inherent content. It provides the means to *encode* language, to translate thought into speech and writing, and to *decode,* to transform language into meaning and thought. The process of encoding draws on the *expressive* language arts skills—speaking and writing. Decoding, on the other hand, draws on the *receptive* skills—reading and listening.

Listening is the fundamental means by which children gain most of their experience with language. Because it occurs first, listening is considered the most basic of the language skills. Ironically, it is one of the most neglected skills of the formal language arts program. Teachers and parents assume that when children start to school they have already learned to listen. It would be just as rational to assume that they have already learned to read and write.

Speaking is said to be the second most necessary language skill for children to learn. But, although children frequently use oral language, speaking is another skill neglected in the language arts program. Many children are taught not to speak but to stay quiet.

Reading, an important component of the formal school curriculum, provides students a key that opens the door to the experience and wisdom of others. Reading is different from listening and speaking in that there is no question about whether it should be taught. Historically, it has taken the lion's share of instructional time.

Writing, the fourth component of the language arts curriculum, provides one of the most satisfying means of communicating with other people. An effective writing program teaches children that writing will enable them to put their thoughts, opinions, and ideas into a permanent form for sharing with others.

THE LANGUAGE ARTS

RECEPTIVE

READING
LISTENING

EXPRESSIVE

SPEAKING
WRITING

The language arts are called the communication skills because they include both the receptive and the expressive means by which people exchange thoughts, ideas, and feelings with other persons. (Courtesy of Sally Nielsen.)

The four language arts skills are closely related. Their interrelatedness might be described in this manner: For every reader there must be a writer and for every writer, a reader; for every speaker there must be a listener and for every listener, a speaker. The link between reading and speaking is obvious—printed matter is merely talk written down, and the manner in which a child talks and listens to the oral language of others is precisely the way that same child attends to reading material. The relationships are infinite. Each of the language arts contributes to and reinforces its counterparts. The force that binds the language arts together is literature.

The Benefits of a Literature-based Program

For at least a quarter of a century, teachers have been urged by educational researchers, college professors of methods courses, writers for pro-

A book becomes a conversation piece even at the nursery school level. (Courtesy of the Beaumont Public Library, Beaumont, Texas.)

fessional journals, inservice consultants, and the children themselves to build their language arts and reading programs around children's books. And why not? Every aim of the language arts curriculum can be accomplished with children's books. Listening improves when stories are told and books are read aloud; oral language is extended as children talk about their feelings and reactions to literature. Children find excellent models for writing in books that have been created by writers of stature. They learn to read by reading "books that will become tattered and grimy from use, not books too handsome to grovel with. Books that will make them weep,

books that will rack them with hearty laughter. Books that absorb them so that they have to be shaken loose from them. Books that they will put under the pillows at night. Books that give them gooseflesh and glimpses of glory."[2]

There is a great deal of evidence that teachers agree with those who advocate a literature-based language arts program. Many elementary classrooms contain library centers, book exhibits, posters and charts that promote reading, scrapbooks of students' book reviews, files of poetry, literature bulletin boards, and other visible evidence of book-sharing experiences. Storytelling and reading aloud are as much a part of the daily routine as writing and spelling lessons. These teachers are informed about the best children's books available, and they recognize dependable authors, illustrators, and poets. They use books that have won Newbery and Caldecott awards to judge the quality of the many newcomers from publishing companies. (See Displays 1.1 and 1.2. Award-winning books are listed in Appendix A and Appendix B.)

A rich program of literature for very young children promotes both facility with language and intellectual curiosity. Listening to someone read aloud is a valuable reading-readiness experience, and it is also reading in the fullest sense of the word: The child studies the pictures and follows the story line as the adult unlocks the printed symbols. Both are engrossed in the reading process. From such enjoyable experiences with literature emerges a natural and lasting interest in books and their message.

Practically speaking, school-age children who have grown up with books know how to hold a book, turn its pages, and read from left to right and from top to bottom. They sense the relationship between text and pictures. They are able to point out details in illustrations, repeat a rhythmic refrain, and recognize the sequential devel-

[2]Robert Lawson, "The Caldecott Medal Acceptance," *Horn Book Magazine* (August 1941), p. 284.

Independent reading in a relaxed environment refines and extends language skills. (Courtesy of Belinda Burns, Dick Dowling Elementary School, Port Arthur, Texas.)

opment of a story. In essence, such children are ready to read and will enter the formal reading program with confidence. Their primary and intermediate teachers will build upon and extend their previous experiences with literature as sequential language arts skills are being taught.

Our premise in this book is that the language arts—listening, speaking, reading, and writing—are irrevocably linked by literature. They cannot be separated, nor should they be. Together they form a holistic framework in which there is a functional relationship among the four parts. As children read books, they should be writing some of their own. Good readers are always

keenly aware of an author's style of writing and are influenced by it. As they participate in structured speaking activities, effective listening becomes a concomitant value. The kinship goes on and on.

Barre Toelken tells in his folklore book a story that could be directed at teachers who attempt to divide the language arts: Black Elk explains the Sun Dance to onlookers. The sun dancer is pierced above both breasts and is attached to the center cottonwood tree by what appears to be two rawhide thongs. Black Elk points out, however, that only one thong is looped around the center tree, a symbol of unity

Display 1.1 The Newbery Award

The Newbery Medal. Used by permission.

Each year the Newbery Medal is awarded to the author of the most distinguished contribution to American literature for children published in the United States during the preceding year. (A certain number of Honor Books, formerly called Runners-up, are also named.) The award was established in 1921 by Frederick G. Melcher, editor of *Publishers Weekly* and president of the publishing house of R. R. Bowker. The first medal was awarded to Hendrik Willem Van Loon for *The Story of Mankind.*

In 1921, Melcher commissioned René Paul Chambellan, a French sculptor well known for his low-relief sculpture in Rockefeller Center, to design the Newbery Medal. One side of the handsome medal, struck in bronze, shows an adult flanked by two children. The scene represents a writer sharing creative talent with children. The other side of the medal shows an open book inscribed with the words "For the most distinguished contribution to American literature for children."

The award was named for John Newbery,

an eighteenth-century English bookseller and publisher who wrote and published books for children. He featured children's books prominently in his bookstore at a time when other booksellers were concentrating solely on books for adults. The purpose of the award, in Melcher's words, is "To encourage original and creative work in the field of books for children. To emphasize to the public that contributions to the literature for children deserve recognition as do poetry, plays, or novels. To give to those librarians who make it their life work to serve children's reading interests an opportunity to encourage good writing in this field."

The Association for Library Service to Children, a division of the American Library Association, sponsors the Newbery Award, and *Horn Book Magazine* publishes in its August issue the author's acceptance speech, which is delivered at an award banquet. In the speech, authors usually tell how they feel about their work. A replica of the Newbery Medal is attached to the jacket of winning books.

Display 1.2 The Caldecott Award

The Caldecott Medal. Used by permission.

Each year the Caldecott Medal is awarded to the artist of the most distinguished American picture book for children published in the United States during the preceding year. A "picture book for children" is defined as one that provides the children with an essentially visual experience. In a picture book, the unity of the story, theme, or concept emerges from a series of pictures rather than from any printed text. There are no limitations on the character of the picture book except that the illustrations be original work.

The Caldecott Award is named for Randolph Caldecott, a nineteenth-century illustrator who is said to be the first artist to draw pictures from a child's point of view when illustrating his books for children. The award was established in 1938 by Frederick Melcher, and the first medal was awarded to Dorothy Lathrop for *Animals of the Bible.*

In making arrangements for the Caldecott Medal, once again Melcher turned to René Paul Chambellan for the design. To help the sculptor understand the spirit of Caldecott's art, Melcher gave him a collection of Caldecott's books. Chambellan was so delighted by Caldecott's draftsmanship that he said he could do nothing better than put some typical scenes from the books on the medal. The face of the bronze medal shows John Gilpin taking his famous ride, accompanied by scattering geese and barking dogs. The other side pictures the pie with four-and-twenty blackbirds being set before the king.

Like the Newbery Award, the Caldecott Award is sponsored by the Association for Library Service to Children. The artist's acceptance speech is published in the August issue of *Horn Book Magazine.* Prior to 1980, a single Newbery-Caldecott committee determined the winners of both awards at the midwinter conference of the American Library Association. Since 1980 there have been two committees of fifteen members each, one for each medal.

within seeming diversity. "It is only the ignorant man," he says, "who sees the many where there is only the one."[3]

To exclude literature from the language arts program is to create a program that deprives children of their right to improve their language arts skills in the most honest and enjoyable way. As Figure 1.1 shows, the study of a single book can be the basis of many activities and experiences that help students with their listening, speaking, reading, and writing. In subsequent chapters, we will examine many of them in detail.

An Overview of This Book

The chapters of this book are related to each other, just as the language arts are interrelated, but each one may be read as a separate entity. In the summaries that follow, we will briefly survey the book's contents. Before we begin, however, we must call attention to an important feature in each chapter.

Proponents of the language arts program with a strong emphasis on literature suggest units of study not only on the literature itself, but also on creators of literature. To meet those recommendations, we have included an *author profile* as a focal point of each chapter. We have given in the profiles the kinds of information that a language arts teacher might find helpful in introducing children to authors, artists, and poets. E. B. White is the focus author for Chapter 1.

At the end of each chapter, in "Best Books for Children," many of the focus author's works, as well as related books by other authors, are briefly reviewed. It is our belief that teachers should become familiar, not only with children's literature, but also with the creators of that literature. In turn, they may lead children to appreciate fine

[3]Barre Toelken, *The Dynamics of Folklore* (Boston: Houghton Mifflin, 1979), p. 43.

books and to care about the art and skill of writing. For the teacher's convenience, each book is labeled according to its approximate grade level.

Chapter 2: A Look at the Language Arts Unit Plan

Every beginning language arts teacher faces the task of learning how to develop and evaluate instructional units. In this chapter we will present a format for a unit plan (based on the Little House books by Laura Ingalls Wilder), and we will describe the factors to be considered by a teacher interested in putting one together. Teachers may use children's books to great advantage when developing units and plans. They provide the constant needed to lessen the harmful effects of the modern curriculum, which tends to be fragmented and compartmentalized. Some books are especially well suited for in-depth study and may become the focal point of an instructional unit or module.

The habit of evaluating learning experiences and activities, in both formal and informal ways, is another professional skill to be mastered by the language arts teacher. Self-evaluation is the key to improving teaching practices, behavior, and attitudes. Children also benefit from recording and analyzing their own progress in communication skills. We will explain how they may be encouraged to do so on a routine basis.

The focus author for this chapter is Laura Ingalls Wilder.

Chapter 3: Personalizing the Language Arts Program

Many girls and boys fail to reach optimum efficiency in reading and writing skills because the teaching of those skills has not been personalized or tailored to their individual needs. As a result,

A CORRELATED LANGUAGE-LITERATURE PLAN

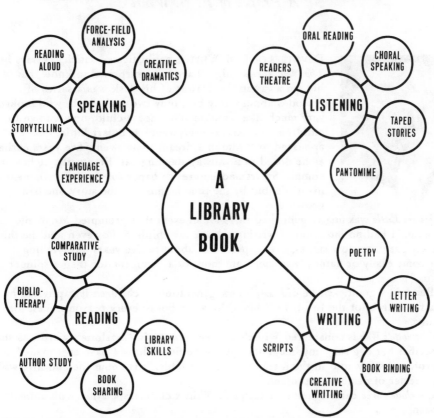

Figure 1.1 *A Correlated Language-Literature Plan. (Courtesy of Peggy Flynn.)*

the student is unable to see the usefulness of language arts skills and their bearing on everyday life. Guides and instruments have been developed to help the teacher determine how much or how little individualization is taking place in the classroom. In this chapter we will describe the elements common to any personalized language arts program, and then we will discuss the requisites of an individualized reading plan.

A personalized reading program in the classroom depends on a collection of library books, time for students to browse and choose books, a system of record keeping, and a program of student-teacher conferences. The success of an individualized language arts program depends on efficient organization and management. It calls for cooperation among teachers, librarians, administrators, and parents.

The focus author for this chapter is Marguerite Henry.

Chapter 4: Improving Listening and Nonverbal Communication Skills

Listening as a skill has been neglected, for the most part, in teachers' manuals, curriculum guides, and preparatory courses. Nevertheless,

A Profile of E. B. White

DEVOTEES OF E. B. WHITE'S sophisticated satirical essays in *The New Yorker* might have been surprised to know that hidden away in the drawer of his desk was a series of episodes about a tiny boy, only two inches tall, who looked very much like a mouse. The mouse-child, now known to children and parents everywhere as Stuart Little, had appeared to White in a dream some twenty-five years earlier as he dozed in a railway sleeping car. Eventually, he began to commit Stuart's adventures to paper for the entertainment of his niece, but by the time he finished the story, she had grown up.

Stuart Little was finally published in 1945, an event that prompted Mr. White to explain: "I had no intention of writing a book for children, however, and the thing merely grew, by slow stages, over a period of about twelve years. Storytelling does not come easily or naturally to me; I am more of a commentator than a spinner of yarns."[1]

But spin a good yarn he did. Each new generation of children is captivated by Stuart's search for the lovely bird Margalo, a symbol of every person's quest for beauty.

Charlotte's Web is considered White's masterpiece, or in Charlotte's words, as she describes her egg sac, "my 'magnum opus'—the finest thing I have ever made." It is a profound story, told in the form of an animal fable. It is about life and love with the specter of death ever present.

Charlotte's Web came about as a result of White's close association with animals in a barn:

> The barn with its creatures and its swallows, has always been a place where I have felt at peace, and I deliberately tried to bring it to life in a story for youngsters. Many of the characters are taken right from life, including the pig and the spider. The tragedy of animal death by murder, which always haunts a farm, haunted me and I guess I was trying to write my way out of the dilemma in the story of Charlotte, and with her able assistance.[2]

Due to the enormous popularity of his books, E. B. White receives from children many more letters than he can answer personally. In a printed letter mailed by his publisher, he attempts to answer the questions asked most frequently by young readers: How old were you when you started writing? What made you want to write? Are your stories true?

"I started writing early," White tells the children, "as soon as I could spell. In fact I can't remember any time in my life when I wasn't busy writing and I see no relief in sight." As to why he wanted to become a writer, White explains:

> I don't know what caused me to do it, or why I enjoyed it, but I think children often find pleasure and satisfaction in trying to set their thoughts down on paper, either in words or

E. B. White photo courtesy of Donald E. Johnson.
[1]Muriel Fuller, ed., *More Junior Authors* (New York: H. W. Wilson, 1963), pp. 225–226.
[2]Ibid.

in pictures. I was no good at drawing, so I used words instead. As I grew older, I found that writing can be a way of earning a living.[3]

White earns a living by writing poems, essays, and editorials for *The New Yorker.* He joined the magazine's staff more than fifty years ago, when it was still in its infancy. He is also the author of eighteen books of prose and poetry. He edited and amplified William Strunk's *The Elements of Style,* a manual well known to high school and college English students.

In reply to the question "Are your stories true?" White reminds children that in real life a child does not look like a mouse, a spider does not spin words in a web, and a swan does not blow a trumpet. "But," he points out, "real life is only one kind of life—there is also the life of the imagination. And although my stories are imaginary, I like to think that there is some truth in them, too—truth about the way people and animals feel and think and act."

A bit of conversation in *The Trumpet of the Swan* shows White's genius for portraying animal behavior that mirrors typical human behavior. One evening the mother swan reveals to her cob that one of their cygnets has never uttered a sound. The cob replies:

Goodness! What are you getting at? Do you wish me to believe that I have a son who is *defective* in any way? Such a revelation would distress me greatly. I want everything to go smoothly in my family life so that I can glide gracefully and serenely, now in the prime of my life, without being haunted by worry and disappointment. Fatherhood is quite a burden, at best. I do not want the added strain of having a defective child, a child that has something the matter with him.[4]

Though well past the conventional age for retirement, E. B. White continues to write as he always has done. He was born in Mt. Vernon, New York, on July 11, 1899, and attended both grade school and high school there. He graduated from Cornell University in 1921 and served for a time in the United States Army. In 1929, he married Katharine Sergeant Angell, literary editor of *The New Yorker.* Their family had grown to include a son and three grandchildren when Mrs. White died in 1977.

For his total contribution to American letters, E. B. White was awarded the 1971 National Medal for Literature. In 1963, President John F. Kennedy awarded him the Presidential Medal of Freedom. He has received honorary degrees from seven colleges and universities. In 1978, White was honored with a special citation from the Pulitzer Prize Committee. "I guess they're trying to catch up on things," Mr. White commented. "They think time is running out."

CHILDREN'S BOOKS BY E. B. WHITE

Stuart Little, 1945
Charlotte's Web, 1952
The Trumpet of the Swan, 1970

---

[3]Information provided by White's publisher, Harper & Row.
[4]E. B. White, *The Trumpet of the Swan* (New York: Harper & Row, 1970), p. 36.

language arts specialists agree that the skill of effective listening can be learned if it is carefully and systematically taught by teachers who consider it a legitimate part of the language arts program. In this chapter we will present many activities that have proved quite successful in promoting active listening. Storytelling, reading aloud, dramatization, and other literature-related activities improve all language arts skills—including listening.

We believe that girls and boys should be taught to notice and respond to nonverbal modes of communication—to gestures, facial expressions, body movements—as well as to speech. Thus we will briefly relate the findings of the science of kinesics to the sharpening of students' perception of nonverbal cues. Illustrations in children's books provide excellent examples of nonverbal cues to be discovered and discussed in the classroom.

The focus author for this chapter is Robert Lawson.

Chapter 5: Enriching Oral Language

A major responsibility of the language arts teacher is to improve each student's facility with oral expression. The ability to provide a stimulating environment in which speech can flourish is an important teaching skill. Furniture arrangement, learning centers, classroom management policies, and student governance privileges are incidental factors that have an impact on students' oral fluency. Experiences with literature provide impetus for many kinds of speaking opportunities. Writers of children's books use language in unique and imaginative ways that serve as fine models for children in their own oral language development. In this chapter we will describe several planned and structured activities, such as panel discussions, force-field analysis, and oral reports, that give students practice expressing themselves in group settings.

Surveys reveal that students are able to make greater gains in oral proficiency when they are given the opportunity to evaluate their efforts with checklists and in other informal ways. We will discuss several useful tools for evaluating speaking skills.

The focus author for this chapter is Theodor Seuss Geisel—Dr. Seuss.

Chapter 6: Handwriting and Spelling

Functional writing—the ability to write legibly and spell accurately—is extremely important and deserves a prominent place in the language arts curriculum. The goals of handwriting instruction are legibility and ease. Legibility depends on the shape, size, slant, and spacing of the letters, and on the speed of the writer. In this chapter we will present activities that will give students a chance to practice handwriting and to realize how important written communication is.

Spelling is quite difficult for some students and needs persistent, effective teaching. Strategies that make use of basal spelling lists as well as lists and activities devised by the teacher are set forth. The chapter concludes with a brief discussion relating the mastery of handwriting and spelling to children's appreciation of books and creative and expository writing.

The focus author for this chapter is Maurice Sendak.

Chapter 7: Grammar and the Mechanics of Writing

By the time most children begin school, they have made significant progress toward developing language proficiency. They have mastered the sound system and most of the basic sentence structures. They have ordinarily acquired a relatively large vocabulary including the most frequently used words of the language, and they

Speaking situations occur frequently in elementary classrooms, and range from informal to formal. (Courtesy of Lorraine Garner and Clark Winslow, *South Park Independent School District, Beaumont, Texas.)*

have learned to adjust their use of language to fit various social situations. Despite the remarkable linguistic proficiency acquired by students before formal schooling, much more language learning takes place during the succeeding years. Writing is fundamental to that learning. Students should be given frequent opportunities to show their mastery of grammar and the rules of punctuation and capitalization in functional writing. By writing, with an effort toward improvement, girls and boys learn to write effectively.

In this chapter we will describe the traditional, structural, and transformational approaches to the study of grammar. Familiarity with all three will facilitate the teaching of grammar. We will also enumerate basic punctuation and capitalization skills to be taught in the primary and elementary grades. The most satisfactory program of grammar instruction combines the language-experience, basal, and literature approaches. Children's literature itself may provide models of proper language usage. Consequently, language arts teachers should draw examples from the books their students enjoy.

The focus author for this chapter is Judy Blume.

Chapter 8: Creative Writing

Psychologists are largely in agreement about the leading characteristics of creative ability, and their composite profile of a creative individual provides a guide for the language arts teacher trying to plan an effective program of creative writing. In this chapter we will describe ways to foster a classroom environment conducive to creativity, and we will present numerous suggestions aimed at helping children undertake creative writing. When properly used, the motivating experiences, activities, and materials we will describe can help students express themselves in writing.

Creative writing is not incidental learning; it can and must be taught throughout the elementary school years. Language arts teachers have the responsibility to provide students with something to write about, a reason for writing, help in the mechanics of writing, and a way to "publish" the finished products of writing. Our aim in this chapter is to help teachers live up to that responsibility. While writing is being taught in many structured and overt ways, children's literature will provide excellent models of creative writing for girls and boys to emulate.

The focus author for this chapter is Marcia Brown.

Chapter 9: Beginning Reading

A variety of reading readiness activities are described in this chapter—activities to be offered those children who need additional language experiences before entering the more formal reading program of basals, workbooks, and other printed materials. Once children are ready to read, ways are suggested for easing them into the reading process.

The two broad goals of beginning reading are to build reading skills, both word attack and comprehension, and to develop a positive attitude toward books and reading. In addition to basal readers and related materials, the beginning reader is provided with easy-to-read library books, magazines, newspapers, labels and consumer materials, and reading games. Teachers in nursery school and kindergarten programs also use language-experience charts as very effective reading matter. This approach continues through the primary grades and beyond. Field trips, resource persons, learning centers, art activities, and outdoor play are the kinds of stimuli that young children can think and talk about. The language arts teacher records the talk on a chart to use as personalized reading material. In the beginning reading period the teacher helps each student to recognize a body of basic sight words—words that are needed most often in primary reading and writing and that children must learn to recognize instantaneously.

The focus author for this chapter is Robert McCloskey.

Chapter 10: Having the Skill and Will to Read

The term *reading* refers to a complex language process that requires the accurate interpretation of written symbols. The teaching of reading is a process of systematic instruction that encourages personal experiences in many different types of reading materials. Initial instruction in reading typically begins with the teaching of word recognition techniques that readers may use to identify unfamiliar words. In this chapter we will examine four of them—recognizing words on sight, recognizing context clues, decoding by means of phonic analysis, and decoding by means of structural analysis.

A preschool child listens to a cassette of the familiar voice of one of her parents reading a picture book. (Courtesy of Michael Coody.)

We will also focus on the topic of reading comprehension. It is important that language arts teachers lead students toward complex levels of understanding. Some reading materials require only literal comprehension; others require interpretation and have the substance to provoke critical analysis and creative responses. It takes skill and practice on the teacher's part to move questioning about a piece of literature from surface questions to those that call for attitudes and value judgments. Activities and materials that will help improve children's comprehension of diverse reading matter are presented.

The focus author for this chapter is Scott O'Dell.

Chapter 11: Creating an Environment for Poetry

Poetry is a special kind of literature much loved by children when presented to them enthusiastically by a teacher who appreciates it. Children reject poetry, however, when inappropriate selections are used or when the teacher's treatment of it is cursory. Since so much inane poetry is to be found in school textbooks and journals, it becomes essential for the language arts teacher to take the time to study and learn as much as possible about good poetry and to recognize the outstanding poets for children. Developing the skill of reading poetry aloud also takes effort and practice on the teacher's part.

In this chapter we will survey the characteristics of poetry that appeals to children and is of a high quality. We will also present a number of activities such as reading poetry aloud, making an anthology, planning a poet-of-the-month display, writing poetry, and dramatizing poetry through choral reading, which serve to create an interest in poetry of various types. We will touch briefly on the importance of having students write poetry of their own and on the difficulties faced by teachers who seek to evaluate such creative writing.

The focus author for this chapter is David McCord.

Chapter 12: Creative Dramatics and Children's Books

Creative dramatics is one of the most enjoyable of all classroom activities. It is unsurpassed as a means of helping children understand and interpret literature. The young child begins dramatizing with his or her first encounters with literature, and the process continues through the elementary grades as long as boys and girls read and react to literature. In this chapter we will describe four types of creative dramatics that may easily be undertaken in the elementary classroom—story-acting, puppetry, readers theatre, and choral speaking.

Story-acting is the dramatization of a story with boys and girls playing the various roles before an audience of their peers. Puppetry is used to dramatize many kinds of literature. Successful puppetry experiences promote better speaking habits, encourage effective listening, stimulate creative writing, and provide an outlet for releasing pent-up emotions and feelings. Readers theatre is the oral reading of literature before an audience. It is used in the classroom not only to entertain, but also to improve oral reading skills. Choral speaking is an excellent way to share poetry. It should be carefully planned and supervised by a teacher who knows how to make the most of it. All four types of creative dramatics tend to sharpen students' language arts skills.

The focus author for this chapter is Margot Zemach.

Chapter 13: Books and Nonbook Materials in Partnership

A well-stocked elementary school library lies at the heart of any language arts program that focuses on literature. For this reason, it is essential that the classroom teacher and the librarian work together to create interest in the library and to teach the skills needed for using it effectively. Every instructional unit taught in the classroom should be calculated to get children into the library, and every library activity should reinforce and enhance classroom work. In this chapter we will describe the basic library skills needed by children in the primary and intermediate grades, and we will discuss ways in which the teacher and librarian can make the library appealing to students by means of book-related art activities, displays, and contests.

Many nonbook media may be used to enhance children's experiences with books and to develop their visual literacy. Television, filmstrips, photographs and slides, overhead transparencies, cassette tapes, and bulletin boards may be put to good use. No material should be used at the expense of books or to replace them. On the contrary, every activity with nonbook media should lead to more and better reading.

The focus author for this chapter is Ezra Jack Keats.

Chapter 14: Using Books to Help Children Cope with Problems

For more than two centuries, teachers have relied on literature to help accomplish the aims of education. They have used books for instructional purposes and to help students resolve their personal problems. Many of the early trade and school books are now considered didactic and not suitable for the modern language arts curriculum. Newer books are more appropriate for bibliotherapy in the classroom. In them, minority groups are more realistically portrayed, girls and women are shown in nonstereotyped roles, and themes and issues of contemporary life are described. In a wide array of excellent books, students are able to meet people who are coping successfully with the everyday problems of living. In this chapter we will show that literature can help children to satisfy life's basic needs, if the teacher is acquainted with many excellent books and makes them available.

The focus author for this chapter is Taro Yashima.

Chapter 15: Meeting the Special Needs of Children

The passage in 1975 of Public Law 94-142, the legislative mandate to provide equal learning opportunities for all children, has brought about important changes in the language arts curriculum. We will consider the impact of that law in this chapter. Teachers are now required to meet the diverse needs of handicapped learners in the regular classroom, where they are integrated with nonhandicapped peers. Teachers are learning to meet the needs of the newcomers by modifying the way the content is presented, by modifying the way the child is asked to respond to the content, and by modifying the position of the child in the content sequence.

Other children requiring special assistance within the regular classroom are broadly defined as "culturally" or "linguistically" disadvantaged. By employing methods such as the language-experience approach, by teaching English as a second language, and by using appropriate trade books to individualize instruction, teachers will ensure that these children have the opportunity to achieve language competency.

The focus author for this chapter is Virginia Hamilton.

Chapter 16: Traditional Literature in the Language Arts Program

In this chapter we will explain why of all the literature available to teachers for use in the language arts program, none offers more advantages than traditional folk tales. They are rich in vocabulary, characterization, and imagery. They form the basis for much of the great literature, art, music, and dance that students will encounter throughout life. Folk tales introduce students to world cultures and provide them a certain world-mindedness that will continue to enrich and inspire them long after the tales themselves have been left behind. Many psychologists and child development specialists are now convinced that folk tales hold deep psychological value for children as well as for adults. Such tales have a way of giving readers insight into themselves and others.

The focus authors for this chapter are Leo and Diane Dillon.

The basic philosophy of this book has been generally supported by language arts and reading teachers for many years. As a matter of fact, it would be difficult to find a person who disagrees with the fundamental idea of using children's books to improve language arts skills. To find the theory being practiced in the classroom, however, is not so common and to locate a textbook outlining the procedure is next to impossible. The need for such a textbook prompted the writing of this one. It is intended basically for students at the college level, but our greatest wish is to have its principles reach children in the elementary school classroom.

Bibliography

Anderson, William, and Patrick Groff. *A New Look at Children's Literature*. Belmont, Calif.: Wadsworth, 1972.

Braun, Carl. "A Boost for the 'Basics' Through Children's Literature." *Reading Horizons*, Fall 1978.

Brown, Roger. "Commentary: Some Priorities in Language Arts Education." *Language Arts*, May 1979.

Chenfeld, Mimi Brodsky. *Teaching Language Arts Creatively*. New York: Harcourt Brace Jovanovich, 1978.

Cianciolo, Patricia. *Illustrations in Children's Books*, 2d ed. Dubuque, Iowa: Wm. C. Brown, 1976.

Cullinan, Bernice E., and Carolyn W. Carmichael, eds. *Literature and Young Children*. Urbana, Ill.: National Council of Teachers of English, 1977.

DeHaven, Edna P. *Teaching and Learning the Language Arts*. Boston: Little, Brown, 1979.

Fuller, Muriel, ed. *More Junior Authors*. New York: H. W. Wilson, 1963.

Huck, Charlotte. "Commentary: Literature for All Reasons." *Language Arts*, April 1979.

Johnson, Lucetta A. "Children's Literature and the Classroom Teacher." *Reading Horizons*, Spring 1977.

Lukens, Rebecca. "The Child, the Critic, and a Good Book." *Language Arts*, April 1978.

Odland, Norine. "Commentary: Children's Literature." *Language Arts*, April 1978.

———. "Planning a Literature Program for the Elementary School." *Language Arts*, April 1979.

Rudman, Masha Kabakow. *Children's Literature: An Issues Approach*. Lexington, Mass.: D. C. Heath, 1976.

Sloan, Glenda Davis. *The Child as Critic: Teaching Literature in the Elementary School*. New York: Teachers College Press, 1975.

Toelken, Barre. *The Dynamics of Folklore*. Boston: Houghton Mifflin, 1979.

Chapter 2

Planning Instruction and Evaluating the Plan: A Look at the Language Arts Unit Plan

EVERY LANGUAGE ARTS teacher must develop the ability to plan children's learning activities, keeping in mind the skills, knowledge, and attitudes to be taught. Planning is making decisions about what content to teach and how to teach it. It is important to focus more on the process of planning than on the specific form in which the plans are prepared; yet a model is a convenient way to organize units of instruction. An example of unit planning is included in this chapter as part of the focus on Laura Ingalls Wilder and the Little House books.

The preservice teacher should realize that a good plan, written or unwritten, takes into account the goals of the instructional sequence, the specific objectives to be achieved, the procedures and materials to be used by both teacher and students, and the evaluation of anticipated outcomes. Effective planning and implementation are required if the goals of the curriculum are to be successfully realized. In this chapter we will examine some of the fundamental requirements for planning and evaluating a literature-based language arts program for the elementary classroom.

Elements of the Unit Plan

To meet the needs of children, a curriculum must provide experiences that relate to students' personal goals and take into account their interests, purposes, abilities, and maturity. The use of a unit plan will help you accomplish those objectives in an efficient and interesting manner that will relate to social studies, science, art, music, and other areas of the curriculum. A basic outline to be used to develop any literature-based unit is shown in Display 2.1. We will discuss each major element separately.

Brief Description

A general statement about the source materials

to be used and the duration of the plan should begin the outline.

Major Concept

The basis of a unit plan is a general statement setting forth the theme of the unit and the major concept to be developed. You must keep the major concept, or main idea, uppermost in your mind as your students work with the unit. If you are able to devise a unit that focuses steadily on a well-defined major concept, students completing the unit will have internalized complex thoughts and ideas.

Goals

In most cases teaching begins with the identification of goals—deciding what is to be learned. To establish goals and to move toward accomplishing them, you must be thoroughly familiar with the content of the unit. You must also be aware of what your students already know about a particular subject. What specific knowledge or skills are prerequisites to understanding the unit you are planning? If some of your students lack the appropriate background, how will you shape your unit to meet their needs? The worth of a unit increases with the teacher's ability to establish appropriate learning goals. Activities designed to meet specific goals help to eliminate the "bag of tricks" syndrome so common to teaching.

Teaching Objectives

Having identified the learning goals to be attained, your next task is to select short-term objectives that will help your students meet the broader learning goals. You must decide what specific "bites" of material students are to master and at what points in the unit this learning

Display 2.1 Outline Plan for a Literature-based Unit

Title
Brief Description
I.   Major Concept
II.   Learning Goals
       A.
       B.
       C.
III.   Teaching Objectives
       A.
       B.
       C.
IV.   List of Materials
       A.
       B.
       C.
V.   List of References
       A. For the Teacher
          1.
          2.
          3.
       B. For Students
          1.
          2.
          3.
VI.   Motivating Questions

       A. Cognitive
          1.
          2.
          3.
       B. Affective
          1.
          2.
          3.
VII.   Learning Experiences
       A.
       B.
       C.
VIII. Projects and Activities (Options for Students)
       A.
       B.
       C.
IX.   Culminating Activities
       A.
       B.
       C.
X.   Evaluation
       A.
       B.
       C.

Used with permission.

should take place. Your teaching objectives should be simple, brief, precise, measurable, and immediate; learning goals, in contrast, are broader and more generalized.

List of Materials

You will need to draw up a complete inventory of materials that you and your students must have to ensure the accomplishment of the learning goals and objectives. This list might be compared to a shopping list prepared in advance of a

gourmet dinner. It will help you to determine which materials are available, which must be acquired, and which can be made on the spot. A list of materials should also be written into your daily lesson plan.

List of References

Successful language arts units require the use of many resources for both the teacher and the student. At the planning stage make a list of references that you and the class will be consulting.

A Profile of Laura Ingalls Wilder

TO ADULT READERS, Laura Ingalls Wilder's "Little House" books bring back memories of days when the frontier was not something reserved for the official history books, and to children they stimulate a keen and lasting interest in the past. In the stories, Mrs. Wilder skillfully and artfully rewove her life into the history of the American Middle West in the 1870s and 1880s, one of the most fascinating periods of time in the story of our country.

Laura's father was restless and moved his family from a Wisconsin forest to Indian Territory to Minnesota and finally to the Dakota Territory. The nine books in the "Little House" series vividly describe the hardships and pleasures of their pioneer living and of their travels by covered wagon from one home to the other. In looking back on the good and bad times, Mrs. Wilder considered them the "sunshine and shadow" of her life and accepted both quite philosophically.

What hardships the family shared! Not just the bitter-cold winters of Dakota, but the stifling summer heat, the makeshift homes, serious illnesses, and always the spectre of poverty:

> For the second meal of the day she boiled twelve potatoes in their jackets. Little Grace needed only one, the others had two apiece, and Ma insisted that Pa take the extra one. "They're not big potatoes, Charles," she argued, "and you must keep up your strength. Anyway, eat it to save it. We don't want it, do we, girls?"[1]

Interestingly enough, the "Little House" books are different from most other pioneer stories in that the characters are also shown at play and rest. They sing and dance, and they invent toys and games to entertain themselves. The constant struggle is tempered with fun and laughter. Laura fondly recalls those times when life was easier and food was more plentiful:

> When Butchering Time was over, there were the sausages and the headcheese, the big jars of lard and the keg of white salt-pork out in the shed, and in the attic hung the smoked hams and shoulders. The little house was fairly bursting with good food stored away for the long winter. The pantry and the shed and the cellar were full, and so was the attic.[2]

Laura Ingalls Wilder was born in the "little house in the big woods" of Wisconsin on February 7, 1867. From that time until young adulthood, she tells her readers, "I lived everything that happened in my books."

After Laura and Almanzo were married, they lived for a few years in the little gray house on the tree claim. In 1894 they took their small daughter Rose, left Dakota, and moved to a farm in the Ozarks of Missouri. In a letter to her readers, Mrs. Wilder explains, "We cleared the land and built our own farmhouse. Eventually we had 200 acres of improved land, a herd of cows, good hogs, and the best laying flock of hens in the country."

This photo of Laura Ingalls Wilder was taken during Children's Book Week in 1952 while she was autographing her books in a Springfield, Missouri, bookstore. It turned out to be one of the last pictures made of her. Used with permission.

[1]Laura Ingalls Wilder, *The Long Winter* (New York: Harper & Row, 1953), p. 227.

[2]Laura Ingalls Wilder, *Little House in the Big Woods* (New York: Harper & Row, 1953), p. 18.

Laura Ingalls Wilder was in her sixties when she began writing the story of her childhood. The first book, *Little House in the Big Woods,* was published in 1932 and became a runner-up for the Newbery Award. In discussing the success of her first book with an interviewer, Mrs. Wilder said:

> I thought that would be the end of it. But what do you think? Children who read it wrote me begging for more. I was amazed because I didn't know how to write. I went to "little red school houses" all over the west and I was never graduated from anything.[3]

In 1949 Almanzo died at the age of ninety-two; they had been married sixty-three years. Laura Ingalls Wilder died in their home on Rocky Ridge Farm on February 10, 1957. She was ninety years old.

THE LITTLE HOUSE SERIES

Little House in the Big Woods, 1953
Little House on the Prairie, 1953
Farmer Boy, 1953
On the Banks of Plum Creek, 1953
By the Shores of Silver Lake, 1953
The Long Winter, 1953
Little Town on the Prairie, 1953
These Happy Golden Years, 1953
The First Four Years, 1953

OTHER BOOKS BY LAURA INGALLS WILDER

On the Way Home, 1962
West from Home, 1974

[3]William Anderson, *Laura Wilder of Mansfield,* p. 9. Copyright 1968 by William Anderson.

As you work through the unit, annotate the list for future use. With conscientious record keeping, you will be able to accumulate lists of appropriate and useful references that will become indispensable if a unit is to be taught to more than one group of children. Your evaluation of books, pamphlets, records, artifacts, and other source materials will become the basis for a complete language arts unit that should improve with age.

Motivating Questions

The ability to ask provocative questions is an important skill to develop. You need to be able to pose different types and levels of questions to create interest in a topic and lead into a lesson or unit. Such questions may motivate students to listen, speak, read, and write about the unit. Your questions should progress from objective questions of the cognitive type to thought-provoking questions of the affective type.

Learning Experiences

The heart of the unit is children's day-to-day learning experiences in the classroom. Such experiences should be both highly interesting and heavily weighted toward the development of language skills. You can obtain suggestions for learning experiences from textbooks, manuals, curriculum guides, professional journals and magazines, resource and supplementary materials, and from the children themselves.

Projects and Activities

All language arts units should present ample jobs to which students may become totally committed if they choose. If such projects involve the use of a wide variety of materials and experiences geared to their own needs and interests, many students will prefer them to any other activity the school has to offer.

Culminating Activities

The learning experiences that conclude work on a unit of study are culminating activities. The major purposes of such activities are to review previous learning, enable children to evaluate personal learning, and provide a transition to the next major unit. The act of tying an exciting unit up into a neat package at the end gives students a feeling of achievement and accomplishment.

Evaluation

The complex final component of the unit plan involves the measurement of students' learning and the evaluation of the teaching process. The teacher who thoughtfully and objectively evaluates the success of a unit will automatically become more effective in preparing future units to meet the needs of children. Because of its importance, we will discuss the evaluation process in detail after we present a sample outline for a unit plan based on the Little House books by Laura Ingalls Wilder. Portions of this unit have been taught at all levels in the elementary school. It may be adapted and revised for use in any classroom.

Example of a Unit Plan

The language arts unit that follows is based on the outline shown in Display 2.1.

Title: *Looking at Our Own Past Through the Little House Books*
Brief Description: A six-week unit of study based on Laura Ingalls Wilder's Little House books.

I. MAJOR CONCEPT: By understanding the events of the past, a person is able to comprehend the present and plan wisely for the future.

II. LEARNING GOALS
    A. To help students understand that some of the pioneer courage shown by early settlers prevails today as people work to meet basic human needs and to satisfy common aspirations.
    B. To acquaint students with two remarkable pioneer families, the Ingallses and the Wilders, and with the warm family relationships described in the Little House books. To help them compare and relate early family living with their own family life.

III. TEACHING OBJECTIVES
    A. To teach factual information about the following aspects of frontier life:
        1. Shelter and clothing
        2. Government
        3. Education
        4. Religion
        5. Recreation
        6. Travel
        7. Farming
        8. Hunting
        9. Cooking and sewing
        10. Music and dance
    B. To study a particular author and illustrator to help students gain certain insights about all authors and illustrators.

IV. LIST OF MATERIALS
   A. Little House books (several sets)
   B. Related books and pamphlets
   C. Art paper, paint, and brushes
   D. Boxes, colored paper, scissors, and paste
   E. Map of the United States
   F. Antiques—churn, coffee mill, sunbonnet, etc.
   G. Scrap materials for constructions
   H. Records, tapes, filmstrips

V. LIST OF REFERENCES
   A. Books
      1. *Little House in the Big Woods*
      2. *Little House on the Prairie*
      3. *Farmer Boy*
      4. *On the Banks of Plum Creek*
      5. *By the Shores of Silver Lake*
      6. *The Long Winter*
      7. *Little Town on the Prairie*
      8. *These Happy Golden Years*
      9. *The First Four Years*
      10. *West from Home*
      11. *On the Way Home*
      12. *The Laura Ingalls Wilder Songbook*
      13. *Let the Hurricane Roar*
      14. *Woman's Day Book of American Needlework*
   B. Pamphlets—Available from Laura Ingalls Wilder Museum, Mansfield, Missouri
      1. "Horn Book Magazine Reprint from the LIW Issue"
      2. "A Wilder in the West," edited by William Anderson
      3. "The Ingalls Family from Plum Creek to Walnut Grove via Burr Oak, Iowa," by Irene V. Lichty
      4. "Laura Ingalls Wilder, 1867–1967," reprinted from April 1967 *Top of the News*, American Library Association
      5. "Laura Wilder of Mansfield" by Doris K. Eddins
      6. "A Teacher's Tribute to Laura Ingalls Wilder" by Doris K. Eddins
      7. "The Story of the Ingalls" by William Anderson
      8. "Getting to Know Laura," excerpts of letters from children

VI. MOTIVATING QUESTIONS
   A. Cognition
      1. Recognition and Recall
         a. Who wrote the Little House books?
         b. When were they written?
         c. In what order were they written?
         d. Who illustrated the second edition of the books?
         e. What was the setting of each book in the series?
         f. Which one of the books was not about Laura and her family?
         g. Which book is about Laura's courtship and marriage?
      2. Demonstration of Skill
         a. Locate Wisconsin, Minnesota, and South Dakota on a map of the United States.
         b. Locate the Kansas-Oklahoma border on the map.
         c. Locate Mansfield, Missouri, on the map.
         d. Draw a line on the map tracing the trail Laura and her family traveled.
         e. Pinpoint on the map the origin of each one of the books.
         f. Describe a dugout home.
         g. Describe a covered wagon.
      3. Comprehension
         a. Explain what is meant by the terms "homestead" and "tree claim."
         b. Can you give examples of other books similar to the Little House series?

c. How do your Christmases compare with Laura's and Mary's? Why were they so happy with simple handmade gifts?

d. What did Ma mean when she said, "There's no great loss without some small gain"?

e. Why did Pa finally leave farming to go to work in a railroad camp?

4. Analysis

a. Why did Pa continue to move his family from place to place?

b. Why was Ma willing to move with him from place to place?

c. Why was Ma anxious for the girls to attend school?

d. Why did Mary have to go so far away from home to attend college?

e. Explain why Garth Williams's illustrations are so authentic and realistic. [See Figure 2.1.]

f. Why did Laura and Almanzo move to Missouri?

g. Why was Missouri then called "The Land of the Big Red Apple"?

5. Synthesis

a. How would the lives of the pioneers have been different if they had not helped each other?

b. What if the government had not opened up Western lands to settlers?

c. What general statement can you make about the contributions that were made by the pioneers to music, art, and literature?

d. Is it necessary for modern people to adapt to the environment and to cope with natural disasters? Explain your answer.

e. Why is conservation of natural resources more crucial today than it was when Laura was a child?

B. Affectivity

1. Opinion

a. Why do you suppose Laura accused Pa of being partial to Mary?

b. Do you feel that he actually did like Mary better?

c. Why did the early settlers have to trust each other to survive?

d. How would you feel if you were suddenly moved from your own home to a completely different part of the country?

e. Why do you think so many modern young people want to move from the city to the country?

f. Why did Laura say she hated Sundays? Do you feel the same way about Sundays?

2. Attitudes and Values

a. Do most Americans still believe in the value of hard work? Defend your answer.

b. In reading these books, are you aware of Laura's values? Explain.

c. How do we know that Laura's family held deep religious faith?

d. Are churches still important to community life? Explain.

e. Do you agree that Laura was unselfish in serving as "Mary's eyes"? Defend your answer.

VII. LEARNING EXPERIENCES

A. Read the nine books in the Little

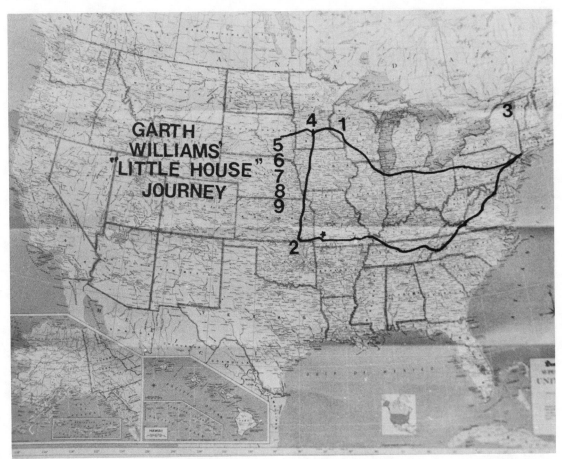

Figure 2.1 *When Garth Williams was asked to illustrate the second edition of the Little House books, he visited Laura Ingalls Wilder in Mansfield, Missouri, and then drove the route that the Ingalls family had taken in their covered wagon. Numerals represent the locale and chronological order of the books. (Based on a map published in* Horn Book Magazine, *December 1953.)*

House series. Divide the class into nine groups (according to book titles) for discussion. Group leaders may then make brief oral reports on each book. [See Figure 2.2.]

B. Study other books and materials related to the Little House books, e.g., *On the Way Home, West from Home, Let the Hurricane Roar,* and pamphlets from the Wilder museum.

C. Write a class letter to the museum in Mansfield, Missouri, for order blanks listing Laura Ingalls Wilder artifacts for sale.

D. Arrange a classroom display of antiques reminiscent of the items Mrs. Wilder described in her books.

E. Compare the popular television series "Little House on the Prairie" with the books to see how closely the TV

Figure 2.2 *A bulletin board containing book jackets placed in order of publication enables students to see the sequential development of the Little House books. Even though students seldom read the books in order, they are curious about the sequence of events in Laura's life.*

version follows the writing of Laura Ingalls Wilder.

    F. Research the Laura Ingalls Wilder Award and the authors who have won it for their lasting contribution to children's literature.

VIII. PROJECTS AND ACTIVITIES (Options for Students)

    A. Construction—Following printed instructions provided by the teacher, construct the following items:

1. Patchwork quilt
2. Braided rug
3. Hornbook
4. Quill pen
5. Sampler
6. Pioneer shot pouch
7. Hunting knife and sheath
8. Decorated Christmas stocking
9. Candles
10. Cornhusk dolls
11. Rag dolls

12. Miniature covered wagon
13. Miniature log cabin
14. "What-not" shelf
B. Cooking—Following recipes provided by the teacher, prepare the following foods:
   1. Churned butter
   2. Laura's gingerbread
   3. Ma's pumpkin pie
C. Art activities—Using materials from the art center, complete the following projects:
   1. Painted mural of the "little town on the prairie"
   2. Shoebox diorama of a favorite episode
   3. Scroll of favorite scenes labeled with captions
   4. Character puppets

IX. CULMINATING ACTIVITIES
A. Plan a Christmas party similar to the one described in *On the Banks of Plum Creek*. Invite friends.
B. Plan a "literary" with a spelling contest, poetry recitation, and prose reading similar to the one described in *Little Town on the Prairie*.
C. Arrange an exhibit of all completed projects and hold "open house" for visitors.
D. Review learnings and record them on an experience chart.
E. Sing favorite songs from the *Laura Ingalls Wilder Songbook*. [See Figure 2.3.]

X. EVALUATION PROCEDURES
A. Creative writing—Students write reactions to the "Laura" unit. [See Figure 2.4.]
B. Students evaluate the "Laura" unit on specially prepared checklist.
C. Teacher-made paper-and-pencil objective test on factual information.

D. Restate motivating questions as an oral post-test.
E. Make plans for another literature unit. Observe student behavior and attitudes.

Evaluating the Plan

No teacher of language arts teaches as well as he or she would like. In varying degrees, we all fail to achieve the goal of successful teaching because of ineffectual procedures, paucity of ideas, lack of experience, or limited understanding of the language arts. Nevertheless, for various reasons, we are often reluctant to use evaluation procedures. There is no way to escape the inevitable round of teaching, testing, grading, and reteaching that evaluation will give rise to. We know teachers play a vital role in providing for the cognitive, social, and emotional development of children. And we realize that to do so effectively, we must strive to improve our understanding of our students, monitor their achievement, make educational decisions about them, and appraise the success of classroom programs, materials, and methods. Moreover, we ought to assess the many tools of evaluation, use them with care, and remain aware of their strengths and weaknesses. Evaluation, however, is difficult and time-consuming work, and if the feedback is largely negative, it may be emotionally draining as well.

But in the constant struggle to improve our techniques, evaluation is an important tool. Defining goals, collecting and recording evidence, making judgments, and revising strategies are the necessary forerunners of improvement.

One of the most perplexing problems in the language arts is determining how appropriate evaluation should occur. How should the beginning teacher assess language outcomes? What measures are appropriate in rendering judgment? What is the difference between formal and infor-

Love's Old Sweet Song

Words by Clifton Bingham   Music by James L. Molloy   1884

James Lyman Molloy, an Irish lawyer, was also well-known as a composer.
This is the most famous of his songs.
The evening before Laura's wedding Pa played all the old tunes that she had
known ever since she could remember and finished with "Just a song at twilight. . . ."   HGY, *page 277*

Figure 2.3 *"Love's Old Sweet Song," words by Clifton Bingham, music by James Molloy, from* The Laura Ingalls Wilder Songbook: Favorite Songs from the "Little House" Books, *compiled and edited by Eugenia Garson. Arranged for piano and guitar by Herbert Haufrecht. Illustrated by Garth Williams. Musical arrangements copyright © 1968 by Herbert Haufrecht. Pictures copyright 1953 by Garth Williams. Used by permission of Harper & Row, Publishers, Inc.*

Old Jack
Tune: "On Top of Old Smokey"

CHORUS: Old Jack was a fine dog
He was fine till the end
He understood Laura
She understood him.

VERSE 1: Jack didn't want to go West
Like all of the rest
He loved the old home place
'Cause it was the best.

VERSE 2: Old Jack was a good dog
All covered with gray
And Laura still loved him
'Til he passed away.

VERSE 3: He'll not run the prairie
As he used to do.
'Cause he went to Heaven
As all good dogs do.

Figure 2.4 During a language arts unit on the Little House books, one class of sixth-grade students composed a folk song in tribute to Old Jack. (Courtesy of Louise Schenkewitz, Dick Dowling Elementary School, Port Arthur, Texas.)

mal evaluation? In fact, what do the terms "evaluation," "testing," and "grading" mean?

To many persons, evaluation is synonymous with testing and grading. In reality, the three terms have not only dissimilar meanings but different implications for instruction. Elliot W. Eisner has summarized the differences between them:

1. *Evaluation* can be conceived of as a process through which value judgments are made about educationally relevant phenomena.
2. *Testing* is one procedure used to obtain data for purposes of forming descriptions or judgments about one or more human behaviors.
3. *Grading* is the process of assigning a symbol standing for some judgment of quality relative to some criterion.[1]

Eisner's definition of evaluation as a process—something that one does in order to make value judgments about educationally relevant events—

is general but has two major implications for the teacher of the language arts. First, value judgments are built into the process. In other words, the teacher does not merely describe some classroom activity as raw scores on a spelling test; the teacher also appraises the worth and implications of such scores. Quiz results provide data that reveal the relative effectiveness of a particular teaching style, the appropriateness of instructional materials, the progress of individuals, or the elements of the program that need to be retaught.

Second, according to Eisner's definition, any language arts experience may be evaluated in some manner. Although some language arts behaviors (such as spelling tests) may be easier to measure than others (such as creative writing), the primary aim of evaluation is to secure information that will shed some light on the effectiveness of the instructional process.[2] Evaluation, then, is an educational tool through which pro-

[1]Elliot W. Eisner, *Educating Artistic Vision* (New York: Macmillan, 1972), p. 201.

[2]Ibid.

fessional intelligence may be exercised on behalf of the students for whom the language arts program is designed.

Many classroom teachers view evaluation from a single perspective—teachers' evaluation of pupils. Evaluation in the language arts, however, is much more complex. It involves teachers evaluating pupils, teachers evaluating themselves, and students evaluating themselves.

Teachers Evaluating Pupils

A great many approaches to the evaluation of the language arts are currently being employed. These assessment procedures range from simple observations of the child to complex diagnostic testing. We will not attempt to cover every technique. Instead we will briefly consider common approaches to evaluation used in typical school settings.

Observation Checklists. One way for teachers to assess individual children or classroom groups is simply by watching them objectively for a period of time. Such observation plays a significant role in language instruction. Many reading problems, for example, may be discovered and remedied through the evaluation of a child's oral reading. Preservice teachers are often asked to observe an elementary school child at work in the class-room and to use a checklist to structure their assessment.

Such instruments, like the one reproduced in Display 2.2, are usually made up of a list of specific behaviors indicative of the ideal or appropriate stage of learning progress. They are designed to improve communication between teachers, parents, and students because they give concrete examples for comparison.

Teacher-made Tests. Tests constructed by teachers may be the single most important tool for evaluating teaching objectives. They provide a direct measure of major learning outcomes and

indirect evidence about other instructional variables. The chief advantage of a test made by the teacher is that it is specific; it usually covers exactly what has been taught in the classroom. Such tests include the precise content of the lessons and may reflect the teacher's particular style and vocabulary.

Unfortunately, teacher-made tests are often poorly constructed. A good one requires not only a sound understanding of the language arts but also a clear view of intended outcomes. Steps to help guide you in developing appropriate test instruments in the language arts are listed in Display 2.3.

Criterion-referenced Measures. In recent years, the use of criterion-referenced tests has spread widely. Also known as objective-based tests, these instruments attempt to measure the extent to which pupils have mastered specific learning objectives. Proponents of criterion-referenced testing point to promising research results and to the benefits of systematically monitoring pupils' progress. Objective-based instruction can provide a useful road map for teachers and students if it is used as a diagnostic teaching tool.

Diagnostic Language Evaluation. The major purpose of a diagnostic test is to measure an individual child's strengths and weaknesses in significant areas of language. The results of such a test are used to help the teacher provide a more effective instructional program.

Assessments of this type fall into one of two broad categories—formal and informal. Formal diagnostic procedures are most often performed with standardized paper-and-pencil instruments by trained educational diagnosticians. They are used as a tool for what has been termed "diagnostic-prescriptive" teaching. Informal diagnostic tests, usually administered on a one-to-one basis, measure a student's language achievement by means of oral reading, listening, speaking, or spelling.

Display 2.2 Observation Checklist to Assess Reading Attitudes

In the two-week period, has the child:

		Yes	No
1.	Seemed happy when engaged in reading activities?	___	___
2.	Volunteered to read aloud in class?	___	___
3.	Read a book during free time?	___	___
4.	Mentioned reading a book at home?	___	___
5.	Chosen reading over other activities (playing games, coloring, talking, etc.)?	___	___
6.	Made requests to go to the library?	___	___
7.	Checked books out of the library?	___	___
8.	Talked about books she/he has read?	___	___
9.	Finished most of the books she/he has started?	___	___
10.	Mentioned books she/he has at home?	___	___

From Betty S. Heathington and J. Estill Alexander, "A Child-based Observation Checklist to Assess Attitudes Toward Reading," *The Reading Teacher* (Newark, Del.: International Reading Association, April 1978), pp. 769–71. Used with permission.

Display 2.3 Devising Teacher-made Tests

1. Plan for a test before attempting to teach the material.
2. Make a careful plan for the test so that you know and the students know "what is expected."
3. Compare each objective and assign a percent to each one; the test should reflect these relative weights.
4. Have the objectives of the unit clearly in mind when you write the test questions.
5. Write each question with an eye toward clarity, objectivity, and ease of grading.
6. Include a representative sample of the subject matter in the test items.
7. Develop test items at the appropriate level of difficulty for the students.
8. Develop the test progressively as the unit is being taught.
9. Use various types of questions—long answer (essay), short answer, and objective (true-false, matching, completion, multiple choice).
10. Use the test results as a means for self-assessment and for reteaching, once data have been collected.

Standardized Survey Tests. Of all the printed formal tests administered in the United States, the standardized survey test is the most common. Those most frequently used are part of a battery of achievement tests that purport to measure major language elements such as vocabulary, reading, grammar, word usage, spelling, punctuation, and capitalization. Since standardized tests yield a number of individual and specific test scores, they provide information about individuals and groups. Survey tests are usually administered once a year as a periodic check on the educational growth of individual children and also on the entire school program. A word of caution: It is more beneficial for future planning to look at *trends* revealed by test scores than to concentrate on a single child's progress.

Teachers' Self-Evaluation

One of the most effective strategies for improving teaching is self-evaluation. Many teachers have had the experience of reading a professional magazine or journal and being attracted by self-appraisal tests designed to appraise teachers' behavior. Such instruments not only pose thoughtful questions but also present a yardstick for self-measurement. The completion of such an examination can produce insight about an individual's teaching practices, behavior, and attitudes. The purpose of such instruments is to provide stimulation for positive change and professional growth.

As unscientific as such tests are, their value lies in the awareness they create of the positive characteristics needed by language arts teachers. Those who respond to such instruments should do so seriously and honestly. In many cases, a simple awareness of desirable attributes can bring about change or growth. For purposes of comparison, the use of informal self-appraisal instruments should be repeated frequently. An example of one, "Developing-Appreciation-for-Literature Inventory," is reproduced in Display 2.4.

Students' Self-Evaluation

In most language arts programs, evaluation procedures are focused on the students' performance at the conclusion of a unit of instruction or on the completion of an instructional module. Although such testing is a vital part of the process of evaluation, it is incomplete; the learner needs to be directly and personally involved. Self-evaluation, sometimes called process evaluation, calls for students to evaluate their own work or progress many times during the course of the school year. Since the language arts are a group of interrelated skills interwoven into the total school program, self-evaluation becomes an integral part of language development.

Self-evaluation may be directed toward the assessment of a child's understanding of the ideas and processes being taught, or it may simply try to ascertain an individual child's satisfaction with the elements of the language arts program. Very young children may not be able to evaluate themselves in other than general terms. On the other hand, middle- and upper-grade students may express amazing candidness. A self-appraisal questionnaire for students is shown in Display 2.5.

Self-evaluation is an effective way to inspire children to greater achievement. Teachers have devised many procedures to help students increase awareness of their personal progress in the language arts. Among them are reading record charts, color graphs of wide reading, handwriting samples, scrapbooks of creative writing, spelling bar graphs, and folders of dated work.

Grading

Generally, the purpose of testing is to decide who will be permitted to go on to the next level of instruction. Test results, along with the teacher's judgment, are the basis of a grading system in which all students are classified several times during the year. Grades are often used to make

Display 2.4 Developing-Appreciation-for-Literature Inventory

Circle the numeral on each five-point scale below that best describes the teaching practices under consideration. One (1) is the lowest rating and five (5) is the highest. Add total points and refer to key.

1. Do you provide a wide collection of books in the classroom that range from easy to difficult?   1 2 3 4 5
2. Do you schedule a period each day for independent reading?   1 2 3 4 5
3. Do you conduct private conferences with students in regard to self-selected reading?   1 2 3 4 5
4. Do you provide students with an efficient record system for keeping a personal account of self-selected reading?   1 2 3 4 5
5. Are your students given an opportunity for creative "reporting" on favorite books?   1 2 3 4 5
6. Do you invite resource persons to your classroom to discuss literature?   1 2 3 4 5
7. Do your students make use of puppetry to enhance literature?   1 2 3 4 5
8. Do you read aloud to students on a regular basis?   1 2 3 4 5
9. Do you use the procedure of storytelling on a regular basis?   1 2 3 4 5
10. Do you study children's books and reviews of children's books on a regular basis?   1 2 3 4 5
11. Do your students frequently write and illustrate their own books?   1 2 3 4 5
12. Do you discuss with students the parts of a book and the people who work to make a book?   1 2 3 4 5
13. Do you have an organized plan of parent involvement in the literature program?   1 2 3 4 5
14. Do you help select books for the school library and do you have a voice in determining library policy?   1 2 3 4 5
15. Do your students read widely and do they appear to enjoy the literature program?   1 2 3 4 5

Interpret your total score as follows:

. Below 50   You definitely need to enrich your literature program.
. From 50 to 65 Your literature program is about average.
. From 65 to 75 You have an excellent literature program.

Betty Coody, *Using Literature with Young Children*, 2d ed. (Dubuque, Iowa: Wm. C. Brown, 1979), p. 177. Used with permission.

Display 2.5 Self-Rating of a Student's Language Arts Skills

Name: _____	Almost Always	Most of the Time	Some of the Time	Seldom	Never
1. I listen carefully.					
2. I ask relevant questions.					
3. I organize my materials logically and clearly.					
4. I follow directions carefully.					
5. I know what is being asked of me as I read.					
6. I read books that are not assigned.					
7. I write effective sentences.					
8. I go beyond the minimum requirements.					
9. I check my work for errors.					
10. I make good use of my time.					

critical judgments on whether the student's performance has been successful (A or B), adequate (C), or unsatisfactory (D or F). Unfortunately, grades are seldom used to determine whether a student learned what the school considered important.

In the past few years there has been much concern and criticism about the assignment of a letter grade to a child in a subject area like language arts. Some critics maintain that grades have been inflated and represent not actual achievement but rather a subjective view of performance, attitude, and effort. Others argue that a single grade is a meaningless form of communication from a teacher to a parent and child. Questions about specific strengths and weak-

nesses are not communicated when a single grade is issued. For example, does an A in spelling identify a child as a terrific speller or simply as the best in a class of poor spellers?

There are no simple answers that satisfy all persons—professional or lay. What is clear, however, is that teachers and administrators have a responsibility to inform parents and other responsible adults, as sincerely and accurately as possible, about the achievement of children and the success of the educational program. Such reports need to be made in a variety of ways.

The most common means of reporting progress to parents is by some type of report card, a device that has been with us since the days of the little red schoolhouse. The various changes undergone by report cards over the years are mute testimony to the fact that neither teachers nor parents have been satisfied with them. At issue is the interpretation of letter grades. It is not likely that this controversy will be resolved in the near future. The best that can be said to the prospective teacher is to make grading as fair as possible, recognize its limitations, and manage it in a way that does not interfere with effective teaching of the language arts. In Chapter 3, we will present a plan for personalizing instruction that improves on the traditional method of teaching, testing, grading, and reteaching.

Summary

The language arts program forms the heart of the elementary school curriculum, and its main task is to assist all children in expressing their thoughts and feelings more fluently by improving their listening, speaking, reading, and writing skills. Every language arts teacher must develop the ability to plan and evaluate children's learning activities and experiences. One of the most effective techniques is to interrelate the language arts with other broad areas of the elementary curriculum such as social studies and science. The unit and project method is the most natural and child-centered means of relating language arts to other elements of the curriculum. It is an approach that is favored by both teachers and students.

The plan for a unit based on Laura Ingalls Wilder's Little House books was presented in this chapter as a guide to the beginning language arts teacher who may be unfamiliar with correlating language arts, literature, social studies, science, and other areas of study. The unit is basic; and the format may be altered as needed, or it may be used as a model for other language arts units featuring different children's books.

Self-evaluation is emphasized in this chapter as the most likely way to bring about change and improvement. Self-appraisal by both teachers and students is considered to be equally important.

Best Books for Children

By the Shores of Silver Lake, written by Laura Ingalls Wilder and illustrated by Garth Williams. New York: Harper & Row, 1953. The Ingalls family moves from Minnesota to the Dakota Territory, where Pa finds a suitable homestead and files a claim. They spend the first winter in a borrowed house sixty miles from the nearest neighbor. Mary and Laura have a thrilling time on their first train ride. The happiest Christmas the family ever had is described in this book. (U)*

Farmer Boy, written by Laura Ingalls Wilder and illustrated by Garth Williams. New York: Harper & Row, 1953. The story of Almanzo Wilder and his boyhood on a big farm in northern New York. While Laura is growing up out West, Almanzo parallels her life by planting, harvesting, and hauling wood in another part of the country. He looks forward to the annual county fair the way Laura and Mary look forward to Christmas. (P-M)

The First Four Years, written by Laura Ingalls Wilder and illustrated by Garth Williams. New York: Harper & Row, 1953. Laura and Almanzo spend the first four years of their marriage on a homestead and tree claim on the South Dakota prairie. They enjoy warm companionship and many happy hours with the baby, but the struggle to create a productive farm is overwhelming. This book ends Laura Ingalls Wilder's chronicle of frontier life with its "sunshine and shadows." (U)

The Laura Ingalls Wilder Songbook, compiled and edited by Eugenia Garson and illustrated by Garth Williams. New York: Harper & Row, 1968. A collection of favorite songs sung by the American pioneers who moved westward over the prairies in the nineteenth century. The tunes have been arranged for piano and guitar by Herbert Haufrecht. These sixty-two well-known songs from the Little House books

*The following code is used throughout the book to indicate appropriate grade levels: P (Primary, grades K–3), M (Middle, grades 4–5), and U (Upper, grades 6–8).

HAVE A BALL - READ

The chart shown here is used to illustrate the student's progress in independent reading. (Courtesy of Sabine Pass Independent School District, Sabine Pass, Texas.)

are organized into the following categories: "Home and Memories," "Favorites of Long Ago," "Ballads, Games, and Dances," "Patriotic Songs," "Love and Courtship," "My Heart Is Sair," and "Hymns and Sacred Songs." (P-M-U)

Laura: The Life of Laura Ingalls Wilder, written by Donald Zochert. Chicago: Regnery, 1976. Besides exploring first-hand the documented records of the life of Laura Ingalls Wilder, the author draws on her unpublished memoir, composed before she began writing the Little House books. A biography to be enjoyed by children and adults alike. (U)

Let the Hurricane Roar, written by Rose Wilder Lane. New York: McKay, 1961. This novel is a romance based on the lives of Charles and Caroline Ingalls, who were the author's grandparents. It is a pioneer story of courage and hardships, of love and happy times set in the Dakota Territory during the nineteenth century. (U)

The Little House Cookbook, written by Barbara M. Walker and illustrated by Garth Williams. New York: Harper & Row, 1979. Carefully researched by the author and tested in her own kitchen are more than one hundred recipes from Laura Ingalls Wilder's pioneer childhood. The recipes are for dishes described in the Little House books. They range from a full-course Christmas dinner to the Ingallses' daily bread. All recipes are adapted to modern measurements and to today's kitchen equipment. (P-M-U)

Little House in the Big Woods, written by Laura Ingalls Wilder and illustrated by Garth Williams. New York: Harper & Row, 1953. Laura Ingalls and her family live in a log cabin on the edge of the big woods in Wisconsin. The days are spent in hunting and trapping, cooking and churning, sewing and mending. The winters are long and cold, but Ma makes special games and toys for the girls, and Pa entertains them by playing his fiddle. (P-M)

Little House on the Prairie, written by Laura Ingalls Wilder and illustrated by Garth Williams. New York: Harper & Row, 1953. Ma and Pa, Mary, and Laura make the long move by covered wagon from the big woods of Wisconsin to the Kansas-Oklahoma border (Indian Territory in those days), where Pa finds a suitable place to build a log cabin. Their days become filled with plowing and planting, hunting wild game, chopping firewood, and gathering grass for their livestock. (P-M)

Little Town on the Prairie, written by Laura Ingalls Wilder and illustrated by Garth Williams. New York: Harper & Row, 1953. The settlers who weathered the long winter now set about starting a school and a church for their new town. The girls are growing up. Mary goes to a college for the blind, and Laura receives her certificate to teach school. Almanzo Wilder walks Laura home from church, and she gives him her calling card. Their courtship begins quietly and naturally. (M-U)

The Long Winter, written by Laura Ingalls Wilder and illustrated by Garth Williams. New York: Harper & Row, 1953. By studying signs and omens, the Indians predict that the winter of 1880–81 will be a long and hard one. Pa takes the warning seriously and moves his family from the claim into the town. Blizzards rage for seven months, and the little town is cut off from the outside world. In May the snow finally melts, and the train arrives bringing the Ingallses a belated Christmas barrel. It is one of the happiest celebrations they ever had. (M-U)

On the Banks of Plum Creek, written by Laura Ingalls Wilder and illustrated by Garth Williams. New York: Harper & Row, 1953. Laura and her family leave the log cabin home in Indian Territory and travel in their covered wagon across Kansas, Missouri, and Iowa to Minnesota, where Pa builds them a sod house in the bank of Plum Creek. Mary and Laura go to school and spend their spare time playing in the creek. The family survives a grasshopper plague and a terrible blizzard. (P-M)

On the Way Home, written by Laura Ingalls Wilder. New York: Harper & Row, 1962. In 1894, Laura and Almanzo leave their drought-stricken farm in South Dakota and travel by buckboard across the United States to begin a new life in the Ozarks of Missouri, "Land of the Big Red Apple." They are accompanied by their seven-year-old daughter Rose. This book is Laura's personal diary faithfully recorded day by day on the long journey. (U)

These Happy Golden Years, written by Laura Ingalls Wilder and illustrated by Garth Williams. New York: Harper & Row, 1953. Not yet sixteen, Laura begins teaching school in an abandoned claim shanty, twelve miles from her home and family. She is forced to take room and board from a very quarrelsome and unpleasant couple. This homesick period in her life causes Laura to appreciate her own family even more. Laura and Almanzo marry and stake a tree claim. (M-U)

West from Home: Letters of Laura Ingalls Wilder, San Francisco, 1915, edited by Roger Lea MacBride. New York: Harper & Row, 1974. Letters from Laura to Almanzo, written during a cross-country train trip from Mansfield, Missouri, to San Francisco in 1915. After Laura's death in 1957, Rose found the letters among her mother's papers and clippings, but they were not published until many years later. (U)

Woman's Day Book of American Needlework, written by Rose Wilder Lane. New York: Simon and Schuster, 1963. Rose Wilder Lane was taught needlework by her mother while they still lived in the Dakota Territory before the turn of the century. This book is a beautifully illustrated collection of American needlework from colonial times to the present. Excellent for use with a Laura Ingalls Wilder unit. (U)

Bibliography

Armstrong, Robert; Terry D. Cornell; Robert E. Kraner; and Wayne E. Robertson. *The Development and Evaluation of Behavioral Objectives.* Worthington, Ohio: Charles A. Jones, 1970.

Clark D. Cecil. *Using Instructional Objectives in Teaching.* Glenview, Ill.: Scott, Foresman, 1972.

Coody, Betty. *Using Literature with Young Children*, 2d ed. Dubuque, Iowa: Wm. C. Brown, 1978.

Duffy, Gerald. "Maintaining a Balance in Objective-based Reading Instruction." *The Reading Teacher,* February 1978.

Eisner, Elliot. *Educating Artistic Vision.* New York: Macmillan, 1972.

Fein, Ruth L., and Adrienne H. Ginsberg. "Realistic Literature About the Handicapped." *The Reading Teacher,* February 1978.

Fox, Barbara J., and Bruce G. Beezer. "State Mandated Assessment: What's Happening in Reading?" *Journal of Reading,* October 1978.

Heathington, Betty S., and J. Estill Alexander. "A Child-based Observation Checklist to Assess Attitudes Toward Reading." *The Reading Teacher,* April 1978.

"Impact of Minimum Competency Testing in Florida." *Today's Education,* September–October 1978.

McDonald, Thomas F. "Pro: Minimal Competency Testing As Viewed from the Front Line." *Journal of Reading,* October 1978.

McNeil, John D. *Curriculum: A Comprehensive Introduction.* Boston: Little, Brown, 1977.

Moffett, James, and Betty Jane Wagner. *Student-centered Language Arts and Reading, K-13,* 2d ed. Boston: Houghton Mifflin, 1976.

Petre, Richard M. "A Statewide Competency-based Reading Program in Maryland." *Journal of Reading,* October 1978.

Ragan, William B., and Gene D. Shepherd. *Modern Elementary Curriculum,* 5th ed. New York: Holt, Rinehart and Winston, 1977.

Shields, Merrill. "Why Johnny Can't Write." *Newsweek,* December 8, 1975.

A Statement on the Preparation of Teachers of English. Urbana, Ill.: National Council of Teachers of English, 1976.

Stoops, Joyce King. *The Child Wants to Learn.* Boston: Little, Brown, 1977.

Tierney, Robert J. "Con: Minimal Competency Testing Won't Do It." *Journal of Reading,* October 1978.

Chapter 3

Dealing with Diversity:
Personalizing the Language Arts Program

THERE IS NO NEED to review here the many reasons why instruction in the elementary school should be individualized. Most educators have long acknowledged that it is the only way to live up to the cardinal principle of American education—comprehensive education for all children.

To believe in democracy is to believe in the uniqueness of the individual, and the democratic ideal of education holds that each individual has a right to develop self-potential to the fullest. Personalized instruction is not just a method to be adopted at the teacher's discretion. It is a child's inherent right.

G. Ray Musgrave describes the attitude that educators should take toward the concept of individualized instruction:

Complete individualization is a goal for educators much as democracy is a goal for Americans or Christianity is a goal for Christians. Everyone in education should strive to reach the goal, knowing that complete individualization is rare, if not impossible. Anytime, however, that the school situation is focusing on the individual student in the teaching-learning process, another step is being made toward the ultimate goal.[1]

In this chapter we will examine some techniques for personalizing instruction in the language arts and describe an individualized reading program. In Appendix C we have provided an inventory for a teacher seeking to determine how well a specific language arts program meets the needs of students. The self-rating instrument is intended to point out strengths as well as deficiencies in the teacher's efforts to individualize instruction. We recommend that it be completed periodically during the school year for the purpose of monitoring and upgrading teaching practices.

[1]G. Ray Musgrave, *Individualized Instruction: Teaching Strategies Focusing on the Learner* (Boston: Allyn and Bacon, 1975), p. x.

Components of Individualized Instruction

Writers advocating the individualization of instruction have described many ways to achieve that goal. We will describe five practices to be used in a language arts program that focuses on the individual child. They are (1) intraclass, task-oriented grouping, (2) multimedia teaching, (3) self-direction in learning, (4) differentiated assignments, and (5) tutorial practices.

Intraclass, Task-oriented Grouping

Two misconceptions about individualizing instruction are that the practice automatically rules out grouping of any kind, and that students involved in such a program must work alone at their own speed. These notions are completely erroneous. It is neither possible nor desirable to completely individualize all learning activities. Some group work is essential. A child's language development depends on group living and group interaction. Intraclass grouping is a system of organizing students in the class to solve certain problems and to accomplish specific tasks.

There are many positive behaviors that a person would like to perform but, because of certain self-restraints, is not able to carry out unless given the support and encouragement of a group. The ability of group work to satisfy individual needs makes group interaction enjoyable, and the perceptive teacher will take advantage of positive group dynamics to accomplish complex tasks. It appears that in groups fewer errors are committed and the mistakes that are made are minor ones. This benefit is due in part to the tendency of group members to reject incorrect ideas.

Another important advantage of working in groups, as borne out by research, is that learning takes place more quickly and information is retained longer.[2] Each member of a group makes use of information put forth by other members, even in groups of two or three. For many years, teachers have known that the review of previous learning is most effective when it is carried out as a group activity. What one person has forgotten, another remembers, and as a result of the pooling of knowledge, information is multiplied many times over.

Intraclass grouping has been defended because of its socializing merits:

Experience with intraclass grouping during the past twenty or more years has resulted in the recognition of a variety of additional educational values. Among these values are opportunities for assisting isolates, neglectees, and overzealous stars to become more acceptable group members, learning leadership and followership skills, group planning and evaluation, assuming responsibility, and critical thinking.[3]

The language arts teacher cannot afford to ignore the tremendous influence the group exerts on individuals. In a group effectively supervised by a teacher, decisions are made and problems solved, attitudes and behaviors are improved, and learning proceeds at an accelerated pace.

The key to successful intraclass grouping lies in the teacher's ability to make groups flexible and task oriented. Groups of various sizes are formed to carry out certain cognitive tasks, and once those tasks have been completed satisfactorily, the group is disbanded. (The idea is similar to ad hoc committee work common in adult organizations.) Groups may be formed to practice an acquired skill, to learn a new skill, to conduct research, to complete a project, to stage a performance, or for a dozen other worthy reasons. There is a place in the individualized language arts program for both independent study and group interaction. There is no reason for one to preclude the other.

Multimedia Teaching

In increasing numbers, teachers are becoming aware that appropriate audiovisual materials can help to enrich the language environment of children while teaching them the basic skills of communication. Modern resource centers include video-taped lessons, learning packets, programmed modules, computer-assisted lessons, and other materials and devices designed to individualize learning.

Even when a needed piece of equipment is not available, a teacher can provide for the needs of children by using teacher-made and student-made materials. Textbooks and trade books may be supplemented with student-made, one-of-a-kind books. Professional recordings may share top billing with cassettes and tape recordings made by students and teachers. Student-dictated experience charts can be displayed with commercial language charts. In many classrooms, when students are not busy preparing their own learning material, they may be found making audiovisual aids for younger children.

Language arts materials made by teachers and children have a special appeal for students. They seldom stay on the shelf collecting dust as many commercial materials are prone to do. School-made audiovisuals are colorful, attractive, and inexpensive. They are usually designed to strengthen a specific skill and for that reason are highly individualized. They are easily accessible and relatively free from the restrictions surrounding expensive commercial aids. There is cognitive value in having students make many of the materials they use for learning. The creative process involved in making audiovisual aids is itself a learning experience.

[2] Paul A. Hare, Edgar F. Borgatta, and Robert F. Bales, *Small Groups* (New York: Knopf, 1961), p. 194.

[3] Henry J. Otto and David C. Sanders, *Elementary School Organization and Administration* (New York: Meredith, 1964), p. 124.

An undergraduate student tutors a child in a specific language skill. (Courtesy of Lamar University, Beaumont, Texas.)

Self-Direction in Learning

Progress in the development of language facility depends not only on planned instruction, but also on guidance in a wholesome environment where language can take place naturally. The most successful language arts teachers constantly guide children toward self-education in communication skills.

Dinkmeyer and Dreikurs picture the "self-directed learning" climate as one in which "valuing, showing faith, stimulating belief in self, giving recognition for effort, utilizing the group to enhance development, pacing, and recognition of the focus on strengths are all basic principles. Positive methods will dominate the teacher's relationship with children in an atmosphere that is encouraging and stimulating."[4]

Self-direction in learning means making choices open to students. It means making available a variety of materials, assignments, and activities from which they are allowed to select. The content of the language arts curriculum

[4]Don Dinkmeyer and Rudolf Dreikurs, *Encouraging Children to Learn* (Englewood Cliffs, N.J.: Prentice-Hall, 1963), p. 111.

should be presented in many stimulating ways. Individual students should be permitted to embrace the methods and materials that help them learn most efficiently.

Also included in the concept of self-direction is the idea of *specialization:* Each student should be allowed and encouraged to study in depth a particular topic of personal interest. The student is supplied with time, materials, and assistance needed to become expert in a chosen subject and is allowed to share newly acquired expertise with other members of the class. This kind of ego-building experience leads a student toward self-direction not only in language arts, but in every area of living.

Differentiated Assignments

It is not uncommon for five or six grade levels of ability and achievement to be represented in a single elementary class. This situation tends to make the class-as-a-whole assignment a waste of time for most students.

Teachers concerned with providing the best learning climate seldom prepare identical academic assignments for all students. Instead, some undertake advanced or enrichment work; others are provided with assignments that are average for their grade level; and still others receive less difficult material or a partial assignment. At least part of the time, an array of assignments, ranging from easy to difficult, is provided and boys and girls are given the privilege of choosing among them.

Differentiated, individualized assignments are based on students' ability, interest, achievement, and past experiences. Activities are challenging and purposeful, but no student is asked to complete an assignment that is too difficult. Teachers now realize that there is no reason for every child in a class to learn the same thing, in the same way, in the same amount of time, from the same material, and with the same amount of interest.

Tutoring

Individualized instruction in the language arts calls for a child having difficulty in any area of reading, writing, listening, or speaking to receive immediate, personal, pinpointed help in the specific area of weakness. Such diagnostic and corrective help may come from a teacher, aide, parent volunteer, intern, student teacher, remedial specialist, peer, older student, or from any other person who is able to offer assistance. In all cases, the language arts teacher arranges, coordinates, and supervises the tutoring.

Tutorial practice sessions are most successful if they are conducted in an unobtrusive manner without undue pressure. Each session should concentrate on a specific area of difficulty and should be accompanied by positive reinforcement and encouragement. The narrow focus of tutoring makes it an excellent way to teach something quickly. When well done, tutoring can keep many a small problem from mushrooming into a large one.

Requisites of an Individualized Reading Plan

A reader is always alone in the act of reading. Parents and teachers may have the strongest interest in a child's ability to read, and they may give every possible help to develop it. But in the final analysis, no one except the child can actually do the reading. Reading is and always will be a personal and private matter between the reader and the printed page. Because reading is so personal, the teaching of reading must be personalized.

Although most teachers are convinced of the efficacy of individualized reading programs, for many they are an ideal rather than a reality. Some have hesitated to develop a fully individualized plan out of concern for the basal reading program. In increasing numbers, however, they are coming to recognize that the two approaches are not mutually exclusive. Basal reading (which is discussed in Chapters 9 and 10) with its related activities can be an efficient way to teach reading skills. But it is usually exposure to trade books that makes a student *like* reading.

Individualized reading is not a cure for all the ills of elementary school reading programs. It does not promise phenomenal reading success for all students, and it does not take the place of the basal reading program. The setting up of a library center in the classroom, independent reading, book sharing, and other individualized activities, however, improve and refine reading skills. Comprehension becomes more accurate, vocabulary increases, and the decoding skills become more efficient. Moreover, individualized reading has the advantage of helping students to enjoy reading and to see the importance it plays in their daily lives. This result alone makes it a superior teaching practice.

The teacher who wishes to individualize the reading program for children must be sure to bring together certain basic elements.

A Library Center in the Classroom

For an individualized reading plan to work effectively, students need many interesting books, close at hand, from which they may choose at will. No magic number is required, but there must be enough titles to give students a wide selection. The book shelves should be restocked from time to time, and the center should be updated each month with appropriate seasonal and holiday books.

Since most elementary schools now enjoy the benefits of a well-stocked central library, it is easy for the teacher to bring books in ample numbers to the classroom. The collection may be supplemented with paperbacks from clubs, books on loan from students, and bequests from

parents, as well as with magazines, newspapers, and student-made books. Such a classroom library in no way replaces or diminishes the regular library program; it actually enhances it by turning indifferent students into active bibliophiles.

In deciding on books to place in the classroom library, the teacher and a committee of students will do well to keep in mind the needs and interests of the boys and girls for whom the books are intended. An open-ended interest inventory completed by each student can provide data to guide the committee in the initial selection (see Display 3.1). If students are continually allowed and encouraged to express their preferences, the library center will become the hub of reading activity and a vital source of learning.

The popularity of the library center will increase if the books are arranged in an attractive way with many of the jackets showing. Books are beautiful in their own right, but artifacts and realia can add to their appeal. Sculpture, paintings, green plants, cushions, and carpeting help to create a veritable oasis in the classroom where students may go to read or to select books for reading elsewhere. The daily maintenance of an orderly and functional library center should be one of the routine tasks rotated among students in the class.

Time for Students to Browse and Select Books

The most successful bookstores invite browsing. Their books are temptingly arranged to be touched and handled, thumbed through and purchased. It takes strong willpower to leave such a store without buying at least one book. Books in the classroom should be displayed in much the same way.

Browsing, scanning, pondering, rejecting, and deciding take time, but it is time well spent. The coveted instructional time so used will pay divi-

Display 3.1 Open-ended Interest Inventory to Aid in the Selection of Books

1. My hobbies are:

2. My main hobby is:

3. I have a collection of:

4. I like to read about:

5. The television show I like best is:

6. My favorite sport is:

7. The most interesting book I ever read was:

8. A movie I really enjoyed was:

9. If I could take only one book on a long trip, I would like it to be:

10. My favorite author is:

11. I usually read books recommended to me by:

12. In our library center I would like to have:

13. My favorite illustrator is:

14. The next book I plan to read is:

15. Of the books I own, my favorite is:

dends in improved reading skill and in positive attitudes toward reading. When students are rushed during the crucial book selection period, the decision too often goes against the book in question. Many students will go away empty-handed rather than take out a book they consider unsuitable.

Students trying to select a book eventually learn to look for features that say a book is fairly easy to read. They begin to study reviews and summaries provided by teachers and publishers, and to seek out the opinions of friends. As students grow and mature in the ability to be discriminating, fewer and fewer mistakes are made in their book choices. Most of the books they choose will be books they can read and will read. Such maturity is gained by a great deal of trial and error on the student's part and much patience and encouragement on the teacher's part.

Time for Independent Reading

More and more elementary schools are setting aside a regular period each day for students in all classes to be able to read silently and independently the books they have selected for themselves. In other instances, individual teachers are making time available for free reading. There seems to be a growing awareness that many students do poorly in reading because they simply do not have time to practice the reading skills so carefully taught them. Fifteen or twenty minutes a day of uninterrupted silent reading may not sound like much, but it can whet the appetite for reading and may well prompt a child to find more time to devote to it.

To designate a block of time for silent reading is to give it the priority it deserves. The ritual of a regularly scheduled period for independent

A cozy, inviting classroom library center. (Courtesy of Barbara Ellis.)

reading leaves the impression with students that reading is an important part of life. For too long it has been relegated to the status of a spare-time activity, "When you have finished all your other work, you may read a library book."

A System of Record Keeping

A chart showing what each child has read is of utmost importance in an individualized program. Because it is a graphic reflection of accomplishment, it helps to satisfy a child's need for the recognition of achievement and encourages sustained silent reading. Such a chart on display in the classroom is more significant to the student than a record kept by the teacher because it

makes the child responsible for the manipulative activities necessary to update the record. Positive reinforcement is gained each time a card is filed.

To make a reading record chart, attach a series of pockets to poster board or plywood or to a bulletin board. When names or numbers are fastened to the pockets, they become personal storage spaces for book cards. As each library book is completed, the student writes its title, author, and the date on a small card and files it in his or her special pocket. Enjoyment comes first from reading the book and second from watching the card pack grow. The chart should not encourage competition among students, however. Each pocket should be considered the child's private property, and no comparisons should be made. The only competition should be with a child's own past record. Since reading the books and keeping the record are sufficiently pleasurable, tangible rewards are not necessary.

The chart should be attractive. Since it will remain in view over long periods of time, it should also be used as a beauty spot in the classroom. The chart should contain a caption that promotes books and reading. Famous quotations from Bartlett's *Familiar Quotations* are excellent for captions and may also provide a theme for the chart (see Display 3.2).

The chart should be durable. Since it is posted at eye level and is in constant use by children, it must be well constructed of sturdy materials. The chart should also be expandable. Be sure to prepare extra pockets so that newcomers to the class can participate in the project without delay.

A graphic record of independent reading in trade books is excellent evidence of progress to show parents. The chart will reveal much about a student's interest in reading, the amount of practice taking place, the level of reading achievement, taste and preference in literature, and the child's basic attitude toward books and reading. No grade on a report card can tell as much.

Planned Book-sharing Sessions

The next best thing to reading a good book is talking about it with someone else. In fact, sharing books in creative and interesting ways remains one of the most popular of classroom activities with boys and girls in the elementary school.

Students searching for unique and original ways to report on reading should be given the freedom to decide how to present their book to the class. The teacher serves as a guide, consultant, and facilitator in the process. When a student cannot think of a nonstereotyped way to present a book, the teacher should be prepared with a file of ideas. The student may either use one of them outright or improvise and improve

A display based on a single author or theme may prompt some students to reread some of their favorite books and introduce others to writers or topics new to them. (Courtesy of Darlene Oliva, Beaumont, Texas.)

on it. A list of alternatives to written book reports is given in Display 3.3.

Planned book sharing is much more than a pleasant diversion for students; it is one of the basic features of a reading program that focuses on children's books. Many benefits accrue from a successful program of book sharing. To be able to hold the attention of a group of peers by discussing an impressive piece of literature is deeply satisfying and encouraging. It almost always leads to repeat performances by the student doing the reporting. Frequent opportunities to respond to literature in meaningful ways help girls and boys to develop the habit of reacting to

Oh for a book and a shady nook.
—*John Wilson*

There is no frigate like a book
To take us lands away.
—*Emily Dickinson*

'Tis the reader that makes the good book.
—*Ralph Waldo Emerson*

A good book is the best of friends, the same today and forever.
—*Martin Tupper*

Man builds no structure which outlives a book.
—*Eugene Fitch Ware*

Life being very short, and the quiet hours of it few, we ought to waste none of them in reading value-less books.
—*John Ruskin*

The peace of great books be with you.
—*Carl Sandburg*

Books are the ever-burning lamps of accumulated wisdom.
—*G. W. Curtis*

I go to books and to nature as a bee goes to the flower, for nectar that I can make into my own honey.
—*John Burroughs*

Reading maketh a full man.
—*Francis Bacon*

Some books are to be tasted, others swallowed, and some few to be chewed and digested.
—*Francis Bacon*

reading material. Such response, in turn, has the effect of creating a higher level of reading comprehension, and one that is more applicable to life. Oral book reports developed from a wide array of excellent children's books are a sound means of teaching literature. In an incidental way, students learn about plot, theme, characterization, style, and other literary elements.

Routine book sharing that is lively, interesting, and informative actually promotes the cause of independent reading. Students read books that are recommended by their friends. To fail to take advantage of the influence of students' peers in the selection, reading, and sharing of library books is to ignore a natural motivating force not found with other methods. Successful book-sharing programs build positive attitudes toward books and reading—attitudes that keep students reading independently not only in school but outside of school as well.

Keeping Parents Informed and Involved

Most parents did not learn to read in individualized programs. For that reason, the teacher must fully explain the program to parents at the outset, seek their help and support, and keep them apprised of their child's progress throughout the school year.

Parents, like many teachers and administrators, may be concerned about any method of teaching reading that seems to be a drastic departure from what they know best—the basal reading program. If parents are shown in many and varied ways that individualized reading supplements the basal program—that it is the other side of the basal reading coin—and will improve reading skills and attitudes, most parents will give it their full and continuing support.

Teachers who conduct personalized reading programs find many ways to keep parents abreast

Display 3.3 100 Creative Alternatives to Written Book Reports

1. Prepare a book or story for readers theatre.
2. Write a personality sketch of a book character.
3. Decorate a classroom door like a book jacket.
4. Make a felt and burlap wall hanging of a book scene.
5. Construct a table-top village representing a book scene.
6. Create tissue paper "stained-glass windows" showing book characters.
7. Debate the pros and cons of an issue from literature.
8. Compose a folk song about a story character or event.
9. Embroider quilt squares with symbols of favorite books.
10. Demonstrate a procedure from a how-to-do-it book.
11. Decorate wastebaskets and storage boxes with storybook scenes.
12. Conduct a used-book auction.
13. Prepare a classroom rating chart for library books.
14. Select poetry for choral reading.
15. Compile a scrapbook of student book reviews.
16. Prepare stories for reading aloud to younger children.
17. Collect magazine pictures and illustrate favorite poems.
18. Construct a mobile of book characters.
19. Wear "sandwich board" posters to promote a book.
20. Write a letter to the publisher giving your impression of a new book.
21. Rewrite an old story as a modern soap opera.
22. Make a frieze to illustrate a narrative poem.
23. Write a newspaper advertisement for a favorite book.
24. Develop a series of crossword puzzles based on popular books.
25. Plan a cooking activity to accompany a book about food.
26. Create an alphabet book with each letter representing a book character.
27. Make an illustrated time line of important events in a book that is historical.
28. Compile a scrapbook about an author, poet, or illustrator.
29. Use a comic strip format to depict episodes in a story.
30. Make a collection of travel brochures and postcards to illustrate a travel book.
31. Arrange a display of artifacts to accompany a book.
32. Use an opaque projector to show illustrations in a picture book.
33. Paint life-size book characters by tracing around each other.
34. Use colored chalk to create a chalk talk about a book.
35. Construct a flip chart depicting scenes from a book.
36. Rewrite a book as a radio play with sound effects and music.
37. Set up a display of old textbooks and library books.
38. Compare an easy-to-read textbook with an easy-to-read trade book.
39. Take a survey to determine which books are favorites throughout the school, and set up a display of the winners.
40. Demonstrate some of the art techniques used in Caldecott Award books.
41. Prepare a "Book of the Week" display.
42. Compare two or more biographies of the same person.
43. Cooperate with a local bookstore to arrange a book fair for the school.
44. Arrange a display of familiar books written in different languages.

45. Make a cumulative book review by adding a sentence as students finish a book.
46. Construct advertising posters to promote favorite books.
47. Arrange a hobby collection to promote a book on collecting.
48. Create poster-board bookmarks and illustrate them with storybook scenes.
49. Make a book report in one of the silent languages—signing, finger spelling, or pantomime.
50. Make a chart of figurative language found in a book.
51. Create humorous newspaper headlines and apply them to book characters.
52. Conduct a quiz show similar to "What's My Line?" and use book characters as contestants.
53. Conduct a panel discussion on the themes in popular books.
54. Locate the setting of travel books on a world map.
55. Write an original poem to summarize a book.
56. Rewrite a book as a play and stage it for another class.
57. Conduct a quiz show similar to "I've Got a Secret" and use the "secrets" of book characters.
58. Dramatize a book, or a scene, as a puppet play.
59. Play bingo by matching books and authors.
60. Make a new jacket for a book and write a blurb about it.
61. Compare and contrast two books.
62. Compare and contrast two book characters.
63. Compare and contrast two authors.
64. Compare and contrast two illustrators.
65. Make story characters for the felt board.
66. Prepare a paper scroll using scenes from a story.
67. Construct a shadow box with a storybook scene.
68. Write a new ending to an old story.
69. Dress in costume as book characters and have a parade.

70. Create paper mosaics of story scenes.
71. Model book characters from clay or papier-mâché.
72. Paint a poster of a story scene.
73. Build a structure as described in a how-to-do-it book.
74. Write a newspaper article about a story episode.
75. Plan storytelling sessions for younger children.
76. Prepare a literature newsletter.
77. Role-play familiar book characters.
78. Prepare monopoly-type board games using book clues.
79. Conduct a panel discussion on science fiction books.
80. Organize a scavenger hunt using book clues.
81. Use magazine advertisements to make a collage of a book scene.
82. Write a letter of recommendation for a well-liked book.
83. Carve story characters from bars of soap.
84. Write an imaginary letter between two characters from a book.
85. Dress dolls in costume to create a storybook family.
86. Write an additional chapter to a book made up of separate episodes.
87. Make place mats of book scenes and laminate the mats for table use.
88. Compile an imaginary diary as it might have been kept by a book character.
89. Tape-record a book report and play it for the class.
90. Write an imaginary autobiography of a book character.
91. Interview another student who is impersonating the main character from a biography or autobiography.
92. Make a collection of famous quotations from literature and post them on the bulletin board.
93. Make a comparative study of children's classics and rate them on a bar graph.
94. Exchange a series of letters with a pen pal in which books are the main topic of discussion.

95. Select a holiday and at the appropriate time set up an exhibit of books suitable for holiday reading.
96. Make a collection of poems on various themes.
97. Illustrate an oral book report with taped excerpts from the book.
98. Write a television commercial advertising a favorite book.
99. Write an essay entitled "The Wisest Book I Have Ever Known" and share it with the class.
100. Plan a literature program to be performed for parents, teachers, and other students.

of what is happening in the classroom. Class visitation by parents during times of browsing, independent reading, and book sharing is the best way for parents to learn about the individualized program. Such firsthand observation helps them appreciate the merits of allowing students to select their own reading material and shows them ways to assist and encourage their child's reading outside of school.

Three-way conferences are an opportunity for parents, teachers, and students to sit down together to discuss the reading program informally face to face. The teacher should be sure that positive strong points are emphasized and discussed and specific plans are made for improvement in areas of weakness.

Newsletters prepared as a cooperative venture between students and the teacher are popular reading material when circulated throughout the school. They may be sent home for parents to enjoy. Parent-Teacher Association programs may be devoted to explaining the workings of an individualized reading program. A slide presentation of the entire process might be prepared in the classroom and narrated by students.

Routine Interviews with Students

Students read many more library books in classes where teachers find time to talk with them privately about their personal reading. Once boys and girls become aware that the teacher knows and cares about what they read independently, they tend to read with greater interest and enthusiasm.

Talking with each student on an individual basis may seem like an impossible task; but if the session is kept brief, and if the teacher follows a plan, it can be managed. A few minutes two or three times a month of the teacher's undivided attention focused on the student's independent reading can be extremely encouraging and motivating to a child. A simple pocket chart is useful for keeping both students and the teacher apprised of upcoming interviews as well as oral book reports that are pending.

While the rest of the class is engaged in independent work of various kinds, the teacher sets up an interview station in a quiet, out-of-the way corner of the classroom and begins the series of conferences with the student whose name appears first on the chart.

In a short period of time, the teacher should be able to ask pertinent questions about the current library book a student is reading, listen to the student read a passage from the book (a passage chosen by the student and thoroughly prepared for oral reading), and make recommendations for further reading. On completion of the interview, the teacher will wish to make notations on findings and impressions, on problems that might need corrective measures, and on points that call for follow-up in future inter-

CHEAPER BY THE DOZEN

A visual aid prepared by a sixth-grade student to accompany an oral report on Frank Gilbreth's popular book.

views. Admittedly, all this is a pretty big order to accomplish, but with practice it can become a smooth and efficient operation that need not lose the elements of friendly and informal personal counseling.

Studying a Book in Depth

"Some books are to be tasted, others to be swallowed, and some few to be chewed and digested." Francis Bacon was stating a universal truth about literature. While students are reading many books of their own choosing, a small number of very special books are earmarked by the teacher and students for a thorough and more analytical study.

The in-depth study of literature has been given various labels by educators—"correlated literature units," "integrated literary studies," "book webbing." The label is not important, however; the process is. In an in-depth study the language arts teacher builds a series of lessons and learning experiences around a particular book or a small group of related books.

Books selected for such in-depth treatment should be well written, appropriate to grade level, interesting to both students and teachers, and easy to adapt to various areas of the curriculum. Obviously, the language arts teacher should se-

Creative use of natural materials to illustrate The Happy Owls *by Celestino Piatti. (Courtesy of Dianne Baker.)*

come yardsticks by which future reading will be measured.

For one group of students, *Amos Fortune: Free Man* by Elizabeth Yates became such a book. A language arts teacher of a combined fifth- and sixth-grade class introduced her students to Amos, one of the most memorable characters in children's literature, by reading the book aloud to them episode by episode over a period of weeks. As she had hoped, the students responded by asking many questions about the book and by checking out the paperback copies that had been provided. Following their lead, and on the basis of their questions, the teacher launched a study of the slave trade as it existed in Amos's youth; the leather-tanning industry, which was his profession in later years; and the memorial museum that was established for him after his death.

In a "total immersion" atmosphere, references were consulted, letters of inquiry composed and mailed, resource persons interviewed, artifacts collected, and displays set up. Because the unit cut across all subject areas—language arts, social studies, science, and art—the teacher could afford the luxury of allocating large blocks of time for research without worrying that other components of the curriculum were being short-changed.

As a culminating activity, the class decided to design and embroider a lap quilt in which each piece would symbolize a dramatic milestone in the long life of Amos Fortune. Scenes were agreed upon and designs first drawn on graph paper were transferred to cloth squares. Small groups collaborated on the needlework until each square was completed. The teacher assisted with the quilting.

The boys and girls themselves suggested a photograph of the quilt be sent to Elizabeth Yates, who in turn recommended that they present the quilt as a gift to the Amos Fortune Museum in Jaffrey, New Hampshire. The entire

lect books for lengthy study that lend themselves to speaking, listening, reading, and writing activities.

Teachers who know their students very well, who are acquainted with many children's books, and who have observed the drawing power of certain books are in a good position to make wise choices of books to be singled out for concentrated study during a school year. Since available hours for literature study are all too few, none of the time should be wasted on mediocre writing; only excellent books by the best writers should be considered for detailed study. These are the books that are likely to permanently influence a child's taste in literature and be-

Reading Activities

I am ready to share a book.

| Sally | Todd | Tim | Jill |

Have an interview with the teacher.

| Ellen | Alice | Robb | Paul |

Pocket chart of reading activities to organize the book-sharing and student-teacher conference periods. (Courtesy of Barbara Ellis.)

class joined in wrapping the package and walking to the nearest post office, where it was carefully and fondly sent on its way. The museum's curator wrote and promised that the quilt would be proudly displayed "for other boys and girls to enjoy in the years to come."

Marguerite Henry is another author whose books have been chosen by countless numbers of students and teachers for in-depth study. Some of her books, such as *Five O'Clock Charlie,* are well suited to the mini-unit idea preferred by teachers of very young children (see Display 3.4). Older students may study the majority of her books individually or as a series. Although most of Marguerite Henry's books are about horses, a wide variety of characters, places, and events make them excellent resource material for a personalized language arts program.

Summary

In order to individualize instruction effectively, the language arts teacher must be aware of the basic components of personalized teaching. Most writers on the subject of individualization agree

Each square in this lap quilt made by a fifth- and sixth-grade class represents an episode in the life of Amos Fortune. Top row, left to right: (1) Africa, (2) slave ship, (3) implements of slavery, (4) the American flag, (5) the Bible, (6) Amos's wagon, (7) tanning tools. Center row, left to right: (1) tanning bark tree, (2) Cyclops, Amos's horse, (3) Mt. Monadnock, (4) the title of the book about Amos and name of the author, (5) Amos Fortune, *(6) Amos's top hat, (7) Celyndia's corn-husk doll. Bottom row, left to right: (1) the church, (2) the home of Amos and Violet, (3) the iron kettle, (4) the school, (5) "Swing Low, Sweet Chariot," (6) tombstones of Amos and Violet, (7) communion service provided by Amos's will. (Courtesy of Helen Boudreaux, Robert E. Lee Elementary School, Port Arthur, Texas.)*

that the following practices will be in evidence in a language arts program that focuses on the individual child: (1) intraclass, task-oriented grouping, (2) multimedia teaching, (3) self-direction in learning, (4) differentiated assignments, and (5) tutorial practices. Each involves a set of teacher behaviors and methods that must be studied, practiced, and evaluated consistently. A self-rating instrument can be of value as a teacher attempts to personalize language arts teaching.

Individualized reading deserves special attention in any instructional program that attempts to meet the unique needs of students. The basic

Display 3.4 Mini-Unit Based on Five O'Clock Charlie[1]

With the publication of *Five O'Clock Charlie* in 1962, young children were at last able to enjoy one of Marguerite Henry's wonderful horse stories. It is an excellent introduction to her other books, which are so widely read by students in the middle and upper grades.

Charlie is a lovable old horse who is retired by his master. He finds a way to make a useful and interesting life for himself by ringing the bell at the Boar's Head Inn every day precisely at five o'clock to notify the countryside that Bertie's good apple tarts are hot out of the oven. Of course, he is rewarded for his effort with the "biggest, brownest, juiciest tart of all." An excellent follow-up activity to a study of *Five O'Clock Charlie* is the baking of apple tarts according to the following recipe:

Recipe for Easy Apple Tarts

2 cans crescent dinner rolls
1 can apple pie filling

Make each rectangle of dough slightly larger and thinner by rolling it gently with a floured rolling pin. Cut five circles from each piece with a 2½" cookie cutter or drinking glass. Place one tablespoon of pie filling on 20 circles. Top with remaining circles and seal edges together with the tines of a fork. Bake 15 to 20 minutes at 375° in preheated oven. Cool and serve with milk.

These small round tarts baked golden brown look very much like those Bertie served each day to Five O'Clock Charlie. Wesley Dennis features them several times in his illustrations.

Language Arts Activities

Read *Five O'Clock Charlie* aloud. Discuss the story. What kind of a horse was Charlie? What is a workhorse? Why was Charlie retired by Mister Spinks? How does a horse of twenty-eight years compare with a person of that age? What is meant by the expression "put out to pasture"? Why did retirement make Charlie unhappy? How could Charlie know when to ring the bell? What is an inn? What was the most popular food served at the Boar's Head Inn? Why?

Prepare a vocabulary chart of descriptive words used by Marguerite Henry to describe Charlie—frisky, bored, useless, forlorn, free, stately, bold, good-for-nothing, happy.

Social Studies Activities

Study the illustrations for a realistic look at the English countryside.

Locate England on a map or globe.

Compare Charlie's retirement with that of elderly people in our society.

Discuss the emotions of loneliness and boredom.

Science and Mathematics Activities

Discuss Charlie's rheumatism as a characteristic of the aging process. At age twenty-eight, why was it so remarkable that Charlie could still roll over, "not just half way, but a complete once over"?

Point out the three geometric shapes to be seen in the dough for the crescent dinner rolls—triangles, two triangles placed together to form a rectangle, and a rectangle cut into circles.

Art Activities

Study Wesley Dennis's illustrations in *Five O'Clock Charlie* and in Marguerite Henry's other books.

Make a collection of horse pictures, prints, or posters for the bulletin board.

[1]Betty Coody, *Using Literature with Young Children*, 2d ed. (Wm. C. Brown, 1979). Used by permission.

elements of a personalized program are a collection of trade books in the classroom, time for girls and boys to browse and select their reading material, time for independent reading, a system of student record keeping, planned book-sharing sessions, a plan for parent involvement, and regularly scheduled student-teacher interviews.

Another important way to personalize the teaching of reading, writing, listening, and speaking is the practice of studying in detail outstanding pieces of literature. Elizabeth Yates and Marguerite Henry are examples of authors whose books offer the kind of information and substance needed for long-term in-depth study.

A group of young girls constructed papier-mâché horses to represent the ones in Marguerite Henry's books. (Courtesy of Lamar University.)

Best Books for Children

Black Gold, written by Marguerite Henry and illustrated by Wesley Dennis. New York: Rand McNally, 1957. This is the story of a coal-black racehorse who grew up in the midst of an Oklahoma oil field. Because the Osage Indians called oil "black gold," he was given that name as a foal. Black Gold continued to run and to win races even during the initial stages of lameness caused by a crack in his hoof: "Yet in spite of his tortured foot, Black Gold kept on racing, and by sheer willpower won his races. Now, people somehow began to identify themselves with him. If he could go on winning over such a handicap, they too could go on living with their own lameness, deafness, whatever their burden." (M-U)

Born to Trot, written by Marguerite Henry and illustrated by Wesley Dennis. New York: Rand McNally, 1950. Marguerite Henry had wanted to write a book about Rysdyk's Hambletonian, the famous Standardbred, but decided instead to build her story around a young, modern-day mare named Rosalind, who was a world champion trotting horse. The heroes of the book are Gib White, the young man who owned Rosalind, and Gib's father, who trained her. The characters in the story, both Rosalind and her fellow creatures, are real. (M-U)

Brighty of the Grand Canyon, written by Marguerite Henry and illustrated by Wesley Dennis. New York:

Rand McNally, 1953. An old prospector who roamed the Grand Canyon looking for pockets of copper found the little burro, made friends with him, and named him Brighty for Bright Angel Creek, which tumbles down the north wall of the canyon into the Colorado River. It is said that Brighty's hoofs tramped out the original trail down into the canyon, still used by explorers, rangers, artists, and tourists. (M-U)

Dear Readers and Riders, written by Marguerite Henry. Chicago: Rand McNally, 1969. As the number of her books increased and as they grew in popularity, Marguerite Henry found herself with many more letters from children than she could possibly answer. After several years of publishing a newsletter that attempted to answer a dozen or more letters at a time, she decided to write a book of replies to questions of all kinds—but mostly about horses. A librarian friend who suggested the idea said, "It could be a kind of jolly encyclopedia." The "jolly encyclopedia" makes delightful reading for horse lovers and lovers of horse stories. (M-U)

Five O'Clock Charlie, written by Marguerite Henry and illustrated by Wesley Dennis. Chicago: Rand McNally, 1962. Based on a true incident, *Five O'Clock Charlie* is the story of an endearing old workhorse who refuses to accept retirement with its life of ease

A Profile of Marguerite Henry

MANY OF THE LETTERS received by Marguerite Henry have asked, "Why do you like to write about horses?" "It is exciting to me," she answers in her newsletter to readers, "that no matter how much machinery replaces the horse, the work it can do is still measured in horsepower—even in this space age." People of all ages seem to feel as she does. Her books are read and loved the world over. Without doubt she is one of the greatest, if not *the* greatest, writers of horse stories of all time.

When Marguerite Henry was eleven years old, a woman's magazine paid her $12 for her first piece of writing, called "Hide and Seek in Autumn Leaves." She has told her readers that she is sorry that she kept neither the check nor the article, for they were responsible for starting her on a writing career that she still considers "the most delightful way to make a living."

Practically every book written by Marguerite Henry, whether about characters with four legs or two, is based on fact. She has traveled widely to glean information and background for her books—to Italy for *Gaudenzia, Pride of the Palio,* to Austria for *White Stallion of Lipizza,* to Morocco for *King of the Wind.* She stayed in Colorado while gathering material for *Mustang, Wild Spirit of the West,* and in Arizona's Grand Canyon she walked the trails Brighty the burro had beaten out with his hoofs. Thorough research not only makes her books authentic and accurate, but creates characters that ring true.

Though fictionalized, all of Marguerite Henry's books are written from a certain historical perspective and are usually considered historical romances. Children, however, seldom think of her books as a study of history, which is just as well. James E. Higgins writes:

> It is partly because children do not come to her books thinking of them as historical works that they are so especially appealing. Teachers, and far too many writers, often ignore the needs of children, forgetting that if they are to be attracted to the study of history their interests must be aroused and their sympathies enlisted; and also forgetting that they want action, drama, adventure, and heroes. All of these can be found by children in the historical animal romances of Marguerite Henry.[1]

Marguerite Breithaupt Henry was born on April 13, 1902. The family home was in Milwaukee, Wisconsin, where her father owned a printing business. She has said that it was in her father's shop that "I first got printer's ink in my blood." After graduating from Milwaukee State Teacher's College, she was married to Sidney Crocker Henry. They now live in Rancho Santa Fe, California, where Mrs. Henry continues her research and writing.

Marguerite Henry photo is used with permission.
[1]James E. Higgins, "Marguerite Henry," *Twentieth Century Children's Writers* (New York: St. Martin's Press, 1978), pp. 589–91.

To date, Marguerite Henry's books have won practically every award granted in the field of literature for children and adolescents. The awards, citations, and honors that have come to her include the Newbery Award, the Boys' Club of America Award, the Lewis Carroll Shelf Award (for a book deemed worthy of being on the shelf with Carroll), the Junior Literary Guild Selection, the Friends of Literature Award, the William Allen White Award, the Sequoyah Children's Book Award, the Western Heritage Award, the Society of Midland Authors Award, the Mark Twain Award, and the Clara Ingram Judson Award.

At the conclusion of *Brighty of the Grand Canyon,* Marguerite Henry states simply her philosophy of life and death:

> Of course, everyone knows that Brighty has long since left this earth. But some animals, like some men leave a trail of glory behind them. They give their spirit to the place where they have lived, and remain forever a part of the rocks and streams and the wind and sky.[2]

The same might be said of her. She will surely give her spirit to the place where she has lived, in the hearts of countless readers young and old.

BOOKS BY MARGUERITE HENRY

Always Reddy, 1947
Misty of Chincoteague, 1947
Benjamin West and His Cat Grimalkin, 1947
King of the Wind, 1948
Sea Star, Orphan of Chincoteague, 1949
Born to Trot, 1950
Album of Horses, 1951
Brighty of the Grand Canyon, 1953
Justin Morgan Had a Horse, 1954
Cinnabar, the One O'Clock Fox, 1956
Black Gold, 1957
Muley Ears, Nobody's Dog, 1959
The Wildest Horse Race in the World, 1960 (Formerly titled *Gaudenzia, Pride of the Palio*)
All About Horses, 1962
Five O'Clock Charlie, 1962
Stormy, Misty's Foal, 1963
White Stallion of Lipizza, 1964
Mustang, Wild Spirit of the West, 1966
Dear Readers and Riders, 1969
San Domingo, the Medicine Hat Stallion, 1972

[2]Marguerite Henry, *Brighty of the Grand Canyon* (New York: Rand McNally, 1953), p. 222.

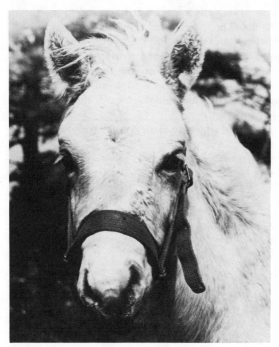

Misty of Chincoteague. From Misty of Chincoteague *by Marguerite Henry, illustrated by Wesley
Dennis. Copyright © 1947 by Rand McNally
& Company. Renewal copyright 1975. Used by
permission.*

and boredom. Charlie finds a way "to make his loneliness vanish like a fog when the sun comes out." Most
of Marguerite Henry's horse stories are too difficult
for young readers. This one is an exception. (P-M)

Justin Morgan Had a Horse, written by Marguerite
Henry and illustrated by Wesley Dennis. New York:
Rand McNally, 1954. Justin Morgan was a singing
master and owner of the horse that became founder
of the famous Morgan breed. Marguerite Henry
quotes passages from some of Morgan's songs in her
story. When the manuscript was finished, she went to
the library to study horse paintings and fell in love
with the drawings of Wesley Dennis in his book
called *Flip*. He agreed to illustrate *Justin Morgan*, and
from there grew a team that lasted through many
years and many books. (M-U)

King of the Wind, written by Marguerite Henry and
illustrated by Wesley Dennis. New York: Rand
McNally, 1948. The Godolphin Arabian, a famous
thoroughbred stallion known as Sham, lived more
than two centuries ago. It is his blood, however, that
gives speed and stamina to modern racehorses. Marguerite Henry tells her readers that while she was writing this story, her own horse became Sham: "It was
not his eyelashes that brushed my hand as I held
the water bucket, but those of Sham, the fleet one."
(M-U)

Misty of Chincoteague, written by Marguerite Henry
and illustrated by Wesley Dennis. Chicago: Rand
McNally, 1947. Of all Marguerite Henry's horse stories, *Misty* is probably the one most loved by children. The book is built around the dreams of two
children of Chincoteague, Virginia, to own a wild
mare and her foal, Misty. The annual wild-pony
roundup, channel swim, and auction held each July
on Chincoteague Island was the inspiration for the
book about Misty and the Beebe family. Many reviewers have called it the best horse story ever written.
(M-U)

Mustang, Wild Spirit of the West, written by Marguerite Henry and illustrated by Robert E. Loughied.
Chicago: Rand McNally, 1966. Wild Horse Annie
was a Colorado woman who fought to have legislation passed and enforced that would protect wild
mustangs from slaughter by men who wanted to sell
them for a few dollars to dogfood factories. Annie
and her crusade became the inspiration for this book.
Children by the thousands wrote letters to the government on behalf of the mustangs, "the last free spirit of
the West." (M-U)

Sea Star, Orphan of Chincoteague, written by
Marguerite Henry and illustrated by Wesley Dennis.
Chicago: Rand McNally, 1949. After Misty became
so well known to children everywhere, it was decided
that she should be sent to Illinois to live with
Marguerite Henry. Maureen explains to Grandma
Beebe: "Misty really doesn't belong to us any more.
She's grown bigger than our island. She's in a book,
Grandma. Now she belongs to boys and girls everywhere." To take the place of Misty, Paul and Maureen
adopt a small orphan colt they find on the beach. He
was named for the white star on his forehead and for
the way he wound himself around the children "just

the way sea stars wind themselves around oysters." (M-U)

Stormy: Misty's Foal, written by Marguerite Henry and illustrated by Wesley Dennis. Chicago: Rand McNally, 1963. The wind and waves of a raging storm wrecked a Spanish ship and brought ponies to Chincoteague Island many years ago. Now Misty is brought into Grandma Beebe's kitchen to wait out another storm and to give birth to a mare foal. From all the suggestions sent by Misty's fans, Stormy was the unanimous choice of the Beebe family as a name for the foal. Misty and Stormy were later taken on a theatre tour to raise money for the restoration of the pony herds that were drowned in the storm. (M-U)

White Stallion of Lipizza, written by Marguerite Henry and illustrated by Wesley Dennis. Chicago: Rand McNally, 1964. The hero of this book is Borina, one of the most famous stallions of the white Lipizzan breed. Marguerite Henry was inspired to write the story when she saw the horses perform in the Spanish Court Riding School in Vienna. This is an authentic account of the amazing intelligence of the horses and the infinite patience and skill of their trainers: "The Lipizzaners are not performing tricks, they are doing natural movements—with the rider's help." (M-U)

The Wildest Horse Race in the World, written by Marguerite Henry and illustrated by Wesley Dennis. New York: Rand McNally, 1960. This book tells the story of one of the most dangerous horse races in all the world—the Palio. Ten men elected to represent each *contrada* in the region race bareback three times around the square in the ancient hill town of Siena, Italy. Each summer people travel from all over Italy and other parts of the world to the sweeping hills of Tuscany to marvel at the medieval pageantry of the Palio. (M-U)

Bibliography

Coody, Betty. *Using Literature with Young Children*, 2d ed. Dubuque, Iowa: Wm. C. Brown, 1978.

Coody, Betty, and Ben M. Harris. "Individualization of Instruction Inventory." *Elementary English*, March 1971.

Croft, Doreen J. *Parents and Teachers: A Resource Book for Home, School, and Community Relations*. Belmont, Calif.: Wadsworth, 1979.

Dinkmeyer, Don, and Rudolf Dreikurs. *Encouraging Children to Learn*. Englewood Cliffs, N.J.: Prentice-Hall, 1963.

Dunn, Rita, and Kenneth Dunn. *Practical Approaches to Individualizing Instruction: Contracts and Other Effective Teaching Strategies*. West Nyack, N.Y.: Parker, 1972.

Forgan, Harry W. *The Reading Corner*. Santa Monica, Calif.: Goodyear, 1977.

Hare, Paul A., Edgar F. Borgatta, and Robert F. Bales. *Small Groups*. New York: Knopf, 1961.

Harris, Larry A., and Carl B. Smith. *Individualizing Reading Instruction: A Reader*. New York: Holt, Rinehart and Winston, 1972.

Howes, Virgil M. *Individualization of Instruction: A Teaching Strategy*. London: MacMillan, 1970.

Huck, Charlotte S. *Children's Literature in the Elementary School*, 3d ed. New York: Holt, Rinehart and Winston, 1979.

Musgrave, Ray G. *Individualized Instruction: Teaching Strategies Focusing on the Learner*. Boston: Allyn and Bacon, 1975.

Otto, Henry J., and David C. Sanders. *Elementary School Organization and Administration*. New York: Meredith, 1964.

Oxley, Mary Boone. *Illustrated Guide to Individualized Kindergarten Instruction*. West Nyack, N.Y.: Parker, 1976.

Petreshene, Susan S. *Complete Guide to Learning Centers*. Palo Alto, Calif.: Pendragon House, 1978.

Rapport, Virginia, ed. *Learning Centers: Children on Their Own*. Washington, D.C.: Association for Childhood Education International, 1970.

Raymond, Dorothy. *Individualizing Reading in the Elementary School*. West Nyack, N.Y.: Parker, 1973.

Spache, George D., and Evelyn B. Spache. *Reading in the Elementary School*, 4th ed. Boston: Allyn and Bacon, 1977.

Thomas, George I., and Joseph Crescimbeni. *Individualizing Instruction in the Elementary School*. New York: Random House, 1967.

Veatch, Jeannette. *Reading in the Elementary School*, 2d ed. New York: Wiley, 1978.

Yates, Elizabeth. *Amos Fortune: Free Man*. New York: Dutton, 1950.

Chapter 4

"Is Anyone Out There Listening?": Improving Listening and Nonverbal Communication Skills

WE ARE LIVING in a time when no one listens to anyone else. Husbands do not listen to wives; wives do not listen to husbands. Parents do not listen to children; children do not listen to parents. Most assuredly, teachers do not listen to students. It may be an overstatement to say that *no one* listens; yet to find one person actively listening to another—listening with empathy and understanding—is a rare experience.

Having another person truly listen to us is one of life's great joys. To have someone's undivided attention, no matter how briefly, is extremely satisfying and therapeutic. It enhances our sense of self-worth.

Lorraine Hansberry captures the strong desire for an understanding listener in a scene from her play *A Raisin in the Sun*. At breakfast, Walter attempts to tell his wife about an investment plan he hopes will take them out of the ghetto, but she is too preoccupied with breakfast and other matters to listen. Exasperated, Walter exclaims:

That's it. There you are. Man say to his woman: I got me a dream. His woman say: Eat your eggs. Man say: I got to take hold of this here world, baby! And a woman say: Eat your eggs and go to work. Man say: I got to change my life, I'm choking to death, baby! And his woman say— Your eggs is getting cold! . . . Damn my eggs . . . damn all the eggs that ever was![1]

The search for a sympathetic listener is a recurring theme in literature. People will go to incredible lengths to find a listening, caring companion. In "The Lament," a short story, Anton Chekhov portrays a man's desperate need for someone to share his grief.

Each night, to earn a few kopecks, Iona Potopov drives a horse-drawn cab through the streets. One bitterly cold evening he turns and says to the army officer who is his passenger,

"My son died this week." When he tries to tell the officer how his son died of a fever, he finds the man has dozed off. Iona's next fare is three rowdy young men on their way to a tavern. During a pause in their joking, he turns around and murmurs, "My son died this week." One of the young men replies: "We all must die. Now hurry up, hurry up!"

When the old man is alone again, he searches among the crowds on either side of the street to see whether there might be just one person who will listen to him. But people hurry by without noticing him or his distress. Iona returns his horse to the stable and finds all the other cab-drivers asleep around the stove. Finally, a young driver stirs and Iona says, "Listen, mate, this week my son died." He looks to see what effect his words have had and finds the young man has hidden his face and is fast asleep again. Iona is overwhelmed by his grief.

"I'll go and look after my horse," he thinks. "There's always time to sleep." The horse munches his feed and breathes on his master's hand. Overcome by his feelings, Iona tells the animal his story.[2]

Educators have long extolled the virtues of effective listening, but until recently there was little evidence that they were doing anything to bring it about. In college, prospective teachers have received training neither in methods of teaching listening skills nor in methods of teaching listening as a process. In spite of new college textbooks and elementary curriculum materials containing information on listening, it remains the most neglected of all language arts skills. Listening, however, not only can but must be taught.

In recent years, language arts teachers have come to realize that girls and boys need to be taught to notice and respond to nonverbal as well as verbal cues. Thus they are bringing to the

[1]Lorraine Hansberry, *A Raisin in the Sun*, in *Plays of Our Time*, ed. Bennett Cerf (New York: Random House, 1967), p. 556.

[2]Anton Chekhov, "The Lament," *Masters and Masterpieces of the Short Story*, ed. Joshua McClennen (New York: Holt, 1957), pp. 5–6.

classroom some of the findings of the new science of kinesics—the study of body movement and gestures. In this chapter, we will describe activities aimed at improving children's listening habits, and we will show how students' sensitivity to the nuances of body language can be sharpened in the language arts class.

Active Listening in the Classroom

Hearing is the special sense by which sounds are perceived. Listening occurs only when the listener pays attention or attends to the sounds. Actual listening, as we know it in the language arts, takes place *only when* a listener interprets what is being heard and reacts to or takes action on it. Hearing is a passive response; listening is an active skill.

It is believed that the teaching of listening has been neglected because language arts teachers assume that children entering school already have the ability to listen. This assumption is based on the fact that listening is the primary communication skill. Children begin listening in early infancy and have several years of listening experience before entering school. Unfortunately, in most cases, only bad listening habits will have developed. Just because children have played with crayons and pencils at home, we do not assume that they know how to write or that planned writing instruction is unnecessary. Similarly, we should not assume that their listening skills are well developed.

At home, children are bombarded with sounds from television, radio, and stereo, and with increasingly higher levels of noise pollution from every direction. Moreover, these auditory stimuli follow children to school. Unless teachers help girls and boys distinguish between sounds that are important and those that must be blocked out, children may never develop the listening skill needed for effective social interaction and optimum intellectual growth.

In one of the oldest and best-known studies on listening, Paul Rankin found that his adult subjects spent well over half of the workday in verbal communication. Eleven percent of the time spent in verbal communication was taken up by writing, 15 percent by reading, 32 percent by speaking, and 42 percent by listening.[3] Figure 4.1 shows this breakdown graphically.

Miriam Wilt reported in 1950 that elementary school students, on the average, were spending 158 minutes listening during a school day—more than half of the time they were in the classroom.[4] Most of that time was spent listening to the teacher. More recent studies have corroborated Wilt's findings that listening in school is one-sided—students listening to teachers. A better balance is long overdue.

Any discussion of improving the listening ability of elementary students must begin with the classroom teacher. The teacher must learn to listen to children, to give sincere, reflective consideration to their interests and concerns. It is futile to expect children to listen to teachers, parents, or even to each other, if important adults in their lives refuse to listen to them.

Despite growing awareness that students tend to fail or succeed in school in accordance with the way they are treated by teachers, most teachers do not listen to students' concerns. They seem to lack understanding of students' problems, and they respond to their questions in a variety of ways that actually cut off communication. Lynette Long has enumerated common strategies used by teachers who wish to avoid the issue of listening to students:

1. *Let me show you how smart I am.* This teacher uses a student's problem to demonstrate a clever ability to solve all problems,

[3]Paul T. Rankin, "Listening Ability," *Proceedings of the Ohio State Education Conference*, 9th annual session (Columbus: Ohio State University, 1929), pp. 172–183.

[4]Miriam E. Wilt, "A Study of Teacher Awareness of Listening as a Factor in Elementary Education," *Journal of Educational Research* (April 1950), pp. 626–636.

| Listening | Speaking | Reading | Writing |

42% spent listening 32% spent speaking 15% spent reading. 11%

Figure 4.1 Verbal Communication During the Workday. (Courtesy of Barbara Ellis.)

and bombards the student with ready solutions without showing any genuine concern.

2. *Let me tell you a story.* Without actually listening to the student, this teacher seizes the opportunity to share a personal experience.

3. *Not now . . . later.* This teacher uses postponement to avoid the problem altogether.

4. *Everything's going to be all right.* This teacher circumvents the problem with cheery platitudes and never deals seriously with a student's concerns.

5. *Let's talk about this instead.* This teacher is quick to change the subject and constantly moves to a more pleasant topic.

6. *Parables, parables, parables.* This teacher gives general advice, never specific enough to relate it to the problem at hand, and bases the advice on a set of beliefs or values. The advice amounts to little more than a cliché.

7. *I'm too busy.* This teacher leaves the impression of preoccupation and conveys to students that there is no time to listen to them.

8. *I'm a teacher, not a counselor.* This teacher is ready and willing to discuss subject matter problems with students, but not personal ones.[5]

Any teacher embarking on a plan to improve the listening skills of students, as well as their

[5]Adapted from Lynette Long, *Listening/Responding: Human-Relations Training for Teachers.* Copyright © 1978 by Wadsworth, Inc. Reprinted by permission of the publisher, Brooks/Cole Publishing Company, Monterey, Calif.

speaking, reading, and writing skills, should first become dedicated to the idea of becoming a model of a sympathetic listener.

Be an active listener. Make eye contact with girls and boys who are speaking to you. Ask appropriate questions, and use gestures that encourage openness. In short, behave like a good listener.

Allow students to express themselves. In listening to their thoughts and feelings, leave room for disagreement. Withhold adult judgment and censure. Avoid sarcasm and ridicule. Children are always at a serious disadvantage before any adult who resorts to sarcasm. Since children are seldom sophisticated or secure enough to return it in kind, ridicule only serves to sever the lines of communication.

Study nonverbal signals. A child's body movements and gestures can reveal a great deal about what she or he really means. Ask the child to clarify if the meaning is obscure. Ask, for example, "Is this what I hear you saying?" Always keep in mind the importance of being a thoughtful listener. When answers are not possible or appropriate, just serving as a sounding board for a child who needs a listener can be beneficial.

Activities to Sharpen Listening Skills

Children in the classroom are expected to attend to and take action on words and phrases, voice

Display 4.1 General Listening Skills

1. To remember significant details accurately.
2. To remember simple sequences of words and ideas.
3. To follow oral directions.
4. To understand denotative meanings of words.
5. To understand meanings of words from spoken context.
6. To listen, to answer, and to formulate simple questions.
7. To paraphrase a spoken message.
8. To understand connotative meanings of words.
9. To identify main ideas and to summarize (the who, what, when, where, why).
10. To listen for implications of significant details.
11. To listen for implications of main ideas.
12. To understand interrelationships among ideas expressed or implied and the organizational pattern of spoken materials well enough to predict what will probably come next.
13. To follow a sequence in: (a) plot development, (b) character development, (c) speaker's argument.
14. To impose structure on a spoken presentation, sometimes including notetaking, by: (a) realizing the purpose of the speaker, (b) remaining aware of personal motives in listening, (c) connecting and relating what is said later in the presentation with earlier portions, (d) detecting transitional words or phrases that refer the listener back or carry him along, (e) detecting the skeleton of main and supporting points and other interrelationships.
15. To connect the spoken material with previous experience.
16. To listen, to apply, and to plan action.
17. To listen, to imagine, and to extend for enjoyment and emotional response (includes appreciation for aesthetic, artistic, dialectic richness, felicity of phrasing, rhythmic flow).

Sara W. Lundsteen, *Listening: Its Impact on Reading and the Other Language Arts*. Copyright © 1971 by the National Council of Teachers of English. Reprinted by permission of the publisher and author.

intonation, and body language. The actions they take include following directions, remembering information, and paraphrasing or summarizing something they've heard. An expanded list of such *general listening skills* appears in Display 4.1. When a student moves beyond general listening to analyzing and criticizing what is being heard, to comparing the message received with something already internalized, the listener is said to be engaged in critical listening. A list of *critical listening skills* is given in Display 4.2.

Displays 4.1 and 4.2 will help teachers plan activities that will offer children a wide variety of listening experiences. They may also facilitate the preparation of tests and checklists to evaluate how well listening skills are being acquired.

The language arts teacher should have a well-stocked arsenal of activities that will enable boys and girls to become good listeners. In addition to familiarizing yourself with the following procedures, which we have found effective, you should keep a file of your own ideas for teaching

Display 4.2 Critical Listening Skills

1. To distinguish fact from fancy, according to a criterion.
2. To judge validity and adequacy of main ideas, arguments, hypotheses.
3. To distinguish well-supported statements from opinion and judgment and to evaluate them.
4. To distinguish well-supported statements from irrelevant ones and to evaluate them; to sort relevant from irrelevant information.
5. To inspect, compare, and contrast ideas and to arrive at some conclusion in regard to them, e.g., the appropriateness and appeal of one descriptive word over another.
6. To evaluate use of fallacies such as: (a) self-contradiction, (b) "skirting" the question at issue, (c) hasty or false generalization, (d) false analogy, (e) failure to present all choices, (f) appeal to ignorance.
7. To recognize and judge effects of devices the speaker may use to influence the listener, such as: (a) music, (b) loaded words, (c) voice intonation, (d) play on emotional and controversial issues, (e) propaganda, sales pressure, i.e., to identify affective loading in communication and evaluate it.
8. To detect and evaluate bias and prejudice of a speaker or point of view.
9. To evaluate the qualifications of the speaker.
10. To plan to evaluate ways in which the speaker's idea might be applied in a new situation.

Sara W. Lundsteen, *Listening: Its Impact on Reading and the Other Language Arts.* Copyright © 1971 by the National Council of Teachers of English. Reprinted by permission of the publisher and author.

listening. Also keep in mind that any well-planned activity designed to promote speaking will also help to develop better listening habits, and that thoughtful, attentive listening by students should be commended with the same respect and admiration that are extended for skillful speaking.

Art and Listening

Mount several inexpensive art prints on cardboard. Divide the class into small groups and distribute a print to each group. Ask the children to take turns describing the paintings while others listen. Encourage the use of colorful adjectives.

Display a large, realistic landscape or seascape painting and ask students to listen while a class member responds to the following questions:

If I were in this place,

what sounds would I hear?

what sights would I see?

what scents would I smell?

what thoughts would I think?

what feelings would I have?

Read aloud a descriptive scene from a favorite children's book and ask the students to depict the scene with colored chalk on textured art paper.

Give oral, step-by-step directions for an art project and allow time for students to carry out each step:

1. Use a black crayon to draw 5 fish on your paper.
2. Color 2 fish yellow and 3 orange.
3. Paint over the entire page with green tempera paint. (The crayoned fish will resist paint and show through, creating a watery effect.)

Listening Walks

Take students on short "listening" walks around the school yard. At the beginning of each walk ask them to listen for different kinds of sounds. After returning to the classroom, discuss the sounds heard on the walk and list them on a chart. Some contrasting sounds to listen for might include

- High sounds/Low sounds
- Loud sounds/Soft sounds
- Nearby sounds/Faraway sounds
- Pleasant sounds/Unpleasant sounds
- Human sounds/Nature sounds
- Rhythmic sounds/Erratic sounds
- Soothing sounds/Irritating sounds

Sound Barrels and Boxes

Cover twenty-six small boxes with contact paper and label each with a different letter of the alphabet. Ask students to fill each box with small cut-out pictures representing words that begin with each letter. For practice in beginning sounds, have students take out the pictures, spread them on a table, say the name of each picture, and reclassify the picture according to its beginning sound.

A variation on this activity is to fill boxes, cartons, or cans with small objects instead of pictures. The objects may then be spread out, discussed, and reclassified by beginning sound. A soft-drink case with twenty-four compartments also works well for these activities if each "box" is labeled with a letter of the alphabet (y and z may be combined with w and x).

Listening to Literature

Tape-record one of the popular folk tales or poems of the accumulative type in which events mount up in a spiral and then unwind again. Ask students to retell the story and place the events in proper sequential order. Check for accuracy by playing the tape back again. The following accumulative tales and poems are popular with children:

- "Drummer Hoff"
- "This Is the House That Jack Built"
- "Over in the Meadow"
- "There was a Crooked Man"
- "The Old Woman and Her Pig"
- "If All the Seas Were One Sea"
- "Chicken Little"
- "The Little Red Hen"
- "The Gingerbread Boy"
- "The Bremen Town Musicians"
- "Clever Elsie"
- "One Fine Day"
- "There Was an Old Woman Who Swallowed a Fly"

Read aloud a narrative poem such as "The Pied Piper of Hamelin." Ask students to paint the various scenes in sequential order and to

Lionel the Listener

1. Sits in a comfortable position.

2. Looks at the speaker.

3. Thinks about what is being said.

4. Picks out the main idea.

5. Listens for supporting facts.

6. Takes advantage of body language.

7. Thinks over what has been said.

8. Evaluates what has been said.

Figure 4.2   Lionel the Listener's Guide to Effective Listening. (Courtesy of Barbara Ellis.)

write two- or three-sentence captions for each scene. Check throughout for effective listening.

Name Games

Write the names of children on 5 × 7 cards. Arrange them into groups according to beginning sounds and display them in a pocket chart with each name showing. Use the name groupings to dismiss students from the classroom for daily activities: "All of those persons whose name begins like Susan's may go outside to play." "If your last name begins like Bill's last name, you may go to the cafeteria." Continue until all students have been dismissed. Eventually this game can be played without the visual clues.

Compose name riddles for students as a listening activity. "I am thinking of someone in this class who baby-sits to earn spending money. She is smiling at us. Her name is _____." "I am thinking of a boy in our class who has a new baby brother. His name is _____." Students listen to each riddle and supply the correct name. When they become familiar with the activity, they may help the teacher compose the riddles.

The Listener's Guide

With the students' help, draw up a list of criteria for effective listening. Write the characteristics on a chart or poster and illustrate it with an appropriate picture (see Figure 4.2). Review the characteristics periodically for reinforcement and commend the students when they follow the criteria.

Rhyme Time

Make a collection of small objects that can be paired to rhyme with each other—for example, a block and a sock, a plane and a train, a star and a jar. Store them in small boxes and ask a student to pair them. Check the work by having another student name the paired objects.

Compose rhyming riddles for children and ask them to supply the correct answers. "I know a word that rhymes with *blue*. It comes in a bottle and you paste things with it." "I know a word that rhymes with *train*. It flies through the air and you can ride in it."

Cross-Age Listening

Plan a storytelling session in which older students prepare stories for telling to younger children. Assist them in making felt-board illus-

The older child is telling a story to younger children. She will check their listening skills by asking them to reconstruct the story. (Courtesy of Caldwood Elementary School, South Park Independent School District, Beaumont, Texas.)

trations to accompany their stories. To encourage better speaking by older students and better listening by younger ones, allow the younger children to retell the story and place the visuals on the board in proper sequence.

Exotic Listening

Use commercial tapes and records to introduce students to unusual and sometimes mysterious sounds that not only appeal to the ear but stir the imagination as well. The following types of recordings might be used:

- Bird calls
- Songs of humpback whales
- Sounds of the desert
- Sounds of the jungle
- Foreign languages
- Regional dialects
- Exotic musical instruments
- Music from foreign countries
- Morse code

Listening to Poetry

The teacher who reads poetry well, shares it on a daily basis, and makes wise selections in light of the age group for whom the poetry is intended is well on the way to improving the appreciative listening skills of children. David McCord's poem "Speak Up," presented in Display 4.3, is an excellent example of a selection containing many sounds and words to be repeated and enjoyed by young listeners.

An End-of-the-Day Routine

Reserve the last few minutes of the school day to review the main events and major learnings that have taken place during the day. Encourage students to listen carefully to the information in order to share it with their parents when they ask the inevitable: "What did you do in school today?"

Variety in Listening

To learn to listen in an efficient and discriminating way, children need to hear many kinds of language usage. They should encounter a variety

An upper elementary student listens to her own oral reading of a textbook story. (Courtesy of Lamar University.)

of dialects, voices, and sounds as they listen to recordings made by themselves and their peers, as well as by teachers and other professionals.

Increasing Awareness of Nonverbal Communication

Within the past decade, the study of body language has emerged as a new science called kinesics. Kinesics is the systematic study of how human beings communicate through body movement and gestures. The science recognizes that words alone may give a distorted picture of what a person is trying to communicate.

More than four hundred years ago Shakespeare recognized the significance of body language when he wrote: "There's language in her

---

Display 4.3 Speak Up
by David McCord

Lambs *bleat*
While gamboling on four springlike sprunglike
    feet.
Whoever thought up *bleat?*
Whoever? I repeat.

Cows *moo?*
They do for me; perhaps for you.
Look into *Webster,* though, where cows say
    Boo.
Wonder what cows old Mr. Webster knew?

Horses? Resources zero. They just *neigh.*
The word is spelled that way.
Perhaps to side with *sleigh,*
Some people say.

Frogs *croak?*
I'm glad you spoke
Of that old joke:
Poetic license, which most frogs r-r-r-r-*revoke!*

Dogs *bark?*
Quite likely back in Noah's Ark.
How now? *Bowwow!*—especially after dark.
Leashwise they row *bowwow* in every park.

Cats howl, *meow,* spit, *purr:*
Purr when you stroke their fur.
Meow for milk—yes, sir!
Cats, of course, aren't kittens. Wish they were.

The grunts of big pigs don't have much
    appeal.
It's little pigs who *squeal*
And somehow make you feel
That being a pig's O.K., if not ideal.

Owls *hoot?* That isn't true.
No "t." Just hoo, hoo—*hoo!*
Three, four times; maybe two.
Screech owls, though, screech at you.

Crows *caw,* they do. Their caws
Come singly, spaced. Each pause
Means something in crows' laws.
Can't tell you what, because . . .

The thrushes sing. The hermit thrush
Makes other singers sound like mush.
Clear, lonely flute—the notes don't rush
Deep woods at dusk. You hear him? *Hush!*

But yet again:
Don't let's forget the winter wren
In Canada. So small! But when
He fills a valley, you will listen then.

Moles? Don't know what they say
In tunnels. Doesn't pay
To crawl down there by day.
It's too dark anyway.

Some far-off northern lake in June,
Night settling down to welcome the full
    moon.
You wait. No sound . . . no sound . . . From
    nowhere soon
That watery wild voice calls loon to loon.

eye, her cheek, her lip. Nay her foot speaks; her wanton spirits leak out at every joint and motive of her body." Only in recent years, however, has there been widespread interest among language arts teachers to move beyond the study of speech and listening to a consideration of nonverbal kinds of communication such as facial expression, gestures, posture, personal space maintained, and tonal quality of the voice. Yet such signals, when properly observed and analyzed, can reveal a lot about another person.

Teachers who realize that both spoken language and nonverbal language convey meaning, have begun planning and devising experiences and activities to help students perceive nonverbal clues.

Recognizing and Analyzing Body Language

Dorothy Grant Hennings has suggested that students be taught to analyze the body language—both gestures and gross movements—of peers, parents, teachers, and television personalities.[6] She recommends that students take notes describing the message being conveyed plus the nonverbal expressions the person is using to convey it. The notes, written in the format shown in Figure 4.3, could then be used as a basis for classroom discussion and other follow-up activities.

The illustrations in children's books, for instance, offer a wealth of examples in which nonverbal behavior can be observed and studied. Skillful artists show characters experiencing a range of emotions—joy, sadness, fear, love, hate—familiar to young readers. With the teacher's help, boys and girls can learn to analyze illustrations and, in doing so, better understand the writer's intent. They also learn to pick up nonverbal signals given by their peers and by adults.

More than thirty years ago, before the term "body language" had been coined, Robert Lawson wrote and illustrated an animal fable that contains many expressions of body language. The leading character in *Robbut: A Tale of Tails* is a young rabbit who admires and envies the tail of every nonrabbit friend he meets. Finally, Little Old Man, who is deeply indebted to Robbut, agrees to provide him with any tail he desires.

While taking Robbut through the trials and tribulations of many unsuitable tails, Robert Lawson uses body language as well as written text to reveal Robbut's state of mind. The theme of the story is based on a biblical passage: "I have learned, in whatsoever state I am, therewith to be content." Eventually, Robbut settles for

[6]Dorothy Grant Hennings, "Learning to Listen and Speak," *Theory into Practice* (Columbus: College of Education, Ohio State University, 1977).

his own small, tufty cotton tail, which he "can twitch just a little."

Robert Lawson, the focus author for this chapter, was especially gifted at characterization in both his writing and his illustrating. Whether his characters are drawn from the human population or from the animal kingdom, they express their thoughts and feelings openly with warmth and humor. They listen to and care for each other.

Finger Spelling

Finger spelling is a way of communicating by means of hand gestures representing the twenty-six letters of the alphabet (see Figure 4.4). The manual alphabet was developed for deaf people, who must depend almost entirely on visual communication. It is a very efficient system for conveying messages, especially when shortcuts such as signs for whole words or phrases are used.

Although finger spelling was developed for the deaf, it has a place in the language arts program for hearing children. As they learn the twenty-six finger positions, a few at a time, and begin sending and receiving messages by means of finger spelling, they grow to appreciate one of

Figure 4.3 Interpreting Nonverbal Communication

Message Sent	Nonverbal Expression That Communicated the Message

Robbut's moods are revealed by his appearance. His bright, direct gaze; grin; and erect ears and whiskers show that he is pretty pleased with himself. Drooping whisker and ears, sad eyes staring at nothing, head resting forlornly on his paws, all are *nonverbal signs that Robbut is in disgrace. (From* Robbut: A Tale of Tails *by Robert Lawson. Copyright 1948 by Robert Lawson. Copyright © renewed 1976 by John W. Boyd. All rights reserved. Reprinted by permission of Viking Penguin, Inc.)*

many forms of silent communication. More importantly, finger spelling can serve as a bridge between deaf and hearing children, giving them the means to talk with each other, to understand and respect each other.

Pantomime

The word *pantomime* is from the Greek and literally means "all imitation." It is the art of telling a story without benefit of dialogue—with body movements alone. Marcel Marceau, the world's greatest pantomimist, has said that pantomime is a universal art that speaks to us in a "speechless" tongue. Marceau believes that pantomime is enjoying a revival because it has the power to communicate with all people, regardless of their race or language.

Pantomime has a place in today's classroom as a means of improving students' listening and observing skills. It can be very effective in helping

children understand the importance of familiar hand gestures and body movements as means of communication. A convenient and natural way to make pantomime part of the language arts program is to use it to interpret literature silently. In the words of Robert Whitehead:

Children find pantomime activities to be genuine fun, literature comes alive as children give lifelike reenactments of situations and characters from books and stories. This is especially true if the teacher is willing to demonstrate techniques through her own pantomimes, and if she shows sincerity and empathy with the children in their interpretations of characters and scenes.[7]

Literary pantomime is at its best when the characters and events mimed are well known to the students. Otherwise the activity becomes a guessing game no more artistic than a game of charades. Familiar stories with dramatic central

[7]Robert Whitehead, *Children's Literature: Strategies of Teaching* (Englewood Cliffs, N.J.: Prentice-Hall, 1968), p. 169.

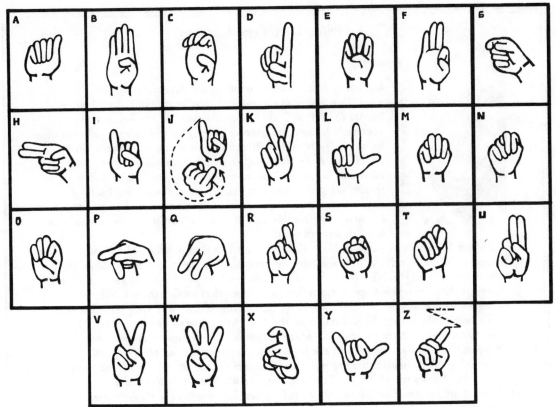

Figure 4.4   The Manual Alphabet Used in Finger Spelling. (Courtesy of Barbara Ellis.)

characters suitable for miming are

- "Rapunzel"
- "Sleeping Beauty"
- "Cinderella"
- "Rumpelstiltskin"
- "The Princess and the Pea"
- "The Bremen Town Musicians"
- "Jack and the Beanstalk"
- "Little Red Riding Hood"

Marcel Marceau has created a book of pantomime for children, *The Marcel Marceau Alphabet Book.* In it he mimes each letter of the alphabet.

By studying the photographs in this beautiful book, children can better appreciate pantomime, "the art of silence," and be inspired to express their own moods and emotions through body movements; and equally important, they can better learn to empathize with the moods and emotions of others.

Summary

Although people are asked to spend much of their time listening to others, few are really good listeners. They hear the sound of voices but pay scant attention to them. Likewise, many people

A Profile of Robert Lawson

IN 1940 ROBERT LAWSON won the Caldecott Medal for
They Were Strong and Good and four years later the Newbery
Medal for *Rabbit Hill.* To be so honored was an amazing
accomplishment and placed Lawson in the unique position of
being the only author/illustrator to win both awards. In an
article for *Horn Book Magazine,* his wife described his first
efforts as an artist: "He neither drew pictures nor wrote
stories, as many children do. It was not until high school
days when a poster contest was announced that he produced
his first drawing. He won first prize and the prize money was
his first earned dollar."[1]

Robert Lawson was born in New York City on October 4, 1892. His family
moved to Montclair, New Jersey, where he grew up and went to school. After high
school he entered the New York School of Fine and Applied Arts in 1911, studying
there for three years. He spent the following three years in Greenwich Village
doing various kinds of commercial art work. During World War I he served a year
and a half in the Camouflage Section of the U.S. Army Corps of Engineers.

In 1922, Robert Lawson married Marie Abrams, a well-known author and
illustrator in her own right, and the following year they moved to Westport,
Connecticut. A dramatic turning point in his career came in 1930 when he began
illustrating books for children. The first was *The Wee Men of Ballywooden* by Arthur
Mason. One reviewer wrote of this work: "When *The Wee Men of Ballywooden*
appeared, its lovely black and white drawings of delicate humor and rich
imagination instantly attracted children's book lovers of all ages. Here was
something new and lovely—an artist to be watched."[2]

In spite of the fact that many people were fond of the illustrations in *The Wee Men
of Ballywooden,* Robert Lawson did not win popular acclaim until he collaborated
with Munro Leaf in creating what turned out to be a modern classic, *The Story of
Ferdinand.* On first seeing the drawings of Ferdinand, Lawson's Aunt Emma said,
"I just don't see any sense to this thing at all; I don't see why you're wasting your
time on it. The idea of a bull smelling flowers; it just doesn't make sense." He
explained to her that the story was not supposed to make sense. "It is only supposed
to make nonsense."

Of all the books written and illustrated by Robert Lawson, the favorite of
children is *Rabbit Hill,* an animal fable in a class with *Peter Rabbit, Charlotte's Web,*
and *Wind in the Willows.* This tale of Little Georgie and his friends was inspired by

Robert Lawson photo is used with permission.

[1]Marie A. Lawson, "Master of Rabbit Hill, Robert Lawson," *Horn Book Magazine* (July–August 1945), p. 240.

[2]Helen Dean Fish, "Robert Lawson: Illustrator in the Great Tradition," *Horn Book Magazine* (January 1940), p. 21.

the small animals living in the woods and fields surrounding the Lawson home in Connecticut. In his Newbery Award acceptance speech, Lawson gave credit to all those who contributed to the creation of the book:

> And of course the largest slice should go to Little Georgie or whoever it was who wrote the thing, because I don't remember doing that at all. I pushed the pencil and pecked at the typewriter, but someone else certainly must have written it. With every other book I've ever done I've always made a complete outline and had everything planned up to the last line, but for this one I had nothing at all. I hadn't the faintest idea of what it was going to be or how it was to come out. In fact it started to be something completely different, but once it was begun someone took hold of it and it just went ahead and wrote itself.[3]

Mae Massee, children's book editor at Viking Press at the time *Rabbit Hill* was published, describes in eloquent terms the way book lovers young and old feel about the book:

> I have heard this story called "slight." It is slight as a beautiful sunny day or a deep moonlit night in the Connecticut country; it is slight as a brook that sparkles through that countryside; it is slight as the relationship between humans who have a home in the country and all the little animals who share that home. They will share your house if you let them, but they will share your grounds whether or no. For the earth is theirs—they owned it before you did and you would not have it at all except for them.[4]

In 1939, Lawson began writing and illustrating his own books, and for the rest of his life he continued to create literature for children. He considered his readers the most perceptive and understanding of all readers: "I would hesitate a long, long time before pronouncing *anything* as above the head of a ten-year-old child." Lawson died suddenly at his beloved "Rabbit Hill" in Connecticut in 1957, leaving behind an abundant treasure in art and story for children of all ages.

BOOKS WRITTEN AND ILLUSTRATED BY ROBERT LAWSON

Ben and Me, 1939
They Were Strong and Good, 1940
I Discover Columbus, 1941
Rabbit Hill, 1944
Mr. Twigg's Mistake, 1947
Robbut: A Tale of Tails, 1948
Smeller Martin, 1950
McWhinney's Jaunt, 1951
Mr. Revere and I, 1953
The Tough Winter, 1954
Captain Kidd's Cat, 1956
Watchwords of Liberty, 1957
The Great Wheel, 1957 (published posthumously)

[3]Robert Lawson, "The Newbery Medal Acceptance," *Horn Book Magazine* (July–August 1945), p. 234.
[4]Mae Massee, "Robert Lawson, 1944 Newbery Award Winner," *Library Journal* (June 15, 1945), p. 560.

fail to observe and respond to nonverbal cues—to various kinds of body language.

Teachers expect girls and boys to listen to them, but many refuse to listen to the students. This is not surprising since prospective teachers receive little training in listening and the subject is often slighted in textbooks and other curriculum materials. Nevertheless, language arts specialists agree that listening can be learned and must be taught. But it must be carefully taught and consistently practiced. Teachers should be familiar with a variety of classroom activities that will sharpen children's listening skills. Storytelling, reading aloud, and other literature-related activities have the advantage of improving all language arts skills—including listening.

In recent years language arts teachers have begun to realize the importance of nonverbal modes of communication. They have turned their attention to the new science of kinesics, which studies the meaning of body movements and gestures, and they are helping their students to be aware of, and to interpret, their own body language and that of others.

Best Books for Children

Adam of the Road, written by Elizabeth Janet Gray and illustrated by Robert Lawson. New York: Viking Press, 1942. This inspiring story set in thirteenth-century England, was so carefully researched that both the text and the illustrations are considered to be accurate and authentic down to the last detail. (U)

Ben and Me, written and illustrated by Robert Lawson. Boston: Little, Brown, 1939. An impertinent and egotistical little mouse named Amos claims he is the real key to Benjamin Franklin's success. For his part in inventing the stove, Benjamin Franklin agrees to deliver to him, twice a week, "1 two-ounce piece best quality cheese, 1 one-inch slice of rye bread, and 88 grains unhulled wheat." (M-U)

Captain Kidd's Cat, written and illustrated by Robert Lawson. Boston: Little, Brown, 1956. Captain Kidd's cat explodes some of the myths surrounding the infamous pirate. And who should know Captain Kidd better than his own faithful cat? Cat lovers and non–cat lovers enjoy this story. (M-U)

Country Noisy Book, written by Margaret Wise Brown and illustrated by Leonard Weisgard. New York: Harper & Row, 1940. Noises made by machines, people, animals, and insects, and other sounds associated with farm life, are illustrated in this book for very young children. One in a series. (P)

Four and Twenty Blackbirds, collected by Helen Dean Fish and illustrated by Robert Lawson. New York: Lippincott, 1937. A collection of favorite old nursery rhymes and stories, each one excellent for reading aloud to preschool and primary level children. (P)

The Great Wheel, written and illustrated by Robert Lawson. New York: Viking Press, 1957. Conn's Aunt Honora reads in the tea leaves that he will leave Ireland and make his fortune in the West. She also predicts that he will ride the greatest wheel in the world. Six years later Conn does sail West to America. He finds work at the World's Fair in Chicago and helps Mr. Ferris build his famous wheel. (M-U)

Handtalk: An ABC of Finger Spelling & Sign Language, by Remy Charlip, Mary Beth Ancova, and George Ancova. New York: Parents' Magazine Press, 1974. A photographic guide to finger spelling (forming words letter by letter with the fingers of one hand) and signing (making a picture or sign with the hands for each word or idea). (M-U)

I Discover Columbus, written and illustrated by Robert Lawson. Boston: Little, Brown, 1941. "A true chronicle of the great admiral and his finding of the new world, narrated by the venerable parrot Aurelio, who shared in the glorious venture." In the foreword to this book, Robert Lawson has drawn himself taking notes on a large pad while the parrot looks over his shoulder and tells him what to say. (M-U)

McWhinney's Jaunt, written and illustrated by Robert Lawson. Boston: Little, Brown, 1951. Professor Ambrose Augustus McWhinney invents Z gas for his bicycle tires and finds that his bicycle can scale buildings, fly through the air, and skim across wide rivers. He entertains himself until Mrs. McWhinney finishes her needlework and becomes more companionable. (M-U)

Mr. Popper's Penguins, written by Richard and Florence Atwater and illustrated by Robert Lawson. Boston: Little, Brown, 1938. Mr. Popper, the house painter, was a dreamer. Once he even painted three walls of a kitchen green and the fourth yellow. But in his wildest dreams, Mr. Popper never imagined how his life would change because of a pet penguin named Captain Cook. (M-U)

Mr. Revere and I, written and illustrated by Robert Lawson. Boston: Little, Brown, 1953. A rollicking account of Paul Revere's famous ride as seen through the eyes of his horse, Scheherazade. Since there is no historian to tell the story fittingly, the horse must tell it as it actually happened. (M-U)

Mr. Twigg's Mistake, written and illustrated by Robert Lawson. Boston: Little, Brown, 1947. Mr. Twigg, "the man of science," makes a mistake in mixing the Bita-Vita cereal, a mistake that causes Arthur Amory and his pet mole to get an undiluted dose of Vitamin X, the growth-producing vitamin. What happens next makes an exciting adventure story. (M-U)

Noisy Nora, written and illustrated by Rosemary Wells. New York: Dial Press, 1973. The middle child in a mouse family, Nora feels neglected. She retaliates by making as much noise as possible to attract her parents' attention. A story in rhyme. (P)

Oh What a Noise! written and illustrated by Uri Shulevitz. New York: Macmillan, 1971. A little boy entertains himself before bedtime by listening to all kinds of imaginary noises: "Lions roaring; Gnats snoring"; "Twenty parrots screaming 'Carrots.'" When he finally becomes sleepy, the animals retreat and leave him in silence. (P)

Pilgrim's Progress, written by John Bunyan and illustrated by Robert Lawson. New York: Lippincott, 1939. The immortal classic of English literature retold and shortened for modern readers by Mary Godolphin. One-fifth the length of the original, this version becomes a fast-moving story of adventure. (U)

Rabbit Hill, written and illustrated by Robert Lawson. New York: Viking Press, 1944. A humorous, lively, and sensitive animal fable comparable to *Peter*

Rabbit and *Wind in the Willows*. Many people consider the illustrations to be the best drawings ever made by Robert Lawson. (M-U)

Robbut: A Tale of Tails, written and illustrated by Robert Lawson. New York: Viking Press, 1948. Inspired by the biblical verse "I have learned, in whatsoever state I am, therewith to be content," Robert Lawson weaves a fine tale about Robbut the Rabbit, who finally learns to be satisfied with his stumpy cotton tail. (M)

Smeller Martin, written and illustrated by Robert Lawson. New York: Viking Press, 1950. Smeller, like Homer Price, is an all-American boy. But Smeller has a talent that makes him famous far and wide—an amazing sense of smell. He can tell where people have been and what they've been doing. He announces accurately, and well in advance, what is cooking in the school cafeteria. A book of fun and adventure. (M-U)

The Story of Ferdinand, written by Munro Leaf and illustrated by Robert Lawson. New York: Viking Press, 1936. Ferdinand, who refuses to fight in the bullring and chooses instead to smell the flowers, represents the nonconforming, rugged individual in our society. He is a memorable character. (P-M)

Symbols, written and illustrated by Rolf Myller. New York: Atheneum, 1978. A colorful and attractive book designed to show children that a symbol stands for something else and makes possible the quick communication of an idea. Rolf Myller conveys the idea that symbols are everywhere and are a vital part of one's life. (P-M-U)

The Terrible Thing That Happened at Our House, written by Marge Blaine and illustrated by John C. Wallner. New York: Parents' Magazine Press, 1975. A little girl describes how her life changes for the worse when her mother goes back to work as a teacher. One of the things she misses most is that there is no one to listen to her. She says: "Then, one night at dinner, when my brother kept talking and talking, and no one was really listening to him or even heard me when I asked for some milk, I got mad. I got so mad I started yelling." Suddenly, everyone listens. (P-M)

The Tough Winter, written and illustrated by Robert

Lawson. New York: Viking Press, 1954. Uncle Analdas, Little Georgie, and all the other lovable animal characters from *Rabbit Hill* are back again to face a long hard winter. One of the best sequels in children's literature. (M-U)

They Were Strong and Good, written and illustrated by Robert Lawson. New York: Viking Press, 1940. This is the story of Robert Lawson's family tree. In the introduction Lawson writes of his ancestors: "None of them were great or famous, but they were strong and good. They worked hard and had many children. They all helped to make the United States the great nation that it now is." (P-M)

Wee Gillis, written by Munro Leaf and illustrated by Robert Lawson. New York: Viking Press, 1959. Wee Gillis is a boy of Scotland trying to decide whether to stay in the valley with his family and raise long-haired cattle or go up in the mountains with his relatives to stalk stags. He finally settles for halfway up and halfway down. (M-U)

Your Silent Language, written by Elizabeth McGough and illustrated by Tom Huffman. New York: Morrow, 1974. A young person's guide to the new science of kinesics. The author investigates body language from the young person's point of view, showing how it affects behavior in familiar teen and preteen social situations. (M-U)

Bibliography

Christopher, Dean A. *Manual Communication*. Baltimore University Park Press, 1976.

Fast, Julius. *Body Language*. New York: M. Evans, 1970.

Fish, Helen Dean. "Robert Lawson: Illustrator in the Great Tradition." *Horn Book Magazine*, January 1940.

Hennings, Dorothy Grant. "Learning to Listen and Speak." *Theory into Practice*. Columbus: College of Education, Ohio State University, 1977.

Kean, John M., and Carl Personke. *The Language Arts: Teaching and Learning in the Elementary School*. New York: St. Martin's Press, 1976.

Lawson, Marie A. "Master of Rabbit Hill, Robert Lawson." *Horn Book Magazine*, July–August 1945.

Lawson, Robert. "The Newbery Medal Acceptance." *Horn Book Magazine*, July–August 1945.

Long, Lynette. *Listening/Responding: Human-Relations Training for Teachers*. Monterey, Calif.: Brooks/Cole, 1978.

Lundsteen, Sara W. *Listening: Its Impact on Reading and the Other Language Arts*. Urbana, Ill.: National Council of Teachers of English, 1971.

Massee, Mae. "Robert Lawson, 1944 Newbery Award Winner." *Library Journal*, June 15, 1945.

Rankin, Paul T. "Listening Ability." *Proceedings of the Ohio State Education Conference*, Ninth Annual Session. Columbus: Ohio State University, 1929.

Stewig, John Warren. "Nonverbal Communication: 'I *See* What You Say.'" *Language Arts*, February 1979.

Whitehead, Robert. *Children's Literature: Strategies of Teaching*. Englewood Cliffs, N.J.: Prentice-Hall, 1968.

Wilt, Miriam E. "A Study of Teacher Awareness of Listening as a Factor in Elementary Education." *Journal of Educational Research*, April 1950.

Wolff, Sydney, and Caryl Wolff. *Games Without Words*. Springfield, Ill.: Charles C. Thomas, 1974.

Chapter 5

The Wonder of Words: Enriching Oral Language

ORAL COMMUNICATION plays a significant role in all human interaction. Since it takes place in a variety of settings, most people have several different levels of speech. The level they use, ranging from slang to highly formal diction, depends on the situation in which they find themselves. Each has its own vocabulary, grammar, and syntax. Skillful speakers make sure that the level is appropriate to the occasion.

Children entering school differ greatly in their ability to speak. A major responsibility of the language arts teacher is to improve students' facility with oral expression—to teach boys and girls to speak with logic and clarity for a definite purpose. Instruction in oral expression depends on the development of a plan that capitalizes on speaking situations that occur naturally and spontaneously in the schoolyard and classroom, and that creates opportunities for more formal oral work.

In this chapter we will examine informal speaking situations and planned and structured activities such as panel discussions, oral reports, and force-field analysis, which give children practice expressing themselves in group settings. And we will describe evaluation techniques that let students participate in the evaluation of their speaking skills.

The Goals of Oral Language Instruction

Just as children must learn to walk before they can run, and run before they can perform the more complicated physical task of skipping, so do children progress through various stages of language development. Therefore, oral language instruction is a vital component of a sequential program of language instruction. Like listening, however, it has not received the attention it merits.

When curriculum planners really believe that language arts skills have a long-term, functional

value, then oral language will assume its rightful place in the curriculum. As C. Van Riper writes: "No other skill has so powerful an influence in determining whether we will succeed or fail. It is hard to understand why we have neglected so vital a subject as the teaching of talking."[1] Since language is essentially a social phenomenon, learned in a social context and used to communicate with others in society, efforts to improve students' ability to speak must be made at all grade levels.

Teachers working to improve students' proficiency in speaking should keep four goals in mind as they plan activities. The objectives of instruction in oral language are

1. the accurate articulation of words that appropriately convey meaning
2. the fluent expression of ideas and information
3. a logically organized presentation
4. the ongoing appreciation and pleasure that accompany the efficient use of language

Settings That Limit or Encourage Learning

Achieving speech-improvement goals is more easily accomplished in some classrooms than in others. In many schools, talking among students is considered a negative form of behavior, and teachers are expected to maintain a quiet classroom at all times. Oral expression is discouraged by restricting speaking opportunities to little more than formal recitations before the teacher. The rank and file seating often found in such traditional classrooms allows only narrow communication between students and the teacher (see Figure 5.1).

In an elementary classroom that encourages controlled speaking and listening experiences,

[1]Charles Van Riper, *Helping Children Talk Better* (Chicago: SRA, 1951), p. 3.

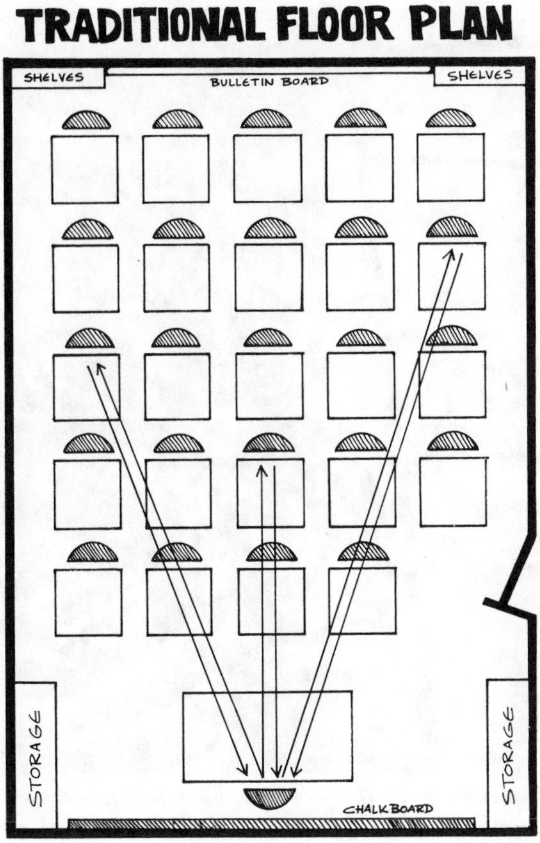

TRADITIONAL FLOOR PLAN

FLEXIBLE FLOOR PLAN

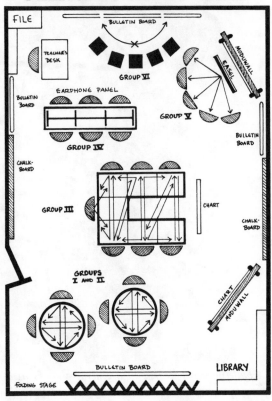

Figure 5.1 *The traditional seating arrangement limits oral expression to communication between students and the teacher. (Courtesy of Barbara Ellis.)*

Figure 5.2 *The goals of oral language instruction are more easily achieved when the classroom arrangement promotes the free flow of speaking. (Courtesy of Barbara Ellis.)*

the furniture can be, and often is, moved around to accommodate groups of various sizes and activities of many kinds. The focus of students' attention is not the teacher standing before a chalkboard in the front of the room; rather it is the group or activity they are involved with. A physical environment that is altered to meet specific needs is much more likely to promote informal as well as planned oral expression than is the inflexible setup of the traditional classroom (see Figure 5.2).

Informal Conversations as Aids to Proficient Speech

Watching and listening to preschool children is a fascinating experience. They seem to talk *at* one another rather than *with* each other. One important sign of language maturity is the ability to both express thoughts and ideas effectively and absorb and appreciate what is being communicated. Informal conversation is probably the

A bulletin board located in a central place is used for displaying "success awards," presented to individual girls and boys for academic achievement, sportsmanship, or citizenship. The teacher may take *advantage of the record to have a personal talk with a student. (Courtesy of Mike Holloway, Sam Houston Elementary School, Port Arthur, Texas.)*

most natural way to practice this communication interaction. The best conversations are spontaneous and free flowing, a balance between speaking and listening.

Initiating a conversation with children in the elementary classroom is easy. Personal conversations between the teacher and a student are an effective way to say, "I care." They may be the only warm personal contact some children have with an adult. Such conversations may occur on the playground, before school, or in any situation where the teacher can interact with an individual child in an "unofficial" way. The tone

should be light but mutually respectful. Teachers often use such opportunities to help children develop a more positive self-concept.

Classroom situations that give rise to interpersonal communication are plentiful. Children should be encouraged to converse with each other. The principles of successful conversation should be reinforced by the teacher's example and by overt instruction. To some listeners, courtesies such as attentiveness, respectfulness, politeness, and tact do not come naturally. The language arts teacher should promote such habits and provide meaningful situations for them to occur. The teacher should keep in mind that children possess varying degrees of interest and ability in conversation. Some are shy; others are gregarious. To compensate for such divergence, the teacher should arrange to have conversations take place among small groups of children.

Planned Activities to Improve Speaking Skills

Formal discussions, oral reporting, and class meetings are some of the structured activities that give students a chance to speak before a group. Children's books present in the classroom or obtained from the library can be the springboard for such activities.

Group Discussions

Discussions are similar to conversations in several ways. Both involve the use of oral language in a relatively small group. Both involve the exploration of an issue or topic, and both give students the opportunity to use a variety of speaking skills. The major difference between a discussion and a conversation is the degree of formality. John Savage has defined a discussion as "problem solving by cooperative thinking."[2] The goal of any discussion is to answer a question or resolve a problem.

The "shape" of any given discussion is largely determined by its purpose, its participants, and the materials used as its basis. There are many different types of discussion. The discussion that most elementary teachers conduct, however, may be defined as a meaningful exploration of a central idea or problem by a classroom group.

In a true discussion, the communication is structured in some formal manner, and the par-

[2]John F. Savage, *Effective Communication: Language Arts Instruction in the Elementary School* (Chicago: SRA, 1977), p. 134.

ticipants expect resolution of the problem. To accomplish this challenge, facts are presented and various alternatives are explored by the students. Teachers often pose leading questions to guide student participants. Each member of the group has an equal opportunity to contribute to the discussion.

Many problems cannot be resolved in a classroom discussion, but meaningful alternatives can be considered. A decision-making stage follows the initial exploration of the problem; an evaluation of the various alternatives is rendered by the participants. No vote is required, but some kind of consensus should emerge.

A discussion in the elementary classroom is more formal than casual conversation and is aimed at formal learning. Specific guidelines to help teachers plan and carry out successful classroom discussions may be found in Display 5.1. What are the requirements for a successful discussion? Perhaps the most important prerequisite is to insist that children use pertinent facts, information, or data. This means that students should prepare for a discussion, usually by reading. For elementary children, what is more important than how much information has been obtained is how such information is interpreted. Differences of interpretation are likely to occur; and when they do, the discussion should be considered successful. The "correctness" of the interpretation is less important than the discovery of the relevant issues as determined by student participation. In this setting girls and boys learn the value of logical and sequential thinking, good diction, and relevance.

A discussion group may range in size from as few as six members to the entire class. A discussion among more than twenty-five children, however, may be unwieldy, and fewer than six will probably not provide enough diversity of thought. A carefully planned discussion can involve all children in both language cognition and divergent thinking.

Panel Discussions

A panel discussion is a popular vehicle for sharing different kinds of information. The panel, usually containing from three to eight presenters, conducts a discussion before a class or other audience. The topic, issue, or question is predetermined. The panel format is most effective when the presentation is lively and informative rather than argumentative or uncontrolled. When the panelists conclude their presentations, the audience is usually invited to participate by asking questions. The questions may be addressed either to the panel as a whole or to individual members.

It is suggested that the teacher or panel members select a moderator. The moderator will be responsible for organizing the panel to ensure that various points of view are represented and for monitoring the discussion so that all members get a chance to participate. A time limit should be placed on individual participation and audience questions. With practice, elementary students will gain confidence in presenting information to their peers. Teachers are often surprised by how deeply student panelists have researched a topic.

Controlled Participation

A variation on panel discussions is an activity known as controlled participation or CONPAR.[3] It is one of the best methods to guarantee the participation and involvement of all members in a group, regardless of group size or the age of the participants. It is a democratic approach to problem solving. The following steps should be taken by the classroom teacher:

1. Identify and define the problem to be approached.

[3]CONPAR as a process was developed by General Motors for use with sales personnel in training sessions. It is modified here for use with children.

2. Elect a group of four or five students to serve as panel members.
3. Give the panel members ample time to research the topic.
4. Divide the remaining class members into small groups and seat them around tables.
5. Number or label each table in some manner.
6. Select a chairperson for each table to start the discussion and to keep it going.
7. Elect a recorder at each table to take down the key points.
8. Allot ten minutes for group discussions and then cut them off with a bell or buzzer.
9. Ask each recorder to write on index cards the three best questions to come out of the discussion.
10. Read aloud the question from the top card submitted by the first table.
11. Allow one or more panel members to respond to the question.
12. Limit each response to two minutes. A small bell may be used to expedite matters.
13. Ask if there are further comments from the floor.
14. Read a card from the next table and again ask the panel to respond. Continue in this manner as long as time permits or until all questions have been covered.
15. Use one minute at the end of the CONPAR session to summarize the key points that were made.

If the CONPAR session is successful, some problems and concerns will have been aired, all students will have had an opportunity for input, and a set of solutions and resolutions will have been established. Effective CONPAR sessions help students to become more self-directed, self-disciplined, and independent.

Class Government

Children in the primary grades do not usually participate in formal classroom government. Sim-

Display 5.1 Teacher-guided Discussion

1. Plan for the discussion by
   A. Asking the students to read selected materials and gather as much background information as possible
   B. Defining the specific issue or issues to be discussed
   C. Preparing some leading questions
   D. Establishing a time limit for individual participation
2. Introduce the discussion by
   A. Making a brief statement or quotation
   B. Outlining the major topics with a handout or agenda
3. Keep the discussion "moving" by
   A. Encouraging spontaneity
   B. Limiting the time for the oral presentations
   C. Recording the oral responses on paper or the chalkboard by means of a class recorder
4. Encourage total participation by
   A. Discouraging the domination of the meeting by a few students
   B. Encouraging less verbal students to participate
5. Bring out all sides of the question by
   A. Asking students to think of arguments on the other side
   B. Using readings that support the various points of view
   C. Playing the role of "devil's advocate"
6. Be systematic by
   A. Keeping the discussion on the subject
   B. Considering one topic at a time
   C. Following the agenda
7. Arrive at a consensus by
   A. Summarizing the major points presented by the various students
   B. Restating the agreed-upon solutions
   C. Stating the conclusion to include possible follow-up action or subsequent discussion

ple experiences, however, can prepare them for active involvement during the middle grades, improve their speaking skills, and help them develop a positive self-image. Very young class officers can deliver simple announcements, read the daily menu, and participate in the presentation of the day's schedule. With little difficulty, primary teachers can determine other activities that will prepare children for more formalized class government.

The most common form of class government consists of a secretary, treasurer, vice-president, and president. Many classrooms also elect committees to help the officers. The number of officers, of committees, and the length of service of both should be strictly regulated. One way to ensure equitable participation is to place the names of all class members in a container and draw a different name for the various offices each week. Thus, every child will have an equal opportunity for selection to every office without regard to sex or popularity, and every child will perceive the fairness of such a drawing.

The secretary, aided by the entire class, can note which children are absent, participate in the lunch count, and record important events in the class journal. Such a journal, available to the entire class and kept in a special location, should be read aloud at regular intervals, with corrections and additions supplied by the class. The duties of the secretary draw upon the skills of notetaking, proofreading, and speaking.

The vice-president of the class should also have defined responsibilities. One role might be that of program coordinator. As part of the morning routine, the vice-president might plan and organize activities that promote oral language. Programs might include jokes, riddles, poems, songs, show-and-tell, or classroom visitations. A bulletin board, organized by the entire class, will help to structure such activities.

The class president presides over class meetings, leads the Pledge of Allegiance, and assists the teacher in matters of general concern.

Children in the intermediate grades of four, five, and six may be ready to participate in class meetings conducted in accordance with *Robert's Rules of Order*. The first step in teaching parliamentary procedure is to stress the importance of structured participation. Children should be introduced to the basic principles and practices simply, as the need arises. A poster, chart, or bulletin board listing the elements of parliamentary procedure will help the presiding officer to maintain a smooth flow during class meetings (see Figure 5.3). Teachers may wish to use the basic terminology as part of a vocabulary or spelling lesson. With practice in parliamentary procedure, children will find class meetings more interesting and extend their oral language skills at the same time.

Parliamentary Procedure

1. Call the meeting to order.
2. Call for the reading of minutes.
3. Call for corrections.
4. Call for treasurer's report.
5. Call for corrections.
6. Call for committee reports.
7. Call for old business.
8. Call for new business.
9. Call for motion to adjourn.
10. Announce adjournment.

Figure 5.3 A prominently displayed chart listing parliamentary procedures in their proper sequence will help the presiding class officer. (Courtesy of Barbara Ellis.)

Informational Oral Reports

Teachers in elementary classrooms, particularly those in content areas, often ask individual students to prepare formal, oral reports on specific topics. The student sharing the information carries all the responsibility for the presentation. Frequently these informational reports are not well delivered or well received. With the teacher's direction and guidance, however, student speakers can gain skill and confidence in oral reporting.

Force-Field Analysis

Force-field analysis is the study of positive and negative forces that have a bearing on human behavior. In the classroom, force-field analysis is used to solve problems, to change behavior, and to improve the quality of human interaction. It is an excellent matrix for the verbalization of opinions, attitudes, and values.

The process is based on the work and theories of Kurt Lewin and has been used widely with adults in the areas of management and supervi-

The chalkboard is a convenient place to list forces for analysis and to organize them for group discussion. (Courtesy of Sam Houston Elementary School, Port Arthur, Texas.)

room, the teacher should keep in mind these suggestions:

1. Identify the problem to be analyzed.
2. Create an environment for open discussion.
3. Introduce the problem with an appropriate example or anecdote.
4. Elicit from students their perceptions of the reasons for the problem.
5. Restate each student's comment for clarification and accuracy.
6. Write each statement on one side of the chalkboard or chart paper. The other side is to be used for possible resolutions (see Display 5.2).
7. When the problem has been fully explored, summarize the students' statements.
8. Ask students to verbalize a realistic solution to each listed aspect of the problem.
9. When the group agrees that a feasible solution has been offered, erase (or draw a line through) the affected item.
10. In summary, help students to internalize the fact that they have within themselves the resources to solve most of their own problems.

The following passage is an excerpt from an actual force-field analysis dialogue between a teacher and a group of sixth-graders who were concerned about the problems surrounding homework assignments:

TEACHER: Based on your comments, I'm pretty sure that homework is a topic you'd like to dig into. Right?

VERNON: Yes.

TEACHER: Why is it such a big problem?

VERNON: I can't do my homework because of television. The good shows come on right after my paper route is finished.

BUD: My problem is football practice. It comes at homework time.

TEACHER: What time does practice begin?

sion. Its main purpose is to establish the parameters of a problem and to diagram the specific elements of a problem. To "freeze" the problem in such a way helps to identify conflicting forces and set them up for possible resolution.

Force-field analysis combines two oral language activities into an effective technique for successful problem solving—the discussion group and the class meeting. It has seldom been used with children; yet it may help students assume responsibility for their own behavior. For a force-field analysis in the upper elementary class-

Display 5.2 Problem to Be Resolved by Force-Field Analysis: Homework Assignments

No, I Can't! (Interferences)	Yes, I Can! (Solutions)
Hard to understand	Pay attention to directions. Ask for help.
Football practice	Do homework first.
Telephone conversations	Unplug telephone. Ask friends to call later.
Too many chores and errands	Do chores before or after homework.
Movies, carnivals, the fair	Reserve for weekends. Do some homework at school.
Company comes over	Ask them to wait or help.
Mealtime takes too long	Do homework before mealtime.
Watching television	Turn it off. Watch only selected programs.
Trips with family	Work in car.
Going to bed too early	Set alarm. Get up earlier.

Written by the sixth-grade class at Sam Houston Elementary School, Port Arthur, Texas.

BUD: At 4:30.

TEACHER: What time do we get out of school?

BUD: At 3:30.

TEACHER: Then you have one hour between?

BUD: Yes.

MELISSA: When I start my homework, someone calls me on the telephone and we talk and talk a long time.

ANGELA: Sometimes I just go to bed early. I don't want to do the homework or I'm tired.

ROSE: My mother gets me in the car after school and we go to visit relatives. Then I don't get my homework done.

ETC. . . .

TEACHER: Well, anything else standing in the way? You really have a lot of interferences and distractions after school, don't you? I think we have listed just about all the excuses ever invented for avoiding homework. Let's see now, can you come up with a solution to any of these problems? If you can think of an answer to any one of the problems, just tell me.

MELISSA: You can get better directions for the homework. You can pay attention, look it over, and ask for help if you don't understand it.

TEACHER: Then do you think we could cross out the statement that homework is too hard to understand?

GROUP: Yes.

LORI: We could turn off the television set, or go in the other room to work.

CHRIS: We could watch just one or two of our favorite programs and no more.

TEACHER: All right. Do you agree that we can eliminate the TV problem?

GROUP: Yes.

ETC. . . .

Force-field analysis has four major results. First, it personalizes a problem at a level that an elementary student can understand. Second, as the dialogue widens, each student begins to assume personal responsibility for solving the problem. Third, force-field analysis works toward the resolution of a problem by promoting interaction and joint commitment. Finally, students come to realize that positive changes in behavior are brought about by a thoughtful process, not by chaos, confusion, or crisis.

Making Announcements

Announcements are common in all classroom situations and at all grade levels. Thus the elementary classroom is an appropriate place to teach students how to make announcements clearly.

Some announcements are ineffectual because they do not convey the essential information. Others are incomplete or fail to capture the listener's attention. As usual, the teacher should serve as an example worthy of imitation. When preparing an announcement, the teacher (or student) should use an introduction that will attract the listener's attention. Then the essential information (who, what, when, where, how, why) should be stated and restated. The message should be brief without sacrificing accuracy or clarity. The information may be written on the chalkboard as an aid to comprehension. Before

the announcement is delivered, the speaker should practice reading it aloud.

The announcement should be made only after the listeners are paying attention. The speaker should make eye contact with the audience and emphasize the most important words.

Children can practice making announcements by reading the lunch menu for the week, participating in the morning routine of opening exercises, and explaining school activities on the school's public address system.

Giving Directions

Children have many opportunities to give and follow directions during the school day. They may issue directions for playing a game, for participating in a dramatic event, for performing a science experiment, or for getting to a friend's house. An excellent opportunity for giving directions may be achieved through cooking activities. Cooking as a language arts activity builds on the children's natural desire to create something similar to what they have read about.

Books that might give rise to cooking experiences include:

- *The Poppy Seed Cakes* by Margery Clark
- *The Egg Tree* by Katherine Milhous
- *Rain Makes Applesauce* by Julian Scheer
- *Stone Soup* by Marcia Brown
- *Blueberries for Sal* by Robert McCloskey
- *Chicken Soup with Rice* by Maurice Sendak
- *Bread and Jam for Frances* by Russell and Lillian Hoban
- *The Thanksgiving Story* by Alice Dalgliesh
- *The Duchess Bakes a Cake* by Virginia Kahl
- *Journey Cake, Ho!* by Ruth Sawyer
- *Nail Soup* by Harve Zemach
- *The Carrot Seed* by Ruth Krauss

Display 5.3 Activities Based on "The Gingerbread Man"

The oral language in this old folk tale has inspired children to tell and retell the story of a fleet-footed cookie who outruns one pursuer after another. The slippery Gingerbread Man adds insult to injury as he repeats the same insolent taunt to everyone who tries to stop him:

> "Run! run! as fast as you can!
> You can't catch me, I'm the
> Gingerbread Man!"[1]

Each time the Gingerbread Man outruns another pursuer, another line is added to the story. Finally outwitted by a wily fox, the Gingerbread Man and the story come to an abrupt end: "As soon as the fox reached the shore, he threw back his head, and into his mouth fell the little Gingerbread Man."

(Courtesy of Barbara Ellis.)

Recipe for Gingerbread Men

4 cups sifted flour
1 tablespoon cinnamon
1 teaspoon salt
1 teaspoon baking powder
1 teaspoon ginger
½ cup shortening
½ cup firmly packed brown sugar
1 cup molasses
1 egg

Sift the first five ingredients together and set aside. Cream the shortening. Gradually add the brown sugar, creaming until fluffy after each addition. Continue creaming while adding the egg. Blend in the molasses. Stir in the sifted ingredients. Chill the dough overnight in the refrigerator.

Pinch off a ball of dough for each child who is working at the table. Let the children roll or pat dough to ¼-inch thick on a lightly floured surface. (If they have a tendency to roll too much flour into the dough, powdered sugar may be substituted for flour.) Cut dough with gingerbread man cookie cutter or cut around a cardboard pattern of a gingerbread man. A good plan for making a more creative gingerbread man is to form a ball for the head, one for the body, and four smaller ones for the arms and legs. Flatten and mash them together slightly so the pieces will adhere. No two gingerbread men will be alike, and that is part of the fun. Using a large spatula, transfer each cookie to a large cookie sheet that has been lightly greased. Each child's cookie may be marked with a small piece of foil on which the child's name has

[1]Ed Arno, *The Gingerbread Man* (New York: Scholastic Book Services, 1967).

been printed with a magic marker. Bake at 350° for 10 to 15 minutes.

Oral Language Activities

1. Prepare a rebus chart showing the various ingredients for making gingerbread men.
2. Make an experience chart indicating the directions for making gingerbread men. Emphasize the sequential order.
3. Discuss new words learned such as "dough," "knead," "ginger," "molasses," "cinnamon," "spatula."
4. Create a bulletin board of the story *The Gingerbread Man*.
5. Ask children to retell the story by playing various roles in the story. Dramatize the story through pantomime or puppetry.
6. Encourage the class to listen to the story *The Gingerbread Man* on a record or cassette tape. Have a small group of children tape their own version of the story and play it back to the class.
7. Design shape books in the form of gingerbread men from brown paper sacks. The shape books may then be used as a means for children to "save" their experiences or as a book in which to write an unusual ending for the story. The stories should be shared with other members of the class.
8. Read the story aloud as the cookies are baking.
9. Discuss the humor and language of the story.
10. Compare *The Gingerbread Man* to the Russian version, *The Bun* by Marcia Brown.

Telephoning

As children learn how to use the telephone correctly, they are practicing skills that relate to all aspects of the language arts curriculum. A telephone unit is easily developed and may feature the following topics:

1. How to use telephone equipment
2. How to speak on the telephone
3. How to listen on the telephone
4. Telephone manners
5. Making emergency telephone calls
6. Using the telephone directory

Most local telephone companies have a device called a Teletrainer, which can be loaned to schools. It provides a way for children to learn how to place a call and to practice telephone courtesy. This device can simulate telephone calls, busy signals, and dial tones. The Bell System has a package of books, pamphlets, and audiovisual materials that have been designed to accompany a telephone unit and training with the Teletrainer; it is entitled *Telezonia*. This useful kit also includes materials helpful in giving children practice using the telephone directory. It is available from local Bell offices or from the American Telephone and Telegraph Company (AT&T) in New York.

Interviewing

Interviewing offers a child the opportunity for a unique encounter with another person. The atmosphere for the interview should seem relatively formal, at least to the child.

Divide the class into committees of three and have each group select someone it would like to interview. The principal, the school secretary, the school librarian, or a local celebrity might be invited to participate. Prior to the interview, the

The Teletrainer, made available to schools by local telephone companies, can be used to simulate real- *life telephone conversations. (Courtesy of Caldwood Elementary School, Beaumont, Texas.)*

committees should investigate the subject's background, occupation, interests, and unique skills. After the preliminary research is completed, each group should draw up a series of questions to ask during the interview (see Display 5.4).

The following guidelines for conducting an interview were developed by one third-grade class:

1. Schedule a specific time and tell the person the purpose of the interview.
2. Plan the questions to be asked and write them down.
3. Be prompt for the appointment.
4. Tell the person to be interviewed the names of the committee members.
5. Ask questions slowly and clearly and listen carefully to the answers.

6. Write down a few key notes. Be especially accurate about names, dates, places, and other specific information.
7. Ask additional questions if needed.
8. Be polite. Thank the person for the interview.
9. Recopy the interview from notes soon after the meeting.
10. Ask the whole committee to help in writing the final report.

Ideally, the interview will lead to further reporting and additional reading.

Telling Jokes and Riddles

Jokes and riddles are an integral part of most language arts programs and all language arts textbooks. They are used to bring a hearty laugh to children while heightening opportunities for speaking. A good story well told enhances any social situation and for that reason story telling can be defended as a necessary part of the language arts program.

Some teachers provide a mini-center where children can peruse joke and riddle books such as *Peanuts Revisited: Favorites Old and New* by Charles Schultz, *Spooky Rhymes and Riddles* by Lillian Moore, *Book of Giggles* by William Cole, *It Does Not Say Meow* by Beatrice Schenk deRegniers, and *Riddle Walk* by Lillian Moore. Theodor Seuss Geisel, known to millions of children and their parents as Dr. Seuss, provides an excellent example of books containing rich humor that children understand, tantalizing word play, and tongue-twisting riddles that they can repeat.

Some teachers begin the school day with a joke or humorous story selected and delivered by a student. Prior to the development of such a routine, however, specific guidelines for telling humorous tales should be formulated. Such information might be listed on an experience chart as a reminder to the class. Rules listed on the chart should include suggestions about what is or is not appropriate for retelling and advice on how to present a joke in the classroom.

Riddles are an age-old form of word play that elementary children have always enjoyed. Once the basic pattern of the riddle is recognized, children like creating their own. Some teachers maintain a riddle box as a delightful diversion for a rainy afternoon or for the last few minutes before the end of the school day.

Evaluating Speaking Skills

Formal classroom tests for evaluating children's ability to use oral language are not available, but this does not mean that speaking skills cannot be evaluated. As John Savage has written: "Speech is

Telephone Courtesy

1. Answer promptly.
2. Hold the phone correctly.

3. Speak courteously. 4. Write down any message.

5. Good manners are essential.

One project in a telephone unit might be the creation of posters to be taken home for display near the family's telephone. (Courtesy of Barbara Ellis.)

a temporal activity. It passes from the mouth of the language user and is gone, so most of the evaluation of oral language activities has to be done on the spot, while speaking experiences are in progress."[4] Most of the evaluation of such activities will be casual and impressionistic.

Relatively informal oral language activities such as conversation or the retelling of humorous tales are most likely to be evaluated by teacher observation. More formal activities such as panel discussions, CONPAR, or informational reports can be evaluated by teacher-developed checklists. Checklists provide standards for planning and gauging the success of an activity. No teacher can evaluate every speaking situation, but

[4]Savage, *Effective Communication*, p. 176.

Display 5.4 Interview Data Sheet

Name of subject:

_____

Time and place of interview:

_____
_____

Name of interviewer:

_____
_____

Where do you live?

_____
_____

What is your job?

_____
_____

What do you like best about your job?

_____

What makes you feel happy?

_____

Do you have a hobby?

_____

What are your future plans?

_____
_____

What message do you have for students our age?

_____

If you could be someone else, who would you be?

_____

What is your favorite food?

_____

What was your favorite book when you were in elementary school?

_____

Why did you like it?

_____

Other questions:

_____
_____
_____
_____
_____
_____

Photo or student-made picture of subject

Display 5.5 Speaking Skills Checklist

Directions: The following items are characteristics of effective oral communication. The purpose of this checklist is to evaluate an individual's speaking skills and abilities so that the student can work toward self-improvement. Students will first rate themselves and then the teacher will evaluate them. The following criteria are to be used:

5 = Always   4 = Usually   3 = Sometimes   2 = Seldom   1 = Never

	Student's Response	Teacher's Response
1. Do I organize my thoughts before I speak?	_____	_____
2. Do I pronounce words correctly?	_____	_____
3. Do I explain things clearly?	_____	_____
4. Do I talk at the proper speed (not too fast, not too slow)?	_____	_____
5. Do I use words that accurately communicate what I am trying to say?	_____	_____
6. Do I make notes before I give a speech before the class?	_____	_____
7. Do I participate in a variety of oral language activities?	_____	_____
8. Do I use new words in my speech?	_____	_____
9. Do I avoid using "er," "uh," or "ah" when I speak?	_____	_____
10. Do I read widely so that I have a good background for speaking?	_____	_____
11. Do I use different types of sentence patterns in my speech?	_____	_____
12. Do I use inflection in my voice when I speak?	_____	_____
13. Do I use appropriate nonverbal gestures when I speak?	_____	_____
14. Do I stand correctly when I speak?	_____	_____
15. Do I respond easily when people ask me questions?	_____	_____
16. Do I show interest in what others are saying before it is my turn to speak?	_____	_____
17. Do I adjust my volume when I speak in different language situations?	_____	_____
18. Do I enjoy speaking in a variety of different situations?	_____	_____
19. Do other people listen to me when I speak?	_____	_____
20. Do other people ask me questions after I speak?	_____	_____

intermittent checks on various skills may indicate that some children have specific difficulties that need to be resolved, perhaps with the assistance of professional speech therapists. Also, checklists can be useful at parent-teacher conferences. A model checklist that may be used in the classroom is shown in Display 5.5.

Children in the middle and upper elementary grades should be encouraged to use a checklist to evaluate their own oral language skills. Occasionally, students may be allowed to critique the performance of their classmates. This should be done with caution, however, for it is easy for students to focus too strongly on others' weaknesses. During a class meeting, the teacher can guide peer evaluations by encouraging an emphasis on the positive aspects of oral language. After both the student and the teacher have responded to the ratings on the checklist, the next step is to identify areas of weakness. While building on strengths, together the teacher and student can establish specific strategies to help solve individual problems.

Another way to evaluate oral language is by preserving children's speech on a cassette tape. Tapes allow students and teachers to carefully evaluate one or more skills such as vocabulary, sentence construction, articulation, organization, and delivery. Some schools also have videotape recorders available for classroom use. This versatile device can record both verbal and nonverbal characteristics of speech and can also show the response of the audience. It is a very effective tool for teachers to use in evaluating their own oral language skills.

Summary

Oral language proficiency must be continually developed in the language arts program, for speech is the most widely used of the expressive language forms. Speaking precedes and forms the basis for reading and writing.

Oral communication is the ability to express oneself with logic and clarity for a definite purpose. The major goals of instruction in oral language are accurate articulation, fluent expression, logically organized presentation, and ongoing appreciation of skillful speech.

The foundation for a sound oral language program is the variety of spontaneous and planned speaking situations that occur during the school day. Opportunities for instruction in speaking occur frequently in the elementary classroom. They include casual conversation, discussions of various kinds, the presentation of oral reports, class government, the teaching of social skills, and force-field analysis. It is the teacher's obligation to take advantage of each opportunity. Activities and experiences with literature provide inspiration for all kinds of speaking opportunities. Writers use language in unique and imaginative ways that serve as fine models for children in their own language development.

Informal procedures such as teacher-developed checklists and tape or videotape recordings are efficient tools for evaluating the development of oral language skills. They permit students as well as teachers to take part in the evaluation process.

Best Books for Children

Alligator Pie, written by Dennis Lee and illustrated by Frank Newfeld. Toronto: Macmillan, 1974. A delightful collection of tongue twisters, poems, and humorous stories that are enhanced by some extremely colorful (and funny) pictures. A unique book that will certainly add to a mini-center featuring jokes and riddles. This selection is aimed toward children in the middle elementary grades. (M)

The Bun, written and illustrated by Marcia Brown. New York: Harcourt Brace Jovanovich, 1972. Marcia Brown has taken a Russian folk tale, equivalent to *The Gingerbread Boy,* and transformed it into a marvelously illustrated story that young children will easily recognize. A teacher could read the two selections together with a follow-up discussion on their similarities. (P)

Charlie and the Chocolate Factory, written by Roald Dahl and illustrated by Joseph Schindelman. New York: Knopf, 1964. What happens when five children are allowed into Mr. Willy Wonka's chocolate factory? What happens when the children come upon factory workers who talk in rhyme? What happens when the children disobey Mr. Wonka's orders? Answers to these questions form the basis for this com-

A Profile of Theodor S. Geisel (Dr. Seuss)

ONCE, WHILE RETURNING FROM Europe by ship, Theodor Geisel found himself mumbling a refrain over and over again to the rhythm of the ship's engines:

> And that is a story that no one can beat,
> And to think that I saw it on Mulberry Street.

His wife persuaded him to write a book that would make good use of the couplet. The result was his first book for children, *And To Think That I Saw It on Mulberry Street.*[1]

Clifton Fadiman, in an essay comparing Dr. Seuss with Kenneth Grahame (author of *Wind in the Willows*), recalled that this first book was rejected by twenty-seven publishers on four grounds:

1. Fantasy doesn't sell.
2. Verse doesn't sell.
3. It had no "pattern," whatever that meant.
4. It wasn't "practical"—that is, it didn't teach the child how to become a better child, or grownup, or mortician.

The twenty-eighth publisher was densely ignorant of the juvenile market. He published the book for a fantastic reason: He liked it.[2]

In a writing career that spans more than four decades, Dr. Seuss has produced some forty books that have sold 80 million copies. He has had as many as five books on the best-seller list at one time!

At the suggestion of author John Hersey, who contended that children would learn to read faster if their parents were not so dull, Dr. Seuss wrote and illustrated *The Cat in the Hat.* Published in 1957, the book began a revolution in primers. It is written in a controlled vocabulary of 220 words and tells the story of a saucy cat who gives children a vicarious experience in misbehavior. In 1958, he wrote a sequel entitled *The Cat in the Hat Comes Back.* Because of the enormous popularity of those two books, Beginner Books, a publishing company devoted to young readers, was founded. Its publications are written with a limited vocabulary and are devoted to the idea that children learn to read more quickly when books are entertaining. Since 1960, Beginner Books has been a division of Random House with Theodor Geisel as president and chief editor.

Ted Geisel was born in Springfield, Massachusetts, in 1904. He developed an early interest in drawing, "always doodling in my notebook," he recalls. After high school he entered Dartmouth as an English major; at college he edited copy, drew cartoons, and wrote articles for *Jack-O-Lantern,* the campus humor magazine. After graduation, he spent the next two years working toward a doctoral degree at

Dr. Seuss photo courtesy of Anthony Di Gesu.

[1] Lee Bennett Hopkins, "Mother Goose's Sons and Daughters," *Teacher* 95 (May–June 1978): 36.

[2] Clifton Fadiman, "Professionals and Confessionals," in *Only Connect: Readings on Children's Literature,* ed. Sheila Egoff, G. T. Stubbs, and L. F. Ashley (New York: Oxford University Press, 1969), p. 321.

Oxford University. On leaving there short of graduation, he decided to add "Dr." to his middle name (his mother's maiden name) to form a pseudonym for his work. He said by doing that he gave himself the title and saved his parents a great deal of money. As far as children are concerned, every doctor should be a Dr. Seuss.

Pamela Marsh has perhaps best summarized the long-lasting popularity of Theodor Seuss Geisel:

> However much adults may yawn over Dr. Seuss and sigh over their children's delight, he does seem to know exactly what children just beginning to read find unbearably funny, how to turn zany almost-logic topsy-turvy, how to make his rhymes sing and how to do it all in simple words.[3]

Whatever his secret, one fact is undeniable: Dr. Seuss is one of the most successful writers of children's books. He has single-handedly modified and improved the reading habits of millions of children in the United States and in other parts of the world. As Clifton Fadiman has suggested, "Somebody ought to give him that Ph.D. he's always hankered after."

BOOKS BY THEODOR S. GEISEL (DR. SEUSS)

And to Think That I Saw It on Mulberry Street, 1937
The 500 Hats of Bartholomew Cubbins, 1938
The King's Stilts, 1939
Horton Hatches the Egg, 1940
McElligot's Pool, 1947
Thidwick: The Big-Hearted Moose, 1948
Bartholomew and the Oobleck, 1949
If I Ran the Zoo, 1950
Scrambled Eggs Super, 1953
Horton Hears a Who! 1954
On Beyond Zebra, 1955
If I Ran a Circus, 1956
How the Grinch Stole Christmas, 1957
The Cat in the Hat, 1957
The Cat in the Hat Comes Back, 1958
Yertle the Turtle and Other Stories, 1958
Happy Birthday to You, 1959
Green Eggs and Ham, 1960
One Fish, Two Fish, Red Fish, Blue Fish, 1960
The Sneetches and Other Stories, 1961
Dr. Seuss's Sleep Book, 1962
Dr. Seuss's ABC Book, 1963
Hop on Pop, 1963
Fox in Socks, 1965
I Had Trouble in Getting to Solla Sollew, 1965
The Cat in the Hat Songbook, 1967
The Foot Book, 1968
I Can Lick Thirty Tigers and Other Stories, 1969
My Book About Me, 1969
I Can Draw Myself, 1970
Mr. Brown Can Moo! Can You? 1970
The Lorax, 1971

[3]Pamela Marsh, *Christian Science Monitor,* May 12, 1960, p. 4B.

Marvin K. Mooney, Will You Please Go Now! 1972
Did I Ever Tell You How Lucky You Are? 1973
The Shape of Me and Other Stuff, 1973
Great Day for Up! 1974
There's a Wocket in My Pocket! 1974
Oh! The Thinks You Can Think! 1975
The Cat's Quizzer, 1976
I Can Read With My Eyes Shut, 1978
Oh Say Can You Say? 1979

edy tale that has become even more popular because of its movie version. (M-U)

Dinosaur Dos and Don'ts, written by Jean Burt Polhamus and illustrated by Steve O'Neill. Englewood Cliffs, N.J.: Prentice-Hall, 1975. Tyrannosaurus is just one of the cast in this guide to prehistoric behavior designed for young readers just catching on to good manners. An entertaining collection of dos and don'ts for social situations. (P)

The Egg Tree, written and illustrated by Katherine Milhous, New York: Scribner, 1950. The theme of this 1951 Caldecott Medal book is the Easter tradition in a Pennsylvania Dutch family. It is an entertaining story of cooking, decorating, hiding, hunting, and eating Easter eggs. The how-to-do-it directions for making the Easter egg tree assist young children in the skill of giving and following directions. (P-M)

The First Book of Words: Their Family Histories, written by Sam and Beryl Epstein. New York: Franklin Watts, 1954. A humorous treatment of a difficult subject—words and word origins. It considers subjects such as "What is a word?" and "What is a spoonerism?" The delightful answers will bring a smile to the faces of middle and upper grade elementary readers. Such answers also give students insight into the etymology of language. (M-U)

The Gingerbread Boy, written and illustrated by William Curtis Holdsworth. New York: Farrar, Straus and Giroux, 1968. A perennial favorite of many young readers, this version of the familiar tale is illustrated with soft black-and-white drawings. Young readers find the story easy to remember and easy to retell because of unforgettable lines such as: "Run!

run! as fast as you can! You can't catch me, I'm the Gingerbread Man!" (P)

Green Eggs and Ham, written and illustrated by Theodor Seuss Geisel. New York: Random House, 1960. Sam-I-Am insists that his friend try some green eggs and ham and finally wears down his resistance. One in the series of Dr. Seuss's easy-to-read books. (P)

Happy Birthday to You, written and illustrated by Theodor Seuss Geisel. New York: Random House, 1959. On your day of all days, anything is possible. You can fly over the housetops to a fantasy land where the Birthday Bird treats you to the best time you've ever had. (P)

Horton Hears a Who! written and illustrated by Theodor Seuss Geisel. New York: Random House, 1954. Horton the elephant protects the tiny Whos from banishment until they can be saved by the "Smallest of All." Teaches a sound lesson regarding each person's role in society. (P)

How the Grinch Stole Christmas, written and illustrated by Theodor Seuss Geisel. New York: Random House, 1957. A very popular book that gives young readers a frightful glimpse of what the world would be like without their favorite holiday. Made even more popular by the television version. (P)

Man Must Speak: The Story of Language and How We Use It, written and illustrated by Roy A. Gallant. New York: Random House, 1969. A nonfiction book for older students that provides enough information to develop a unit of instruction on words. It gives a lucid account of how oral speech, languages, and writing have evolved. (M-U)

Many Hands Cooking, written by Terry Touff Cooper and Marilyn Ratner with illustrations by Tony Chen. New York: Thomas Y. Crowell (available through UNICEF), 1974. Savory recipes from over forty different countries highlight this unique book. Each recipe is marked with a code for difficulty: one, two, or three hands. The recipes take readers around the world with food. At the end of the book, international menu ideas for meals and parties are given. A book that can be adapted to many enjoyable oral language activities. (P-M-U)

One Fish, Two Fish, Red Fish, Blue Fish, written and illustrated by Theodor Seuss Geisel. New York: Random House, 1960. One of the most popular of the easy-to-read books created by Dr. Seuss. It relies on many basic sight words plus new ones to enlarge vocabulary. (P)

The Poppy Seed Cakes, written and illustrated by Margery Clark. Garden City, N.Y.: Doubleday, Inc., 1924. A nonsensical book made up of a series of short stories about the misadventures of a small boy named Andrewshek. These stories about one mishap after another are excellent for reading aloud and are perfect for storytelling. One excellent follow-up activity to promote oral language development is actually making the poppy seed cakes referred to throughout the book. The recipe is included in one of the stories. (P)

Q's Are Weird O's: More Puns, Gags, Quips, and Riddles, collected and illustrated by Roy Doty. Garden City, N.Y.: Doubleday, 1975. One of many such books in a series by Roy Doty. Clever illustrations highlight the playful riddles that can be read and retold by children throughout the elementary grades. (M-U)

The Riddle Pot, collected and illustrated by William Wiesner. New York: Dutton, 1973. What goes up and never comes down? Why is a large coat like a banana skin? These and other unlikely questions (and answers) appear in a book of bafflers for elementary readers. (M)

The Rooster Crows, written and illustrated by Maud and Miska Petersham. New York: Macmillan, 1945. A collection of rhymes, jingles, finger games, rope-skipping rhymes, counting-out rhymes, and games drawn from America's oral language heritage. This treasury can aid in promoting a young child's oral language development. Caldecott Award winner. (P-M)

The Sneetches and Other Stories, written and illustrated by Theodor Seuss Geisel. New York: Random House, 1961. The Star-Belly Sneetches hate all the other sneetches who have no "stars on thars," and the con-artist Sylvester McBean makes a fortune with his star-on machine. (P)

Stone Soup: An Old Tale, written and illustrated by Marcia Brown. New York: Scribner, 1947. Marcia Brown has made a carnival of activity from this old tale. So much goes on in the pictures that children who have once heard the story will turn to them again and again, retelling the story for themselves. A suggested follow-up activity is the making of stone soup. (P)

Thidwick: The Big-Hearted Moose, written and illustrated by Theodor Seuss Geisel. New York: Random House, 1948. Thidwick is one of the most memorable characters ever created by Dr. Seuss. He is a friendly, gullible fellow (like Horton) until he finds he is being used by his friends. (P)

Tomfoolery, written by Alvin Schwartz and illustrated by Glen Rounds. Philadelphia: Lippincott, 1973. Trickery and foolery with words collected from American folklore mark this collection of riddles. This sophisticated version of traditional word play is intended for older elementary readers. (M-U)

What Do You Do Dear? written by Sesyle Joslin and illustrated by Maurice Sendak. New York: Young Scott Books, 1961. The author accurately describes the book as "a second handbook of etiquette for young ladies and gentlemen to be used as a guide for everyday social behavior." Maurice Sendak's illustrations support the humorous text that has a subtle message for young readers: Etiquette can be overdone. (P)

Yertle the Turtle and Other Stories, written and illustrated by Theodor Seuss Geisel. New York: Random House, 1950. Yertle, the king of the turtles, decides that the kingdom he rules is too small. He plans to make his throne higher by making each turtle stand on another's back until a plain little turtle named Mack topples the throne with a well-timed burp. (P)

Bibliography

Burton, R. W. "Evolution of the Objectives of an Oral Language Program." *Elementary School Journal,* Dec. 1973.

Carlson, Ruth Kearney. *Speaking Aids Through the Grades.* New York: Teachers College Press, 1975.

Henry, Mabel W. *Creative Experiences with Oral Language.* Urbana, Ill.: National Council of Teachers of English, 1967.

Lenneberg, Eric. *Biological Foundations of Language.* New York: Wiley, 1967.

Lundsteen, Sara W. *Children Learn to Communicate.* Englewood Cliffs, N.J.: Prentice-Hall, 1976.

Possien, Wilma M. *They All Need to Talk: Oral Language in the Language Arts Program.* New York: Appleton-Century-Crofts, 1969.

Savage, John F. *Effective Communication: Language Arts Instruction in the Elementary School.* Chicago: SRA, 1977.

Stewig, John Warren. "Instructional Strategies: The Owl, the Pussycat, and Oral Language." *Elementary English,* Feb. 1973.

Tiedt, Sidney W., and Iris M. Tiedt. *Language Arts Activities for the Classroom.* Boston: Allyn and Bacon, 1978.

Van Riper, Charles. *Helping Children Talk Better.* Chicago: SRA, 1951.

Chapter 6

A Nice Letter to Aunt Martha:
Handwriting and Spelling

MORE THAN FOUR THOUSAND years ago, the Egyptians used a hieratic script, comparable to our cursive handwriting, to conduct their daily intellectual and business affairs. With the invention of a kind of paper made from the stems of the papyrus plant, cursive writing became a practical and widely used tool of communication.

Cyperus papyrus was a marsh reed growing along the banks of the Nile. Workers harvested the green canes, peeled back the bark, and cut the white pithy stalks into sections approximately a foot long. The sections were then sliced into very thin lengths, which were placed horizontally side by side on a cloth. Another layer was placed vertically on the first, and a second cloth was placed on top. With a wooden mallet, the stack was beaten until the plant fibers were woven together into a thin mat. The cloths were taken away, and the "paper" (also known as papyrus) was placed in the sun to dry. Flour paste was used to glue pages together to form a roll of paper. The Egyptians found the papyrus far superior to heavy clay tablets. It was thin, flexible, durable, easy to store, and convenient to carry.

Thousands of years after the invention of paper spurred written communication, critics deplore the lack of expertise shown by many students and adults. A popular newspaper columnist recently wrote a scathing attack on modern methods of teaching writing. In the article she called today's high school graduates "notoriously bad letter writers who can't compose an acceptable letter to Aunt Martha to thank her for a Christmas gift." An exaggeration perhaps, but close enough to the truth to make language arts teachers a bit uncomfortable.

It is probably safe to say that students are not as interested in perfecting the skills of functional writing—legibility, mechanics, and usage—as they were at one time. In *The Story of Helen Keller,* a biography for young readers, we are given a vivid picture of Helen Keller's desire, despite severe handicaps, to create the best writing possible in her day-to-day correspondence:

The maid, who came to help them during the day, brought in the mail. There were lots of letters. Helen Keller had been one of the most famous people in the world for more than seventy years— ever since she was a little girl. Famous people get a great deal of mail.

Polly read the important letters first, and spelled them to Helen with her fingers. Those that were not so important she laid aside. She would answer these. Helen would answer some of those that were important.

They spent the morning at their typewriters. Polly's desk was downstairs, in a room off the front hall. Helen had a study upstairs.

Next to her typewriter was a Braille machine, which works somewhat like a typewriter. On this she wrote letters to her blind friends and things which she herself wanted to read over later, such as speeches.

Before lunch Polly came in, and Helen handed her the letters she had written. Polly looked them over carefully. If there was one single mistake in the letter—even the tiniest mistake in typing—Polly would give the letter back to Helen, and Helen would do it over. This was something Teacher had always made Helen do, and she insisted that Polly make her do it, too. But today there were no mistakes. Polly held a heavy piece of cardboard underneath the space where Helen would sign her name, so that her signature would be even, and Helen signed each one.[1]

Older students who read this dramatic anecdote about Helen Keller's personal correspondence can scarcely avoid examining their own attitudes toward everyday writing tasks. Many are indifferent about their handwriting and ability to spell because they take for granted the alphabet and the miraculous way it works. The manner in which writing and writing materials have developed through the ages is a fascinating story of human genius. Learning about it might help students appreciate the alphabet and their unique ability to communicate with others by

[1]From *The Story of Helen Keller* by Lorena A. Hickok. Copyright © 1958 by Lorena A. Hickok. Reprinted by permission of Grosset & Dunlap, Inc.

Papyrus reeds painted on a swatch of newly made papyrus, from the Papyrus Institute of Cairo.

means of writing, and it might foster in them some of the profound regard in which Helen Keller held written communication.

In this chapter we will describe procedures to help children write legibly and spell accurately—functional skills they will need throughout life.

Writing Readiness

Parents who encourage their preschool children to cut and paste, color with crayons and markers, model with clay or plasticine, and write (scribble) with pencils and chalk might not realize that those activities are preparing their children for handwriting, but they are. Such activities demand the same coordination of eye, hand, and mind that is necessary for handwriting. In fact they are the same experiences that kindergarten and first-grade teachers provide to help girls and boys develop the coordination and motor control needed for handwriting.

A child who is ready for formal instruction in writing is able to make effective use of oral language on which writing is based, understands the relationship between writing and literature, is able to handle writing implements with correctness and ease, and has a certain interest in learning how to write.

The Manuscript Style: Printing

Since the manuscript style of writing, or printing as it is commonly known, is based on two strokes—the straight line and the circle—it is considered easier than the cursive style for young children to both learn and read (see Figure 6.1). It is a beautifully plain and unadorned form of writing, and the fact that it resembles the print in books is strong argument for teaching it to beginning writers who are at the same time beginning readers.

Manuscript is a modified form of the handwriting used by medieval scribes in England. It has been used widely in the United States for approximately sixty years. Americans have found it very functional, and most people continue using it to some extent from kindergarten throughout adulthood.

The Cursive Style: "Real Writing"

Because our culture seems to hold cursive writing in higher regard than printing, most children are eager to learn it. First-grade teachers are quite familiar with the child who links printed letters together by drawing a straight line from one to

A young child at the prewriting stage. Her scribbles will begin to have recognizable shape with the development of motor control and visual perception. (Courtesy of Deidra Coody.)

ciples should be followed. The transition should be made gradually, over a period of months. Throughout the transition period, children should be allowed to use both manuscript and cursive. Any child experiencing undue difficulty with cursive writing should be allowed to revert to printing for a period of time.

Children should be taught to respect both forms of writing. In other words, printing should not be considered infantile or inferior in any way. Students' ability to use the manuscript form should be reviewed occasionally throughout the elementary school years. It will prove useful in making posters and labels, in filling out forms, and on all occasions when "please print" is requested.

Five Keys to Legibility

To ensure that all students achieve the worthy goal of legible handwriting, teachers must understand and stress the five S's of writing—shape, size, space, slant, and speed.

Shape

Each letter and numeral has a standard, commonly accepted configuration or shape. Guides to letter formation are available to the classroom teacher in basal textbooks, workbooks, worksheets, and on commercial writing cards and posters.

Although students will refer to the same examples of handwriting, it is not necessary for them to conform to one particular style or perfectly duplicate a printed model. The emphasis of instruction should be on legibility rather than on perfection and sameness. Under such a plan, the student's natural writing style will be allowed to emerge. Individuality in handwriting, much desired by students, will become a reality, and it need not interfere with legibility.

the other. Hearing parents and older brothers and sisters refer to cursive as "real writing," it is no surprise that the young child is eager to experiment with it. This cultural bias is the strongest factor determining that young children be taught cursive writing. That it is slightly faster to execute is the one other significant argument in its favor (see Figure 6.2).

The language arts teacher should be aware that cursive writing is extremely difficult for many young children. It should be presented without pressure in practice sessions that are relaxed and brief.

The proper time to make the transition from printing to cursive writing has been a controversial issue among early childhood educators for many years. Whether it is made in the first, second, or third grade, or even later, certain prin-

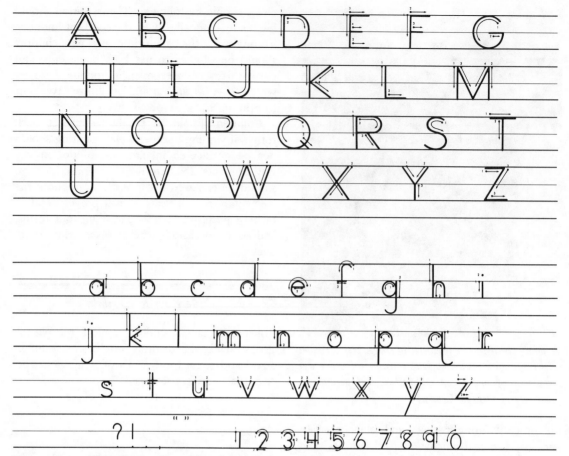

Figure 6.1 *The Manuscript Style of Writing.* *(From* Creative Growth with Handwriting. *Copy-* right © 1975. *Zaner-Bloser, Inc., Columbus, Ohio. Used by permission.)*

Size

The beginning writer who is practicing correct letter formation should also be made aware of the appropriate size for handwriting. Legibility is diminished when writing is extremely small or abnormally large. In cursive writing, upper-case or capital letters are generally one space high and lower-case letters (with the exception of tall lower-case letters) are half that height. Whether the writing is on the chalkboard, chart tablet, or standard writing paper, the same proportion should be maintained.

The handwriting (printing or cursive) of very young children may be larger than that of older boys and girls. As students' motor skills become more refined, the size of their writing may be gradually reduced toward a more mature style.

Space

A major factor affecting legibility is the white open area surrounding letters and words on a page. Letters crowded together to form words and words packed closely together to form sen-

Figure 6.2 Cursive Writing. *(From* Creative Growth with Handwriting. *Copyright © 1975.* Zaner-Bloser, Inc., Columbus, Ohio. Used by permission.)

tences are extremely difficult to read. Oddly enough, too much space between letters also makes a word difficult to read, and too much space between words makes sentences and paragraphs annoyingly hard to read even for an efficient reader.

Words printed on paper should have the width of a child's finger between them, and words printed on the chalkboard should be separated by the width of a hand. Such a guideline, of course, makes it very easy for a child to actually measure the space until the crutch is no longer necessary and spacing is done visually.

The most effective way for boys and girls to acquire a feeling for spacing is to practice writing. During practice sessions, the students should be able to refer to the spacing on a good printed guide, and the teacher should point out spacing errors.

Slant

The departure from the perpendicular characteristic of cursive writing is known as slant. A moderate, consistent slant from left to right is con-

(Courtesy of Barbara Ellis.)

With a sharp knife, cut the thick end of a large feather to a sharp point as shown in the accompanying drawing. Some possible sources of feathers are zoos, poultry farms, and poultry markets.

To make berry ink, mash a cup of ripe blueberries, blackberries, or raspberries through a strainer. To the berry juice add a teaspoon of vinegar and a teaspoon of salt. Store in a small jar.

With practice, students may become fairly skillful at dipping the quill pen into the home-made ink and making smooth writing strokes without blots.

sidered easy to read and fortunately is easily achieved. Legibility suffers when handwriting slants too much, when it slants from right to left, and when the slant is inconsistent (one letter slanting in one direction, the next letter slanting in another).

Achieving the correct slant and consistency in slant is difficult for students; but because legibility depends so much on the proper slant, it must be carefully taught. Once again, practice with a good printed guide to follow and individualized assistance from the teacher will help children produce handwriting that is pleasing to look at and easy to read.

Speed

A fairly rapid rate of writing makes for a smoother, more legible script. Obviously, in the beginning stages of handwriting, when letters are carefully "hand drawn," children cannot be expected to speed up the process. Only when correct letter formation, proper slant and size, and accurate spacing have been accomplished should students be challenged to write faster. Even then it should be done in a low-key way and without pressure. Legibility should never be sacrificed for speed. After all, students in elementary school have no need to write at an astronomically fast rate. They should, however, learn to write with fluency and ease—two characteristics of mature handwriting that do call for a certain amount of writing speed.

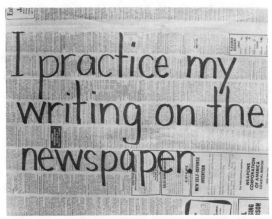

Figure 6.3 *Using the classified and stock market sections of the daily newspaper for handwriting practice. Columns turned horizontally serve as excellent guides.*

To help students appreciate the variety of excellent writing tools available to them, the teacher might help them undertake the task of making their own pen and ink just as early American children did before the invention of pencils, fountain pens, and ball-points. This simple activity is described in Display 6.1.

Activities to Teach Handwriting

Fluent handwriting, like any other skill, is achieved mainly through consistent practice. To make such practice interesting, a variety of activities emphasizing shape, size, spacing, slant, and speed are needed. The following are examples of such practice exercises.

Using a Variety of Writing Tools

Crayons, charcoal, pencils, ball-point pens, lettering pens, felt-tip markers, brushes, and chalk are all instruments that should be explored by beginning writers. Experimentation adds interest to the often mundane activity of writing practice. With increasing independence in writing, a child should be able to use with ease several kinds of instruments.

Writing on Many Different Surfaces

Children should be encouraged to practice writing on both lined and unlined paper, on newspapers (see Figure 6.3) and chart tablets, on chalkboards and slates, and on stationery of assorted sizes. If handwriting instruction is successful and functional, a child will eventually be able to write legibly on any writing surface and with any writing tool, including a stick in the sand.

Practicing Letter Formation Strokes

A paper cup of water, a large soft brush, and the chalkboard are the ingredients needed for this activity. Forming letters on the chalkboard with a wet brush gives children a unique opportunity to do large, bold writing and provides a respite from paper-and-pencil drill. The writing dries at once, and the chalkboard is ready to be reused.

Observing the Teacher

In addition to providing printed copies of the alphabet showing proper letter formation strokes, the teacher should write often before the children. Such writing should be slow and deliberate, giving students time to observe how letters are formed, the posture of the writer, and the grip of the pencil or chalk.

Letter Writing

The handwriting activity with the most carry-over value is letter writing. The practice, however, must be meaningful, or the exercise will quickly become an excruciating bore. Letters written in class should be mailed and appropriate replies elicited.

The teacher should post large colorful charts showing the format of various types of letters—the position of the date, greeting, body, closing, and signature. The teacher should encourage students to refer to the charts. If it is not practical or convenient to actually mail letters, students may exchange them with classmates or pen pals. The importance of accurate spelling, appropriate punctuation, and legibility becomes clear to children when they are conscientiously trying to communicate with another person.

Studying the History of Writing

The origin of our alphabet and the evolution of writing tools and writing surfaces are fascinating stories. They not only inform and entertain, but also help children to appreciate the genius inherent in the skill of handwriting and the effect of writing on culture.

While students are learning to write, they might enjoy looking at samples of early American fancy writing. At a time when few people knew how to write, the ability to write was considered a sign of education and refinement. The fancier and more elaborate the writing, the better.

Early American teachers of penmanship emphasized the attractiveness of the script. Students spent many hours copying letter forms over and over again until their writing looked exactly like the teacher's decorative script. School notebooks were filled with such writing, usually in the form of platitudes and proverbs such as "An ounce of prevention is worth a pound of cure"; "A stitch in time saves nine"; or "Cleanliness is next to godliness."

Copies of early American documents featuring the ornate penmanship with its many flourishes are usually available in school libraries. The signatures on such documents are especially decorative. For fun, some students might like to try fancy writing, but it should be pointed out that fancy strokes are not necessary in today's writing. We now believe that the plainer the writing, the better.

Left-Handedness

An "oppressed minority" that never protests, pickets, or sues is the 20 million persons in the United States who are left-handed. The discrimination against them is neither overt nor intentional. It stems from the fact that common articles are designed for members of the right-handed majority. Left-handers must make a special and concerted effort to learn to use scissors, pencil sharpeners, spiral notebooks, and wrist watches. To complicate matters, right-handed persons are so unaware of the problem that they

Display 6.2 A Petition to Those Who Have the Superintendency of Education[1]

I address myself to all the friends of youth, and conjure them to direct their compassionate regard to my unhappy fate, in order to remove the prejudices of which I am the victim. There are twin sisters of us; and the eyes of man do not more resemble, nor are capable of being on better terms with each other than my sister and myself, were it not for the partiality of our parents, who made the most injurious distinction between us. From my infancy I have been led to consider my sister as being of a more educated rank. I was suffered to grow up without the least instruction, while nothing was spared in her education. She had masters to teach her writing, drawing, music and other accomplishments, but if by chance I touched a pencil, a pen, or a needle I was bitterly rebuked; and more than once I have been beaten for being awkward, and wanting a graceful manner. It is true, my sister associated with me upon some occasions; but she always made a point of taking the lead, calling upon me only from necessity, or to figure by her side.

But conceive not, sirs, that my complaints are instigated merely by vanity. No; my uneasiness is occasioned by an object much more serious. It is the practice of our family, that the whole business of providing for its subsistence falls upon my sister and myself. If any indisposition should attack my sister— and I mention it in confidence, upon this occasion, that she is subject to the gout, the rheumatism, and cramp, without making mention of other accidents—what would be the fate of our poor family? Must not the regret of our parents be excessive, at having placed so great a difference between sisters who are so perfectly equal? Alas! We must perish from distress; for it would not be in my power even to scrawl a suppliant petition for relief, having been obliged to employ the hand of another in transcribing the request which I have now the honor to prefer to you.

Condescend, sirs, to make my parents sensible of the injustice of an exclusive tenderness, and of the necessity of distributing their care and affection among all their children equally.

I am, with profound respect, Sirs,
Your obedient servant,
THE LEFT HAND

[1]An essay written by Benjamin Franklin about two hundred years ago.

seldom offer assistance. Left-handers teach themselves, and their efforts often strike others as awkward, peculiar, or comical. Over two hundred years ago, Benjamin Franklin described the plight of the left hand in a clever essay, which we present in Display 6.2.

With one person in ten being left-handed, an elementary teacher should be prepared to work with two or more left-handers in nearly every class. In teaching the left-handed student to write legibly and with ease, the teacher must be especially concerned with the grip of the pencil and the slant of the paper.

The left-hander should be taught to grip the pencil or pen two inches above the point, about one inch higher than the right-handed grip (see Figures 6.4 and 6.5). Such a high grip allows the left-handed writer to see what is being written

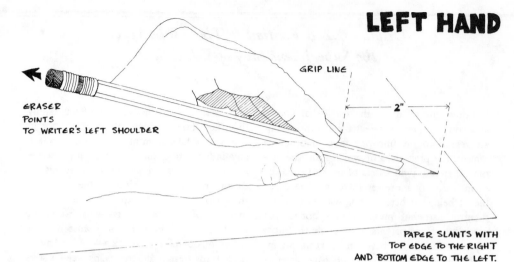

LEFT HAND

GRIP LINE

2"

ERASER POINTS TO WRITER'S LEFT SHOULDER

PAPER SLANTS WITH TOP EDGE TO THE RIGHT AND BOTTOM EDGE TO THE LEFT.

Figure 6.4   The Correct Pencil Grip for a Left-handed Writer. (Courtesy of Barbara Ellis.)

and helps to avoid the "hook" grip that many left-handers adopt to keep their hand from dragging across the writing. A notch carved in the pencil, a stripe of red nail polish, or a rubber band wrapped tightly around the pencil at the proper grip point may aid left-handed writers until they become accustomed to the higher grip. It should be noted that, in spite of everything, left-handers are much more likely to smudge handwriting than are their right-handed peers, and this awareness calls for some tolerance and patience on the teacher's part.

During cursive writing, the left-hander's paper should slant toward the writer's left shoulder (exactly the opposite from the way the right-hander slants it), and the eraser end of the pencil should point toward the left shoulder.

Many years ago, a wise teacher said, "Left-handed children have not been taught to write with the left hand; they have only been *permitted* to do so." Things have not changed much for left-handers in American schools. As willing as most teachers are to offer individual assistance to children with special problems, they have all but ignored the plight of the left-handed. It is time these boys and girls were given the tools, atten-

tion, and help they need and deserve. For a definite psychological boost, left-handed students might be given research topics such as the following:

- Left-handed presidents of the United States
- Left-handed sports heroes and heroines
- Left-handed actors and actresses
- Left-handed musicians
- Left-handed historical figures
- Superstitions surrounding handedness
- Organizations for left-handers (for example, Lefthanders International, One Townsite Plaza, Topeka, Kansas 66607)

Spelling: Basal Versus Teacher-made Lists

Spelling is one of the most difficult of all tasks for the elementary school child to master. Ironically, it is also one of the most essential. Without the ability to spell correctly, the child is handicapped in all writing efforts, no matter how informal or fundamental. A great deal of the

RIGHT HAND

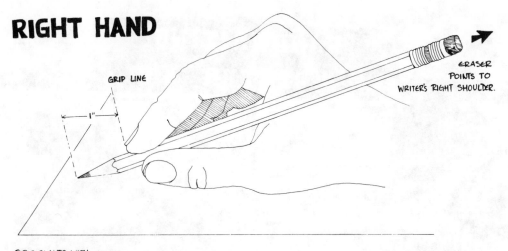

GRIP LINE

1"

ERASER POINTS TO WRITER'S RIGHT SHOULDER.

PAPER SLANTS WITH TOP EDGE TO THE LEFT AND BOTTOM EDGE TO THE RIGHT.

Figure 6.5   The Correct Pencil Grip for a Right-handed Writer. (Courtesy of Barbara Ellis.)

teacher's time will be spent in planning ways to simplify spelling principles and to make spelling practice more palatable to children.

At the present time, most elementary language arts teachers rely mainly on basal textbooks for spelling instruction. Students study a prescribed list of words by means of various exercises, and after a period of time their learning is evaluated with a paper-and-pencil test. Teachers defend such a program by saying it is sequential, systematic, and convenient, which of course it is.

The main criticism of this traditional approach is that the words studied are not always related to the life of the child. Under the basal plan, spelling often becomes a fragmented and isolated exercise that to many students is misunderstood, frustrating, and irrelevant. There is nothing inherently wrong with basal spelling lists. For the most part they contain words that children should learn to spell correctly. The problem is not the list per se but how to make the words themselves meaningful to the students.

Many teachers believe that spelling lists should reflect a child's personal needs. Two major sources of such words are the child's oral language and the child's creative writing. Advo-

cates of this personalized approach to spelling maintain that it encourages children to learn words that they need and words in which they have a keen interest.

Both the basal list and the teacher-made list have certain strengths, which the most effective spelling programs attempt to take advantage of. The basal list is used as prescribed, and the teacher-made list is used to supplement it.

Activities to Teach Spelling

To improve spelling instruction grounded in the basal method, the individualized approach, or a combination of the two, the language arts teacher should engage students in a variety of activities.

Taking Seven Steps Toward Accurate Spelling

Many girls and boys seem to have no plan or system for learning to spell. Relying on a hit-or-miss method, they look at a word and hope for

A well-planned handwriting center that provides practice aids for both left-handed and right- *handed students. (Courtesy of the Beaumont Independent School District, Beaumont, Texas.)*

the best. By taking the seven steps listed below, a student should be able to learn to spell easily and quickly.

1. Look at the word.
2. Pronounce the word.
3. Think what the word means.
4. Spell the word out loud.
5. Write the word from memory.
6. Check the spelling.
7. Repeat steps 1 through 6 several times.

The teacher should walk students through this important sequence until they are able to use it routinely. For students who find spelling unduly difficult, it may be advisable to add an additional step—tracing the word. In this way all senses become involved in learning to spell—visual, auditory, kinesthetic, and tactile.

The "Frequency Approach"

It is well known that students use some words much more frequently than others in their writing. Because frequently used words hold personal, colorful, and interesting words together in sentences, they are aptly called *service words*. (See Chapter 9, Display 9.1.) It stands to reason that such a body of words should be emphasized in spelling as well as in reading.

Unfortunately, most service words are abstract and therefore difficult for many children to learn. Obviously, students need many encounters with them, and they should meet them in a variety of writing situations. Basic words may be emphasized in experience charts, creative writing, word games, and basal texts. For ready reference, especially in primary classrooms, the words should be printed in alphabetical order on a large chart. Frequent checks should be made to ascertain how well girls and boys are learning them.

Improving Handwriting

Students often lose credit for a word spelled correctly because of the poor quality of their handwriting. In fact, according to some estimates, approximately 27 percent of all spelling errors made in the elementary classroom can be attributed to poor handwriting. Such a pervasive problem makes it essential that elementary students at all levels receive individualized, diagnostic instruction in handwriting, followed by supervised practice on specific problems.

Correct formation of letters is only a part of the writing-spelling problem. Certain letters in cursive writing are difficult to link together and must be given frequent special attention if writing is to be fluent and legible. The most difficult combinations for most children are: *bo, be, bi, br, by, oa, oi, os, va, vi, vo, vu, wa, we, wi,* and *wr.*

Only when letters are formed correctly, are in good alignment, and are linked together properly will words spelled correctly also *appear* accurate. In other words, when handwriting improves, spelling improves.

Developing Efficient Dictionary Skills

In today's classrooms, even primary children can have access to excellent dictionaries that are well

Sequential steps that will help children learn to spell are displayed on a colorful poster.

organized, easy to use, and beautifully illustrated. To find out which dictionary skills should be taught and reinforced at each level, the teacher should check students individually.

Dictionary skills recommended for elementary students include the following:

1. Recognizing names of letters
2. Arranging letters consecutively
3. Relating one letter to another in the alphabet
4. Alphabetizing a group of words by their first letter
5. Alphabetizing a group of words by their second and third letters
6. Using guide words to find information
7. Using diacritical marks as pronunciation aids

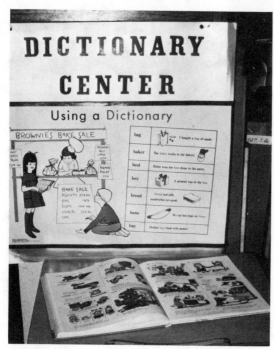

A mini-center promoting the use of the dictionary.

8. Understanding how accent marks affect pronunciation
9. Understanding principles of syllabication
10. Selecting the most suitable definition
11. Understanding the significance of word derivation
12. Making use of special tables and other features in the dictionary

Making Deposits in a "Word Bank"

Any word that the teacher is asked to spell for a student (one that the student has not been able to find in a dictionary) should be written on a small piece of paper. The child uses the word as needed and then files it in a personal "word bank" (an envelope or small box) for later use. The chances are that a word needed once will be needed again. As the word is used and reused in the course of daily writing activities, it will automatically become part of the student's spelling vocabulary. Because such spelling is completely functional, the learning takes place without lengthy drill or forced memorization.

Periodically the teacher should check each student's word bank and give an informal test on its contents. All words that can be spelled easily and correctly may then be sent home as a progress report to parents. The others are redeposited into the bank for further practice.

Charting Seasonal Words

The changing seasons of the year with their holidays, festivals, traditions, and symbolism make life exciting for children and at the same time provide them with excellent raw material for writing. To keep spelling from being a barrier to such writing, the teacher may wish to prepare charts for each season and post them in the classroom as the need arises. It is not difficult to predict, for example, many of the nouns young children will need in writing stories about Halloween, Thanksgiving, Christmas, Valentine's Day, Memorial Day, or the birthdays of famous men and women. To give students more independence in using such charts, each word may be identified with a small picture. The chart actually becomes a facsimile of a page in a child's picture dictionary.

Spelling Games

A teacher who takes advantage of the countless excellent commercial spelling games now available, who makes additional word games for children and helps them create some of their own, is setting the stage for spelling practice of the most valuable kind. In a game format, a great deal of

Halloween Vocabulary Words

Jack-o-lantern   witch

ghost   pumpkin

apples   bat

cat   mask

trick-or-treat   moon

A rebus chart may be used to familiarize children with words relating to special holidays or times of the year. (Courtesy of Barbara Ellis.)

spelling drill can take place without the drudgery so many students associate with it.

Spelling games include crossword puzzles of all types, phonograms, alphabet cards, letter blocks, "spill and spell" games, tachistoscopes, and Scrabble. All games should be organized, labeled, and stored together in an accessible place in the classroom. Keeping them in order and attractively arranged can be one of the routine tasks rotated among students. Obviously, if word games are to have any marked impact on spelling achievement, time must be allotted for game playing, the rules for each one must be carefully taught, and a certain amount of supervision by the teacher must take place.

An old typewriter in the classroom can be an excellent aid to spelling and writing when students are permitted to take turns using it. Typing is also a great asset to the student who has poor coordination and whose spelling suffers because

Display 6.3 100 Words Commonly Misspelled in English

absence	fascinate	meant	ridiculous
accommodate	February	minute	roommate
all right	forty	misspelled	schedule
analyze	fulfill	necessary	seize
anoint	government	ninth	separate
anonymous	grammar	noticeable	sergeant
benefit	guarantee	occurrence	sheriff
boundary	guerrilla	often	sophomore
business	height	optimistic	subtle
category	hoarse	pamphlet	supersede
committee	holiday	parallel	surgeon
conscience	hygiene	peculiar	tongue
conscious	icicles	persistent	tragedy
corroborate	imagine	phenomenon	truly
counterfeit	indispensable	plebeian	tyranny
dealt	innocent	principal	undoubtedly
definitely	irresistible	principle	until
despair	irritable	privilege	vacuum
dilemma	jealousy	procedure	vengeance
disappoint	league	pursue	vicious
ecstasy	leisure	receipt	warrant
eighth	license/licence	receive	weird
embarrass	losing	recommend	wholly
exceed	maneuver	repetition	yacht
existence	marriage	rhythm	yield

of illegible handwriting. Other manipulative materials that students enjoy using—materials that incidentally improve spelling—are printing sets, letter stencils and templates, stick-on letters, tape writers, and label makers.

Isolating Troublesome Words

Among the most significant barriers to correct spelling are the different sounds produced by the same letter combinations, various alternate spellings for one word, silent letters in words, and homonyms. As new words are presented to students, the teacher should anticipate problems and help the student stay on guard against errors by pointing out the difficult parts of a word.

Mnemonic (a spelling demon in itself) devices can be helpful in the case of certain word confusions such as "principal" and "principle." "Just remember your school principal is a 'pal.'" In deciding whether to spell "dessert" with one *s* or two, students may be reminded that a popular dessert, strawberry shortcake has two *s*'s. Of course, not every difficult word has such a mnemonic association, but many do. Students and teachers together can create others.

Over the years, many persons interested in the problem of spelling have compiled lists of the most commonly misspelled words in English (see Display 6.3). Such words need much more attention and practice than others. Since many of these frequently misspelled words are used in upper elementary writing, the language arts teacher may wish to point out features that make each of them difficult.

Proofreading

One of the most troublesome problems in correcting students' written work is the way they feel about recopying their writing to achieve a "perfect" paper. By the time students reach the

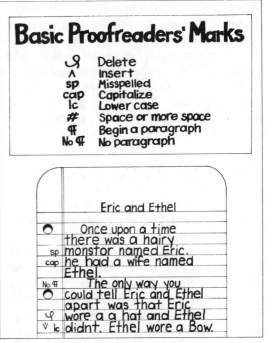

(Courtesy of Barbara Ellis.)

proofreading and revising stage, they are often tired of their work and ready to go on to something else. The teacher who recognizes this persistent problem and gives students a respite from their writing before asking them to correct errors will reap the rewards of better writing and improved attitudes toward the task.

In fact, there is probably no harm done in waiting three or four days to return a set of papers. Students are then able to look at their writing with a fresh perspective, and errors seem to come into sharper focus after such a cooling-off period.

Another way to solve the problem of recopying is to avoid it altogether. A simple procedure makes this possible. The teacher prepares a large chart of basic proofreaders' marks and posts it in a prominent place. As papers are corrected, the teacher uses the code marks to signify various errors in spelling and writing. The marks are made lightly with a soft-lead pencil in the far left margin preceding each line of text. The student interprets the code, corrects the error, erases the teacher's marks (or with scissors clips off a strip containing the marks), and enjoys a fairly neat-looking corrected paper. Only for special purposes should it be necessary for a student to recopy the paper. The eventual goal is to have students do their own proofing, and the process described here is a means to that end.

Keeping a Record of Spelling Progress

In spelling programs utilizing a basal textbook, it is customary to administer a test at the end of each week of study. Most basals cover from ten to twenty words per week, and evaluation usually takes the form of a written test. An effective way to show students and their parents a graphic picture of progress is by means of a bar graph (see Figure 6.6). A grid drawn on 8×10 paper should contain vertical squares equal to the number of words on each weekly test and horizontal squares equal to the number of weeks in a school semester. The grid is duplicated for each class member and stapled inside the back cover of the notebook in which each weekly test is to be taken. The student colors in a square to represent each word spelled correctly.

Relating Literature to Writing and Spelling

Today's students are more likely to appreciate the importance of writing and spelling skills if they can be led to care about books and the people who make them. Such sensitivity will never emerge from the reading of any odd assortment of books that happens to be on hand. To say that girls and boys need interesting and exciting books to read is to belabor the obvious. What may not be so apparent is the fact that they need books that are beautiful to the eye and tantalizing to the touch. Rich, textured bindings; distinguished illustrations; and handsome type printed on fine paper are features that may awaken an appreciation of literature and art, as well as an awareness of the value of legibility and accurate spelling.

An author and illustrator who has devoted his life to creating such books for children is Maurice Sendak. In a National Children's Book Week program Sendak described his first encounter with a fine book:

My sister brought me my first book, *The Prince and the Pauper.* A ritual began with that book which I recall very clearly. The first thing was to set it up on the table and stare at it for a long time. Not because I was impressed with Mark Twain; it was just such a beautiful object. Then came the smelling of it. I think the smelling of books began with *The Prince and the Pauper,* because it was printed on particularly fine paper, unlike the Disney books I had gotten previous to that, which were printed on very poor paper and smelled poor. *The Prince and the Paper—Pauper*—smelled good and it also had a shiny cover, a laminated cover. I flipped over that. And it was very solid. I mean, it was bound very tightly. I remember trying to bite into it, which I don't imagine is what my sister intended when she bought the book for me. But the last thing I did with the book was to read it. It was all right. But I think it started then, a passion for books and bookmaking. I wanted to be an illustrator very early in my life; to be involved in books in some way—to make books. And the making of books, and the touching of books—there's so much more to a book than just the reading; there is a sensuousness. I've seen children touch books, fondle books, smell books, and it's all the reason in the world why books should be beautifully produced.[2]

Many elementary school students have a similar experience when they first see and handle a fine book in the classroom or library. More than once such an encounter has been the beginning

[2]Maurice Sendak, *Quarterly Journal of the Library of Congress* (October 1971), "Questions to an Artist Who Is Also an Author," p. 263.

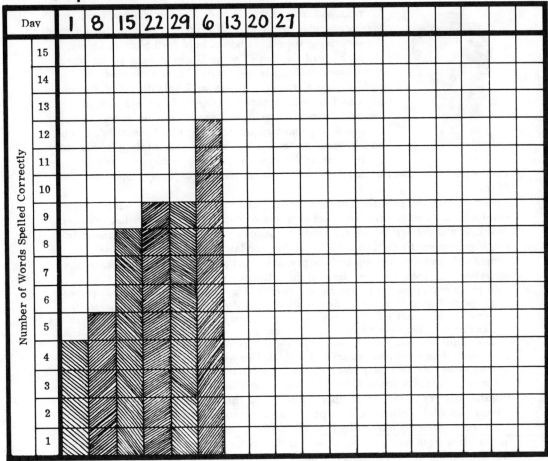

Name __Brian James__

Month __September   October__

Day	1	8	15	22	29	6	13	20	27								

Figure 6.6   Bar Graph to Record Spelling Progress. (Courtesy of Barbara Ellis.)

* To be stapled in the back of a spiral notebook in which a student takes a weekly spelling test. The student colors in a square to represent each word spelled correctly, thus working to excell past performance. Hopefully an upward trend will be noted.

of a long and loving relationship with books. Binding, paper, print, and illustration—the physical features of a book—all combine to create a lasting impact on children at a time when their attitudes toward reading and writing are being formed.

When a literature-based language arts program is successful, children become more and

A Profile of Maurice Sendak

TO TAKE A CLOSE LOOK at *Kenny's Window,* the first book Maurice Sendak wrote and illustrated, is to better understand the surprising appeal his books hold for children. In the 1950s, he read *One Little Boy* by Dorothy Baruch, the noted child psychologist. Sendak recalls, "It was the study of a child named Kenneth who was so deeply disturbed that he couldn't function." Kenneth's parents had taken him to Dorothy Baruch for help, and she in turn set down the step-by-step therapy undertaken to bring him back to full mental health. Maurice Sendak was moved and inspired by her story. He remembers, "It gave me my subject matter, which is children who are held back by life, and then the wonder of leading them out of that."

Kenny's Window, published in 1956, is the poetic story of a deeply withdrawn child who daydreams and fantasizes as a way of coping with the harsher realities of life. It was the first of several books by Sendak that have been instrumental in helping emotionally disturbed children. Yet Sendak maintains that he does not consciously and deliberately include psychological principles in his work. In an interview with John Culhane, he told the following story:

> A group of psychiatrists invited me to a meeting. They wanted to know if I had purposely put psychological things into *Where the Wild Things Are* to help autistic or emotionally damaged children. I said, "No, you cannot have good art when you consciously put things like that in." They were astonished. They were going along one route to help kids, and I as an artist was going along another; yet we discovered we sometimes achieved exactly the same thing—to make contact with a child. That was wonderful to me, because it went back to my original Kenny, and my hope that a fictional work of art could help a child."[1]

Maurice Sendak's books have sold over 15 million copies. Translated into the major languages of the world, they are loved by children everywhere. A small minority of adults, however, have not found them so appealing. Some have labeled them too frightening and realistic in theme for young children. But Sendak writes for children from *their* viewpoint, and to the critics he responds: "Kids think about sex. They think about eating. They think about going to the bathroom. They think about dying. They think about everything we think about—but more obsessively since they don't have the answers to anything." He has not allowed the objections of a few critics to diminish his work in any way. At one time he was called "the Picasso of children's books," an analogy that is still appropriate.

Maurice Sendak has written and illustrated ten books of his own and has been the illustrator of some seventy others. He was awarded the Caldecott Medal in 1964 for *Where the Wild Things Are* and in 1970 was the first American to win the Hans Christian Anderson Award, the highest international honor bestowed on an illustrator of children's books.

Maurice Sendak photo by Philippe Halsman.
[1]John Culhane, "The Fantastical World of Maurice Sendak," *Reader's Digest* (February 1977), pp. 1–6.

The youngest of three children, Maurice Sendak was born June 10, 1928, in Brooklyn, New York. He received his formal art training at the Art Students' League. He now lives and works in a two-story apartment in Manhattan. In addition to writing and painting, he collects rare children's books and antique toys.

BOOKS BY MAURICE SENDAK

Kenny's Window, 1956
Very Far Away, 1957
The Sign on Rosie's Door, 1960
Nutshell Library, 1962
Where the Wild Things Are, 1963
Higglety Pigglety Pop! or There Must Be More to Life, 1967
In the Night Kitchen, 1970
Maurice Sendak's Really Rosie, 1975
Some Swell Pup: or Are You Sure You Want a Dog? 1976
Seven Little Monsters, 1977

more involved with books. They begin to develop an interest both in the way professional writers use words and in the physical characteristics of books themselves. In books they meet fascinating, strange-sounding new words for the first time as well as familiar standbys combined in unique ways. Not surprisingly the reading child's spelling and speaking vocabulary grows at an amazing rate.

The child's interest in books and words and users of words gives the teacher a perfect entrée into a study of sentence structure, word usage, punctuation, spelling, and other composition skills. It is a short step, of course, from a student's reading of books to a student's writing of books. It is in the writing of stories and essays, biographies, letters and diaries that the need for writing and spelling skills becomes most apparent to the student.

Summary

A tablet found in a schoolhouse in Babylonia in 1894, bears a proverb written by a child forty-two hundred years ago: "He who shall excel in tablet writing shall shine as the sun." Handwriting and spelling remain extremely important in the daily life of every person and should be given the attention they deserve in the elementary school.

Boys and girls need to practice handwriting (both printing and cursive), but opportunities for practicing should be built into daily classroom activities instead of occurring only in isolated drill sessions. The goals of handwriting instruction should be legibility and ease. Legibility depends on the shape, size, slant, and spacing of the letters, and on the writer's speed.

Spelling is a puzzlement to many students. Drill becomes extremely tiresome unless it is tempered with interesting, gamelike activities that actually teach spelling. Both basal spelling lists and lists compiled by the teacher play an important role in spelling instruction.

The most successful teachers of written communication are those who have the ability and take the time to relate spelling and writing tasks to the everyday lives of students. By practicing their newly acquired skills in writing original letters, diaries, journals, poems, plays, stories, and essays, students learn to appreciate the significance of written communication.

To acquire efficient skills in functional writing might not cause a student to shine as the sun, but to be able to write a nice letter to Aunt Martha is an achievement just as significant and much more practical.

Best Books for Children

The Bat Poet, written by Randall Jarrell and illustrated by Maurice Sendak. New York: Macmillan, 1967. Told in a perfect combination of prose and poetry, *The Bat Poet* is the sensitive story of a small brown bat who represents the creative and often nonconforming individual in our society. A book that is as popular with teen-agers and adults as it is with children. (M-U)

Chicken Soup with Rice, written and illustrated by Maurice Sendak. New York: Harper & Row, 1962. This book of months contains hilarious nonsense poems promoting chicken soup with rice for year-round enjoyment. Each month of the year is illustrated with a whimsical full-page illustration by the author. (P)

The Happy Rain, written by Jack Sendak and illustrated by Maurice Sendak. New York: Harper & Row, 1956. The people of Troekan like nothing better than gentle, glorious rain to flood the gardens, patter on the tile roofs, perfume the air, and muddy the streets. "And, because it rained happily ever after, the people of Troekan lived happily ever after." (P)

Higglety, Pigglety Pop! or There Must Be More to Life, written and illustrated by Maurice Sendak. New York: Harper & Row, 1967. Based on an old Mother Goose rhyme, Maurice Sendak has created a delightful fantasy story with a little terrier dog as the leading character. Jennie has everything a dog could want, but her life is not complete. She packs her things in a leather bag and sets out to become very experienced and very famous. (P)

In the Night Kitchen, written and illustrated by Maurice Sendak. New York: Harper & Row, 1970. Influenced by the commercial slogan "Baked While You Sleep," Micky dreams of falling into the night kitchen and into the bread dough. There he shapes the dough into an airplane and flys up to the Milky Way. Illustrated with bold poster-type paintings. (P)

Kenny's Window, written and illustrated by Maurice Sendak. New York: Harper & Row, 1956. *Kenny's Window* was the first book written by Maurice Sendak. It is based on a real child of his acquaintance who was so emotionally disturbed that he could not function. Sendak's Kenny is also a withdrawn, introverted child who uses fantasy as a tool for dealing with reality. (P)

The Left-hander's World, written by Alvin and Virginia B. Silverstein. Chicago: Follett, 1977. At least 20 million people in the United States are left-handed, and this book explains in a very graphic way how they are discriminated against every day. There are some promising new materials and methods for left-handers, and they are included in this unique work. (M-U)

Let's Be Enemies, written by Janice May Udry and illustrated by Maurice Sendak. New York: Harper & Row, 1961. John and James are best friends, but James has some irritating habits that drive John into a tantrum: "I'm going over and poke James." The sun comes out and James begins to mellow toward his enemy: "Let's roller-skate, James." "O.K. Have a pretzel, John." (P)

Mr. Rabbit and the Lovely Present, written by Charlotte Zolotow and illustrated by Maurice Sendak. New York: Harper & Row, 1962. Mr. Rabbit helps a little girl to decide on just the right gift for her mother's birthday—a basket of fruit. A beautiful book of colors filled with dialogue that is childlike, humorous, and extremely sensible. (P)

The Moon Jumpers, written by Janice May Udry and illustrated by Maurice Sendak. New York: Harper & Row, 1959. This rhythmic story shows a group of children enjoying the pleasure of a moonlit summer night. "The warm night tosses our hair. The wind chimes stir. And we all dance, barefooted. Over and over the grass!" Many people consider these to be some of Maurice Sendak's loveliest paintings. (P)

Some Swell Pup: or Are You Sure You Want a Dog? written by Maurice Sendak and Matthew Margolis and illustrated by Maurice Sendak. New York: Farrar,

Straus and Giroux, 1976. Employing the comic-strip approach, Maurice Sendak and Matthew Margolis tell a realistic and factual story of two youngsters who learn to care for a new puppy. The puppy is too young for training at West Pointer Academy, and so the rest is up to them. This is certainly the most entertaining book on puppy care that anyone is likely to read. Young readers of the female sex who accuse Maurice Sendak of being partial to boys will be pleased to note that in this book a leading character is a girl and the puppy also turns out to be a "she." (P-M)

The Story of Helen Keller, written by Lorena A. Hickok and illustrated by Jo Poiseno. New York: Grosset & Dunlap, 1958. This dramatic story of Helen Keller's life has been popular with adolescents and teen-agers for over twenty years. It is printed in large type and is fairly easy to read. (M-U)

What Do You Do, Dear? written by Sesyle Joslin and illustrated by Maurice Sendak. New York: Young Scott Books, 1961. The author and illustrator label this companion volume to *What Do You Say, Dear?* "a second handbook of etiquette for young ladies and gentlemen to be used as a guide for everyday social behavior." Guaranteed to bring laughter to young readers. (P)

What Do You Say, Dear? written by Sesyle Joslin and illustrated by Maurice Sendak. New York: Young Scott Books, 1958. A book of manners for all occasions, and what occasions they are! A tongue-in-cheek account of what happens when social amenities are carried to the extreme. Maurice Sendak's illustrations have never been funnier. (P)

Bibliography

Allen, Roach Van. *Language Experiences in Communication.* Boston: Houghton Mifflin, 1976.

Boyd, Gertrude A., and Gene E. Talbert. *Spelling in the Elementary School.* Columbus: Charles E. Merrill, 1971.

Chambers, Dewey W. *Children's Literature in the Curriculum.* Chicago: Rand McNally, 1971.

Cramer, Ronald L. *Writing, Reading, and Language Growth: An Introduction to Language Arts.* Columbus: Charles E. Merrill, 1978.

Culhane, John. "The Fantastical World of Maurice Sendak." *Reader's Digest,* February 1977.

De Stefano, Johanna S., and Sharon E. Fox, eds. *Language and the Language Arts.* Boston: Little, Brown, 1974.

Donoghue, Mildred R. *The Child and the English Language Arts,* 2d ed. Dubuque, Iowa: Wm. C. Brown, 1975.

Kennedy, Larry D. *Teaching the Elementary Language Arts.* New York: Harper & Row, 1975.

Mellon, John C. "Round Two of the National Writing Assessment—Interpreting the Apparent Decline of Writing Ability: A Review." *Research in the Teaching of English,* Spring 1976.

Petty, Walter; Dorothy Petty; and Marjorie Becking. *Experiences in Language Arts Methods.* Boston: Allyn and Bacon, 1976.

Porter, Jane. "Research Report." *Elementary English,* October 1972.

Rubin, Dorothy. *Teaching Elementary Language Arts.* New York: Holt, Rinehart and Winston, 1975.

Ruddell, Robert B. *Reading-Language Instruction: Innovative Practices.* Englewood Cliffs, N.J.: Prentice-Hall, 1974.

Savage, John F. *"Effective Communication": Language Arts Instruction in the Elementary School.* Chicago: SRA, 1977.

———. "Whatever Happened to the Grammatical Revolution?" *Elementary English,* April 1972.

Sendak, Maurice. "Questions to an Artist Who Is Also an Author." *The Quarterly Journal of the Library of Congress,* October 1971.

Smith, James A. *Adventures in Communication: Language Arts Methods.* Boston: Allyn and Bacon, 1972.

Chapter 7

Language in Blume:
Grammar and the Mechanics of Writing

THERE SEEMS TO BE a widespread belief in the United States that the writing skills of students have deteriorated to a near-crisis level. Blamed for the problem are poor teaching strategies, insufficient time for teaching writing, the influence of media, the difficulty of evaluating students' writing, overcrowded classrooms, broken homes, student apathy; the list could go on and on.

The problem is vexing and has sparked lively debate among educators and parents for years. Some promising trends are emerging, however. First, students are being asked to do more writing of the practical, purposeful type. The Latin proverb *Scribendo disces scribere* is being quoted frequently. It means that by writing one learns to write.

Second, there is a great deal of agreement that literature provides the best model for language usage, and consequently more and more language arts programs are adopting a literature approach. Students' interest in both reading and writing is being engaged more effectively than ever by the use of trade books. Popular books such as those by Judy Blume have become an indispensable part of many language arts programs and are no longer treated merely as recreational reading. Such books are, of course, enjoyable, but (as we will show in this chapter) they are also excellent vehicles for the teaching of grammar, spelling, punctuation, capitalization, sentence structure, and other kinds of language usage.

Approaches to Grammar Instruction

With the current emphasis on "back to basics," it is likely that grammar instruction will receive increased attention in the language arts curriculum. Most people agree that students should learn the grammar of their language. There is little agreement, however, about what should be taught. Proponents of so-called traditional grammar are

confronted by advocates of "modern" grammar. Traditional grammar is a set of prescriptive rules based on Latin; it presents a dogmatic model for students' speaking and writing. Modern grammar takes account of the changing nature of language and the various ways it is used in different situations. The dichotomy between the traditionalists and the modernists places a classroom teacher in the position of being able to select the best elements from each approach.

The most widely used avenue to formal grammar instruction is commercially produced language arts textbooks. Most publishers of such series attempt to strike a balance between the traditional and modern approaches. Their approach is eclectic, selecting what appears to be the best of several possible methods. They encourage teaching techniques that appeal to children's wide interests and unique abilities. Basal language arts series try to combine skill learning and practice in interesting thematic units. The specific content of grammar instruction in most elementary schools, however, is likely to be formulated by local philosophies and guidelines.

In the 1980s grammar instruction is certain to undergo a broadening of scope:

- Greater awareness of children's language development
- Increased appreciation of the grammar children naturally possess
- Expanded use of children's oral language as the logical starting point for grammar instruction
- Extended opportunities for writing situations to improve proficiency in grammar and usage
- Heightened knowledge of language usage at all levels
- Enriched experiences with outstanding grammar models to be found in children's literature

Language arts teachers are aware of the general definition for the term *grammar*, a body of rules (or conventions) for speaking or writing the

A colorful display might spark children's interest in writers whose works are used to teach grammar, punctuation, and capitalization. The center "pock- ets" of these daisies are made of papier-mâché plates.

English language. Many teachers, however, are less familiar with the various applications of grammar. W. Nelson Francis provides not one, but three definitions of grammar. All three are included here because the differences he describes may help to dispel some of the misconceptions that exist about grammar.

Grammar 1: The first thing we mean by grammar is the set of formal patterns in which the words of a language are arranged in order to convey larger meanings. It is not necessary that we be able to discuss these patterns consciously in order to be able to use them. In fact, all speakers of any language above the age of five or six know how to use its complex forms of organization with considerable skill. In this sense of the word they are thoroughly familiar with its grammar.
Grammar 2: The second meaning of grammar is that branch of linguistic science which is concerned with the description, analysis, and formalization of language patterns.
Grammar 3: The third sense in which people use the word *grammar* is that of linquistic etiquette.

The word in this sense is often coupled with a derogatory adjective; the expression "He ain't there" is "bad grammar." What we mean is that such an expression is bad linguistic manners in certain circles.[1]

We will use Francis's model to structure our discussion of grammar, examining the three aspects he describes: natural language development, formal analysis of language patterns, and usage.

Grammar 1: *Natural Language Development*

Speaking and understanding language are among the most complex skills children acquire during the preschool years. Most children do not begin to utter complete thoughts before they are twelve months old. Yet, during their first year,

[1]W. Nelson Francis, "Revolution in Grammar," *Quarterly Journal of Speech* (October 1954), p. 230. Used by permission.

most babies effectively communicate through a wide range of vocalizations, including crying. For example, by three months of age, most infants are *cooing*, producing a series of soft vowel sounds when they are relaxed and contented. Also during this period, babies learn to *gurgle*, producing a series of random noises that contain a variety of speech sounds, both consonant and vowel. At this time, children also become aware of the unique voices of other individuals such as parents, grandparents, and siblings.

By six months of age, *babbling*, a second phase of natural language development, is observed. Babbling is quite different from the random sounds of cooing and gurgling. It combines consonant and vowel sounds such as "ki," "di," and "la." At about nine months of age, the baby begins to put sounds together: "la-la-la-la," "bah-bah-bah-bah," "dah-dah-dah-dah." At this stage, babies begin to vary the pitch and volume of their vocalization in such a way that it resembles real speech. Many parents become ecstatic when their offspring produces a sound that closely resembles "mama" or "dada." Such behavior is greatly reinforced, of course, when the mother or father smothers the child with affection upon hearing such sounds.

The young child communicates not only with words, but by intonation and pitch of voice, and by bodily gestures. For example, the baby who sees mother may simply point to her and utter "ma-ma, ma-ma," probably acknowledging its mother's presence. In another situation the child may raise its voice, stretch out its arms, and cry, "ma-ma, ma-ma," in effect saying, "Mother, please come here." Parents come to know rather quickly what message their child is expressing.

Several months after the child speaks a first word, many other individual words are acquired in rapid succession. By the time a child is eighteen months old, a vocabulary of well over fifty words is likely to be identified, and some children seem to be able to name almost everything in their environment. During this developmental stage the child is also learning to walk. As a

With an appropriate book as a catalyst, two kindergarten girls experience both the form and function of language. (Courtesy of Deidra Coody and Carol Nelson.)

result, the language development of young children may be interrupted and uneven while they master the techniques of walking, for it is difficult to concentrate on two complicated tasks at the same time.

At about twenty-four months of age, most children have acquired and are using a large number of individual words. Also by two years, children are combining two or more familiar words into simple but recognizable sentences. Numerous language studies have counted, categorized, and analyzed the number of words children use and the age at which they are spoken. In recent years, research studies have investigated the development of more complex and perhaps more important language structure—speech patterns and grammar formations. The child's developing grammar system may be of greater significance than is the child's burgeoning vocabulary.

According to language development specialist Martin Braine, the use of two-word language-meaning combinations, called *pivot grammar*,

A Profile of Judy Blume

"WHERE DO YOU GET the ideas for your books?" is the question most often asked of Judy Blume by her young readers. She explains to them that ideas for stories come to her from all directions: In *Blubber* she drew heavily on an incident that took place in her daughter's classroom. The idea for *Deenie* came from a woman whose beautiful young daughter developed curvature of the spine. She wrote *It's Not the End of the World* because she knew many families who were suffering the pains of divorce. She says of her own divorce, "While it wasn't easy, it wasn't the end of the world for any of us either."

The idea for the very popular *Tales of a Fourth Grade Nothing* came to Judy Blume from a newspaper article about a real toddler who actually swallowed a pet turtle. She based the character of Fudge on her son, Larry, when he was that age. A sequel to the book about Fudge and his family is called *Superfudge*.

Quite often Judy Blume writes from her own experiences, as in *Are You There God? It's Me, Margaret.* Margaret was actually Judy when she was in the sixth grade: "Her thoughts, concerns, and feelings were my own." *Starring Sally J. Freedman as Herself* is considered by Judy Blume to be her most autobiographical book. "When I was ten," she writes, "I was a lot like Sally, making up stories inside my head."

Most of Judy Blume's fiction is written in the first person, and her stories have a way of expressing an adolescent viewpoint in a self-critical and humorous way that is also psychologically accurate. Her books are set on the East Coast of America in an environment of relative affluence and material security. Blume says of her background: "I had a typical middle-class suburban upbringing—but somehow along the way I started to think for myself—probably because of my father, who was a bit of a philosopher and shared ideas with us."

With its elements of conflict and resolution, Judy Blume's realistic fiction speaks directly to adolescent-age readers and helps them better understand themselves and others. Ironically, many parents also read the books for insight into the feelings of their own children.

Judy Blume's account of her initial efforts in writing help to explain the phenomenal success of her eleven novels:

> I always wanted to get married and have children, but deep inside was the wish to become a great actress or artist or something very exciting. But it wasn't until my children were both off to school that the urge came back. I knew I had to do something for myself—something that belonged to me as a person, apart from having a family. I was lucky. I have the best of both worlds now, and my husband and children share my excitement.
>
> When I write books for children, I become a child—whether it's a boy or girl doesn't matter. I love my work, and I love to hear from children who read my books. I shall continue writing for children forever.[1]

Judy Blume photo courtesy of E. Hamilton-West.
[1]Anne Commire, *Something About the Author*, Vol. 2 (Detroit: Gale Research, 1971).

Judy Blume was born on February 12, 1938, in Elizabeth, New Jersey, the daughter of Rudolph and Esther Sussman. Her father was a dentist. In 1959, she married an attorney, John M. Blume, and they became the parents of a daughter, Randy Lee, and a son, Lawrence Andrew.

Judy Blume now lives in the mountains of northern New Mexico, "where the scenery is so beautiful I sometimes have to face the wall in order to write."

BOOKS BY JUDY BLUME

The One in the Middle Is the Green Kangaroo, 1969
Are You There God? It's Me Margaret, 1970
Iggie's House, 1970
Freckle Juice, 1971
Then Again, Maybe I Won't, 1971
It's Not the End of the World, 1972
Otherwise Known as Shelia the Great, 1972
Tales of a Fourth Grade Nothing, 1972
Deenie, 1973
Blubber, 1974
Starring Sally J. Freedman as Herself, 1977

does not occur until about age two but then shows a dramatic increase toward more complicated structures.[2] By using only two words, the young child may effectively communicate a wide range of ideas and concepts. The child may locate something: "that car"; ask for something: "more milk"; negate something: "not hungry"; describe an event or situation: "hit ball"; indicate possession: "my shoe"; describe something: "pretty dress"; or ask a question: "where ball?" According to Dan Slobin, such sentences communicate both concrete and abstract ideas as well as demonstrate the fact that children have acquired the rudiments of grammar.[3]

A child who has reached three years of age produces sentences that are substantially longer and grammatically more complex than those of a two-year-old. "My house" is expanded to "my yellow house," for example. Another observed language expansion is the addition of phrases within a sentence, such as, "I want to go *for a walk,*" or "Is Mommy going *to the store?*" A third grammatical expansion results from the complex process of transforming a simple declarative sentence into a question. At first, most children simply add a question word like "who," "what," or "where" to make a sentence such as "Where is my doll?" Later, one of the most difficult of all grammatical functions emerges—word order transformation to ask a question, "Do you have the cookie?"

As studies of language acquisition and language development are examined, we find several maturational patterns that have important implications for classroom instruction. One observable pattern is that children tend to see language as a "whole." They do not learn isolated segments and later reconstruct the individual parts. They seem to embrace a universal lan-

[2]Martin Braine, "The Ontogeny of English Phrase Structure: The First Phase." In *Readings in Language Development,* edited by Lois Bloom. New York: John Wiley & Sons, 1978, p. 113.
[3]Dan Slobin, *Psycholinguistics,* Glenview, Ill.: Scott, Foresman, 1971, pp. 42–43.

Display 7.1 A General Overview of Language Development

Age	General Language Characteristics
3 months	The young child starts with possible language sounds and gradually eliminates those sounds that are not used around him.
1 year	Many children are speaking single words (e.g., "ma-ma"). Infants use single words to express entire sentences. Complex meanings may underlie single words.
18 months	Many children are using two- or three-word phrases (e.g., "see baby"). Children are developing their own language rule systems. Children may have a vocabulary of about 300 words.
2–3 years	Children use such grammatical morphemes as plural suffix /s/, auxiliary verb "is," and past irregular. Simple and compound sentences are used. Understand tense and numerical concepts such as "many" and "few." A vocabulary of about 900 words is used.
3–4 years	The verb past tense appears, but children may overgeneralize the -ed and -s markers. Negative transformation appears. Children understand numerical concepts such as "one," "two," and "three." Speech is becoming more complex, with more adjectives, adverbs, pronouns, and prepositions. Vocabulary is about 1,500 words.
4–5 years	Language is more abstract and more basic rules of language are mastered. Children produce grammatically correct sentences. Vocabularies include approximately 2,500 words.
5–6 years	Most children use complex sentences quite frequently. They use correct pronouns and verbs in the present tense. The average number of words per oral sentence is 6.8. It has been estimated that the child understands approximately 6,000 words.
6–7 years	Children are speaking complex sentences that use adjectival clauses, and conditional clauses beginning with "if" are beginning to appear. Language is becoming more symbolic. Children begin to read and write and understand concepts of time and seasons. The average sentence length is 7.5 words.
7–8 years	Children use relative pronouns as objects in subordinate adjectival clauses ("I have a cat which I feed every day"). Subordinate clauses beginning with "when," "if," and "because" appear frequently. The average number of words per oral sentence is 7.6.
8–10 years	Children begin to relate concepts to general ideas through use of such connectors as "meanwhile" and "unless." The subordinating connector "although" is used correctly by 50 percent of the children. Present participle

active and perfect participle appear. The average number of words in an oral sentence is 9.0.

10–12 years   Children use complex sentences with subordinate clauses of concession introduced by "nevertheless" and "in spite of." The auxiliary verbs "might," "could," and "should" appear frequently. Children have difficulties distinguishing among past, past perfect, and present perfect tenses of the verb. The average number of words in an oral sentence is now 9.5

Donna Norton, *The Effective Teaching of Language Arts* (Columbus: Charles E. Merrill, 1980), pp. 32–33. Used by permission.

guage framework. For example, when children are involved in a conscious study of word order, effective classroom instruction must always relate language principles to the larger, meaningful structures children already possess.

A second language pattern indicates that children formulate language generalizations and later refine them. Initially, children have only a tentative understanding of language. Elementary education involves the process of narrowing and refining the broad language generalizations. A successful language arts program accepts children's language at whatever stage of development it happens to be and helps them achieve maximum proficiency.

A third pattern indicates a positive correlation between language acquisition and language-based activities. For example, young children engage in play activities, yet speech is not an inherent part of the activity. Later, language becomes a logical extension of the activity or the basis for the activity itself. Therefore, language development is an active but largely unconscious process. Mastery requires much opportunity to associate language with real-life situations as opposed to artificial exercises.

Although the rate of language development in pre-school and school-age children varies widely, major stages of development have been identified. They are summarized in Display 7.1.

Grammar 2: Formal Analysis of Language Patterns

This section briefly describes the three main approaches to grammar instruction: the traditional or prescriptive approach, the structural or descriptive approach, and the transformational-generative approach. The latter two grammars may not be familiar to the college student, but since they are an integral part of the modern language arts program, it would be well for the beginning teacher to become acquainted with the terminology. The three types of grammar are discussed in the following paragraphs.

Traditional Grammar

The modification of "grammar" by the adjective "traditional" is a relatively recent phenomenon. For many years, the approach to grammar now called traditional was the only approach known. Most people equated language study with the description and analysis of the English language in terms of rules derived from the study of Latin. The underlying assumption of such an approach is that English and Latin are similar in structure. Traditional grammar places primary importance on written language, with the major emphasis on syntax. Since this is the most common approach, it will undoubtedly remain in the language arts program for many years to come.

The history of traditional grammar may be traced back to 1795 when Lindley Murray wrote *Grammar of the English Language Adapted to the Different Classes of Learners*. From the writing of this early work to the present, rules, definitions, and diagrams showing language relationships have been employed. Often used in association with traditional grammar is the term "prescriptive," implying the existence of precise rules that must be internalized before writing or speaking can take place. Thus, the major aim of traditional grammar instruction is the teaching of what is often called "correct" English.

Conventional wisdom about American education maintains that formal grammar instruction improves a student's writing ability. For over fifty years, research has been conducted to determine the validity of this conviction. Much of the research seems to *refute* the claim that instruction in grammar affects writing skills positively. Conversely, a student's proficiency in written communication has, at best, a minimal relationship to that student's knowledge of traditional grammar. Nevertheless, although newer and more pragmatic systems of grammar are being infused into modern elementary language arts programs, most of the essential concepts and basic terms of the Latin-based model endure.

Instruction in traditional grammar typically requires students to classify the words in a sentence into categories called *parts of speech,* to place the subject-predicate relationship in the proper order, and to study the whole sentence to determine how words are used in that particular context. In short, traditional grammar borrows Latin grammar and attempts to fit English to its model.

One of the most widely held beliefs of traditional grammar is that the English language has eight parts of speech: nouns, pronouns, adjectives, verbs, adverbs, prepositions, conjunctions, and interjections. In the traditional scheme, every word may be classified into one (or more) of the eight parts. The role played by a word in a specific context determines its classification. For example, a word that is the subject of a sentence, the direct or indirect object of a verb, or the object of a preposition is said to be a noun or a pronoun. Likewise, a word that describes the action of a verb is considered to be an adverb. Thus, all words are classified by their function and meaning in a sentence.

Parts of speech are combined into larger units of meaning—phrases and clauses. Traditional grammar identifies them and analyzes their function in sentences of various types—simple, compound, complex, compound-complex. One method of carrying out the analysis is by diagramming.

In the language arts classroom, one of the most widespread practices for analyzing the application of grammar rules is by diagramming a sentence. Diagramming is intended to illustrate a word's function in a particular sentence. For example, in Judy Blume's *Then Again, Maybe I Won't,* the following sentence is used: "We had vanilla ice cream for dessert" (page 98). The diagram for this sentence is shown in Figure 7.1 and reveals the subject-predicate relationship of the sentence.

Traditional grammar is prescriptive. It tells, or attempts to tell, people how to speak and write. Such grammar operates on the assumption that there is a standard English grammar which is changeless and that the school's task is to develop proficiency in understanding its elements. Traditional grammar describes English in great detail by taking apart specific sentences. Other grammar types develop principles for the description of sentences not yet spoken or written as shown in the following section.

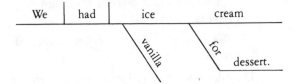

Figure 7.1 *Sentence Diagram Reflecting the Traditional Approach to Grammar*

Structural Grammar

Dissatisfied with the traditional approach to grammar, language scholars such as Leonard Bloomfield in the 1920s and, more recently, Charles Fries and James Sledd have been instrumental in removing English grammar out from under the shadow of Latin. The "structuralists," as they are known, began to explore three different aspects of language: *phonology* (the study of minimal units of sound, or *phonemes*), *morphology* (the study of word formation and minimal units of meaning, or *morphemes*), and *syntax* (the way words are put together to form phrases and clauses). The structuralists categorize words according to the way they change form, the way they change position in a sentence, and the way they change function in a sentence.

Structural grammar identifies four categories or *form classes*, which bear some resemblance to the traditional parts of speech: noun determiners (articles, possessives, demonstratives such as "a," "my," "this"); modals, an auxiliary verb to indicate mood (such as "may," "can," "will"); intensifiers or qualifiers (adverbs and adjectives such as "very," "remarkable"); and conjunctions. Changes in the form or meaning of nouns, verbs, adjectives, and adverbs occur in the following manner:

I. Nouns
  A. A noun changes form by taking certain endings to indicate the plural or to show possession.

     Plural: brother*s*
             bab*ies*

     Possession: it*s*
                 boy*'s*
                 girls*'*

  B. A noun often appears with function words called determiners. Determiners such as articles, possessives, and demonstratives usually precede nouns.

     Articles: *a* carnival
               an elephant
               the mountain

     Possessives: *my* dad
                  your sister
                  their bicycle

     Demonstratives: *that* car
                     this book
                     these houses
                     those women

  C. Nouns usually occur in certain positions in a sentence.

     After the determiner and before the verb: The *workers* rested.

     After the verb, as direct object: Linda hit the *baseball*.

     After a preposition: The students sat in their *chairs*.

II. Verbs
  A. A simple verb may change its form by adding *-s* for the present tense and *-ed* for the past tense.

Present: The mayor react*s* strongly to criticism.

Past: The mayor react*ed* strongly to criticism.

B. A great many verbs are irregular and show the past tense without adding *-ed*. For example:

begin, began, begun
drink, drank, drunk
go, went, gone
lie, lay, lain

C. A verb is usually located after the noun that is the subject of the sentence.

Kevin *broke* the window.

D. The structure words that precede verbs are called *auxiliaries*. Such words include "is," "can," "would," "has been."

We *are* using radioscopes in the treatment of certain diseases.

III. Adjectives
A. Adjectives containing one syllable, and a few with two, usually change form to show comparison by adding *-er* and *-est*.

bright, brighter, brightest
heavy, heavier, heaviest
high, higher, highest
loud, louder, loudest

B. Adjectives containing more than two syllables usually show comparison by adding the intensifiers "more" or "most," or "less" or "least."

studious, more studious, most studious
extravagant, less extravagant, least extravagant
helpful, more helpful, most helpful
willing, less willing, least willing

C. Adjectives often precede the noun they modify.

The *green* pots contain *different* types of cactus.

D. Adjectives may follow a linking verb.

Aunt Helen seemed *unhappy* today.

E. Intensifiers such as "very" and "quite" frequently precede adjectives.

This is a *very* heavy package.

IV. Adverbs
A. Many adverbs are formed by adding *-ly* to an adjective.

brightly
heavily
extravagantly
willingly

B. Adverbs are often found at the end of the sentence.

Our garage doors open *automatically*.

C. Adverbs, like adjectives, usually show comparison by adding the intensifiers "more" or "most," or "less" or "least."

I retraced my steps *more carefully*.
She accepted praise *most graciously*.
After ten hours the light glowed *less brightly*.

According to the structuralists, the essential sentence patterns found in English may be described in terms of the form and function of words. Carl Lefevre has identified four basic patterns and their variations.[4] We will illustrate the four basic sentence patterns with examples from Judy Blume's book *It's Not the End of the World:*

Pattern 1

A. Noun–Verb: "Mom hollered."

[4]Carl A. Lefevre, *Linguistics and the Teaching of Reading* (New York: McGraw-Hill, 1964), pp. 90–91.

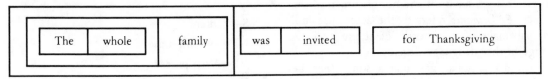

| The | whole | family | | was | invited | | for Thanksgiving |

Figure 7.2 *Sentence Diagram Reflecting the Structuralist Approach to Grammar*

B. Noun–Verb–Adverb: "Mother smiled sadly."

C. Noun–Verb–Adjective: "Mother's face turned red."

Pattern 2

A. Noun–Verb–Noun: "Garfa had chicken pox."

Pattern 3

A. Noun–Verb–Noun–Noun: "Gary Owens wrote our class a letter."

B. Noun–Verb–Noun–Adjective: "Val painted the bedroom green."

Pattern 4

A. Noun–Linking Verb–Noun: "The lawyer's name is Mr. Levinson."

B. Noun–Linking Verb–Adjective: "Jeff feels grown-up."

C. Noun–Linking Verb–Adverb: "Amy is here."

Structuralists use a series of enclosures or boxes to indicate the relationship and function of the words in a sentence. The major parts of a sentence—the subject and predicate—are enclosed first, and then boxes are drawn within those boxes to demonstrate the relationship of words within the subject and the predicate. To illustrate, we have diagrammed a sentence from Judy Blume's book *Then Again, Maybe I Won't* (see Figure 7.2).

Structural grammar recognizes the inadequacies of traditional grammar and proposes a new system for analyzing language. The most significant feature of structural grammar is that it describes grammar rather than prescribing it. By using the approach of structural grammar we are able to identify basic sentence patterns of En-

glish and to describe the form and function of words in those patterns.

Transformational Grammar

Perhaps the most striking difference between structural grammar and transformational grammar is the fact that transformational grammar is *generative:* It provides rules for producing new sentences as well as patterns for the description of existing sentences. Transformational grammar, according to Pose Lamb, divides American English into two main classifications—basic sentences and transforms, or variations, of those basic sentences.[5]

The principles of transformational grammar are set forth in *Syntactic Structures*, a book written by Noam Chomsky in 1957. Chomsky explains that sentences have both a surface structure and a deep structure. The *surface structure*, or sentence form, is what an individual actually speaks, hears, or reads. The *deep structure*, or abstract meaning, is the underlying set of semantic rules implied in the sentence. Transformations are conversions from the deep structure to the surface structure. Therefore, transformational grammar is both an analysis and a description of language processes that people acquire and use naturally. Transformational grammarians distinguish between competence and performance. Language *competence* may be defined as an individual's unconscious understanding of grammar—the ability of a person to differentiate

[5]Pose Lamb, *Linguistics in the Proper Perspective*, 2d ed. (Columbus: Charles E. Merrill, 1977), p. 100.

between a grammatical and nongrammatical sentence. *Performance* refers to the actual use individuals make of this knowledge at any particular stage of their language development.

Transformational grammar distinguishes between phrase structure rules and transformational rules. *Phrase structure rules* are needed for generating basic units of language. *Transformational rules* are the steps to be taken to combine or rearrange units of language into recognizable sentences. Another term used in transformational grammar is *kernel sentence*. It refers to basic or "kernel sentences" from which all other sentences are formed. Kernel sentences are usually short, simple, declarative sentences without details or added phrases.

Phrase Structure Rules. Phrase structure rules provide a guide for producing new sentences as well as patterns for the analysis of existing sentences. Such rules are essentially a series of linguistic equations (similar to those of algebra) by which a sentence is broken down into smaller and smaller language elements. The first step identifies the two essential parts of a kernel, or basic, sentence—the noun phrase (NP) and the verb phrase (VP). Sequentially, each sentence component is further refined as follows:

Key

S—Sentence

NP—Noun phrase

VP—Verb phrase

Det—Determiner (article)

N—Noun

V—Verb

MVP—Main verb phrase

Aux—Auxiliary verb

Tns—Tense

M—Model

**Phrase Structure Rules
for Generating Sentences**

Rule 1 —S → NP + VP

Rule 2 —NP → Det + N

Rule 3 —VP → Aux + MVP

Rule 4 —Aux → Tns = (M) +
(have + en) + (be + ing)

Rule 5 —Tns → past
present

Rule 6 —MVP → V + NP

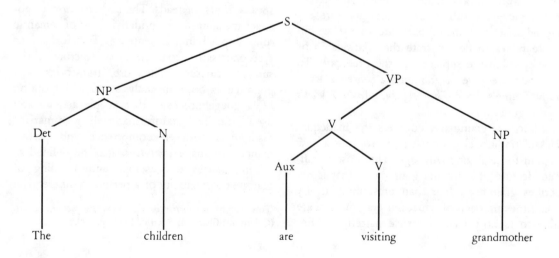

Display 7.2 Grammar Activities Using Automobile Advertisements

Plurals and Possessives. Distribute ads and brochures from car agencies. Ask students to scan them for the names of ten different cars and write them in a list. Beside each name they should write its plural and possessive forms.

Parts of Speech. Ask students to circle all the nouns, pronouns, adjectives, and so on in different colors. Upon completion, they may make a bar graph to show how frequently each part of speech is used.

Synonyms. Ask students to list on 3 × 5 cards adjectives and adverbs used in the ads to describe the automobiles. On a second set of cards, they may write a synonym for each of the original words. When the cards are shuffled, this activity provides a game of the Concentration type.

Etymology. Ask students to look up the history, origin, and background of various automobile names. The list should include a variety of different types—Chevrolet, Omni, Volkswagen, Mustang, Malibu. Interesting information about such names may be found in the dictionary, thesaurus, atlas, or encyclopedia.

Sentence Structure. Print sentences from the car ads onto sentence strips. Cut each sentence apart between the subject and verb. Ask students to match them in a pocket chart and to reassemble the sentences into a meaningful paragraph.

Sentence Expansion. Using the car ads, ask students to write simple sentences (for exam-

1. Write five declarative sentences about the cars in the ads.

2. Make a list of the adjectives used.

3. Find a synonym for each verb.

4. List the car titles in alphabetical order.

5. Prepare a vocabulary chart of car parts.

6. Make a list of the picturesque phrases used in the car ads.

7. Prepare a crossword puzzle of car titles with clues.

8. Write an original automobile advertisement.

(Courtesy of Barbara Ellis.)

ple, "The car stopped."). Illustrate ways to expand such sentences into longer, more elaborate ones (such as "The sporty Trans Am stopped in the pit for a quick transfusion.").

Paragraph Construction. Examine the copy used in car ads. Ask students to identify such features as the topic sentence, controlling idea, and transition sentence. Ask students to write paragraphs similar to those in the ads.

Display 7.3 Grammar Activities Using Books by Judy Blume and Other Authors

1. Show students several sentences from books by Judy Blume. The sentences should have a specific part of speech deleted, for example, "I _____ out the window, but no pigeons were on the ledge." Have the students suggest several possible words that might fit the position. After the completed sentences are discussed, ask the students to pantomime the sentence with a different part of speech deleted.

2. Have the students listen to two sentences found in a book by Judy Blume, one expanded and the other nonexpanded: "Janet grabbed my arm" and "She pulled me through the revolving door and into the store." Ask the students to describe each sentence. Which was more interesting? Which was more informative? Present several other nonexpanded sentences and have the students expand them in various ways.

3. Ask students to listen to a phrase or paragraph written in slang similar to that found in the title of Judy Blume's book *Tales of a Fourth Grade Nothing*. Ask the students to rewrite the passage in standard English.

4. Discuss the fact that speakers and writers such as Judy Blume use clues to indicate time. Duplicate several passages that illustrate a different time period. Ask the students to identify the time element: past, present, or future. Have the class develop topics that would illustrate the various verb tenses.

5. Use a predictable language pattern to help primary grade children experience the concept of subject and predicate. First, read a story such as *Drummer Hoff* by Ed and Barbara Emberley: "General Border, gave the order." The concept is repeated as new charac-

ters are introduced. After the story is read, let the students develop their own characters engaged in various actions to illustrate subjects and predicates.

6. Make a set of sixteen words for the four major parts of speech (four nouns, four verbs, four adjectives, and four adverbs) on different colored paper. Pass the word sets out to a group of four students (one part of speech per student). Ask each group to make as many sentences as possible using the four parts of speech:

Set 1 Nouns	Set 2 Verbs
children	attack
snails	drink
cats	walk
lions	cry

Set 3 Adjectives	Set 4 Adverbs
young	quickly
big	happily
clean	wildly
sad	carefully

Many unique and grammatical sentences are possible, such as:

Young lions attack quickly.
Sad snails walk carefully.

7. Read a line or two from Lewis Carroll's poem, "Jabberwocky." Have the students substitute real words for nonsense ones. Upon completion of the task, reverse the process, having the students substitute nonsense words for real ones in another poem.

Transformational Rules. Phrase structure grammar is based on the rules of formation, like the rule $S \rightarrow NP + VP$. The additional level that Chomsky and his followers have developed is based on rules of transformation, which are simply rules for rearranging the basic elements.

Transformational grammarians see such rules as patterns or directions for sentences not yet spoken. Structuralists, on the the other hand, use the rules for categorizing existing sentences. Therefore, transformation refers to the ways kernel sentences may be altered. The following transformations are among the most common:

1. *Question transformation*—The kernel sentence, "The house is green" is transformed into a question by simply rearranging the words, "Is the house green?" Question transformations often begin with such words as "who," "what," "when," "where," and "why."
2. *Negative transformations*—The kernel sentence, "The house is green" becomes a negative transformation by inserting the word "not" or "n't" after the verb. "The house isn't green."
3. *Passive transformation*—The kernel sentence is in the active voice. A change that affects the action of the verb usually contains a transitive verb. For example, the sentence "The girls ran the hundred-yard dash" may be transformed so that the subject receives the action rather than the object, i.e., "The hundred-yard dash was run by the girls."

Two discussions in this section have dealt with the system of rules that relates the meaning of a sentence to its production. The distinction between the underlying "deep structure" and the string of words uttered aloud or "surface structure" is one of the major contributions of transformational grammar. A generative grammar, therefore, is a set of rules rather than an analysis of a sentence using the parts of speech.

We do not believe that children learn grammatical concepts by means of quiet busy work.

Understanding the proper application of grammar rules to various speaking and writing situations is an active process. Grammar *must* be learned through performance: by participating, by imitating, by experimenting, and by making mistakes.

Grammar 3: Usage

Grammar 2 has been defined as the theoretical description and formal analysis of language. Usage is the convention of language—the choices of words, phrases, and sentences in different situations. Usage is concerned with word choices, the language attitudes and standards of an individual or group. It is related to the speaker (or writer), the audience, and the topic.

How individuals use language is a reflection of personal preference and social standards. The effectiveness of usage is measured not by conformity to fixed rules but by the response of the listener or reader to the communication. Every person uses different styles, or *registers*, of language. Registers are language styles, ranging from the highly formal, at one extreme, to colloquialism and slang at the other. Students should be aware that effective speakers and writers know when to change register to ensure that their message is understood. Boys and girls need to encounter diverse styles of usage and perceive the appropriateness of each in a given situation. An understanding of the concept of register will help them adjust their listening, speaking, reading, and writing to the situation at hand.

Children's literature provides examples of many registers and is an excellent vehicle for sensitizing students to the nuances of usage. The following passages from three Newbery Award books illustrate three registers of usage: formal, general, and informal. These three groupings represent occasions in which most people encounter language, from time to time, in their daily lives.

Register 1: Formality

The regular, orderly, methodical arrangement of "correct" language characterizes formal usage. In *Amos Fortune: Free Man*, Elizabeth Yates describes the epitaphs of Amos and Violet as she observed them in the churchyard in Jaffrey, New Hampshire:

Sacred
to the memory of
Amos Fortune
who was born free in
Africa a slave in America
he purchased liberty
professed Christianity
lived reputably and
died hopefully
Nov. 17, 1801
Aet. 91

Sacred
to the memory of
Violet
by sale the slave of
Amos Fortune by
marriage his wife by
her fidelity his friend
and solace she died
his widow
Sept. 13, 1802
Aet. 73[6]

Register 2: Everyday Informality

General language usage is an expression describing speech and writing consistent with the norms of society. It is natural and generally accepted. This definition, used by the National Council of Teachers of English, has maintained that usage: (1) is determined by the living language of today; (2) recognizes dialect, geographical, and vocational variations; (3) is judged by its appropriateness for the purpose intended; (4) recognizes that

there are situational levels of speech; and (5) takes into account the historical development of the language.

Everyday dialogue between two or more persons is a natural situation in which to observe a flow of general language usage. Literature is filled with examples of such informality. For example, in ... *And Now Miguel* by Joseph Krumgold, Miguel and Gabriel discuss Miguel's draft notice:

With his thumb he shot one of his pebbles, and we watched it splash.

"I've never seen an ocean," said Gabriel.

"I understand," I said. "Not around Los Cordovas. Only mountains and mesas and prairies."

"And so I thought how it would be to see an ocean once. Just for a while, to see an ocean and then to come back here and go on like always. To see all that water and the big waves, how an ocean looks. And the islands with water all around coming up white on the beaches, islands where the coconuts come from."

"To put on the cake," I nodded. "I understand about coconuts."

"It grows like footballs on trees. And on the same islands are girls that wear skirts made out of grass."

"What kind of grass, alfalfa?"

"A straw kind of grass."

"That must be interesting to look at. And cool."

"Well, that's been my wish for a long time, to go see an ocean, the Pacific, and the islands that are down there in the middle of it. And now, I've got my wish."

"But to be a soldier, wasn't part of it?"

"No. That part was the surprise."[7]

Register 3: Slang

Highly informal language consisting of both coined words and extended meanings attached to new words is known as slang. Such language

[6]Elizabeth Yates, *Amos Fortune: Free Man* (New York: Dutton, 1950), p. 18. Used by permission.

[7]Excerpt from ... *And Now Miguel* by Joseph Krumgold. Copyright 1953 by Joseph Krumgold. Used by permission of Thomas Y. Crowell.

A folder providing a picture to write about, a list of needed words, and some general guidelines may en- *courage children to create stories or essays. (Courtesy of Barbara Ellis.)*

quickly passes into disuse or comes to have a more formal status. A popular book whose very title implies slang usage is *It's Like This, Cat* by Emily Neville.

Slang is the body of words and expressions frequently used by a rather large portion of the general public, but not accepted as standard formal usage by the majority. Slang attempts to employ a quick, easy, personal mode of speech. It comes mainly from cant, jargon, and argot words and expressions whose popularity has in-

creased until a large number of the general public uses or understands them. Eventually, a great deal of slang passes into standard usage. Other slang flourishes for a time and is then forgotten. Finally some slang remains in usage but is never fully accepted by the general population. This particular slang includes obscenities, vulgarities, and "taboo" words.

The following passage from the book *It's Like This, Cat* is an example of the esoteric jargon used by teen-agers in the 1950s and 1960s:

I wonder who Nina is. I don't hear her mother come into the kitchen. Then I turn around and there she is. Holy crow! We got some pretty beat-looking types at school, but this is the first time I've ever seen a beatnik mother.

She's got on a black T-shirt and blue jeans and old sneakers, and her hair is in a long braid, with uneven bangs in front.

Mary waves a saucepan vaguely at us both and says, "Nina—Davey—this is my mother."

So Nina is her mother. I stick out my hand. "Uh—how do you do?"

"Hel-loo." Her voice is low and musical. "I think there is coffee on the stove."[8]

The main point to be made in discussing the three registers of grammar is to make students aware that all three are appropriate on occasion. They need to be able to shift from one to the other as the need arises.

Punctuation

Punctuation helps to clarify meaning. In writing, the rhythm and tempo of language are often conveyed through the use of punctuation marks.

Despite the fact that punctuation is taught at almost every grade level, skill mastery and practical application remain a problem for many students. Punctuation errors are among the most common flaws made by students in written composition. In 1929 a research study determined that between one-third and one-half of the mechanical errors made by elementary and secondary students were due to punctuation mistakes.[9] Similar percentages have been found in the National Assessment of Basic Skills, a test designed to measure the acquisition of various academic skills by children across the United States.

Regardless of the emphasis placed on punctuation over the past fifty years, students have shown little relative improvement as they progress through the language arts program. What are the reasons for this shortcoming in language arts learning? Burns and Broman have concluded "that few children have discovered the importance of these items, that they have been inadequately introduced, that there was insufficient review of the items to establish their use, or that insufficient attention was given to their use in genuine writing situations."[10]

Punctuation skills that should be taught in the primary and intermediate grades are listed in Displays 7.4 and 7.5.

Capitalization

Capitalization is another element that helps to clarify the meaning of written discourse. Quite often scope and sequence guidelines suggest strategies for introducing and teaching the various conventions of capitalization. Such a guide is only a suggested framework; considerable variation exists in the introduction and reinforcement of capitalization skills. Most often, children are introduced to capitalization early, through dictated stories, language-experience charts, and other reading activities. For young students in the primary grades, understanding capitalization and applying the rules is a natural process.

Most students do not have difficulty applying capitalization rules. They are much easier to use than the rules of punctuation. Younger students expect to signal the beginning of a sentence, a proper noun, or a special word with a capital

---

[8]Emily Neville, *It's Like This, Cat.* Copyright © 1963 by Emily Neville. Used by permission of Harper & Row, Publishers, Inc.

[9]R. L. Lyman, *Summary of Investigations Relating to Grammar, Language, and Composition* (Chicago: University of Chicago Press, 1929).

[10]Paul C. Burns and Betty L. Broman, *The Language Arts in Childhood Education* (Chicago: Rand McNally, 1979), p. 274.

Display 7.4 Punctuation Skills for the Primary Grades

Punctuation Mark	Example
1. A period at the end of a sentence	Laura always wondered why bread made of cornmeal was called johnnycake.
2. A period after numbers in a list	1. Put your name on the paper. 2. Open the test booklet.
3. A question mark at the close of a question	Why do I have to do that?
4. A comma between the day of the month and the year	September 15, 1882
5. A comma between the name of a city and the state	Mansfield, Missouri
6. A period after abbreviations	Sun., N.J., St., Dr.
7. A period after an initial	E. B. White
8. An apostrophe in common contractions	I'm, can't, wouldn't, I'll
9. A comma between items in a list	hammer, nails, paint, and brush
10. A comma after the salutation of a friendly letter	Dear Aunt Martha,
11. A comma after the closing of a friendly letter	Your friend, Robert

letter. Older students often look for capital letters when they scan a selection in search of the answer to a question requiring a name, place, or object. In fact, only a few rarely-used capitalization rules give students any real difficulty. Most girls and boys seem to internalize the conventions of capitalization and reinforce that understanding with writing and reading experiences.

Basic rules of capitalization usually taught in the primary and intermediate grades are listed in Displays 7.6 and 7.7.

"They Write and They Write"

People learn to speak by speaking, to read by reading, and to write by writing. Dan Fader in *Hooked on Books* describes a successful approach to the teaching and learning of writing:

They write a small mountain of out-of class papers, in-class papers, exercises, paragraphs, sentences . . . they write and they write and they write. With very

Display 7.5 Punctuation Skills for the Intermediate Grades

Punctuation Mark	Example
1. An apostrophe to show possession	girl's, boy's, teachers'
2. A hyphen to separate parts of a word divided at the end of a line	superinten-dent
3. A period following a command statement	Go. Come here.
4. An exclamation point at the end of a group of words that indicate excitement	Let's go home! Oh, no!
5. A comma to set off an appositive	Linda Edwards, our basketball coach, conducts practice every afternoon.
6. A comma between explanatory words in a quotation	She said, "Hi, I'm Mary Louise."

7. A period after numerals and letters in an outline	I.
	   A.
	   B.
	II.
	   A.
	   B.
	      1.
	      2.

8. A comma to set off nouns in direct address	Mary, come in here.
9. A hyphen in compound numbers	forty-three, one-third
10. A colon to set off a list	The following players will start: Earl, James, Albert, Mark, and Harold.
11. A comma before a coordinating conjunction in a compound sentence	Margaret will not be able to attend the party, and she will be missed.
12. A comma to set off a parenthetical expression	I really enjoyed *Freckle Juice*, since I have freckles myself, and I'm now reading it a second time.

Display 7.6 Capitalization Rules for the Primary Grades

Item to Be Capitalized	Example
1. The first word in a sentence	*The Incredible Journey* is the best book I ever read.
2. A person's first and last name	Tom Sawyer, Huckleberry Finn
3. The word "I"	You know that I am proud of you.
4. The date	April 27
5. The first word and other important words in the title of a book or composition	*The Wind in the Willows,* *The Monster's Bathtub*
6. Titles of address that precede someone's name	Mr. Johnson, Mrs. Sharon Harmon, Miss Owens, Ms. Fairchild, Dr. Janet Olson
7. Proper names: month, day, common holidays, places, etc.	Thursday, October, Christmas, Hanover, New Hampshire
8. The first word of a salutation in an informal note	Dear Amy,
9. The first word of a closing in an informal note	Your best friend,

few exceptions, they write more in one semester than they have written before in their lives. And they learn how to write. They have learned to write through the one method they have never before been subjected to, the one method which can be expected to succeed—the constant practice of writing itself.[11]

Plentiful writing assignments help students to understand and internalize principles of grammar, sentence structure, punctuation, and capitalization; and they provide incentives for reading and seeking out people and experiences to write about. The rewards to individual boys and girls, parents, and teachers will be essays like the following, composed by a third-grade student:

OUR FIELD TRIP TO THE CLEANERS

On Tuesday we took a trip to the Longhorn Cleaners. At about 12:30 p.m. we left the school in cars, driven by volunteer parents. At the cleaners Mr. Hancock explained how to clean and wash clothes. His washing machine is much longer than my mother's. I like the way the workers ironed sheets and tablecloths, but best of all I liked watching them fold shirts. The whole laundry was interesting.

[11]Daniel N. Fader and Elton B. McNeil, *Hooked on Books: Program & Proof* (New York: Berkley, 1968), pp. 27–28.

Display 7.7 Capitalization Rules for the Intermediate Grades

Item to Be Capitalized	Example
1. Names of cities and states	Cleveland, Ohio, Phoenix, Arizona
2. Names of organizations	Girl Scouts, Boy Scouts, Indian Guides, Little League
3. "Mother" and "Father" when used in place of the name	Mother is ill, and Father is nursing her.
4. Local geographical names	Big Bend National Park, Rocky Mountains, Mississippi River
5. Names of streets	1600 Pennsylvania Avenue
6. Names of all places, persons, countries, oceans, etc.	Dartmouth College, Stephen F. Austin, Kenya, Atlantic Ocean
7. Roman numerals and letters in outlines	I. 　A. 　B. 　C.
8. Commercial trade names	Xerox, RCA, Chevrolet, Jello, Kleenex
9. Names of the deity and holy books	God, Holy Ghost, the Bible, the Koran, the New Testament
10. Proper adjectives indicating race or nationality	Eskimo, Chinese, German, Hispanic

Summary

Few people give much thought to the complexity of the language they speak and write so casually and so easily every day of their lives. People just speak, almost entirely unaware of the subtleties of the word choices they are making, of the grammar they are using, or of the sentence structure they are creating. Inexplicably, appropriate words come to mind. Sentences emerge without the speaker or writer consciously thinking about the rules of grammar that govern their structure. Effective instruction in the elementary grades is one factor enabling girls and boys to internalize principles of grammar and usage and to use them effortlessly as adults.

Grammar is a body of rules or conventions that describe and prescribe the speaking and writing of English. Grammar is the study of language that deals with the form and structure of words (morphology), with the customary arrangement of phrases and sentences (syntax), and with the meaning of words at a given time (usage). Traditionally, the words in English have been classified into eight groups, called *parts of speech*. In the twentieth century, however, language scholars became dissatisfied with the traditional approach and developed different systems for examining how our language works. Structural and transformational grammarians analyze the production of sentences and describe patterns for new ones. An understanding of both the traditional and contemporary systems will give the language arts teacher a deeper appreciation of how language functions and will facilitate the teaching of grammar in the elementary classroom.

Every person uses several different styles, or *registers,* of language, ranging from slang to formal diction. Matching the appropriate register to a given situation is a skill to be learned. Using examples of various styles of language found in children's books, the teacher can help children develop the ability to change register as social situations warrant. Punctuation and capitalization are other important communication skills initially taught and developed in the elementary language arts program. Literature is a valuable resource for extending children's understanding of grammar and usage and should play an important role in the teaching and learning of grammar.

Best Books for Children

Amos Fortune: Free Man, written by Elizabeth Yates and illustrated by Nora Unwin. New York: Dutton, 1950. This moving story is based on the life of an actual person—a man who was born free in Africa and sold as a slave in America. He lived from 1710 to 1801 and during that time worked to purchase his own freedom and that of his loved ones. (M-U)

. . . And Now Miguel, written by Joseph Krumgold and illustrated by Jean Charlot. New York: Thomas Y. Crowell, 1953. Miguel is older than his brother Pedro, but younger than his brother Gabriel. It seems to Miguel that Gabriel gets everything he wants because he is the eldest son and that Pedro gets everything he wants because he is a baby. Being in the middle brings nothing but trouble. But when Gabriel is about to go away and leave Miguel to assume the role of the eldest son, he does not like that either. A Newbery Award book. (M-U)

Are You There God? It's Me, Margaret, written by Judy Blume. Scarsdale, N.Y.: Bradbury Press, 1970. In a series of small prayers Margaret talks to God about all the problems she faces in moving to a new town and in graduating from elementary school to junior high. She also asks for reassurance in the more frightening task of maturing into young womanhood. (M-U)

Deenie, written by Judy Blume. Scarsdale, N.Y.: Bradbury Press, 1973. Deenie's mother wants her to be a model with her face on magazine covers, but what Deenie wants most is to forget modeling and to spend time with her friends. Judy Blume tells her readers that the idea for the story came from a woman whose daughter had scoliosis. (M-U)

Freckle Juice, written by Judy Blume. New York: Four Winds Press, 1971. Andrew Marcus wants freckles like his friend Nicky's. If he had freckles like Nicky, Andrew reasons, his mother would never know if his neck was dirty. Enterprising Sharon offers to sell him a freckle juice formula for fifty cents. (P-M)

A Gathering of Days: A New England Girl's Journal, 1830–32, written by Joan W. Blos. New York: Scribner, 1979. This Newbery Award book is a novel about early American farm life recorded in journal form by a thirteen-year-old girl. It is a tender story of her family and friends and their life in a small New Hampshire village. (U)

Grammar Can Be Fun, written and illustrated by Munro Leaf. New York: Lippincott, 1934. A popular book with children for many years, *Grammar Can Be Fun* has made the basic rules of correct speech palatable and easy to understand. Like all Munro Leaf's Can Be Fun books, it is illustrated with his own special brand of cartooning. This book is also a helpful guide to the language arts teacher. (P)

I Wish I Had a Computer That Makes Waffles, written by Fitzhugh Dodson and illustrated by Al Lowenheim. La Jolla, Calif.: Oak Tree Publications, 1978. A modern collection of nursery rhymes that teach a young child numbers from zero through ten, the days of the week and seasons of the year, primary and secondary colors, and concepts of time and space. The language is rich, colorful, and repetitive. (P)

It's Like This, Cat, written by Emily Neville and illustrated by Emil Weiss. New York: Harper & Row, 1963. Dave Mitchell is a fourteen-year-old boy growing up in New York City. This Newbery book is the story of his relationships with many different ethnic groups, with his own parents, and with a stray tomcat called Cat. (M-U)

It's Not the End of the World, written by Judy Blume. Scarsdale, N.Y.: Bradbury Press, 1972. Karen's family finds itself in a painful crisis as her father files for a divorce and her teen-age brother runs away from home. As the title implies, all the family members survive the trauma and begin the process of building a new life for themselves. (M-U)

Miss Nelson Is Missing, written by Harry Allard and James Marshall. New York: Scholastic Book Services, 1977. Miss Nelson's class is the worst-behaved group of children in the school until she devises a plan that changes all that. She sends a witch, Miss Viola Swamp, to teach in her place for a few days. "Miss Swamp meant business. Right away she put them to work. And she loaded them down with homework. She even cut out story hour." Miss Nelson returns to a well-behaved class. (P-M)

The One in the Middle Is the Green Kangaroo, written by Judy Blume and illustrated by Lois Axeman. New York: Reilly & Lee, 1969. Freddie Dissel finds it easier to live in the middle between a popular older brother and a pesky little sister once he attains some status for himself by starring in the school play. (P-M)

Otherwise Known as Shelia the Great, written by Judy Blume. New York: Dutton, 1972. Shelia is surprised to find that her girl friends know all her secret fears. She finally begins to overcome those fears by admitting to herself and others that they exist. (M-U)

Ox-Cart Man, written by Donald Hall and illustrated by Barbara Cooney. New York: Viking Press, 1979. A New Englander and his family work all year to produce goods for selling at the Portsmouth Market. Then, with a pocket of coins, the farmer buys provisions for his family and returns home where the cycle begins once more. A lyrical lesson in economics. The art work resembles the early American technique of painting on wood. A Caldecott Award book. (P)

Starring Sally J. Freedman as Herself, written by Judy Blume. Scarsdale, N.Y.: Bradbury Press, 1977. Judy Blume considers *Starring Sally J. Freedman as Herself* her most autobiographical book. She tells her readers that at age ten she was very much like Sally, making up long, elaborate stories in her head. Sally, as a part-time detective, believes for certain that she has found Adolf Hitler living in disguise in Miami Beach. (M-U)

Tales of a Fourth Grade Nothing, written by Judy Blume. New York: Dutton, 1972. This book is an account of the trials and tribulations of Peter Warren Hatcher, a fourth grade nothing whose biggest problem is a two-and-a-half-year-old brother called Fudge. "The only time I really like him is when he's sleeping." (M-U)

Then Again, Maybe I Won't, written by Judy Blume. Scarsdale, N.Y.: Bradbury Press, 1971. Thirteen-year-old Tony Miglione faces the growing-up problems that all boys must face, but to him they seem more serious. "I don't cry any more. I'm too old for that baby stuff, which is why I ran for the bathroom and locked myself in." (M-U)

The Wheel on the School, written by Meindert DeJong and illustrated by Maurice Sendak. New York: Harper & Row, 1954. The dramatic story of six Dutch school children who work to bring the storks back to the small fishing village where they live. It is a story of high adventure and suspense. Winner of both the Newbery and Hans Christian Anderson awards. (M-U)

Bibliography

Barber, Charles L. *The Story of Speech and Language.* New York: Thomas Y. Crowell, 1965.

Boyd, Gertrude. *Linguistics in the Elementary School.* Itasca, Ill.: F. E. Peacock, 1976.

Braine, Martin. "The Ontogeny of English Phrase Structure: The First Phrase." *Reading in Language Development,* ed. Lois Bloom. New York: John Wiley & Sons, 1978.

Burns, Paul C., and Betty L. Broman. *The Language Arts in Childhood Education.* Chicago: Rand McNally, 1979.

Chomsky, Carol. *The Acquisition of Syntax in Children 6 to 10.* Cambridge, Mass.: M.I.T. Press, 1979.

Chomsky, Noam. *Reflections on Language.* New York: Pantheon Books, 1975.

——— . *Syntactic Structures.* The Hague: Mouton, 1957.

DeHaven, Edna P. *Teaching and Learning the Language Arts.* Boston: Little, Brown, 1979.

Elkins, William R. *A New English Primer: An Introduction to Linguistic Concepts and Systems.* New York: St. Martin's Press, 1974.

Espy, Willard R. *The Game of Words.* New York: Bramhill House, 1976.

Fader, Daniel N., and Elton B. McNeil. *Hooked on Books: Program & Proof.* New York: Berkley, 1968.

Francis, W. Nelson. "Revolution in Grammar." *Quarterly Journal of Speech,* October 1954.

Hazlett, James A. *National Assessment of Educational Progress. Report 8, Writing: National Results.* Washington, D.C.: U.S. Government Printing Office, 1972.

Keane, John M., and Carl Personke. *The Language Arts: Teaching and Learning in the Elementary School.* New York: St. Martin's Press, 1976.

Lamb, Pose. *Linguistics in the Proper Perspective,* 2d ed. Columbus: Charles E. Merrill, 1977.

Lefevre, Carl A. *Linguistics and the Teaching of Reading.* New York: McGraw-Hill, 1964.

——— . *Linguistics, English and the Language Arts.* Boston: Allyn and Bacon, 1970.

Lyman, R. L. *Summary of Investigations Related to Grammar, Language, and Composition.* Chicago: University of Chicago Press, 1929.

Norton, Donna. *The Effective Teaching of Language Arts.* Columbus: Charles E. Merrill, 1980.

Pooley, Robert. "Dare the Schools Set a Standard in English Usage?" *English Journal,* March 1960.

Slobin, Dan, *Psycholinguistics.* Glenview, Ill.: Scott, Foresman, 1971.

Tiedt, Iris M., and Sidney W. Tiedt. *Contemporary English in the Elementary School.* Englewood Cliffs, N.J.: Prentice-Hall, 1975.

Wardhaugh, Richard. *Introduction to Linguistics.* New York: McGraw-Hill, 1972.

Chapter 8

Nourish the Urge to Write:
Creative Writing

IN THIS CHAPTER, *creativity* means the ability to produce, or quality of producing, something new, unique, original, not in existence before. This definition has been accepted for many years and will serve the purposes of a discussion on creative writing. We believe that all children have some creative ability, and that nearly all children with careful guidance can develop a high level of creativity in written expression. In this chapter we will describe the creative features that children have in common and outline methods to be used to draw on those resources and talents in the teaching of writing.

Characteristics of Creativity

Many psychologists have worked long and diligently to develop lists of general characteristics of creativity. In 1964, Burton and Heffernan attempted a synthesis of the work of Frank Barron, J. S. Bruner, Jacob Getzels, J. P. Guilford, Philip Jackson, Donald W. MacKinnon, Gardner Murphy, J. Richard Suchman, Calvin W. Taylor, and E. Paul Torrance; they formulated a composite listing of the leading characteristics of creative ability:

1. Curiosity; willingness to ask questions, to question axioms, to wonder, to talk back, to do divergent thinking, to voice "crazy" ideas ("crazy" ideas often turn out to be highly insightful and original), to reject superficial or conventional explanations, to work for more complex and inclusive explanations.
2. Capacity to be puzzled, sensitivity to problems.
3. Self-confident without being dogmatic; poised enough to accept conflict, tension, and resistance to change in others, to manifest suspended judgment, to be tolerant of ambiguity.
4. Willingness to avoid absolutes, certainties,

personal beliefs, to abandon any beliefs when facts so indicate.
5. Flexibility of mental habits, fluency of ideas, many answers suggested, flexibility of association, ability to recall pertinent ideas applicable to a new situation, fluency of expression, ability to redefine familiar objects and concepts, easy and spontaneous personality with marked intuitiveness and insight.
6. Liking for autonomy but recognition of necessity for rules in discussion and production; likes to "fool around" with ideas.
7. Easily activated; often self-motivated; high energy level; early commitment to looking things up, getting the facts, eventually doing research; often chooses unconventional career; persists strongly in any commitment; likely to think critically and to evaluate.
8. Ability to elaborate, ability to start with an idea and develop it into a comprehensive whole; broad intellectual and aesthetic interests.
9. Willingness to take risks.[1]

Observers of children will at once recognize that many children exhibit most or all of those characteristics. This is especially true of young children just entering school. They are spontaneous, eager, and extremely curious. They have a breezy enthusiasm for a variety of experiences, and they have a way of bringing creativeness to all kinds of mundane tasks. There is seldom a motivation problem at this level. Unfortunately, most of these children will not reach their potential and will appear to become less and less creative as they compromise and suppress their uniqueness through the school years. This presents a serious problem to teachers of language arts.

[1]William H. Burton and Helen Heffernan, *The Step Beyond: Creativity* (Washington, D.C.: National Education Association of the United States, 1964), pp. 20–21. Used by permission.

The writing center should contain virtually everything needed by a young creative writer. (Courtesy of Barbara Ellis.)

Barriers to Creativity in the Classroom

At a time where there is a great deal of interest in creativity, with numerous research studies being conducted every year and formal reports being published on the subject, schools are failing to take advantage of available knowledge. Inadvertently, the educational system has erected obstacles that thwart and diminish the creative abilities of many children. Barriers to creativity include

1. Class-as-whole procedures in which a big part of the school day is spent completing exercises and assignments in unison
2. An overemphasis on packaged and programmed materials that require students to work alone for long periods of time on small fragments of information

3. Departmentalization, which has students changing classes and subjects every forty-five minutes or so
4. Rigid curricula built mainly around textbooks and accompanying workbooks
5. Strict promotion and retention policies based on arbitrary and outdated standards
6. Typical marking systems in which all work must receive a letter grade

By recognizing policies and practices that stifle originality and spontaneity, teachers may reverse the situation. In spite of the fact that it is not within their power to change some administrative policies, teachers do have a voice and possibly much more impact on curriculum reform than they realize. The teacher is responsible for the atmosphere that prevails in a particular classroom. In more pointed words, the teacher is professionally and morally obligated to establish and maintain a wholesome learning environment for children.

An Environment for Creativity

There are many factors involved in setting up and operating a classroom that simultaneously facilitates learning and promotes wholesome personality development in children. Students should be encouraged to participate in planning and arranging the facilities they will be using. They have amazing insight into what will and will not work. The teacher should set up a system of learning centers based on students' interests, providing an array of challenging materials that allow for individual differences in taste and ability.

A writing center, for example, should be provided for every classroom. It should be an oasis where students may go at will to put down on paper their thoughts and feelings while the creative urge is present. Each feature of the center should foster creative writing by offering materials that will give information about grammar and spelling, stimulate the flow of ideas, and offer suggestions for sharing the finished product with others. The following materials may be used to set up such a center:

- Writing paper: primary tablets, notebook paper, sentence strips, chart paper, the want ad section of the newspaper, newsprint
- Art paper: colored construction paper, manila paper, shelf paper for scrolls
- Pencils: primary pencils, pencils with soft leads, ball-point pens, magic markers
- Art material: crayons, watercolors, tempera, brushes, scissors, paste
- Writing guides: manuscript and cursive alphabet cards
- Word sources: dictionaries, thesauruses, basic word lists
- Adding machine tape for making personal word boxes
- Pocket chart to hold sentence strips for story building
- Felt board and Pellon to make cutouts for the felt board
- Scrapbooks for mounting finished writing
- Envelopes and stationery for letter writing
- Old magazines for illustrations
- Poetry box to hold students' original poems
- "Browse" box of ideas for writing
- Primary typewriter and typing paper

Teaching should proceed at a relaxed and comfortable pace. To work creatively, children must be relieved of the pressure that comes with verbal hurrying. The teacher should try to establish a warm and friendly relationship with students and encourage them to enjoy and appreciate the companionship of each other. Such esprit de corps exists in every effective elemen-

A Profile of Marcia Brown

MARCIA BROWN is considered one of America's most versatile author/illustrators because she believes each picture book she creates should look different from the others, and she works to make it so. As each new book appears, her readers enjoy a fresh approach. She believes that "books are as individual as people, and each book must elicit from the artist a unique set of feelings if it is to be a unique experience for the child looking at it."

Readers young and old are aware that Marcia Brown has won three Caldecott Awards and has been named runner-up many times. It is remarkable that she has been able to create some twenty books for children and to have each one receive wide acclaim. No other children's author has a more impressive record.

Marcia Brown was born in 1918 in Rochester, New York. Her father was a minister and often moved his family from one small town to another. She tells us: "As a child, when our family moved to a new town, my sisters and I made a trip to the library to make friends with the librarian and to get our library cards before our parents had a chance to unpack the china."

Marcia Brown is living proof that a young child's experiences with literature have a lifelong influence. In her Caldecott acceptance speech of 1955, she graphically described an encounter that she and her older sister had with one of Hans Christian Andersen's fairy tales:

> One night when I was five and she and I were alone, to amuse me she read aloud Andersen's fairy tales. Three of us sat in our old black leather Morris chair—she on one side, our good-sized Airedale on the other, and I in the middle, feeling the warmth of each as an antidote to the sadness of the Little Match Girl.

From the age of twelve, Brown knew that she wanted to be an artist—to illustrate books. After graduation from high school and college, she studied painting at the New School for Social Research and the Art Students' League in New York City. While studying art there she worked as a children's librarian with the New York Public Library, where she used storytelling and puppetry "to tell stories from all over the world to children from all over the world." During this period she wrote and illustrated her first book for children, *The Little Carousel,* a colorful book depicting daily life on the busy street in the Italian neighborhood where she lived.

Everywhere she travels, Marcia Brown fills her sketch pads with drawings of animals—goats, cats, birds, and zoo animals. Many of these drawings eventually become the raw material for a new book. She writes of her travels: "In order not to drag the ideas or techniques that I have developed during work on one book into another, I try to take a good piece of time between books, painting or just taking in impressions by travel, in order to clear the way for the next."

It is our good fortune that Marcia Brown continues to write and illustrate successful books for children. Her most recent award is the 1977 Regina Medal of the Catholic Library Association. Her books continue to reflect a deep affection for folk tales and legends. She explains why they have the power to entertain and nurture modern children: "Today a staunch soldier through circumstances not of his own making, goes through terrible trials but remains steadfast in his devotion to his ideal. Tonight somewhere Cinderella through the magic of kindness has been enchanted into greatest beauty; tonight Cinderella goes to her ball to meet her prince."

BOOKS BY MARCIA BROWN

The Little Carousel, 1946
Stone Soup, 1947
Henry-Fisherman, 1949
Dick Whittington and His Cat, 1950
Skipper John's Cook, 1951
Puss in Boots, 1952
The Steadfast Tin Soldier, 1953
Cinderella, 1954
The Flying Carpet, 1956
Felice, 1958
Peter Piper's Alphabet, 1959
Tamarindo! 1960
Once a Mouse, 1961
The Wild Swans, 1965
Backbone of the King, 1966
The Neighbors, 1977
The Three Billy Goats Gruff, 1968
How, Hippo! 1969
Giselle, 1970
The Bun, 1972
All Butterflies, 1973
The Blue Jackal, 1977
Shadow, 1982

tary classroom. Successful group ventures of the project type will help to reinforce it.

Children's literature should be used to enrich every area of the curriculum. Some of the most creative people in our society spend their time writing and illustrating books for children. A refreshing outlook on life shines through their art and writing, an outlook that serves to sustain and inspire children. Marcia Brown, one of the most outstanding of those authors, is a case in point. Fortunately, she has written books suitable for girls and boys of every age in the elementary school. For correlating various elements of the language arts curriculum through literature, a collection of Marcia Brown's books is unequaled. To children and adults alike, her books serve as models of creative expression.

When Writing Is Creative

Someone has described creative writing as "when the words sing." Certainly not all writing is creative. Much of it is incredibly dull, and if the words do sing, it is only in a monotone. There is a need, obviously, for functional, practical writing; but any student given a steady diet of pragmatic writing is in for a boring existence.

For writing to be creative and unique, words must be put together in ways that are fresh and original. They must express honest emotions and feelings. Words used creatively are filled with love, hate, anger, happiness, fear, and fun. They say something that has not been said before; or if it has been said before, it has never been said in that particular manner.

Years ago, Alvina Burrows and her colleagues conducted experiments in which they attempted to release free expression from children while cultivating the skill necessary for writing with correctness and ease. They arrived at the following conclusion, which might well serve as a guide for today's teachers of creative writing:

We know that if a child is to be an effective, poised personality he must have an awareness and an appreciation of his own power. Such self-knowledge comes only through frequent opportunity to experiment and to fumble along the lines of his desire until out of his effort he fashions something which in his eyes is good. That the product is often crude and clumsy does not matter. The important thing is that the child, out of himself and working in his own way, has produced a thing of which he can approve.[2]

Encouraging Written Responses to Literature

Reacting and responding to a piece of literature by creating literature of one's own may be considered the highest level of reading comprehension. It occurs at the time a reader reacts to the printed material and moves beyond that reaction to take definite action on it by creating some original material. To reach such a creative level, a reader must successfully attack the printed passage, search out the literal meaning, interpret the author's intent, weigh the ideas pro and con, and then respond to the reading in a personal way. In *To Help Children Read,* Frank B. May writes:

Many of us have been inspired, while reading, to do something: to solve a problem, to share our emotions, or translate our feelings into a poem or a painting or some other medium, or to do something better than we've ever done it before. But this creative desire is often stymied by a seeming lack of time or energy or talent—or perhaps more than anything else, by the habit of not responding.[3]

If May's theory is a valid one, it seems reasonable to assume that teachers can help young readers break the habit of *not* responding. In cases where students are consistently encouraged to discuss reading material, to interpret it, to write down and share reactions, they begin to respond to reading as a matter of course.

Herbert Kohl, the author of *36 Children,* is another staunch advocate of creative writing in the classroom as a means of releasing students to respond to reading and other experiences in original and inventive ways. He writes:

It is absurd that young people fear their own writing and are ashamed of their own voices. We have to encourage them to listen to themselves and each other, and to take the time to discover who they are for themselves. If teachers respect the voices of the young, and nurture them instead of tearing them down or trying to develop ones for students, then perhaps school will be less oppressive and alienating to the young.[4]

By providing many rich experiences in the classroom and by drawing on those that occur outside the school, by giving many opportunities for creative writing and sharing, teachers may, as Kohl advocates, encourage students to listen to

---

[2]Alvina Treut Burrows et al., *They All Want to Write* (Englewood Cliffs, N.J.: Prentice-Hall, 1952), pp. 1–2. Used by permission.

[3]Frank B. May, *To Help Children Read* (Columbus: Charles E. Merrill, 1973), pp. 222–223.
[4]Herbert Kohl, "Writing Their Way to Self-Acceptance," *Grade Teacher* (May 1969), pp. 9–11.

---

themselves and others, and to develop a growing pride in their own voices.

Children seem to have an innate urge to create, and fortunately, to some extent, they all have creative ability. According to Petty and Bowen: "Creativity occurs whenever isolated experiences and ideas are put into new combinations and patterns."[5] Writing is creative when a student gives an honest and sincere response to the material he or she has read and then is able to capture that response in writing.

Creative classroom activities in which literature and writing go hand in hand include the following:

1. Writing personal reactions to books that are read aloud by the teacher or aide at story-time. Bind reactions together into a book for the library table.
2. Making new book jackets for favorite books. Use any art process desired to decorate the jacket and then write a blurb that will advertise the book. Write a continuation of the blurb containing a biographical sketch of the author.
3. Compiling a scrapbook of brief book reviews written by children. Let it serve as a source of information to young browsers.
4. Writing a set of provocative questions about books that have circulated in the class. The questions are then compiled into a literary quiz program for the class.
5. Writing letters to the librarian requesting the purchase of books that follow the interests of class members. Such books might include information on hobbies, collections, sports, or pets. Explain why such books are needed.
6. Writing comparative essays in which one book is compared to another. Other comparisons might include authors, illustrators, or book characters.

7. Writing additional adventures to a book that is made up of episodes, such as *Hitty: Her First Hundred Years, Homer Price, My Father's Dragon, Pippi Longstocking,* or *Amelia Bedelia.*
8. Writing a letter to parents explaining why a certain book is wanted as a Christmas or birthday gift.
9. Writing a letter to a classmate recommending a certain book. Justify the recommendation with valid arguments for the book's merit.
10. Writing an essay explaining why a certain book deserved to win the Caldecott Award.
11. Writing a new ending to an old favorite such as *The Pied Piper of Hamelin, Miss Hickory,* or *Down, Down the Mountain.*
12. Writing an imaginary letter to a well-known book character, or an imaginary conversation between two characters.[6]

The Role of Motivators in Creative Writing

The use of motivating devices to trigger creative expression has been a controversial subject among teachers of writing. Some see it as a way of restricting young writers. There should be no problem, however, if students are encouraged to make use of "starters" only when they are needed for ideas and inspiration. It is all too true that many students cannot think of a way to begin writing. Immediate input is needed in such cases, and it is the teacher's responsibility to provide it.

Reluctant writers complain that they have nothing to write about. Occasionally this is a legitimate complaint, but more often the student has many things to write about and simply does not recognize them as suitable topics. The teacher has the task not only of providing experi-

[5]Walter T. Petty and Mary E. Bowen, *Slithery Snakes and Other Aids to Children's Writing* (New York: Appleton-Century-Crofts, 1967), p. 2.

[6]Betty Coody, *Using Literature with Young Children,* 2d ed. (Dubuque, Iowa: Wm. C. Brown, 1979), p. 78. Used by permission.

ences and activities to promote creative writing but also of showing students how such experiences become the raw material for writing.

There is no evidence in modern psychology that the use of models and motivators diminishes creativity. On the contrary, proper use of such materials and activities may release personal expression that would otherwise remain dormant. One good way to judge whether the use of motivators is too pervasive is to study students' work for elements of originality and diversity. If a wide range of approaches to a topic is evident, well and good. If, on the other hand, there appears to be a great deal of sameness in students' writing, the motivator may be too much in evidence. In truly creative writing, children do not copy themselves or each other.

Experiences and Materials That Lead to Creative Writing

Numerous writing opportunities both planned and spontaneous, occur every day in elementary school classrooms. The language arts teacher has only to take advantage of those incidental happenings that students find so interesting and to supplement them with planned writing activities similar to the ones described below.

Field Trips

A field trip need not be a complicated once-a-year happening for it to stimulate oral language and writing. A leisurely, purposeful walk around the block can provide vivid impressions of people, animals, plants, and machines. Back in the classroom, these impressions become the raw material for creative writing.

Resource Persons

Interesting people who are willing to visit the classroom and talk with children are available for

WHAT DO YOU SEE ?

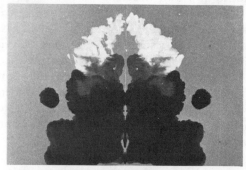
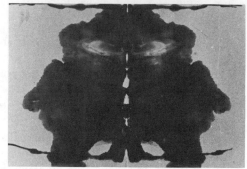

Abstract designs made by painting on one half of the paper and folding the other half over it while the paint is wet. The images students perceive in such designs may stimulate imaginative writing.

the asking—fellow teachers, administrators, custodians, cafeteria workers, the school nurse, parents, local celebrities, and countless others who have good stories to tell. Such visitors to the classroom make excellent subjects for interviews and experience charts as well as for creative writing.

Teaching Pictures

An ample picture file is a necessity for a creative environment. Pictures may include art prints, magazine advertisements, travel posters, and commercial teaching pictures. Some should be mounted, laminated, and stored to form a permanent collection; others should be left un-mounted and available for children to cut and paste as illustrations for their written work.

Exotic Objects

Exotic and unusual objects brought into the classroom spark a great deal of interest that often leads to spontaneous research and writing. Such objects might include a geode, a saguaro boot, a Venus's-flytrap, a Moebius strip, or a hectograph. The object should be dramatically situated alone on a table and labeled with leading questions such as "What is this?" "What will it do?" "Where was it found?" "How old is it?"

Creative Dramatics

Dramatic play, readers theatre, puppet plays, pantomime, and other forms of dramatization are excellent springboards to creative writing. In addition to the many kinds of script writing they call for, the dramatizations themselves elicit welcome written reactions.

Art Activities

Most children thoroughly enjoy writing about their own art work; they are especially fond of writing stories about their paintings. A handsome bulletin board display can be made by mounting the paintings and stories together; later they may be fastened together to make a popular scrapbook for the library table.

Collections and Hobbies

A student's personal collection or hobby provides both an excellent stimulus for the student's own creative writing and interesting material for others to look at and read about.

Pets and Other Animals

Children are partial to animal stories. They like reading them and having them read aloud. They also have a good time writing and illustrating their own talking-beast tales. Such stories make beautiful one-of-a-kind books for classroom use.

Cooking

After reading aloud an entertaining book that has food or the acquisition of food as its theme, children often request a classroom cooking activity as follow-up. Writing is a natural outcome of such an exciting experience.

Photography

Both teacher and students can make good use of photography as a basis for writing. A Polaroid snapshot makes a perfect illustration for a student's autobiography. Appropriate photographs might also inspire expository writing on the environment, weather, festivals, science experiments, and social studies projects.

Writing Stimulated by Visual Aids

For students who have difficulty in deciding on a topic to write about or who have trouble getting started on a writing assignment, a visual aid may be used as a stimulus to get writing under way. The following aids have been successful with many hesitant young writers.

Fantasies

Highly imaginative writing can often be elicited by means of a projective design similar to the Rorschach test. A design is made by painting swatches of color on one half of a page and,

WHAT DO YOU SEE?

Humorous and creative language may be used to describe abstract shapes.

while the paint is still wet, folding the other half over so that the color is transferred to it. The contrasting colors and irregular shapes cause abstract images to appear—images that will be interpreted differently by each student. The oral language that is generated by the design becomes the basis for creative writing. Students show more enthusiasm for this activity if they are permitted to make the designs they will use. When their writing is displayed, it should be accompanied by the design.

A similar procedure may be followed by cutting abstract shapes from colored paper and mounting them on poster board. The shapes should be numbered for easy identification during discussion and writing. A small booklet may be made for each shape, with the writing fastened inside and the shape itself serving as a cover.

Autobiography

Creative writing in which a student reveals true feelings about self is therapeutic. The purpose of such writing is to enhance the self-image and not necessarily to promote reading and writing skills. For this reason, such highly personal writing should be treated with the privacy it deserves; it should not be displayed or shared unless a student chooses to do so. If life stories are to be displayed, they may be illustrated with drawings, Polaroid snapshots, or photographs brought from home.

An effective way to stimulate writing of an autobiographical type is to display a small mirror with the caption "Who am I?" Some teachers prefer to give each student in a writing group a small stand-up mirror. In either case, boys and girls should be encouraged to look beyond obvious physical features to inner characteristics and feelings. One second-grade boy studied himself at length in a mirror and then wrote the following poem:

> MYSELF
>
> He can be good.
> He can be bad.
> But mostly he's good.
>
> He can be happy.
> He can be sad.
> But mostly he's happy.
>
> He stands up.
> He falls down.
> But mostly he stands up.
>
> And I have no idea.
> Who or what he is.

Whimsical Speculation

"It's in the Bag" is the title of a project that creates a lot of fun and laughter. Bags of all kinds, shapes, and sizes are mounted on the bulletin board and numbered for easy identification. Students are asked to write paragraphs speculating about what might be in the bags. There should be no compulsion toward literal reporting in this activity. Anything goes, and the more whimsical the writing, the better. This is an excellent exercise for the student who is too serious and tense about writing and believes all writing should be factual reporting. Finished paragraphs may be trimmed, folded, and stored in the appropriate bag for enjoyable reading.

Puppet Plays

No one knows for sure where or when the art of puppetry originated. Ancient tombs and burial grounds in all parts of the world have revealed carved figures jointed in various ways to permit movement by hand. Puppetry is extremely popular with students in today's classrooms. It is most effective when students construct their own puppets, write the dialogue, and stage the puppet show for an audience of peers or younger children.

Teachers have long recognized the value of dialogue or drama in oral reading practice. Students reading a play almost never have to be admonished to "follow the place" or "read with expression." There is also no need to worry about the readability level of a play written by students; they seem to solve that problem instinctively.

Shape Books

Shape books are just what the name implies— books cut into various recognizable shapes. The novelty of the books motivates both writing and reading. The small size requires students to keep their stories brief, and the shape causes students to stay with one theme throughout a story. Both factors improve the readability, and the end product becomes popular reading material for the classroom library.

A shape book is made by cutting a familiar shape from poster board and decorating it realistically with colored chalk or crayons. Pages are made by cutting lined notebook paper in the same shape as the cover and stapling it between the cover and a firm back. There should be enough pages for several students to contribute stories. It is better to make several thin books of twenty pages or less than one thick one. An overly thick book is likely to become tied up with one writer or reader for too long a time. Construction of the shape book is best done by the teacher.

Books cut into the following shapes will be easily recognizable and should stimulate both writing and reading:

- Football
- Basketball
- Telephone
- Television set
- Guitar
- Airplane
- Ghost
- Christmas tree
- Gift box
- Heart
- Easter egg
- Ice cream cone

Sports Stories

The sports page of the daily newspaper is replete with stories that students can use as models when they set out to write their own sports stories. The newspaper stories are rather easy to read, and they contain a great deal of action in the first few lines. Both of these characteristics are assets in working with reluctant readers and writers.

Some students will need help with the specialized terms found in sports stories, and an interesting vocabulary study may well be the end result. Sports words may be added to a wall chart as the writing project is in progress.

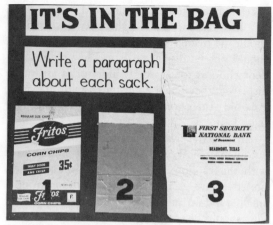

Assorted bags mounted on a bulletin board are used to initiate a writing activity.

Shape books are a departure from traditional writing assignments and provide extra reading material for the library center.

Books made of white wrapping paper stapled together are labeled with the names of the most popular sports and are made ready for students to paste their finished stories in. If the stories are brief, lively, and well illustrated, boys and girls will be more likely to reread the books. The writers might like to personalize their stories by including in them their own names and the names of their friends.

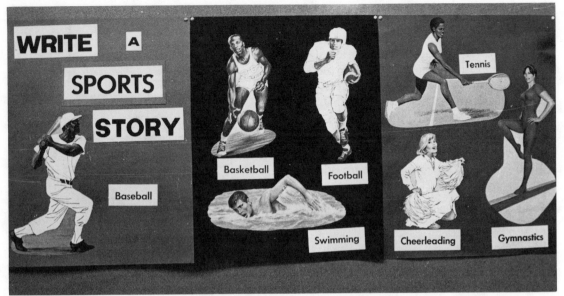

Using the sports page as a point of departure, entertaining stories may be composed and illustrated.

A similar procedure may be used to compose stories about hobbies and collections.

Dialogue

Conversation is very appealing to young readers and so are comic strip characters. Combining the two can make for an exciting writing activity. To find out which cartoons are most favored by students, an informal survey of the class should be made. Committees may then be formed and the various strips distributed.

The cartoon characters are enlarged by hand and painted with water colors, tempera, or felt-point pens. The finished characters are cut out and mounted on colored poster board with an empty "balloon" (white space where dialogue is to be printed) above each figure. The white balloons should be covered with clear contact paper so that students can take turns writing dialogue in the spaces. If a grease-point pencil is used, the writing may be easily wiped off with a tissue or a cotton ball, making the space available for several students. Such a bulletin board becomes a focal point for several days, and its personality changes with each new set of dialogue.

A comic strip writing activity often leads to an interest in cartoonists and their work. In that event, most metropolitan newspapers are able to provide information on the cartoonists whose strips they feature daily.

Comparisons and Contrasts

Comparisons and contrasts are interesting writing projects for students. The analysis necessary to contrast two objects, two people, or two ideas forces girls and boys to think critically and creatively and to defend their viewpoints. Since a new set of descriptive terms is formulated for each comparison, vocabulary is enlarged.

Literary comparisons begin in the primary grades as children informally compare two books such as *Make Way for Ducklings* and *The*

Story of Ping, and they continue into college classes where students are asked to "compare and contrast the writings of Milton and Shakespeare." Two very similar or dissimilar ideas provide the simplest form of comparison for elementary students. A wide variety of ideas from which to choose should be made available:

- Two pieces of fruit: one artificial, one real
- Two masks: one comic, one tragic
- Two paintings: one abstract, one realistic
- Two coins: a penny and a quarter
- Two seasons or holidays
- Two pets
- Two people
- Two books or characters
- Two authors or illustrators
- Two poems
- Two bicycles
- Two cars
- Two toys
- Two movies or TV series
- Two comic strips

In working with reluctant readers and writers, pictures, models, and manipulative objects are needed to create interest and clarify concepts.

An effective drill on adjectives may follow comparative writing. All adjectives used in the essays are transferred to a chart and used as a basis for oral discussion.

Animal Stories

Anyone who knows children is aware of their fascination with animals. Animal fantasies and animals realistically portrayed consume the greatest part of an elementary student's free reading time. Inventories show that when students are given a choice of topics for creative writing, they most often choose to write about animals.

Popular cartoon characters prompt students to write comic dialogue.

Teachers willing to take advantage of this natural affinity for beast tales may use them to teach all aspects of creative writing. Literally hundreds of good books about animals are available for use in reading aloud, independent reading, storytelling, puppetry, dramatization, art activities, and creative writing. The book collection is made even more appealing when it is accompanied by posters, pictures, and models of animals. Animal stories created by students should be classified, illustrated, and mounted in books or on scrolls for future reading.

Accounts of Holidays and Festivals

An appropriate way to celebrate holidays and festivals in the classroom is to use them as raw material for the writing of stories and poems.

Art prints, magazine advertisements, and book jackets provide a stimulus for comparative essays.

The teacher should provide a background of lore and legend for each holiday through storytelling, reading aloud, dramatization, music experiences, and art activities. A collection of seasonal books may be made available for the library center. A display of pictures, art prints, art objects, and posters that depict holiday symbols will create interest in the festival and provide the input needed for creative writing.

Since holiday activities in the classroom seem to foster trite and hackneyed work from students, the teacher will do well to emphasize uniqueness and originality in their writing and to offer many opportunities for fresh, new ways to look at the familiar symbols. Using an international theme to study celebrations around the world is an excellent way to leave clichés behind and, at the same time, to give students some understanding and appreciation of other cul-

tures. An added benefit is gained from seasonal writing if the finished products are mounted in scrapbooks for future reading.

"Why" Stories

Simple myths that tell why something happened or how something came to be are called *pourquoi* tales (French for "why" and pronounced "por-kwa"). Such stories were told orally long before they were written down, as people attempted to explain natural wonders they did not understand. Rudyard Kipling patterned his "Just So" stories after the early *pourquoi* myths. They are perfect for the classroom teacher to read aloud on a day-to-day basis, even though a certain amount of practice is required to read them smoothly. They are suitable for all ages.

Posters, pictures, models, and even live animals may provide input for talking-beast tales.

Students who have become thoroughly familiar with the style of the *pourquoi* myth enjoy writing their own "why" stories, and with a little help they are able to work out a rhythmic refrain that can be repeated throughout the story. Needless to say, their stories provide exciting reading material for peers and also for younger friends. "Why" stories might be about topics such as "Why the Sheep Wears Curly Horns," "Why the Giraffe Has a Long Neck," "Why the Rabbit Has a Cotton Tail," and "Why the Turtle Wears a Shell."

Limericks

Limericks are nonsense poems named for the chief port on the west coast of Ireland where party guests once made up limericks to entertain themselves. Limericks became popular the world over after Edward Lear, an English artist, published in 1846 a collection he had written to amuse young friends.

The limerick meter is one of the easiest forms of poetry for children to cope with. Most girls and boys are able to create an acceptable non-

"WHY" STORIES

Why the Tiger Wears Stripes

Why the Sheep Wears Curly Horns

Why the Bear Wears a Fur Coat

Why the Elephant Wears a Trunk

A bulletin board filled with pictures of wild animals may promote "why" stories of the "Just So" type.

Write a tall tale—a whopper.

A colorful poster of Paul Bunyan is used to begin a study of tall tales.

sense rhyme. They need not observe any hard and fast rules, but humor and nonsense are required. Half of the fun is in the creation of nonsensical line drawings to illustrate each limerick.

Tall Tales

Tall tales are characterized by heroes who accomplish outlandish feats with very little effort. The main ingredients of a tall tale are exaggeration, conflict, humor, and a certain realism or accuracy.

Tall tales are unsurpassed as material to be read aloud by the teacher. Creative writing becomes a natural follow-up to the reading and to the oral language it stimulates. Tall tales written

by students are very effective when told rather than read. Illustrating the tales for felt-board presentation is a good way to involve the class in a storytelling workshop.

Proverbs

A proverb is a short, pithy saying that expresses a well-known truth or fact. It may be referred to as an "adage," "maxim," "epigram," or "old saw," but no matter what the name, it is usually didactic and contains a sound lesson. The classroom teacher might do well to use proverbs as an aid to a writing program that lags.

After students have made a study of proverbs from many countries and from various periods in history, they are usually able to create proverbs that contain a morsel of truth and wisdom. They may write proverbs that are completely original, or they may try to rewrite some of the old ones, bringing them up to date or giving them a new slant.

The Writing Workshop

There is a strong link between creative writing in the classroom and a literature-based approach to the language arts. The teachers who have learned to capitalize on this natural bond have produced the most successful writing programs. On a daily basis, they rely on reading aloud, storytelling, dramatization, and the students' personal reading to motivate effective writing in the classroom. With some variation, good writing programs look very much alike and are organized along similar lines. The key ingredient in each case is children's literature. On the basis of interest inventories, anthologies, and recommended lists, hundreds of good books are made available. Ample time is provided for students to browse and select the right book for personal reading, and class time is then allotted for independent silent reading. Follow-up discussions are organized into planned sharing periods in which the teacher serves as facilitator or moderator.

A natural outgrowth of the library-centered classroom is the creative writing workshop in which students routinely write tall tales, animal stories, holiday essays, myths, legends, fables, and poetry, stimulated by their involvement with many kinds of literature. The teacher serves as catalyst in getting writing underway and as an aide in providing the necessary help in word acquisition, spelling, punctuation, and sentence structure.

Writing in a typical workshop format, students may decide on a topic and begin a first draft one day, work to further develop and refine

it the second day, and recopy and illustrate it the third day. The result is, more often than not, an attractive piece of writing that is accurate, informative, and interesting. Quality writing takes time and diligence; the teacher provides the former, the student the latter.

"Publication"

Once writing has been polished and refined to the satisfaction of both student and teacher, finding an adequate means of sharing it with readers is the next important step. "Publication" is the incentive needed by young writers to urge them toward maximum effort in the difficult, demanding task of writing. Here are some suggested formats for sharing students' writing with readers both inside and outside the classroom.

Scrapbooks

Oversized pages of wrapping paper fastened together make excellent books in which to mount creative writing. Such scrapbooks are especially good for use with young children, who usually find it easier to work on a separate page of lined paper that will be pasted in a permanent book. The oversized pages are also much more suitable for the large handwriting and drawings of young children. After the scrapbooks have served their time in the classroom library, they may be disassembled so that the children can take their individual stories home.

Bound Books

Nothing succeeds like a bound book in giving children a feeling of authorship. Such one-of-a-kind books also leave them with a higher regard for books in general and for authors and illustrators. Binding books in the classroom can be as simple as pasting paper or cloth over two pieces of cardboard and fastening the pages between, or it may be done in a more elaborate way to produce a professional-looking book. In all cases student-made books should be given the prominent place they deserve in the classroom library.

Books for Younger Children

A project that brings much satisfaction to upper level students is the writing of plays, stories, and poems for younger children. The writing, reflecting information gained from interviews with young children, contains the types of characters they prefer, humor they can understand, and best of all, words they can read. An added benefit of a cross-age experiment such as this is the close relationship that grows between older and younger children.

Bulletin Board Displays

Displaying creative writing on bulletin boards remains one of the most effective ways to provide reinforcement for the effort students expend on their writing. No piece of personal writing should ever be placed on display without the willing consent of the student who wrote it, however.

Eye-level displays provide entertaining reading material for passersby. Such bulletin boards will be more interesting if they are developed around a theme and pulled together with a descriptive caption.

Scrolls

"Roller writing" is a fine way to present a group's work for reading by an audience. Stories centered on a theme are colorfully illustrated and then pasted in sequence on a long strip of paper. The ends are fastened to two sticks and rolled together in such a way that the complete story is revealed section by section as the scroll is unrolled.

Children's Books as Models for Writing

Children's literature can stimulate students at all levels to improve their creative writing. Reading and discussing the writing of published authors helps to create an awareness of plot, theme, characterization, style, and other literary elements that students are striving to incorporate into their own writing.

A Gathering of Days by Joan W. Blos, for example, is an excellent model for journal or diary writing in the middle and upper grades. In this Newbery Award novel, thirteen-year-old Catherine Hall is keeping house for her widowed father and younger sister when she begins her journal in the year 1830. Her moving narrative captures both the hardship and the tranquillity of farm life in early America. A study of the young girl's journal can give today's students a deeper appreciation of their heritage and of the men and women who lived in earlier times. Such writing can also help them to express in written form their own feelings, attitudes, and values.

Books such as *Mr. Rabbit and the Lovely Present* by Charlotte Zolotow, *The Runaway Bunny* by Margaret Wise Brown, and *Little Bear* by Maurice Sendak are filled with realistic conversation very similar to the quiet talk that often takes place between two young children. By reading such books, students in the primary grades are able to see dialogue in printed form. Thus, even in a child's first attempts at composition, literature becomes a model for writing conversation.

Summary

"'Tis the reader that makes a good book" is an adage reminding us that reading and writing are two sides of the same coin. Since writing serves as an effective means of responding to literature, fledgling readers should be writing books as they read them.

Psychologists and other researchers in the field of creativity tend to agree about the leading characteristics of creative ability. A profile, based on their findings, of a creative individual will provide a guide for the language arts teacher planning a program of creative writing. If creative expression is to develop properly, an environment conducive to creativity must be provided and practices that are limiting and negative must be avoided.

It is believed that all children have some creative ability, but many need stimulating ideas and experiences to release that ability. Experiences, activities, and materials used to motivate original writing are not deterrents to creativity if they are not overemphasized and if they are used only with students who need an idea to get them started.

Creative writing is not to be treated as incidental learning but should be taught systematically and routinely at all grade levels. All elementary teachers have the responsibility of teaching writing on a daily basis. They must help students with the mechanics of writing, provide them with something to write about, and give them a reason for writing. They must also find ways to "publish" students' writing once it is completed.

Books of all kinds provide excellent models for students. They are not to be copied or duplicated, of course, but to show how professional writers use language to create moods and images.

Best Books for Children

The Adventures of Three Colors, written and illustrated by Annette Tison and Talus Taylor. Cleveland: World, 1971. An explanation of how a rainbow is formed by the division of white light into many colors. As Herbie paints with the three primary colors he has seen in the rainbow, he discovers he can make other colors. Clever overlays show how the primary colors combine to form secondary colors and finally tertiary colors. (P)

The Bears on Hemlock Mountain, written by Alice Dalgliesh and illustrated by Helen Sewell. New York: Scribner, 1952. Jonathan is sent across Hemlock Mountain to borrow a big iron pot so his mother can cook for the many aunts, uncles, and cousins. Jonathan discovers there are bears on Hemlock Mountain and hides under the iron pot. A story long told by the people of Pennsylvania. (P-M)

Christmas in America, written and illustrated by Lillie Patterson. Champaign, Ill.: Garrard, 1969. One of a series of holiday books, clearly written and vividly illustrated for use by children and teachers as reference material. Contains legend, lore, and symbolism of the holiday. Other titles in the series are *Fourth of July, Thanksgiving, Halloween, Spring Holidays, New Year's Day, Patriot's Day, Valentine's Day, Birthdays,* and *Poetry for Holidays*. (P-M-U)

The Complete Nonsense Book, written and illustrated by Edward Lear. New York: Dodd, Mead, 1912. This 480-page book contains all the famous limericks of Edward Lear along with his popular nonsense stories, songs, and verses. Illustrated with his original absurd and foolish drawings. (P-M-U)

Curious George, written and illustrated by Hans A. Rey. Boston: Houghton Mifflin, 1941. This curious little monkey is very much like a child as he explores and examines his environment. His curiosity leads him into trouble, but his friend in the yellow hat always gets him out again. The first in a series of books about Curious George. (P)

Danny and the Dinosaur, written and illustrated by Syd Hoff. New York: Harper & Row, 1958. An easy-to-read book about a dinosaur who leaves the museum to become Danny's friend and pet. All the children are given a ride on his back, and he learns to play hide and seek with them. At the end of a wonderful day of play he goes back to the museum, leaving Danny with memories of the fun. (P)

Finders Keepers, written and illustrated by William Lipkind and Nicolas Mordvinoff. New York: Harcourt Brace Jovanovich, 1951. This is a story of two dogs who live together in peace and friendship until they find a bone. They ask all passersby to decide which of the two deserves to keep the bone. The ridiculous answers they get leave them no wiser. When they are forced to fight for the bone, they decide to share it. (P)

Five O'Clock Charlie, written by Marguerite Henry and illustrated by Wesley Dennis. New York: Rand McNally, 1962. Based on a true incident, as are all of Marguerite Henry's horse stories, *Five O'Clock Charlie* is the story of an endearing old workhorse who refuses to accept retirement with its life of ease and boredom. Charlie finds a way "to make his loneliness vanish like a fog when the sun comes out." Most horse stories are too difficult for young readers. This one is an exception. (P)

The Gingerbread Rabbit, written by Randall Jarrell and illustrated by Garth Williams. New York: Macmillan, 1964. Mary's mother loves her so much that she bakes a gingerbread rabbit for her as a surprise. The warm sun shining into the kitchen brings the rabbit to life, and he is promptly adopted by a pair of rabbits who live in the nearby woods. The mother creates another one, this time from cloth. (P-M)

Harry the Dirty Dog, written by Gene Zion and illustrated by Margaret B. Graham. New York: Harper & Row, 1956. The story of a dog who gets so dirty that he is unrecognizable and finds soap and water are important to him after all. (P)

Hitty: Her First Hundred Years, written by Rachel Field and illustrated by Dorothy Lathrop. New York: Macmillan, 1929. The story of a hundred years' worth of adventures as experienced by a lovable antique doll named Hitty. A Newbery Award winner. (M-U)

Just So Stories, written and illustrated by Rudyard Kipling. Garden City, N.Y.: Doubleday, 1907. These long-popular "why" stories tell how various animals came to be. Similar to ancient folk tales, each story is pure fun and nonsense balanced with the right amount of realism. The stories are excellent for the teacher or aide to read aloud because of the rich vocabulary and rhythmic style. For smooth reading, the stories should be practiced in advance. (P-M-U)

Miranda the Great, written by Eleanor Estes and illustrated by Edward Ardizzone. New York: Harcourt Brace Jovanovich, 1967. According to an ancient legend, Rome will fall if the stray cats ever leave the city. Miranda the Great was Queen Cat of the Colosseum during the founding of the cat dynasty. She was a cat of many accomplishments, and her story is still told in the Eternal City. The glory of ancient Rome is reflected in the superb illustrations. (M)

Miss Hickory, written by Carolyn Sherwin Bailey and illustrated by Ruth Gannett. New York: Viking Press, 1946. Miss Hickory is a doll made from an applewood twig; she has a hickory nut head. She lives in a corncrib house under a lilac bush. This fantasy tells how Miss Hickory lives among neighbors like Crow, Bull Frog, Ground Hog, and Squirrel. The surprise ending teaches a subtle lesson about hope and immortality. (M-U)

Mr. Popper's Penguins, written by Richard and Florence Atwater and illustrated by Robert Lawson. Boston: Little, Brown, 1938. When he is not working at his job of house painting, Mr. Popper reads books on polar exploration. His life is changed completely when Admiral Drake sends him a penguin from the Antarctic. He names the bird Captain Cook. An aquarium sends Mr. Popper a mate for Captain Cook, and soon there are ten more penguins in the house. (M-U)

Mrs. Frisby and the Rats of NIMH, written by Robert C. O'Brien and illustrated by Zena Bernstein. New York: Atheneum, 1972. The story of a mouse named Mrs. Frisby who appeals to the rats of the National Institute of Mental Health for help. The rats have undergone experimentation in the laboratory of NIMH for several years and have developed extremely high intelligence as a result. A Newbery Award winner. (M-U)

My Father's Dragon, written by Ruth Stiles Gannett and illustrated by Ruth Chrisman Gannett. New

York: Random House, 1948. A young boy rescues the baby dragon from his tormentors by outwitting the wild animals who are using the dragon as a ferryboat to cross the river. A humorous adventure story of danger and daring. Chapter titles such as "My Father Meets a Lion" and "My Father Meets a Gorilla" appeal to young readers and listeners. (P-M)

Rabbit Hill, written and illustrated by Robert Lawson. New York: Viking Press, 1944. One of the most irresistible animal fables ever written. Little Georgie compares with Peter Rabbit in popularity and appeal. A Newbery Award winner. (M)

Stuart Little, written by E. B. White and illustrated by Garth Williams. New York: Harper & Row, 1945. A debonair little mouse who acts much more like a person than a mouse becomes involved in one exciting adventure after another. E. B. White's first book for children. (P-M)

The Velveteen Rabbit, written by Margery Williams and illustrated by William Nicholson. New York: Doubleday, undated. A beautiful and sensitive dialogue between Skin Horse and Velveteen Rabbit explains how toys become real: "Generally by the time you are Real, most of your hair has been loved off, and your eyes drop out and you get loose in the joints and very shabby. But these things don't matter at all, because once you are Real you can't be ugly, except to people who don't understand." (P-M)

Bibliography

Applegate, Mauree. *Easy in English*. New York: Harper & Row, 1960.

———. *Freeing Children to Write*. New York: Harper & Row, 1963.

Burrows, Alvina Treut; June D. Ferebee; Doris C. Jackson; and Dorothy O. Saunders. *They All Want to Write*. Englewood Cliffs, N.J.: Prentice-Hall, 1952.

Burton, William H., and Helen Heffernan. *The Step Beyond: Creativity*. Washington, D.C.: National Education Association of the United States, 1964.

Carlson, Ruth Kearney. *Writing Aids Through the Grades*. New York: Teachers College, Columbia University, 1970.

Coody, Betty. *Using Literature with Young Children*, 2d ed. Dubuque, Iowa: Wm. C. Brown, 1979.

Hansen-Krening, Nancy. *Competency and Creativity in Language Arts*. Menlo Park, Calif.: Addison-Wesley, 1979.

Koch, Kenneth. *Wishes, Lies, and Dreams: Teaching Children to Write Poetry*. New York: Vintage Books, Chelsea House Publishers, 1970.

Kohl, Herbert. *36 Children*. New York: New American Library, 1967.

———. "Writing Their Way to Self-Acceptance." *Grade Teacher*, May 1969.

May, Frank B. *To Help Children Read*. Columbus: Charles E. Merrill, 1973.

Petty, Walter T., and Mary E. Bowen. *Slithery Snakes and Other Aids to Children's Writing*. New York: Appleton-Century-Crofts, 1967.

Root, Shelton, ed. *Adventuring with Books*. New York: Citation Press, 1973.

Stewig, John Warren. *Read to Write: Using Children's Literature as a Springboard to Writing*. New York: Hawthorn Books, 1975.

Strickland, Ruth G. *The Language Arts in the Elementary School*. New York: D. C. Heath, 1963.

Trauger, Wilma K. *Language Arts in Elementary Schools*. New York: McGraw-Hill, 1963.

Weiss, Harvey. *How to Make Your Own Books*. New York: Thomas Y. Crowell, 1974.

Chapter 9

I Can Read It Myself: Beginning Reading

ONE OF THE MOST drastic changes to occur in American education in recent years is the manner in which young children are taught to read. Reading instruction has felt the pressure of experimentation and change as methods and materials for use with children are being designed for introduction at younger and younger ages because of increasing numbers of boys and girls entering school at an early age. Many school-age children are ready to read, and some come to school actually knowing how. As a result, early childhood curricula have had to be revised in a hurry, and new courses of study have been developed to meet the needs of the eager newcomers.

There has been much conjecture and debate about why the new crop of children appears more ready to read than girls and boys of earlier years. The causal factor most frequently mentioned is television viewing. The fact that young children watch adult programs by the hour and listen to adult language is bound to affect their language development. With reading readiness and beginning reading so closely related to language development, it is not surprising that many children are ready to read at a younger age.

Moreover, the number of children who have had some form of schooling before they enter kindergarten or first grade is increasing yearly. Thousands of women, on entering the labor market, enroll their young children in nursery schools and day-care centers where broad socialization begins early and plays a large role in children's oral language development at a formative period in their lives. Boys and girls at day-care centers and nursery schools are introduced to reading informally by means of stories, songs, poems, games, and painting. Primary teachers, responsible for formal reading instruction, have been the first to feel the impact of such learning experiences.

It might also be added that many modern parents consider themselves the child's first and most important teacher; educators and psychologists have convinced them of that fact. They are meeting the challenge by reading aloud, telling stories, answering questions, and talking to their children from the time of infancy. Parenting is no longer considered an innate ability; it is seen as a skill to be learned, and thus many parents find themselves working and studying to better understand all aspects of rearing children. The children, of course, thrive on all this positive attention.

Whatever the reasons for the precocity of so many of today's young children, there is no reason to believe that the situation will change in the near future. Therefore school programs must be designed to fit young children as they are. It is obvious that some will not need a long reading-readiness program. Others, however, will.

Unfortunately, there is a darker side to the child development picture. All too many children are denied, for one reason or another, the nurturing care they need for optimum intellectual and emotional growth. A deficiency in language ability is almost always the result of such deprivation. It then becomes the teacher's task to overcome the deficit with a reading-readiness program rich in experiences designed to help children think and talk.

Formal lessons from the printed pages of a book are put off until these children become more fluent in speaking and more skillful at understanding the speech of others. Mature language is not the only characteristic of readiness for reading, but it is a crucial one. Like all areas of language arts instruction, the reading-readiness program must be individualized and tailored to meet the unique needs of each child, no matter what that child's experiences have been prior to entering school.

In this chapter we will examine the concept of reading readiness and describe how it may be fostered in the language arts classroom by means of a rich literature program. It also attempts to show how a readiness program gently and gradually leads into beginning reading.

What Is Reading Readiness?

Children who are ready to read and, with proper sequential instruction, will become successful at it show all or most of the following traits. They talk easily; they have the ability to make their feelings and wishes known by speaking freely and distinctly. They are interested in words. They recognize many brand names, labels, and logos; "read" signs and billboards; and often ask, "What does that say?" They have a broad vocabulary and draw from a large storehouse to find words that best fit a situation. They are quick to try new and strange-sounding words.

Children ready to read are at ease with books. They enjoy looking at books, discussing stories, and dramatizing characters. They study the detail in illustrations and see the humor in ludicrous situations. They know how to handle and care for books, holding a book correctly and turning the pages from front to back. They realize that the printed words carry the story line, and they ask to have books read to them. They like hearing favorite stories repeated, join in on refrains, and may quote long passages verbatim.

Children who are ready to read are able to point out small objects and symbols in illustrations when requested to do so. They are thoughtful listeners, willing to sit still for fairly long periods of time to listen to storytelling, reading aloud, dramatizations, and other literature-related activities.

Experiences to Prepare a Child for Reading

Readiness for reading may be cultivated in the classroom by well-planned activities designed to increase a young child's facility with language. The teacher should provide experiences and opportunities that will stimulate children to talk about what they feel, see, hear, taste, and smell.

Field Trips

Excursions to places of interest such as pet shops, bookstores, museums, zoos, and parks, and even a purposeful walk around the school yard, will provide children with the raw material for oral language. To extend their vocabulary, the teacher may devise a chart carrying notes about the trip and what was said about it. Such charts are very interesting and should be reviewed over several days. The rereading becomes a vicarious means of reliving a pleasant experience while at the same time strengthening skills.

Dramatic Play

Interest centers are areas set aside in kindergarten and primary grade classrooms for the purpose of enriching the quality of dramatic play. They should be stocked with fascinating materials and equipment arranged for easy accessibility on child-size tables. Carefully selected articles encourage curiosity, manipulation, and conversation as children act out or play like various characters from both real life and literature.

Permanent interest centers usually include those labeled home, art, science, music, and the like. Temporary centers focus on more transient topics such as pets, holidays, and hobbies. Permanent centers provide routine and stability for the young child, while temporary ones offer variety and enrichment.

Meeting Interesting People

Men and women who know how to talk with children and have entertaining stories to tell may be invited to the classroom. With prior preparation by the teacher, children can learn something of the art of interviewing. With practice, even very young children can learn to ask provocative questions, to think critically, and to analyze the answers their questions elicit.

Reading Aloud

The teacher who routinely reads aloud from excellent literature is leading children in a natural way into the world of books and reading. This experience often makes girls and boys aware for the first time that reading is a necessary and integral part of life—an understanding that is necessary to success in beginning reading.

Storytelling

The ancient art of storytelling helps to introduce modern children to fine literature and acquaints them with characters with whom they can identify. When well done, storytelling whets the appetite for further literary experiences and creates a lasting interest in reading. On those occasions when the felt board is used by the teacher to illustrate a story, it should be left in place for children to use in retelling the story.

Puppetry

Puppets used on a regular basis are very effective as a means of developing self-confidence in shy children. Through the voice and gestures of the puppet, a child is able to say what she or he would like to say in real-life situations but does not for fear of disapproval. Puppetry may provide some children with their first opportunity to speak freely and openly.

Experimentation

To allow children to explore and experiment with a wide array of art, science, and music materials is to invite oral expression. It is almost impossible to share materials with another person and not engage in conversation with that person. Learning to follow directions in sequential order is an added benefit to be gained from experimentation such as following a recipe to prepare a snack for classmates.

Activities Based on "Found" Reading Matter

Long before formal reading instruction takes place, young children begin to "read" signs, labels, and other "found" items. In today's advertising-conscious society, words virtually scream out from billboards, cereal boxes, movie marquees, and television commercials. It is not uncommon for a child of three or four to recognize dozens of brand names found on boxes and cans in the kitchen pantry, on posters and storefronts, and in countless other places where advertisers and sign painters have left their mark.

Adults may decry the gaudiness and pervasiveness of advertising, but they should realize that a young child's attempts to make sense of the many visual symbols vying for attention are a form of reading and should be encouraged as such.

The teacher should be familiar with a variety of activities that take advantage of children's natural interest in advertising and other "found" reading materials.

1. Attach familiar labels to large cards to be used in matching and word recognition games.
2. From magazines and newspapers, allow children to cut out words and symbols they recognize and paste them on a poster or in a large scrapbook. This is a good first-day icebreaker.
3. Arrange "browse" boxes of popular everyday reading materials such as comics, television guides, menus, recipes, jokes, riddles, and toy catalogs.
4. Organize group discussions of signs and billboards that the children have observed.

Logos, trademarks, and other words and phrases recognized by these two first-graders were cut from *newspapers and magazines to make a colorful poster. (Courtesy of Dianne Baker and James Slayter.)*

Keep a running list of words that the children may add to daily.

5. Help each child to keep a personal word bank of labels and trade names as they become recognizable.

6. Plan art activities that make use of signs or labels—for example, a frieze of a shopping center or grocery store.

7. Make a separate set of cards for warning signals such as "Stop," "Caution," "Danger," "Exit," "Poison," "Railroad Crossing," "Keep Out." Teach the significance of such words and phrases.

8. Develop language-experience charts using trade names observed on a short field trip.

9. Prepare rebus recipe charts using labels to represent key words.

10. Discuss brand names used in childrens' books. A few to be seen in *Charlotte's Web* are: GMC, Plymouth, Ford, Chevvies, Buick, Studebaker, Pontiac, and Jeep.

Using Readiness Books

When used with discretion by a teacher who provides many other experiences, readiness books can play a role in the young child's preparation for formal reading. Ordinarily, readiness workbooks contain pictures of characters children will

In this boy's classroom a browse box of consumer materials and a collection of newspapers and magazines are used to supplement basal readers. (Courtesy of D. J. Boudreaux.)

Introducing Formal Reading: The Basal Reader

Most teachers use a basal reader and the accompanying workbook to introduce girls and boys to formal reading. Over the years, basal reading series have received much criticism from teachers and people not directly concerned with reading in the primary classroom. A great deal of the criticism has been justified, and writers and publishers have responded with improvements. Actually, basal readers and their related materials are better now than they have ever been and are often superior to most subject-matter textbooks.

Heilman has discussed some advantages of a basal program.[2] Modern series have excellent pictures and art work. A number of first books deal with the same characters, thereby giving children a sense of familiarity with the material and adding to their confidence.

Basal readers are graded to provide systematic instruction from the prereadiness level through the upper elementary grades. These graded materials permit teachers a great deal of flexibility in dealing with individual differences and in working with children grouped according to their attained reading skill. Excellent teacher's guides are available for each book or level. They provide suggestions for a step-by-step teaching program. If used properly, a basal reading series deals with all phases of the reading program, guarding against overemphasis on some aspects and neglect of others. New skills are introduced in a logical sequence, and many opportunities for review are provided. The vocabulary is rigidly controlled to prevent frustration in the beginning reader. And, finally, the use of prepared materials saves teachers considerable time.

The teacher who uses basal textbooks and related materials in professional and creative ways, who adapts them to fit the needs and abilities of individual children, and who supplements them

meet in readers at the primer and first-reader levels. Arthur Heilman has offered this description of readiness books:

At the readiness level one might find picture books in which a picture, or series of pictures, suggest a child-centered story. From the pictures, the teacher and the pupils develop a story. The more skillful the teacher is in providing background and involving the pupils in participation and interpretation, the more successful the use of these materials will be. Other readiness books may call for children to identify and mark similar objects, letters, or words, facilitating the development of visual perception. To strengthen auditory discrimination, the child will identify two pictures in a group whose naming words rhyme. Identifying other pairs of pictures which start with the same sound gives practice in the discrimination of initial sounds.[1]

Readiness books introduce boys and girls to formal reading in basal materials.

[1]Arthur Heilman, *Principles and Practices of Teaching Reading,* 3d ed. (Columbus: Charles E. Merrill, 1972), p. 212. Used by permission.

[2]Ibid., p. 215.

"How could I have done it? That word isn't in my sight vocabulary."

Reprinted with permission of Tony Saltzman and the International Reading Association.

with a wide variety of other reading matter is employing an eclectic approach to beginning reading instruction that has every chance of being highly successful.

Words to Be Recognized on Sight

In order for children to read at a fairly rapid rate, to read with ease, and to comprehend what is read, they must be able to recognize certain words instantly, on sight. Familiarity with a body of sight words relieves the beginning reader of the tedious, time-consuming task of decoding every single word in a passage. An adequate vocabulary of sight words is needed also as the basis for the decoding skills of phonic analysis, structural analysis, and contextual clues (these word attack skills are discussed in Chapter 10).

The words that best serve beginning readers are words used most frequently in the printed material they will be reading. A list of frequently used words was developed by Edward Dolch in 1941. It consists of 220 basic sight words occurring most often in basal readers at the first-, second-, and third-grade levels. Even though the list

is rather old, it can still meet the needs of primary teachers if it is regularly supplemented by other words personally selected by the students.

In the primary grades, boys and girls encounter the Dolch basic sight words in basal readers, trade books, teacher-made charts, children's creative writing, picture dictionaries, and word games. The Dolch list of 220 basic sight words is reproduced in Display 9.1.

Basic sight words must be used over and over again in interesting and meaningful ways in order for them to become a part of the young child's reading vocabulary. Many of the words in the Dolch list have no inherent meaning but must be used in a specific context, along with the names of people, places, and things, if they are to be understood. For this reason, it is imperative that frequently used nouns, such as those listed by Roach Van Allen, be taught along with the more abstract words. The two lists in combination enable children to read sentences and paragraphs that are loaded with meaning. Isolated words are then studied only for practice, reinforcement, and perhaps testing. The Van Allen list of 230 frequently used nouns appears in Display 9.2. The words it contains have been culled from

Display 9.1 Dolch Basic Sight Word List

Preprimer	Primer	First Grade	Second Grade	Third Grade
1. a	1. all	1. after	1. always	1. about
2. and	2. am	2. again	2. around	2. better
3. away	3. are	3. an	3. because	3. bring
4. big	4. at	4. any	4. been	4. carry
5. blue	5. ate	5. as	5. before	5. clean
6. can	6. be	6. ask	6. best	6. cut
7. come	7. black	7. by	7. both	7. done
8. down	8. brown	8. could	8. buy	8. draw
9. find	9. but	9. every	9. call	9. drink
10. for	10. came	10. fly	10. cold	10. eight
11. funny	11. did	11. from	11. does	11. fall
12. go	12. go	12. give	12. don't	12. far
13. help	13. eat	13. going	13. fast	13. full
14. here	14. four	14. had	14. first	14. got
15. I	15. get	15. has	15. five	15. grow
16. in	16. good	16. her	16. found	16. hold
17. is	17. have	17. him	17. gave	17. hot
18. it	18. he	18. his	18. goes	18. hurt
19. jump	19. into	19. how	19. green	19. if
20. little	20. like	20. just	20. its	20. keep
21. look	21. must	21. know	21. made	21. kind
22. make	22. new	22. let	22. many	22. laugh
23. me	23. no	23. live	23. off	23. light
24. my	24. now	24. may	24. or	24. long
25. not	25. on	25. of	25. pull	25. much
26. one	26. our	26. old	26. read	26. myself
27. play	27. out	27. once	27. right	27. never
28. red	28. please	28. open	28. sing	28. only
29. run	29. pretty	29. over	29. sit	29. own
30. said	30. run	30. put	30. sleep	30. pick
31. see	31. ride	31. round	31. tell	31. seven
32. the	32. saw	32. some	32. their	32. shall
33. three	33. say	33. stop	33. these	33. show
34. to	34. she	34. take	34. those	34. six
35. two	35. so	35. thank	35. up	35. small
36. up	36. soon	36. them	36. upon	36. start
37. we	37. that	37. then	37. use	37. ten
38. where	38. there	38. think	38. very	38. today
39. yellow	39. they	39. walk	39. wash	39. together
40. you	40. this	40. were	40. which	40. try

Preprimer	Primer	First Grade	Second Grade	Third Grade
	41. too	41. when	41. why	41. warm
	42. under		42. wish	
	43. want		43. work	
	44. was		44. would	
	45. well		45. write	
	46. went		46. your	
	47. what			
	48. white			
	49. who			
	50. will			
	51. with			
	52. yes			

Compiled by Edward W. Dolch. Copyright 1942 by Garrard Publishing Company, Champaign, Ill. Used with the permission of the publisher. (Note: Writers who followed Dolch arranged the words into grade levels for the convenience of teachers.)

primary readers, standardized tests for primary grades, trade books for young children, and school newspapers.

Supplementing the Basal Reading Series

The Classroom Library Center

If trade books are to be used as a supplement to the basal textbook reading program, if they are to afford beginners needed practice on basic reading skills, they must be readily available. A classroom collection should contain picture books, easy-to-read books, magazines, student-made books, informational books, and other materials for browsing and reading. Although such supplementary materials often contain the same basic words as beginning basals, they allow for practice on those words in new and different contexts. In short, the supplementary materials encourage wider reading.

Children appreciate the library center much more if they have had a hand in planning it, if they are permitted to recommend some of the books it will contain, and if they take responsibility for its organization and management. There is no reason, for example, why they cannot operate a simple check-out system. It is to be expected that the more girls and boys become involved with the book collection, the greater will be its worth. And, since lasting attitudes about books and reading are being formulated

Display 9.2 Van Allen List of 230 High-Frequency Nouns

air	church	first	kite	paper	sentence	today
airplane	circle	fish		part	sheet	tooth
animal	city	five	lamp	pencil	ship	top
answer	clock	flag	land	penny	shirt	town
apartment	clothes	floor	leaf	people	shoe	tree
apple	clown	flower	leg	pet	show	truck
astronaut	coat	food	letter	picture	side	turkey
author	cookies	forest	life	pilot	sister	two
	corner	four	light	place	sky	
baby	country	fox	line	play	sleep	umbrella
ball	cow	frame	lion	poem	snow	
balloon	cup	friend	lunch	point	sock	valentine
basement		frog		policeman	something	
bear	daddy	front	man	pony	song	wall
bed	day		men	princess	sound	water
bee	dime	game	miles	purse	spring	way
bell	dog	garden	milk		square	whistle
bird	dollar	girl	money	quarter	stairs	white
block	door	grass	monkey	queen	stamp	wind
boat	dress	ground	moon		star	window
body	drum	guitar	morning	rabbit	stop sign	winter
book	duck		mother	rain	store	witch
box		hand	mouth	raincoat	story	woman
boys	ear	head		refrigerator	stove	word
bread	earth	hill	name	river	street	world
breakfast	egg	home	nest	road	summer	
brother	elephant	horse	next	rock	sun	x-ray
bus	end	house	nickel	rocket	swing	
	example		night	roof		yard
cake	eyes	ice cream	nose	room	table	year
candy		island	nurse	rope	tail	
cap	fall			rose	teacher	zipper
car	family	jacket	one		telephone	zoo
cat	father	jack-o'-lantern	orange	sailboat	television	
chair	feet	jelly		school	thing	
chicken	field		page	sea	three	
children	fire	king	palace	second	time	

This boy is testing himself on a body of sight words. With practice, the words in the "no" can will go in the "maybe" can and from there into the "yes" can.

By keeping a tally, he records his own progress. (Courtesy of Mrs. Claire Hymel.)

during this period, it is imperative that all experiences with library books be enjoyable and free from anxiety.

Once the center is in operation, ample opportunity must be provided for children to look through the books and select the ones they wish to spend some time with. Time for independent silent reading should be set aside during the school day, not relegated to after-school hours. There should also be time for reading with friends, for sharing books, for art activities as a response to books, and for student-teacher conferences in which personal reading is discussed. (A more complete discussion of personalized reading is given in Chapter 3.)

In kindergarten and primary classrooms, the library center should become the focal point for reading aloud, storytelling, book-sharing talks, and other literature-related activities. Since it is a supplement to the basal program, the teacher should constantly evaluate the center's effectiveness. Books that are rarely used should be taken out and replaced with more suitable ones, and multiple copies should be acquired of books that are extremely popular.

Classroom library centers are seldom successful when the teacher simply selects books at random from library or bookstore shelves. To guarantee that books selected for the classroom library center are those that young children want

Display 9.3 Interest Inventory for Use with Beginning Readers

1. What is the name of your favorite book? Why do you like it?
2. How many books do you own? Where do you keep them?
3. Does someone read aloud to you at home? Who?
4. What kind of stories do you like to hear read aloud?
5. If you could change places with someone, who would it be?
6. What do you like best about reading?
7. What do you like least about reading?
8. What is your favorite television show? Why do you like it?
9. What is your hobby?
10. Do you collect anything? If so, what?
11. How do you feel about reading for fun?
12. Do you own a library card?
13. What are the names of some of the books you have at home?
14. If you were to write your own book, what would it be about? Why?
15. What games or sports do you like?
16. What do you like best about reading class?
17. How would you change the reading class?
18. What do you do when you come to a word you do not know?
19. What is the most important thing that happens in school?
20. What is the next book you plan to read?

to read and will read, the teacher would be wise to use aids such as recommended lists, personal observation, and informal questioning to determine students' preferences. Display 9.3 is an interest inventory for use with beginning readers. It is intended to be given orally to individuals or small groups.

A good book may be followed up with a creative activity, such as cooking, art, creative writing, or dramatization.

For read-aloud sessions in the classroom, books by Robert McCloskey are just about perfect. In both interest and content, his books range from the nursery school and primary level (*Make Way for Ducklings* and *Blueberries for Sal*), through the middle grades (*Lentil* and *Burt Dow: Deep-Water Man*), to the upper elementary grades (*Homer Price* and *Centerburg Tales*). Most of McCloskey's books are written in the "comic

anecdote" style, which happens to be the type of story requested most often by students at all grade levels.

Controlled-Vocabulary Books

One of the first easy-to-read, or "controlled-vocabulary," trade books was *Nobody Listens to Andrew* by Elizabeth Guilfoile, published by Follett in 1957. It was immediately popular with beginning readers because they could read it and because it told a good story. Teachers liked it for other reasons. Until that time there had been no reading material for beginners except textbooks and charts made by the teacher. Texts and charts are needed, of course, to teach the skills of reading, but everyone agrees that children should be turned loose to practice those skills in library books—books they can browse in and choose for themselves.

Fortunately, since 1957 many more easy-to-read books have been published. Theodor Seuss Geisel, in particular, must be given credit for his continued and successful efforts on behalf of beginning readers. Just as Edward Lear made the limerick famous by using nonsense rhymes and drawings, Dr. Seuss has made easy-to-read books famous. His *Green Eggs and Ham* has sold well over 5 million copies, making it one of the best-selling children's books of all time. It contains only fifty different words. Because of the repetition of those words, a beginner can read the story fluently and at a rather rapid rate. It is very satisfying to all concerned when a beginner is able to sound like an experienced reader. Not surprisingly, easy-to-read books become threadbare with use.

Teachers, parents, and others shopping for easy-to-read books will have little trouble recognizing them because of certain unique features that keep their readability level low. It soon becomes possible for a teacher or parent to thumb through a book and accurately estimate its relative ease or difficulty. Easy-to-read books have the following characteristics:

1. Open space. Space between words and between the printed lines is ample, and the margins around the perimeter of the page are wide. This openness makes the text inviting to beginning readers.
2. Large print. Fairly large, bold black print on white paper is easiest to read. For beginning readers, the print should be in manuscript form and without flourishes.
3. Graphic illustrations. Realistic pictures to enhance and clarify the story are studied carefully by young children as an aid to both word analysis and comprehension. All pictures should be perfectly coordinated with the text.

So Mother Bear made something

for Little Bear.

"See, Little Bear," she said,

"I have something for my little bear.

Here it is.

12

A typical page from Little Bear, *written by Else Minarik and illustrated by Maurice Sendak, shows the features that make a book easy to read. (Used by permission of Harper & Row, Publishers.)*

4. Short words. The most frequently used words in beginner books are short, for the most part containing only one or two syllables. Such basic words are of course interspersed with proper names and familiar nouns, which may be somewhat longer.
5. Personal pronouns. The frequent appearance of "I," "we," "you," "he," "she," seem to make it easier for a fledgling reader to identify with story characters. The personal nature of these words makes them among the easiest basic sight words to learn.

A Profile of Robert McCloskey

IN ORDER TO MAKE the drawings exactly right for *Make Way for Ducklings*, Robert McCloskey bought four quacking ducks from the poultry market to be used as live models. He carried them home on the subway, quacking in their carton. In his words, "I spent the next weeks on my hands and knees armed with a box of Kleenex and a sketchbook, following the ducks around the studio and observing them in the bathtub." While sketching one little duckling in an appealing pose, McCloskey often found the others wandering off to hide under the furniture. He recalls: "I had to slow those ducks down somehow so I could make the sketches. The only thing that worked was red wine. They loved it and went into slow motion right away." He filled his sketchbooks with "running, walking, standing, sitting, stretching, swimming, scratching, sleeping ducklings." It was his feeling that to draw a duck accurately, "you more or less have to think like a duck." Such attention to details paid rich dividends. *Make Way for Ducklings* won the Caldecott Medal in 1942 and has been exceedingly popular with young children ever since.

A completely different kind of book won a second Caldecott Medal for Robert McCloskey in 1958, making him the first artist to win the award twice. *Time of Wonder* was inspired by an island in Penobscot Bay in Maine, where McCloskey and his family spent many summers while his daughters were growing up. It is the story of a storm and a family's survival. Beautiful water-color paintings show children exploring the land before and after a hurricane.

The beauty of the paintings and the rhythm of the language combine to help children appreciate the wonder of the world they live in. McCloskey shows two little girls examining ancient seashells under the roots of an upturned tree and writes, "Under an old tree by the house you discover an Indian shell heap, and, poking in the thousands of snow-white clam shells, so old they crumble at a touch, you realize that you are standing on a place where Indian children stood before the coming of white men."

Robert McCloskey was born in Hamilton, Ohio, on September 15, 1914. As a boy, he spent his time practicing the piano, inventing mechanical contraptions, and teaching crafts at the YMCA, all experiences that were later to enrich his work. During his senior year in high school he won a scholarship to the Vesper George School of Art in Boston, where he studied for three years. During the next two years he studied at the National Academy of Design in New York City.

In 1940 McCloskey married Margaret Durand, the daughter of Ruth Sawyer, famous storyteller and writer (winner of the Newbery Medal for *Roller Skates*). Their daughter Sally was born in 1945, Jane in 1948. Both girls were later to become subjects for their father's book illustrations. Sal is featured in *Blueberries for Sal,* and Jane is introduced in *One Morning in Maine.* Penny, their dog, also appeared, along with their black cat, Mozzarella.

Robert McCloskey photo courtesy of Mary Velthoven.

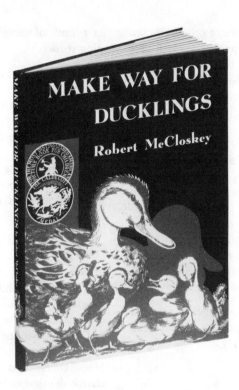

In explaining why he enjoys writing and illustrating books for children and why he has continued to do so over the years, McCloskey has said:

What I'm interested in is communicating with people. I like to know my work is being looked at and enjoyed. When you paint a mural in a bank or post office, you never know whether your work is being seen or not. People who frequent banks and post offices are usually busy cashing checks and licking stamps. They don't notice murals, and if they do, they seldom write and tell you so. Thirty years ago I did the sculpture for a public building, and during all those years I received perhaps six letters from people who have noticed. On the other hand every day brings me more letters than that from children, from parents, from teachers and librarians who've read my books.[1]

BOOKS BY ROBERT MC CLOSKEY

Lentil, 1940
Make Way for Ducklings, 1941
Homer Price, 1943
Blueberries for Sal, 1948
Centerburg Tales, 1951
One Morning in Maine, 1952
Time of Wonder, 1957
Burt Dow: Deep-Water Man, 1963

[1]*The Lively Art of Picture Books* (Weston, Conn.: Weston Woods Studio, 1964).

6. Dialogue. Girls and boys not only find conversation easy to read, but they enjoy it very much, especially when they are given the opportunity to read it aloud.
7. Rhythmic flow. Sentences should flow smoothly and rhythmically as they do in informal conversation.
8. Short sentences. Sentences are short, and end-of-line breaks correspond to natural pauses.
9. Relatively few sentences per page. Too many lines of print on a page are discouraging to a beginning reader.
10. A subject of interest. Beginners find it much easier to read about their favorite topics. Basically they prefer humorous stories about animals and people.

Keeping in mind these characteristics, teachers should have little trouble spotting easy-to-read books for the classroom library.

Language-Experience Charts

To become acquainted with the world, a young child uses all five senses to see, taste, smell, hear, and feel objects in order to understand them. In the classroom these sensory experiences should be used as raw material for the young child's introduction to formal reading. The creation of reading material based on a child's own experiences has proved to be an effective way to demonstrate to young children that reading is oral language in written form. When a child dictates a story based on a personal happening, when the teacher serves as recorder to take it down and then helps the child to read it back from the chart that the teacher has made, certain understandings develop that help the child to internalize what the reading process is all about.

According to Lee and Van Allen, these are the basic understandings that come to the child as a result of using experience charts with beginning readers:

1. A child can talk about what he or she thinks about.
2. What one talks about can be expressed in writing.
3. Anything the child or teacher writes can be read.
4. Individuals can read their own writing and what other people write.
5. What a child has to say is as important as what other people have written for him or her to read.[3]

As a teacher carefully prints the child's words on white or buff chart paper, moving from left to right as the child watches and all the while repeating the child's language for emphasis, the child is able to experience the feeling of both reading and writing. With the teacher's help, the child is soon able to read a brief chart story. Since much ego involvement goes into the chart's development, it becomes one of the easiest pieces of material for a child to read.

The story should not be long. It should stay on one subject and sound like the speech of children. It should have a title and include the names of people, places, and events; but it should also repeat many basic sight words. The completed chart will resemble a page in a book. It will be interesting, informative, easy to read, and best of all, personal.

Spontaneous experiences suitable for discussion and chart making occur frequently in the classroom. But the teacher should be prepared to provide experiences and topics that children can talk, read, and write about. If the experience has been a shared one, the teacher and the class may cooperate in composing the chart, with teacher taking dictation from the children.

[3]Dorris M. Lee and R. Van Allen, *Learning to Read Through Experience* (New York: Appleton-Century-Crofts, 1963), p. 13.

Possibilities for oral language with chart making as a natural outcome include:

- Resource persons
- Field trips
- Storytelling
- Creative writing
- Experiments
- Dramatic play
- Discussions and conversations
- Art activities
- Children's books
- A favorite TV show
- A party at school
- Cafeteria behavior
- Celebrations and holidays
- Show-and-tell
- Outdoor play
- Films and filmstrips
- Pictures and prints
- Objects and models
- Pets and other animals
- Children's magazines
- A popular movie
- Parents' night
- A new game

Children's books will provide numerous experiences for oral language and inspiration for stories to be dictated to the teacher for charting. When children become acquainted with fascinating books such as *Why Mosquitoes Buzz in People's Ears* by Leo and Diane Dillon, *Finders Keepers* by William Lipkind and Nicolas Mordvinoff, and *One Fine Day* by Nonny Hogrogian, lively talk is bound to follow and the making of language-experience charts becomes an easy task. To create a handsome chart in relation to a good book is to say to children: "Books are important and reading is a natural thing to do."

On reading a newspaper account of jeans production, second grade students dictated a story and illustrated it with cut paper appliqued jeans.

Instruction in writing and reading is the main purpose of language-experience charts, but eventually they may be put to many other good uses in the classroom and at home. Some alternatives are listed in Display 9.4.

Reading Aloud to Beginning Readers

For many years teachers have been telling parents, "Children who read were read to," and parents are being convinced. They are finding out how much their young children enjoy having parents read to them from books of all kinds. The child's pleasure is reward enough for most parents, but they also take pride in seeing the child's progress in oral language skills. Perceptive parents recognize that, through shared experiences with literature, their child is developing a lasting interest in books and reading. That is one of the greatest gifts parents can give their children.

Oddly enough, some of the teachers who advocate that much reading aloud be done in the home are not willing to give it its rightful place in the classroom. As children move upward from kindergarten through elementary school, their teachers read to them less and less. It is rare to find a teacher, even at the primary level, who writes the reading-aloud experience into daily lesson plans, who maintains a routine schedule for it, who prepares the material, and who spends time on planned, structured follow-up activities. The children, of course, are the losers.

At the time when boys and girls are learning to read and are bound by the narrow parameters of basal readers and easy-to-read trade books, it is essential that teachers give them a broader view of literature by reading aloud to them from some of the best books available—books the children may not be able to read for themselves for several years to come. The primary teacher who consistently omits reading aloud and storytelling from the daily program cannot be considered an adequate teacher of beginning reading, no matter how effectively he or she teaches word analysis skills. Most children will learn to read. Unfortunately, they will not all learn to like it. Only literature that goes beyond the strictly controlled vocabulary of basal materials has the kind of plot, theme, and characterization to move children to new heights and give them the understanding that reading can do wonderful things for a person.

Kindergarten and primary teachers who wish to make reading aloud an integral part of reading instruction should keep in mind the following suggestions:[4]

1. *Establish a regular schedule for reading aloud.* Reading aloud by the teacher should be a routine part of the daily classroom schedule. Children should be able to look forward to an enjoyable experience with literature at approximately the same time each day. The teacher's lesson plans should indicate the time period for reading aloud, the book to be read, and any planned follow-up activities.

2. *Choose a book with your students in mind.* Interest inventories and personal observation will help the teacher determine the kinds of books preferred by children; and by supplementing that information with recommended lists for each grade level, the teacher will greatly reduce the risk of selecting the wrong book. Generally, nursery, kindergarten, and first-grade children prefer picture books that can be completed in one sitting. Continued stories should be reserved for upper primary children.

3. *Select a book with yourself in mind.* The teacher should not read aloud from a book he or she does not like or finds boring. The children are sure to perceive the dissatisfaction, and the whole experience will be a disappointment. Since time for reading always seems to be at a premium, no part of it should be spent on trite and inane books. A really fine book for children will appeal to adults as well.

4. *Practice reading the book.* A rehearsal will make the reader both aware of the difficult,

[4]Betty Coody, *Using Literature with Young Children*, 2d ed. (Dubuque, Iowa: Wm. C. Brown, 1979), pp. 12–13. Used by permission.

Display 9.4 Alternative Uses of Language-Experience Charts

1. Cut the chart into separate sentences for students to reassemble in proper sequence.
2. Use the chart for word decoding to give students practice in phonics and structural analysis.
3. Cover key words with small flaps to give students practice in using context clues.
4. Circle basic sight words to reinforce and emphasize them.
5. Use the chart to review capitalization, punctuation, and sentence structure.
6. Bind several charts together to make a book of stories for the reading table.
7. Transcribe chart stories on the primary typewriter to make small booklets for classroom reading.
8. Exchange charts with other classes to provide additional practice in silent reading.
9. Send dated charts home for children to read to their parents.
10. Cut up charts to make dictionary boxes and word games.

sometimes tongue-twisting, language of a book and familiar with the story's concepts. Such familiarity will help the teacher look up from the book, making eye contact with the children. Eye contact is a key ingredient in holding the attention of young listeners.

5. *Create an atmosphere for reading aloud.* An area should be set aside for gathering children together in an intimate story circle or, more precisely, a semicircle. The teacher sits on a low chair at the open end of the semicircle and holds the picture book face out, just slightly above the eye level of the children. Obviously, a teacher must master the art of reading from the side so that children are able to see the illustrations at all times.

6. *Eliminate undue distractions.* The best-laid plans amount to little if distractions and interruptions are allowed to interfere with storytime. If the story is carefully chosen and well read, even the most active child can be expected to listen attentively throughout. Good listening behavior, however, should always be recognized and rewarded with a compliment.

7. *Read with feeling and expression.* A sense of the dramatic is always present in oral reading, but it should not be overdone. Over dramatization only causes children to concentrate on the reader rather than the story. On the other hand, careful attention to pitch and emphasis is necessary if printed dialogue is to sound like conversation. If the teacher enjoys a story and has a good time with it, that feeling will shine through and the children will like it too.

8. *Discuss unfamiliar words.* Not every unfamiliar word in a story or book need be analyzed, but the chill should be taken off key words that are certain to have a bearing on comprehension. Some teachers prefer to write the new words on the chalkboard at the outset, others define them unobtrusively as the story is in progress. In either case, one of the values of reading aloud is the enrichment of vocabulary that children experience.

9. *Teach the parts of a book.* A few minutes of each oral reading session should be devoted to pointing out the main parts of a book— the jacket, covers, endpapers, spine—until children are completely familiar and comfortable with the terminology.

10. *Give an opportunity for responses to the book.* Detailed discussions about every book read aloud are not necessary, but children do usually wish to talk about a book they have enjoyed. They like to compare it with other books they know and perhaps request a similar one to be read at the next session.

Summary

To say that the beginning reading period is a crucial time in the life of a child is a cliché; yet it needs to be said over and over again.

Reading readiness activities such as field trips, dramatic plays, resource persons, reading aloud, storytelling, puppetry, science experiments, and paper-pencil exercises help young children develop the oral language skills needed for a successful beginning in formal reading.

In beginning reading, two important factors need to be considered: (1) The sequential building of reading skills, both word attack and comprehension, and (2) the development of a positive attitude toward books. Both are highly significant in reading success.

At the same time a child is working to learn the skills of decoding, some other important reading activities are taking place in the classroom. A library center is in operation where the young reader is able to pick and choose among picture books to look at and easy-to-read books for reading. The teacher reads aloud to the class or tells stories on a daily basis. Both the reading aloud and storytelling sessions are well planned and executed as part of the reading program and not solely for the entertainment of the children.

Since success in reading is based on oral language facility, wholesome language experiences must be provided throughout the primary grades. Such experiences include field trips, resource persons, language-experience charts, and learning centers.

Among other reading materials to be used with beginners are magazines and newspapers, reading games, everyday "found" materials, and labels. Special activities should be provided for adding interest and variety to the task of building a body of sight words.

Best Books for Children

A Baby Sister for Frances, written by Russell Hoban and illustrated by Lillian Hoban. New York: Harper & Row, 1964. Watching her parents care for the new baby in the family, Frances feels alone and neglected until she finally decides to set things right by running away. Her parents understand her feelings and quickly take steps to make amends. (P)

Alligators All Around, written and illustrated by Maurice Sendak. New York: Harper & Row, 1962. A delightful nonsense alphabet book about alligators. A tiny book just right for small hands. Part of the Nutshell Library by Maurice Sendak. (P)

Anatole and the Cat, written by Eva Titus and illustrated by Paul Galdone. New York: Whittlesey House, 1957. Anatole the Cheese Taster is the most honored and respected mouse in all of France. He also turns out to be the bravest by figuring out a way to do something that other mice had been talking about for thousands of years—a way to bell the cat. (P)

Angus and the Ducks, written and illustrated by Marjorie Flack. Garden City, N.Y.: Doubleday, 1930. Angus, a curious little Scotty dog, goes to investigate a quacking sound. The quacking turns to hissing, and Angus quickly loses his curiosity—for three minutes at least. (P)

The Big Snow, written and illustrated by Berta and Elmer Hader. New York: Macmillan, 1948. A realistic story of how various animals prepare themselves for winter, and of a kindly couple who puts out food for them when the big snow arrives. A good story to help make children sensitive to needs of wild animals. (P)

The Big World and the Little House, written by Ruth Krauss and illustrated by Marc Simont. New York: Henry Schuman, 1949. A beautifully illustrated story of an abandoned house being transformed into a real home by a family that moves in and restores it. Throughout the book, emphasis is placed on the little house's relationship to the rest of the world and, in turn, on the world's influence on the little house. (P)

Caps for Sale, written and illustrated by Esphyr Slobodkina. New York: William R. Scott, 1947. A cap peddler who carries all his wares on his head is surprised to find they have been whisked away by a band of mischievous monkeys. How he finally persuades them to give back the caps is delightful fun for young children. (P)

The Happy Lion, written by Louise Fatio and illustrated by Roger Duvoisin. New York: Whittlesey House, 1954. Everyone loves the happy lion as long as he stays at a safe distance, which he does not want to do. (P)

Jeanne-Marie Counts Her Sheep, written and illustrated by Françoise. New York: Scribner, 1951. Jeanne-Marie makes elaborate plans for all the things she will buy when her sheep Patapon has lambs. As she imagines more and more lambs, Jeanne-Marie's list of wanted items grows. Eventually Patapon has one little lamb, and there is just enough wool to knit Jeanne-Marie a pair of new socks. The story is illustrated with bright, poster-like pictures. (P)

The Little Auto, written and illustrated by Lois Lenski. New York: Henry Z. Walck, 1940. Mr. Small drives the little auto exactly like a young child would like to, with all the familiar gestures and movements. A simple story without plot, but one young children request again and again. Other books in the series are *The Little Train, The Little Airplane,* and *The Little Fire Engine.* (P)

The Little House, written and illustrated by Virginia Lee Burton. Boston: Houghton Mifflin, 1942. A little country house is engulfed as the city gradually builds around it. The story shows some of the undesirable aspects of technological and industrial progress. In-cludes a lovely description of the four seasons as observed by the little house. (P)

Little Tim and the Brave Sea Captain, written and illustrated by Edward Ardizzone. New York: Henry Z. Walck, 1955. Tim, a small boy who wants more than anything to be a sailor, stows away on an ocean steamer. He is forced to face storms, hard work, and other perils. Tim proves to be courageous and hard working. He endears himself to the other sailors and especially to the captain, who finally sees Tim safely home again. (P)

Make Way for Ducklings, written and illustrated by Robert McCloskey. New York: Viking Press, 1941. After Mr. and Mrs. Mallard have hatched out a fine family of eight ducklings, they must teach the little ones to swim, dive, walk in a line, come when called, and keep a safe distance from things with wheels. (P)

Petunia, written and illustrated by Roger Duvoisin. New York: Knopf, 1950. Petunia, a humorous, lovable goose, is more like a person than a barnyard fowl. She is a wise philosopher and a unique individual. Other books in the series are *Petunia and the Song* and *Petunia Takes a Trip.* (P)

A Sky Full of Dragons, written by Mildred Whatley Wright and illustrated by Carroll Dolezal. Austin, Tex.: Steck-Vaughn, 1969. The story of how a Chinese boy named Lee Chow and his grandfather use rice paper and paint to make a sky full of dragon kites for Lee Chow's friends. What Lee Chow is given in return is something he wants more than anything. Beautifully illustrated. (P)

The Story About Ping, written by Marjorie Flack and illustrated by Kurt Wiese. New York: Viking Press, 1933. The adventures of a small duck who lives with his brothers, sisters, cousins, aunts, and uncles on a Chinese junk in the Yangtze River. Authentic Chinese legend and background. (P)

The Tale of Peter Rabbit, written and illustrated by Beatrix Potter. New York: Frederick Warne, 1901. One of the most perfect stories for early childhood. Young children see themselves in Peter as he disobeys, finds himself in serious trouble, repents, is punished, and is finally accepted and forgiven. (P)

The Three Billy Goats Gruff, illustrated by Marcia Brown. New York: Harcourt Brace Jovanovich, 1957.

One of the finest versions available of a folk tale that has been a favorite of children for generations. Illustrated by a most versatile artist for children. (P)

Time of Wonder, written and illustrated by Robert McCloskey. New York: Viking Press, 1957. This beautiful book of watercolor paintings tells the story of life on a Maine island before and after a hurricane. Children go about exploring the seashore and the forests beyond just as children have always done. An excellent account is given of the way parents protect children during a crisis. (P)

A Tree Is Nice, written by Janice May Udry and illustrated by Marc Simont. New York: Harper & Row, 1956. The text and pictures are combined to show every child who reads or looks at the book the joys and delights a nice tree has to offer. The book not only gives childlike directions for planting a tree, but describes the pride that comes in watching it thrive and grow. (P)

Two Lonely Ducks, written and illustrated by Roger Duvoisin. New York: Knopf, 1955. Children are given three separate counting situations in this book. They count the eggs laid by the mother duck; they count the days she sits on them; and finally they count the ducklings that hatch out. (P)

Umbrella, written and illustrated by Taro Yashima. New York: Viking Press, 1958. Momo's third birthday brings a new umbrella and red boots, but it is many days before the rain comes. Something special happens to Momo when she carries the umbrella. Beautiful Japanese art. Excellent for reading to very young children. (P)

Wheel on the Chimney, written by Margaret Wise Brown and illustrated by Tibor Gergely. Philadelphia: Lippincott, 1954. This poetic and beautifully illustrated book follows the storks on their migratory flight to Africa and back again to their nest in a wheel on the chimney. (P)

Bibliography

Aukerman, Robert C. *Approaches to Beginning Reading.* New York: Wiley, 1971.

————. *Some Persistent Questions on Beginning Reading.* Newark, Del.: International Reading Association, 1972.

Coody, Betty. *Using Literature with Young Children,* 2d ed. Dubuque, Iowa: Wm. C. Brown, 1978.

Cramer, Ronald L. *Writing, Reading, and Language Growth.* Columbus: Charles E. Merrill, 1978.

Dallmann, Martha; Roger L. Rouch; Lynette Y. C. Char; and John J. DeBoer. *The Teaching of Reading.* New York: Holt, Rinehart and Winston, 1978.

Durkin, Dolores. *Teaching Them to Read.* Boston: Allyn and Bacon, 1978.

Hall, Mary Anne. *Teaching Reading as a Language Experience.* Columbus: Charles E. Merrill, 1970.

Heilman, Arthur W. *Principles and Practices of Teaching Reading,* 3d ed. Columbus: Charles E. Merrill, 1972.

Herrick, Virgil E., and Marcella Nerbovig. *Using Experience Charts with Children.* Columbus: Charles E. Merrill, 1964.

Hittleman, Daniel R. *Developmental Reading: A Psycholinguistic Perspective.* Chicago: Rand McNally, 1978.

Kohl, Herbert. *Reading, How To.* New York: Dutton, 1973.

Lee, Dorris M., and R. Van Allen. *Learning to Read Through Experience.* New York: Appleton-Century-Crofts, 1963.

Smith, Richard J., and Dale D. Johnson. *Teaching Children to Read.* Menlo Park, Calif.: Addison-Wesley, 1976.

Stauffer, Russell G. *The Language-Experience Approach to the Teaching of Reading.* New York: Harper & Row, 1970.

Van Allen, Roach. *Language Experiences in Communication.* Boston: Houghton Mifflin, 1976.

Chapter 10

A Proper Way to Live:
Having the Skill and Will to Read

MANY STUDENTS GO through American schools and graduate without the skills needed to read well. Countless others can read but choose not to do so. Both groups cast a poor reflection on modern methods of language arts and reading instruction. In a recent newspaper interview, Ken Kesey, author of *One Flew over the Cuckoo's Nest*, expressed his personal concern over the way reading is taught today: "One reason for the nation's literacy problems is that education has concentrated on the technicalities of reading and neglected its content." Many reading teachers agree with Kesey's sentiments and are now in the process of tapping the great wealth of content to be found in children's literature to create interest in reading.

Parents and teachers no longer pay only lip service to the merits of reading. They may be seen working together to help children become involved with captivating library books. Several years ago, novelist Leo Rosten wrote an eloquent essay on the priceless rewards of reading (see Display 10.1). In it he reassures us all that the book will never be replaced by television because reading is crucial in deep psychological ways; it helps us to know ourselves. Reading not only teaches us the proper way to live; to read *is* the proper way to live.

As we discussed in Chapter 9, many different approaches are used in beginning reading instruction. Helping children to recognize words, enlarge their reading vocabulary, and understand a writer's ideas are the ultimate goals of every program. In this chapter we will examine some techniques for accomplishing those goals.

Sharpening Word Recognition Skills

Learning to read is a developmental process. It requires systematic instruction, mastery of skills, and meaningful practice. Formal reading instruction typically begins in the primary grades, and one of the first skill clusters to be introduced is

word recognition—the methods and techniques used by a reader to identify, pronounce, and recall words. The four major ways that words may be recognized are on sight, by context, by phonic analysis, and by structural analysis.

Recognizing Words on Sight

Efficient and fluent beginning reading depends on the child's ability to recognize commonly used words on sight. Eldon Ekwall has found that between 60 and 70 percent of the words found in primary reading materials are among the two hundred most frequently encountered words.[1] Furthermore, many of the sight words have irregular or confusing spelling (for example, "their" and "there"), which means that they must be mastered to be instantly recognized.

In 1923 Godfrey Dewey discovered that ten words—"the," "of," "and," "to," "a," "in," "that," "it," "is," and "I"—constituted almost 25 percent of the words in elementary reading materials, and sixty-nine other frequently used words made up almost half of the vocabulary of primary grade readers.[2] Subsequent research has reinforced this early finding. For example, a recent computerized count of primary reading materials determined that the eight most frequently recurring words are the same as those on Dewey's earlier list.[3]

Generally, children master basic sight words by the end of the second or third grade. Some students, however, fail to attain proficiency and need additional practice before they are able to recognize these words. Since such words are often presented in isolation on lists, some elementary teachers introduce and drill students on the

[1]Eldon Ekwall, *Diagnosis and Remediation of the Disabled Reader* (Boston: Allyn and Bacon) 1976, pp. 66–67.
[2]Godfrey Dewey, *Relative Frequency of English-Speech Sounds* (Cambridge, Mass.: Harvard University Press, 1923).
[3]Edward Fry, "The New Instant Word List," *The Reading Teacher*, December 1980, pp. 284–289.

Display 10.1 The Miracles of Print*
By Leo Rosten

If you want to cure a whooping cough, eat a roasted mouse. If you want to end a toothache, drive a nail into an oak tree.

If you want to steal without getting caught, conceal a toad's heart on your person.

Absurd? Well, men no more stupid than you or I once believed these preposterous prescriptions. And have you not heard good men and women declaim that too much reading would injure children's eyes? That movies would kill reading? That television tolls the inevitable doom of print?

None of these bromides is true; all have been proved false by experience. Americans read more today than they ever did before. They read better books and magazines. And any librarian or bookseller will tell you that after a book has been made into a movie, or dramatized on television, the demand for it does not decline but skyrockets.

I have never been able to understand the periodic lamentations we hear about the perils which reading confronts. It has always seemed to me that nothing—no new gadget or gaudy distraction—could long replace the priceless rewards that reading (and reading alone) offers us. It is not only that words possess a power and majesty of their own: the activity of reading itself is so unique that neither movies nor radio nor television can possibly serve as substitutes.

Consider. When you read, you read *alone*—in a solitary, timeless absorption which engages your mind and emotions to enrich your own resources.

When you read a novel, you read at your own pace—not the pace imposed upon the material by a movie producer or television director. You, not they, control how fast, how slowly, with what degree of intensity you may ingest what is before your eyes. With print you can do what you can never do with film or television tube: you can reread, re-experience, explore an idea yet once more, relive a laugh or a tug at the heart.

You can put a book or a magazine down, knowing it will wait for you to return—in a moment or an hour, a day or a year. Print is your slave and you need not rush to "catch" him at a certain time, or fret that he has passed beyond recall.

You can choose reading, from the boundless treasury of print, to match your mood, feed your intellect, satisfy your underlying or transient needs. Above all to read means to enliven your mind with ideas, nourish your heart with insights, lift your spirit with inspiration.

Montaigne spoke for all of us when he said: "I read in order to learn *how to know myself*—and teach myself the proper way to live and die."

*Leo Rosten, "The Miracles of Print," *Reader's Digest Condensed Books* (Pleasantville, N.Y.: Reader's Digest, 1965). Used by permission.

HOW TO MEET A NEW WORD:

1. Read the rest of the sentence and decide what makes sense there.

The boy threw the _____ through the hoop.
...lawnmower?
...elephant?
...basketball?
...bike?

2. Sound out the word.

/bäs'-kət-bȯl/

3. Look to see if you recognize any part of the word.

basket**ball**

4. Check to see if there is a picture to help you.

5. Look it up in the dictionary or glossary.

6. If all else fails, ask the teacher or a classmate.

In becoming independent readers, children learn to apply the major word recognition skills. An attractive chart may show girls and boys how to go about decoding unknown words. (Courtesy of Barbara Ellis.)

individual words. A word in isolation, however, is much more difficult to learn than a word in context. Thus teachers should introduce sight words in context with words the children already know. Three guidelines for teaching basic sight words are:

1. Use new words in a variety of oral language situations before introducing them to children as sight words.
2. Present sight words within the context of a meaningful sentence or phrase.
3. Reinforce the recognition of sight words through an assortment of games and activities.

Configuration Activities Distinctive physical features of words include shape, length, and height. The ability to visualize the configuration of a word often eliminates confusion produced by certain letters and combinations of letters—for example, *b* and *d*, *y* and *j*, and *p* and *q*. To encourage children to take account of the physical characteristics of troublesome words, many teachers create "shape cards," which present in a graphic way the configuration of confusing letters and words (see Figure 10.1). This technique has the obvious limitation of removing words from a meaningful context, but it may be used with other strategies to teach words containing confusing combinations of letters.

Phrase and Sentence Activities Sentence strips are thin cardboard pieces that fit into a pocket chart, sometimes called a "sentence holder." Both the strips and holders are available from school supply stores. Sentences and phrases that utilize sight words may be printed on the strips for students to arrange into various patterns. Teachers should provide a variety of sentence strips and phrase cards so that children may create their own sentences.

Matching Exercises Activities similar to the one below are quite familiar to teachers of young children. The child is expected to circle the two identical words, the purpose being to develop word and letter discrimination.

for	four	for	from
and	and	are	any
saw	was	say	saw
too	to	too	two
not	now	out	not

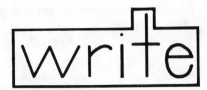 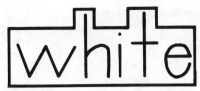

Figure 10.1 *The words* write *and* white *have been paired here to illustrate the close similarity in* the configuration of the two words. To a beginning reader, they are almost indistinguishable.

Tachistoscopic Activities A tachistoscope is a device with an opening through which words are shown. Many different tachistoscopes are commercially available. They range from the simple hand-held type to expensive "controlled readers." The most useful tachistoscopes, however, are probably those made by teachers for specific purposes. The language arts teacher should make several tachistoscopes for use in the classroom. Children may then work together or individually to read the words, either silently or orally, as they appear. Activities with a tachistoscope help children to become familiar with many new words while reinforcing their understanding of known ones.

Recognizing Words in Context

All readers use context clues when they rely on what is said before and after a word or phrase to make sense of the word or phrase. The reader makes a qualified judgment on the basis of what he or she actually knows about the word in question. If, as the reader continues reading, the passage remains coherent, the estimation is considered accurate or accurate enough. Skill in using context clues is a major factor in reading comprehension.

Context Clues There are many kinds of context clues.[4] Some of the most widely used are:

[4]Constance M. McCullough, "Context Aids in Reading," *The Reading Teacher* (April 1958), pp. 225–229.

1. *Picture clues.* Illustrations, pictures, charts, and photographs that aid children in understanding print material.
2. *Verbal clues.* The sentence before or after a sentence containing an unknown word that gives the reader an indication of the word's probable meaning.
3. *Grammar clues.* Sentence constructions and language patterns that provide the reader with language indicators about the general meaning of a word.
4. *Experience clues.* Real or vicarious experiences that help a reader estimate the meaning of a word.
5. *Comparison and contrast clues.* Contrast that enables a reader to "sense" the meaning of an unknown word. For example, figures of speech are a literary device that leads the reader to a forced analogy between two or more ideas.
6. *Synonym clues.* Repetition that employs a synonym for a word that may have been unknown in the previous sentence.
7. *Mood clues.* The tone of a sentence may suggest an emotional climate that gives the reader a "feeling" about an unknown word.
8. *Punctuation and typographical clues.* The use of punctuation marks and typographical aids that serve as subtle language signposts. They provide a useful reference in determining definitions, main ideas, and numerous other context clues.
9. *Summary clues.* Statements that summarize ideas previously stated in context. This review technique is frequently applied in text-

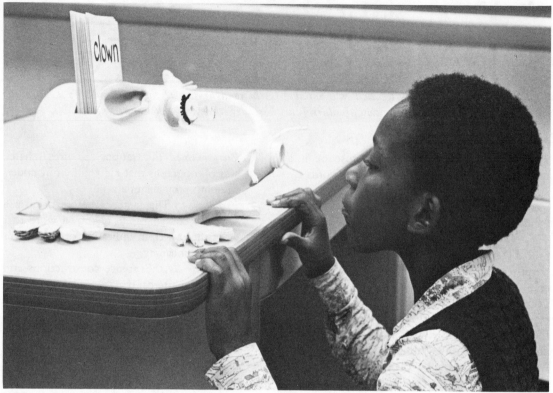

A bleach bottle tachistoscope is being used for practice on nouns. The student pronounces the word exposed and then checks for accuracy by looking through the spout at a small picture on the bottom of *the card. If a word is missed, it goes to the back of the pack for another try. Several card packs may be made to add variety and to enlarge sight vocabulary. (Courtesy of Lamar University.)*

book writing as the author closes one topic before introducing the next.

10. *Definition clues.* A definition following directly on the heels of a unique word that a reader might not be expected to know. Fortunately, most writers for children are careful to define terms within the text of their writing, and children can be taught to look ahead for such definitions.

Cloze Procedure A practical technique for teaching students the effective use of different types of context clues is the cloze procedure.

The term "cloze" comes from the Gestalt principle of closure; it refers to the tendency of an organism to complete that which is incomplete in a predictable direction.[5] The cloze procedure has been described as a "method of systematically deleting words from a prose selection and then evaluating the success the reader has in accurately supplying the words deleted."[6]

[5]Roger Farr and Nancy Roser, *Teaching a Child to Read* (New York: Harcourt Brace Jovanovich, 1979), p. 71.
[6]Richard D. Robinson, *An Introduction to the Cloze Procedure* (Newark, Del.: International Reading Association, 1972), p. 2.

This procedure is frequently used to determine three major levels of proficiency in reading: (1) *independent* (self-reliant reading with no outside assistance), (2) *instructional* (guided reading with moderate assistance from the teacher), and (3) *frustration* (difficult reading with much assistance and frequent errors). The following steps are presented as a guide to the formal use of the cloze procedure:

1. Select a passage of at least 250 consecutive words from graded reading material such as a textbook. The selection should be one that the students have not read previously.
2. Reproduce the passage, leaving the first and last sentences intact. Disregarding all proper nouns, delete every fifth word. Substitute the word with a blank or line of uniform length.
3. Ask the students to read the passage and to fill in the blanks.
4. Score the test by counting as correct only the exact words that were used in the text. Double the number of correct answers to arrive at a percentage; apply the following formula as developed by John Bormuth.[7] (Note: John Bormuth's research has concluded that the overall percentages change very little when synonyms are counted as correct responses.)

   Independent level = 58 to 100 percent
   Instructional level = 44 to 57 percent
   Frustration level   = 43 percent or less
5. Make use of the information from the cloze procedure test in the following manner:
   A. *Independent level.* Assign students material easy enough for reading alone without any help from another person. Also, have on hand a collection of easy materials from which students may select their own reading matter, that is, library books and supplementary materials.
   B. *Instructional level.* Place students in material at this level when instruction is to be provided by the teacher, that is, basal readers and related materials.
   C. *Frustration level.* Since the term "frustration" obviously means that the material is too difficult, no child should be expected to read at this level.

A recent informal adaptation of the cloze procedure is its application to the language-experience approach. The teacher may adapt the principles of cloze procedure to material dictated by students and written by the teacher. For example, the teacher guides the telling of an individual's or group's story and writes the details on a large chart. With the first and last sentences left intact, every *n*th word (that is, every fifth, seventh, ninth, etc., word) is covered by a piece of construction paper hinged with masking tape. Students are asked to read the sentences, making a determination about the identity of each covered word as they go along. To check their responses, students simply lift the flap to see whether their answers are accurate. The higher the comprehension, the more accurate will be the decisions. This adaptation is not intended to be a substitute for the formal application of the cloze procedure. It is not a test per se, but rather is a useful means to teach the concept of context clues using materials made by the teacher and students.

Decoding Words by Phonic Analysis

Phonic analysis, or phonics, is an important aspect of word recognition, and it is given exhaustive treatment in the elementary reading program. Phonic analysis is the process of asking a reader to break a word into its component

[7]John Bormuth, "Comparable Cloze and Multiple-Choice Comprehension Test Scores," *Journal of Reading* (February 1967), pp. 291–299.

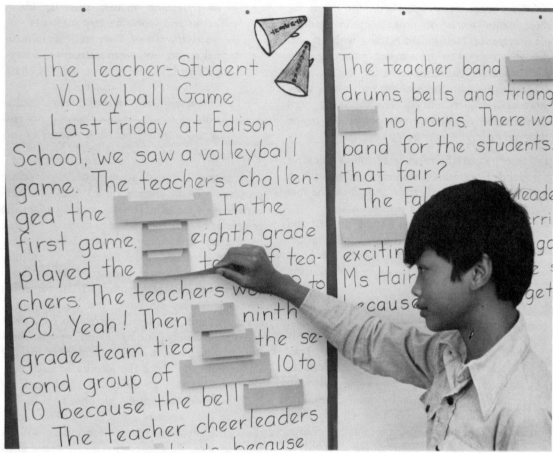

The Teacher-Student
Volleyball Game
     Last Friday at Edison
School, we saw a volleyball
game. The teachers challenged the ▢   In the
first game,   eighth grade
played the   te   f tea-
chers. The teachers w   to
20. Yeah! Then   ninth
grade team tied   the second group of   10 to
10 because the bell
     The teacher cheerleaders
              ▢   because

The teacher band
drums, bells and triang
       no horns. There wa
band for the students.
that fair?
     The Fa   Jeade
                rri
excitin   ga
Ms Hair   s
 cause   get

In a highly modified version of the cloze procedure, a language arts teacher helps students studying English as a second language to develop skill in using context clues. The students not only partici- *pated in the event but also in composing the chart. (Courtesy of Monteel Copple, Edison Junior High School, Port Arthur, Texas.)*

sounds, or phonemes. *Phonics* is the organized correspondence between sounds and symbols. The effective use of phonic analysis helps readers to pronounce and subsequently to understand many new words that are unknown on sight. Phonic analysis also facilitates fluent oral reading. The relationship between pronunciation and spelling is often inconsistent in English. Nevertheless, phonic analysis furnishes readers with a means to decode many unknown words.

Ideally, the major goal of phonics instruction is to provide readers with the ability to relate printed letters and combinations of letters to their corresponding speech sounds. A reader who is capable of translating written symbols into appropriate speech sounds may add previously unknown words to her or his speaking and listening vocabularies. The reader accomplishes this task when, for example, the letter *c* in "cat" is recognized as having the same sound as the letter *k* in "kitten." The child gradually becomes familiar with difficult and often contradictory sound-symbol relationships and understands more and more words. Some reading specialists describe phonic analysis as "cracking the code"—an apt description, since printed material is oral language in the form of a code.

The major problem faced by teachers and students in carrying out a phonic analysis is the imperfect relationship that often exists between the letters and sounds. In English, there are approximately forty-four speech sounds to be expressed by twenty-six letters. To further complicate matters, some letters consistently represent their own sound, other letters are considered superfluous because they lack individual sounds, and still other letters produce a variety of unique speech sounds. Despite the difficulties and ambiguities, the application of phonic rules, called *generalizations*, is easier than might be imagined. In fact, Arthur Heilman maintains that "85 percent of English words are phonetic."[8] A list of generalizations is given in Figure 10.2.

In most basal reading, language arts, and spelling textbooks, phonic skills are introduced and practiced according to a predetermined hierarchy. Commercial publishers usually call such an instructional plan a "scope and sequence" continuum. There is considerable variation in the way phonic skills and subskills may be organized.

Many people do not believe that phonics is being taught in today's schools since it is seldom labeled as a separate topic. Most teachers now include phonics instruction as part of a total reading program that focuses on word recognition, vocabulary development, and comprehension skills. Moreover, the teaching of phonics has changed over the years. Instead of rote drill, children now participate in games and projects that require the use of phonic skills in a more natural and enjoyable way.

"*Not ŏ, dummy, ō̄ō̄.*"

Drawing by Modell. © 1978 The New Yorker Magazine, Inc. Used by permission.

How much and what type of phonics instruction should children receive in the reading program? A definitive response to this question is not possible. However, two important principles should be recognized by all elementary language arts teachers. First, reading instruction should interrelate the four main strategies of word recognition. Second, teachers should be aware that most children dislike isolated phonic drills and endless assignments in workbooks. Their goal is to read books. Charlotte Huck has underscored this point: "Children will want to read because they want to read stories—their own and other persons, real stories where something happens to believable characters."[9]

Decoding Words by Structural Analysis

Essentially, structural analysis is an examination of the individual parts of a word. It requires an understanding of meaning as well as the sound-

[8]Arthur W. Heilman, *Phonics in the Proper Perspective* (Columbus: Charles E. Merrill, 1976), p. 15.

[9]Charlotte Huck, "Literature as the Content of Reading," *Theory into Practice* (December 1977), p. 363.

The Most Helpful Reading/Spelling Generalizations

1. The final *e* is usually silent. (gat*e*)

2. The vowel at the end of a one-syllable word is usually long. (g*o*)

3. When two vowels go walking, the first does the talking and says its own name. (b*ea*n)

4. Every word has one syllable for each sounded vowel. (r*e* l*o* c*a* t*e*)

5. Syllabicate the letter patterns vowel/consonant vowel (V/CV) before the consonant. If a vowel is pronounced long it is probably the last letter in the syllable. (h*e* r*o*, h*o* b*o* consist of "open" syllables)

6. Syllabicate the pattern VC/CV between consonants. If a vowel is pronounced short it is probably closed in from behind by a consonant or two. (m*a* n, r*a* b b*i* t, *i* n t*e* r m*i* t t*e* nt consist of only "closed" syllables)

7. Before syllabicating, clear the deck of all prefixes and suffixes. They generally remain as intact units. (*pre* dic *tion*)

8. *i* is usually long when it comes before *gh*. (l*i*ght)

9. *i* before *e* except after *c*, or when sounded like *a* as in n*ei*ghbor or w*ei*gh. (fr*ie*nd, s*ie* ge)

10. If you need to guess how to pronounce a vowel, it is more often short than long.

11. Most consonants have a consistent sound; it's the vowels and vowel combinations that have varied pronunciations and cause 90 percent of our spelling problems. (h*a*te, h*a*t, h*a*rd)

12. A doubled consonant or vowel usually has one sound. (be*tt*er, b*ee*t)

13. *gh* is usually silent. (si*gh*t, hi*gh*)

14. Consonants *c* and *g* have their soft sound before *i, e* and *y*; otherwise use their hard sound. (*c*ity, *c*at; *g*em, *g*o—major exception: *g*irl)

15. The sound *k* may be made by *c* or *ck*. (*c*at, si*ck*)

16. The sound *ch* is often spelled *tch*. (ma*tch*)

17. The sound *j* is often spelled *dg* or *dge*. (e*dg*ing, do*dge*)

18. When a word ends in *y* with a consonant before it, to make the word plural change the *y* to *i* and add *es*. (tr*y*, tr*ies*)

19. The ending *-tion* may be spelled *-sion, -sian, -cian, -tian*. (na*tion*, ses*sion*, Rus*sian*, musi*cian*, ti*tian*)

20. Vowels in unaccented syllables are often pronounced as a neutral sound represented like this ə—called schwa. (lab*o*r, rabb*i*t, lab*e*l, wom*a*n, *u*pon)

21. The ending *-ance* may be spelled *-ence*, even *-ants* or *-ents* (attend*ance*, excell*ence*, attend*ants*, presid*ents*)—remember that schwa!

22. The ending *-ous* may be used with an *i* or an *e*. (gener*ous*, suspic*ious*, simultan*eous*)

23. Look twice at the common prefixes *in-*, *en-* and *un-*. They are not used interchangeably.

24. Compound words look hard but are relatively easy. (dog house)

Warning! Don't forget that none of these generalizations works all of the time or even most of the time! But they are important!

Figure 10.2 A list of "The Most Helpful Reading/Spelling Generalizations" published in Teacher *magazine uses cartoon illustrations to simplify the generalizations. Used by permission.*

symbol relationships. This important skill depends on the recognition of these elements: (1) prefixes and suffixes, (2) inflectional endings, (3) compound words, (4) contractions, (5) syllabication, and (6) accent.

Prefixes and Suffixes New words are formed by the addition of a prefix or suffix to a root word. A semantic change occurs in a root word when a prefix is placed before it or a suffix is placed at its end. Familiarity with the meaning of prefixes and suffixes will significantly improve a reader's ability to recognize unfamiliar words. Prefixes and suffixes ought to be taught in context rather than in isolation.

Inflectional Endings Elements added to words to indicate a grammatical or syntactical function are known as inflectional endings. The endings -*s* and -*'s*, for example, are added to nouns to denote number and possession. Verbs, adverbs, and adjectives are also inflected.

Children usually learn the correct use of inflectional endings naturally, as they learn to speak. Regular plural endings have usually been mastered by the time a child enters school. Irregular forms such as "mice," "wrote," "ate," however, are confusing and may require special emphasis. With constant reinforcement and meaningful practice, they too will be added to the child's storehouse of sight words. The ability to understand and use inflectional endings also improves boys' and girls' ability to write and spell.

Compound Words Two or more words may be joined together to create a new word, which is said to be a compound word. The English language contains thousands of words that have been linked to produce new words. Some compound words combine two nouns that are easy for children to recognize—for example, "toothbrush," "bathtub," "baseball." An activity to increase children's knowledge of compound words

is discussed in Display 10.2

Contractions Contractions may be thought of as oral language shortcuts. They are often used in conversational speech. The ability to use them correctly in their written form, however, is difficult because they lack one or more letters, they contain an apostrophe inserted where a letter or letters have been omitted, and they have the same meaning as the long form they represent but have their own pronunciation.[10] Children need guidance and practice in both recognizing and pronouncing contractions until eventually they become sight words.

Syllabication A *syllable* is a unit of speech that contains a vowel sound and may include one or more consonant sounds. Syllabication, the division of words into syllables, is an aid to correct pronunciation. A word may consist of one syllable, or it may be polysyllabic. Much criticism of instruction in syllabication has centered on the manner in which it is taught—through the use of generalizations or rules.

Accent Accent refers to the differing degrees of emphasis given to individual syllables in polysyllabic words. The syllable that receives the most stress is said to have the *primary accent—gov'* ern ment. In some words, there is also a secondary accent—en' ve *lope'*.

The location of the emphasis in most words depends on the number of syllables in the word. It should also be noted that words spoken in isolation are frequently pronounced differently from those spoken in context. In the absence of a specific context, for example, "contract" may be pronounced in either of two ways. This is a major reason why many children have trouble correctly pronouncing words in isolation. One way to help them "hear" the difference in word accents is to compare words with similar sounds—for example, "accident" and "accidental."

[10]Heilman, p. 100.

A Proper Way to Live: Having the Skill and Will to Read **211**

Display 10.2 Compounding Words

doghouse

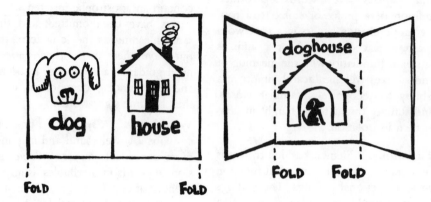

cowboy

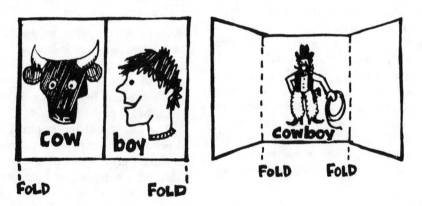

To reinforce students' understanding of compound words, show them how to fold a piece of paper into three parts and have them draw pictures representing the two elements of the compound term on the outside flaps. Then the flaps are opened so that a picture representing the compound word may be drawn on the inside. (Courtesy of Barbara Ellis.)

Guiding Vocabulary Growth

The term "vocabulary" is frequently used as though it had a single meaning—the acquisition of new words. Actually, the word has multiple meanings and connotations. It really should be used in the plural, for we may distinguish between listening, speaking, reading, and writing vocabularies.

Listening vocabulary consists of the words a child understands in oral communication. It is the first vocabulary to be developed and is usually the largest vocabulary at a person's command. *Speaking vocabulary* is the words a child uses when talking. The speaking vocabulary follows closely on the listening one and expands rapidly during the preschool and primary years. *Reading vocabulary* consists of the words a child recognizes in printed form. The reading vocabulary is introduced and enlarged in the language arts and reading program and increases greatly throughout the elementary years. *Writing vocabulary* is the words used in written discourse. This vocabulary is the last to be developed and usually contains the smallest number of words. It is the responsibility of teachers to enlarge each vocabulary with systematic and meaningful instruction.

There are two main types of reading vocabulary—sight and meaning. Sight vocabulary, which we have previously discussed, consists of words a person recognizes instantaneously. According to George Spache, "meaning vocabulary" consists of words the child learned by mental association such as the use of context clues in specific reading situations.[11] Elementary language arts teachers must attempt to develop both aspects of a child's reading vocabulary by making certain that children understand the

[11]George D. Spache and Evelyn B. Spache, *Reading in the Elementary School*, 4th ed. (Boston: Allyn and Bacon, 1977), p. 415.

A pocket chart aids in word classification. Categories may become more and more complex as word recognition and comprehension improve. (Courtesy of Lamar University.)

meaning of words, phrases, and sentences presented.

Cultivating, nourishing, and enriching children's listening, speaking, writing, and reading vocabularies is a major responsibility of the language arts teacher. This difficult task may be accomplished by both planned and natural experiences with words. Planned experiences include the direct teaching of words by means of vocabulary exercises that call for labeling, matching, or categorizing. Such activities, if presented in an interesting way, make a significant contribution to the child's meaning vocabulary. Planned experiences occur routinely in the basal language arts reading program as well as in various content area subjects. Natural experiences with words are indirect and incidental events that teachers take advantage of to integrate language into the curriculum.

The following activities may be used to build a lasting appreciation for words:

Learning About Word Origins (Etymology)
The study of word origins and derivations may spark children's interest in words. Many words have unique backgrounds, and it often proves

This student arranges color-coded word cubes into a meaningful unit, the purpose being to better understand the structure of sentences. (Courtesy of Lamar University.)

fascinating to trace the origin of words such as the following:

- villain
- dandelion
- silly
- corduroy
- parson
- lollipop
- doctor
- meander

Playing Word Games   The language arts teacher may easily create word games that enlarge students' vocabularies. Numerous ideas are regularly presented in educational publications and activity books. The teacher should carefully evaluate the quality and variety of such activities.

Displaying Words   Posters, bulletin boards, and learning centers may be created to emphasize familiar words or present new ones. Such

exhibits should be developed over a period of time with students adding appropriate words to the display as they encounter them.

Using Dictionaries   The dictionary is one of the most useful reference tools with which children may improve their vocabularies. Many types are available, and every child should have at least one version easily accessible. Fortunately, there are excellent dictionaries on the market for all ages and grade levels. The teacher who serves as a positive model and develops interesting lessons and activities requiring students to consult a dictionary will help to develop the dictionary habit.

Using Word Cubes   Girls and boys may understand complex grammatical structures more easily by manipulating word cubes. The cubes are made from half-pint milk cartons covered with construction paper and imprinted with words representing different parts of speech (see Display 10.3). Turning one or more of the cubes will create a new sentence. This activity helps to guide students toward a better understanding of linguistic components and enlarges their meaning vocabulary.

Solving Crossword Puzzles   Crossword puzzles stimulate readers to unlock the meaning of new words. The clues provided in the "down" and "across" columns present an almost irresistible challenge. Crossword puzzles may be used as vocabulary enrichment, as an introduction to new words, or as an evaluation instrument to check a student's comprehension.

Improving Reading Comprehension

Many research studies provide empirical support for the notion that there are levels of reading comprehension. Although it is generally agreed that reading comprehension progresses from a concrete level to a more abstract one, there is a

Display 10.3 Making and Using Word Cubes

Directions for Making

Trim the tops off two half-pint milk cartons and slip one inside the other to form a cube. Make four cubes—one for proper nouns, common nouns, verbs, and articles. Cover the cubes with construction paper, using a different color for each one. Print words on pieces of white paper and glue them to the six sides of the appropriate cube. Cover the cubes with clear contact paper.

Note: The game becomes more challenging if a single color is used for all blocks. For more advanced students, a cube with adjectives and one with adverbs may be added.

Basic Blocks

Proper Nouns	Verbs	Articles	Common Nouns
Andi	finds	a	ball
Father	gets	one	book
Amy	likes	that	boat
Mother	sees	that	game
Pete	takes	the	dog
Betty	wants	this	toy

Directions for Playing

The first player tosses out the cubes and arranges them into a sentence before sand runs down in an egg timer. The turn then goes to the next player, etc. Keep score by tally marks.

Courtesy of Lamar University.

---

great deal of overlap between the literal, interpretive, critical, and creative levels.

Since the levels are not discrete, a certain risk is involved in discussing a taxonomy of reading comprehension skills. The reason for doing so is to emphasize that students must be led toward sophisticated analytical levels of comprehension, but in order to achieve the higher levels they must successfully pass through the lower ones. Teachers need to be aware of the hierarchy so that they are sure to provide classroom experiences designed to strengthen skills at each level. At the same time, teachers should remember that the levels of comprehension overlap and cannot be precisely distinguished one from the other. Figure 10.3 is a simplified diagram that might

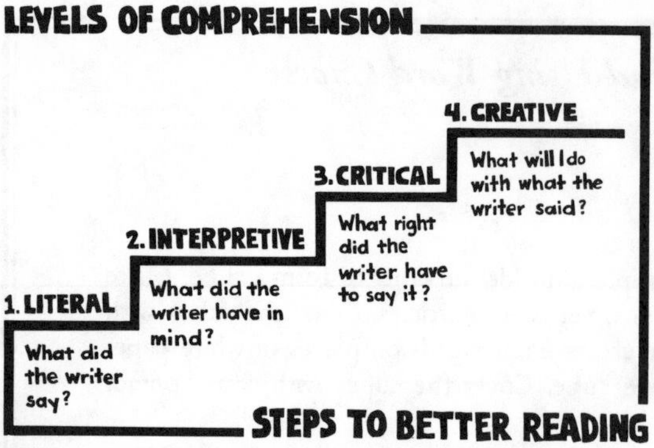

LEVELS OF COMPREHENSION

4. CREATIVE
What will I do with what the writer said?

3. CRITICAL
What right did the writer have to say it?

2. INTERPRETIVE
What did the writer have in mind?

1. LITERAL
What did the writer say?

STEPS TO BETTER READING

Figure 10.3   A diagram, for use with elementary students, that simplifies the idea of reading comprehension levels. (Courtesy of Barbara Ellis.)

be used to help students in the upper elementary grades visualize the necessity of reading at higher, more complex levels of understanding.

The Literal Level: What Did the Writer Say?

Literal comprehension is understanding the basic, factual content of the reading material. It calls for recognition and recall and does not require the reader to interpret or analyze the writer's intent. It is the level of comprehension required for following printed directions, looking up a name in the telephone directory, or reading the description of an item in a hardware catalogue.

The Interpretive Level: What Did the Writer Mean?

Interpretation requires the reader to read between the lines to analyze the writer's intent and, on the basis of that analysis, predict the outcome of the writer's line of thought. At the interpretive level, the reader goes beyond the facts to implied meanings that are not overtly stated. An understanding of figurative language (metaphorical ex-

pressions) is essential if young readers are to develop competence in interpretive comprehension.

The Critical Level: By What Right Did the Writer Speak?

At this sophisticated level of comprehension, the reader makes a judgment about the truth and merit of the writing. The reader questions who the writer is, by what authority the writer speaks, and how accurately the writer has composed. At the critical level of comprehension students benefit from in-depth studies of some of the creators of literature—authors, illustrators, and poets.

The frequent exercise of critical judgment helps young readers to develop opinions, attitudes, and values. For this reason they should become aware of propaganda techniques used by writers to influence the reader. Some types of propaganda are described in Display 10.4.

The Creative Level: What Will I Do with What the Writer Said?

At the creative level of comprehension, the individual is called upon to react or respond to the reading by a change in behavior or attitude. The reaction is often reflected in creative activities such as writing, discussing cause-and-effect relationships, constructing some object alluded to in the reading material; or it may result in a new outlook or perspective on the reader's part. Creative comprehension moves a person to action or to change in some manner.

Activities and Materials to Further Comprehension

When working to help students strengthen their ability to understand printed material, the teacher

Display 10.4 Types of Propaganda

Propaganda is a methodical plan for spreading ideas or opinions to promote a cause or product. Common approaches include the following:

1. *Bandwagon:* The implied message is: "Everyone else is enjoying this product; you should too." Usually employs large crowds of people in a "bandwagon" effect.
2. *Testimonial or personal endorsement:* Very well known athletes, movie stars, and public figures endorsing products. The implication is that if you use the product you will be as successful and popular as they.
3. *Repetition, hypnotism:* A refrain repeated over and over to the point of mesmerizing the listener or reader. Also seeks to have the consumer commit the slogan to memory.
4. *Plain folks or down home:* Ordinary people, neighborly and folksy, promoting products. The implication is that a plain person is more honest and would not cheat or deceive you.
5. *Ego building, snob appeal:* Suggests that if you use a certain product, you too may belong to this exclusive group. Implies that you are superior and should have an advantage over others.
6. *Emotional words, patriotic slogans:* Employs words such as "mother," "grandmother," "church," "U.S.A." Suggests that if you are a good mother, Christian, citizen, or whatever, you will use this product.
7. *Value, durability:* The idea of more for less. A product that promises to last longer and save the consumer more money than competing products.
8. *Straw man:* Creates a problem where none exists in order to sell a product. "If you have trouble sleeping at night, use this product."
9. *Sex appeal:* Features beautiful women and handsome men promoting products. They suggest that if you use their product you will be attractive to the opposite sex.
10. *Card stacking:* Stating all the claims (stacking the cards) in favor of one product.

should keep in mind the fact that comprehension skills are interdependent and overlapping. Even so, certain materials lend themselves better to the skills of literal and interpretive reading and others to the higher levels of critical and creative reading. A variety of reading experiences, ranging from consumer advertising to classic literature, is essential if girls and boys are to become fully efficient readers who can read and do so.

The aim of the following activities is to improve reading comprehension. The list begins with activities to enhance literal comprehension and proceeds through creative comprehension.

Label Game Cards Collect labels, logos, and brand names from boxes, bottles, cans, and packages. Glue the labels to large index cards. Make several of the card packs available for beginning readers to identify and classify.

Browse Boxes Collect menus, catalogues, advertisements, health folders, television guides,

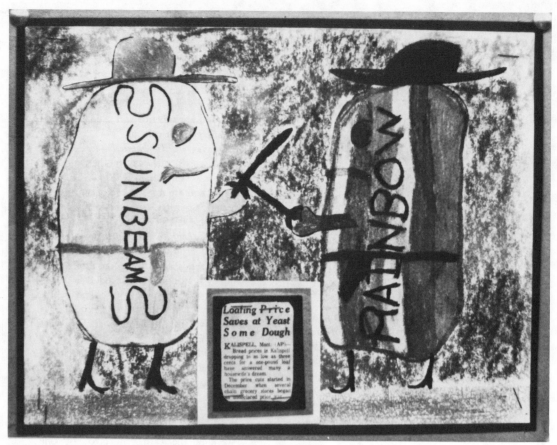

Artistic renderings of newspaper articles help to develop interpretive skills. This drawing tells the story of a price war between two bakeries.

travel folders, and other materials aimed at consumers. Store the materials in brightly covered boxes and make them readily available for students to browse in and read.

Trademark Posters Invite students to cut from magazines and newspapers symbols used by manufacturers to advertise products. Mount the trademarks on poster board for discussion and rereading.

How-to-Do-It Charts Print the directions for experiments, projects, and activities on poster board. Help students to develop the habit of reading directions carefully as they carry out a project.

Student Activity Books Make a collection of books that outline clear directions for constructing items of interest—macrame, candles, model planes, pinatas, origami. Allow time for boys and girls to follow directions and make items of their choosing.

Newspaper Art Ask students to cut interesting articles from the daily newspaper and use art to interpret the articles. Provide crayons, tempera, felt-tip pens, and colored chalk. Mount the articles and drawings together and post them at eye level for others to read.

Figurative Language Cartoons   Allow students to illustrate sayings, expressions, and proverbs in cartoon form. Mount the drawings on a' bulletin board with captions explaining what the expressions mean.

"Old Saw" Quizzes   Compose several multiple-choice tests on figurative language and administer them over a period of time to evaluate student's ability to understand popular idiomatic expressions.

For example: does "walking around with a heavy heart" mean that (1) your heart weighs ten pounds, (2) you are very sad, or (3) you are carrying a box of valentine candy?

Critical Reviews   Compile a scrapbook of brief book reviews and critiques written by students. Display the scrapbook in the school library or in the classroom book center as an aid to browsers.

Propaganda Identification   Make a survey of propaganda techniques used by advertisers. Ask students to cut advertisements from magazines to illustrate the various types. Label the pictures and mount them on a "propaganda" frieze.

Five W's Game   Ask students to read a newspaper article in which they identify who, what, when, where, and why. Ask them to write the answer to each question on a piece of paper folded as shown in Figure 10.4. Store the folded papers and articles in a box for students to match and read.

Author Study   Make a study of authors and illustrators of popular books. Compare an author or illustrator's various works.

Book Making   Assist students in writing and illustrating their own creative stories. Bind the

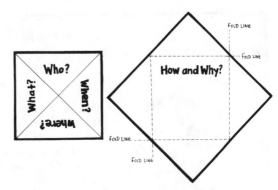

Figure 10.4   Paper Folding for the Five W's Game. (Courtesy of Barbara Ellis.)

one-of-a-kind books and place them in the library to be circulated like any other book.

Creative Book Reports   Allow time for children to make audiovisual aids to accompany favorite books they wish to share with the class.

In-Depth Study of Children's Literature   Total immersion in fine literature is the most effective and natural way to improve reading comprehension at all levels. Novels of substance like those written by Scott O'Dell cut across all levels of comprehension and are unsurpassed as vehicles for teaching factual information, inferential language, ideas for critique and debate, and issues to be acted upon and internalized. Although Scott O'Dell has written some fourteen novels for young people, his masterpiece remains *Island of the Blue Dolphins*. It is one of the most popular of all the books on the Newbery list, and it is ideal for in-depth study to improve comprehension skills.

Summary

The main goals of an elementary school reading program are to develop the tools needed for word recognition and the skills needed for comprehension. At the same time, it is the responsibility of every reading teacher to instill in stu-

A Profile of Scott O'Dell

SCOTT O'DELL was conducting research for *Country of the Sun,* an informal history of southern California, when he happened across an old magazine article about a young Indian woman who had been stranded alone on a desert island for eighteen years. The island was San Nicolas, some seventy-five miles off the coast of southern California, where Scott O'Dell had lived most of his life.

Having visited the island, he knew it to be the loneliest and most remote of all the Channel Islands, and he could picture the Indian girl Karana living there year after year, gradually losing all hope of being rescued. Thus was born the idea for *Island of the Blue Dolphins,* Scott O'Dell's feminine version of the Robinson Crusoe classic.

It is a story told in the first person, in sparse, simple, almost poetic language as if spoken by the Indian girl. Karana is faithfully portrayed as a strong, resourceful woman, "not afraid to face dangerous situations or ultimately to face herself." To so describe the feelings and emotions of a woman would have been an impossibility for most other male writers.

When he began the book, Scott O'Dell was already well established as a writer for adults. Nevertheless, he decided to make *Island of the Blue Dolphins* a children's book. He has explained why: "I had a strong feeling that nothing I could do for adults, as such, would be read or listened to, but that I had a chance to reach children. Hopefully, they would have children and the book would have influence. That's why I wrote it."[1]

Respect for the environment and reverence for every kind of life shines forth in *Dolphins* as in all of O'Dell's writing, and that is exactly as he means it to be:

> Every ten or fifteen pages I have maybe a paragraph about what we have done to the otter, that sort of thing. I want the children to share my interest in ecology. I just got fed up at the hunters that kill everything. It made me so damn mad. I said to myself, what do you do when you're damn mad? You write a letter to the newspaper and what happens? Nothing.
>
> So, I sat down and let this suppressed violent feeling out quietly and coolly in the *Dolphins.* That is what it is all about to me. To talk to children about these things. A child cannot read this book, finish this book, and have the same feelings about nature as he had before he started. It's impossible. This is the only reason I write.[2]

O'Dell's lifelong commitment to ecology is movingly portrayed in his description of Karana as she sits on the reef for hours watching the otters strike hard abalone shells against their breasts to open them:

> After that summer, after being friends with Won-a-nee and her young, I never killed another otter. I had an otter cape for my shoulders, which I used until it wore out, but

Scott O'Dell photo courtesy of Robert C. Frampton.
[1]Edith McCormick, "Scott O'Dell: Immortal Writer," *American Libraries* (June 1973), p. 357.
[2]Ibid., p. 357.

never again did I make a new one. Nor did I ever kill another cormorant for its beautiful feathers, though they have long, thin necks and make ugly sounds when they talk to each other. Nor did I kill seals for their sinews, using instead kelp to bind the things that needed it. Nor did I kill another wild dog nor did I try to spear another sea elephant.

Ulape would have laughed at me, and others would have laughed, too—my father most of all. Yet this is the way I felt about the animals who had become my friends and those who were not, but in time could be. If Ulape and my father had come back and laughed, and all the others had come back and laughed, still I would have felt the same way, for animals and birds are like people, too, though they do not talk the same or do the same things. Without them the earth would be an unhappy place.[3]

Scott O'Dell was born in Los Angeles on May 23, 1902, "where at that time," he tells us, "it had more horses than automobiles, more jack rabbits than people." He grew up in Los Angeles, San Pedro, and Long Beach, California, and "was never far from the sound of the sea."

After graduation from Long Beach Polytechnic High School, O'Dell attended Occidental College, the University of Wisconsin, and Stanford University. He said he had the idea of attending a different college each year as a clever way of seeing the world.

At one time he worked as a cameraman for Metro-Goldwyn-Mayer and, while filming *Ben Hur* in Italy, studied at the University of Rome. He now lives and writes in Westchester County, New York.

Scott O'Dell received the Newbery Medal for *Island of the Blue Dolphins* and three Newbery honor awards for *The King's Fifth, The Black Pearl,* and *Sing Down the Moon.* He has received numerous international awards including the Hans Christian Anderson Medal, an award given for a body of work. His books have been translated into some twenty languages, which should reassure Scott O'Dell that he *is* changing children's feelings about nature—in his own country and in many other parts of the world.

BOOKS BY SCOTT O'DELL

Island of the Blue Dolphins, 1960
The King's Fifth, 1966
The Black Pearl, 1967
The Dark Canoe, 1968
Journey to Jericho, 1969
Sing Down the Moon, 1970
The Treasure of Topo-el-Bampo, 1972
The Cruise of the Arctic Star, 1973
Child of Fire, 1974
Zia, 1976
The 290, 1976
Carlota, 1977
Kathleen, Please Come Home, 1978
The Captive, 1979

[3]Scott O'Dell, *Island of the Blue Dolphins,* p. 156. Published by Houghton Mifflin Company. Copyright © 1960 by Scott O'Dell. Reprinted by permission.

dents a lasting desire to read. Even though reading skills must be taught in a systematic and structured way, students should be allowed to practice those skills in trade books they choose for themselves.

Words may be identified on sight, by context clues, by phonic analysis, and by structural analysis. An important step toward becoming an independent reader is the application of word recognition techniques to self-selected reading material. Enlarging children's listening, speaking, reading, and writing vocabularies is a major aim of language arts instruction. To accomplish this task, teachers must make sure that girls and boys learn new words by means of both planned and natural experiences.

Comprehension of written material may occur at the literal, interpretive, critical, and creative levels. Some materials require only literal comprehension; others provoke critical analysis and creative responses. It takes skill and practice on the teacher's part to move questioning about a piece of literature from surface questions to queries that call for value judgments and evaluations.

Best Books for Children

The Black Cauldron, written by Lloyd Alexander and illustrated by Evaline Ness. New York: Holt, Rinehart and Winston, 1965. In the mythical kingdom of Prydain, the decision is made to destroy the Black Cauldron, chief implement of the evil powers of Arawn, lord of the Land of Death. In the "Author's Note," Alexander relates the conflict to modern times: "Although an imaginary world, Prydain is essentially not too different from our real one, where humor and heartbreak, joy and sadness are closely interwoven." *The Black Cauldron* is probably the most popular book of the Prydain Chronicles. (U)

Black Fox of Lorne, written and illustrated by Marguerite De Angeli. New York: Doubleday, 1956. An adventure story in which two young Norsemen travel across the wild land of tenth-century Scotland in search of their mother and father's murderer. A clever deception helps them to survive: "He was used to hearing this voice, so like his own, in secret speech and secret plotting, for they were twins, so like in voice and look, in manner and motion, that one was easily mistaken for the other." (U)

The Black Pearl, written by Scott O'Dell. Boston: Houghton Mifflin, 1967. *The Black Pearl* is based on an ancient legend and has its setting in the seaport village of La Paz in Baja, California. O'Dell describes it as "a tale of good and evil, a giant Manta ray and a fabulous pearl." (U)

Carlota, written by Scott O'Dell. Boston: Houghton Mifflin, 1977. Carlota, fulfilling the role of her dead brother, takes part in the struggle between the Californians and the Americans in the battle of San Pasqual. When Carlota wounds a young soldier with her lance, she finally comes face to face with her own compassion. Another strong and resourceful female character whom Scott O'Dell defines to perfection. (U)

Chitty-Chitty-Bang-Bang, written by Ian Fleming and illustrated by John Burningham. New York: Random House, 1964. *Chitty* was one of the last literary works written by Ian Fleming (author of the James Bond books) and was published shortly after his death. The idea grew out of a series of bedtime tales concocted for his son Casper about a racing car who had a mind of her own and could fly. He based *Chitty* on a real racing car that existed in the early 1920s. (M-U)

The Dark Canoe, written by Scott O'Dell. Boston: Houghton Mifflin, 1968. *The Dark Canoe* was inspired by one of Scott O'Dell's favorite books, *Moby Dick*. He said that in reading it for the sixth or seventh time, he was struck by the words "dark canoe." The phrase refers to a coffin turned into a life buoy, which saves the life of the man who tells the tale. O'Dell's novel is the story of the search for the coffinlike dark canoe said to be still drifting around the world. (U)

The Gingerbread Rabbit, written by Randall Jarrell and illustrated by Garth Williams. New York: Macmillan, 1964. One of the best contemporary stories containing the motif of inanimate objects personified.

Not only does life come to a gingerbread cookie, but the illustrator, Garth Williams, endows the mixing bowl, rolling pin, soap dish, and other household objects with smiling faces. (P-M)

Island of the Blue Dolphins, written by Scott O'Dell. Boston: Houghton Mifflin, 1960. This book is based on the true story of an Indian girl who was left on an island near the coast of Southern California and lived there alone for eighteen years before being rescued. Winner of the 1961 Newbery Award. (M-U)

Journey to Jericho, written by Scott O'Dell and illustrated by Leonard Weisgard. Boston: Houghton Mifflin, 1969. Scott O'Dell as a young child was taken across the country to visit an aunt and uncle who lived in a small coal-mining town of West Virginia. Fascinated by the miners with lamps on their caps and the blind mules that shoved the carts back and forth in the mines, years later he unfolded the story as a book for children. (P-M)

The King's Fifth, written by Scott O'Dell and illustrated by Samuel Bryant. Boston: Houghton Mifflin, 1966. This book describes the adventures of a band of young Spaniards who in the sixteenth century searched for the Seven Golden Cities of Cibola. Scott O'Dell tells his readers that to gather material for this book he followed the trail of the Spaniards for more than a thousand miles by boat, automobile, and on foot. (U)

Paddle-to-the-Sea, written and illustrated by Holling Clancy Holling. Boston: Houghton Mifflin. An Indian boy living in the Canadian wilderness carves the figure of an Indian in a small canoe and names him Paddle-to-the-Sea. He places Paddle in a melting snowbank, where the long journey to the Atlantic Ocean begins. This book, like Holling's other books, is carefully documented with accurate diagrams, maps, and labeled drawings interspersed with beautiful full-color paintings. (P-U)

Poor Richard, written and illustrated by James Daugherty. New York: Viking Press, 1941. Like James Daugherty's other works, this is a rich, lively, and very readable biography of a great American statesman. Both prose and illustrations help to capture the qualities of Benjamin Franklin that make him as fascinating to people living today as he was to his contemporaries. Young readers are especially fond of Daugherty's treatment of the *Almanac,* with its saws and sayings: "Those who in quarrels interpose must often wipe a bloody nose." (P-M)

Sing Down the Moon, written by Scott O'Dell. Boston: Houghton Mifflin, 1970. In 1961 Scott O'Dell spent part of the summer in Navaho country, where the states of Arizona, New Mexico, Colorado, and Utah meet. This story about Bright Morning and her flock of sheep is a result of that stay among the Navaho. He tells his readers, "I think of it as a modest tribute not only to this Indian girl but also to the courage of the human spirit." (M-U)

The Treasure of Topo-el-Bampo, written by Scott O'Dell and illustrated by Lynd Ward. Boston: Houghton Mifflin, 1972. Topo-el-Bampo is the poorest village in Mexico, and yet it is the site of the country's richest silver mine. Heroes of the story are two small burros named Tiger and Leandro who are forced to carry the king's gold out of the silver mine to the harbor. Striking two-color illustrations point up the poverty of the village. (P-M)

The 290, written by Scott O'Dell. Boston: Houghton Mifflin, 1976. In this novel for young readers, Scott O'Dell tells the story of an apprentice shipbuilder who becomes profoundly involved with a new ship being built for the Confederate navy. The young apprentice decided to ship aboard "The 290" and it turned out to be one of the most famous vessels of the Civil War. (U)

The Westing Game, written and illustrated by Ellen Raskin. New York: Dutton, 1978. Rich old Samuel W. Westing has a sense of humor and intrigue, which he uses to plan a dangerous game for his sixteen heirs. The story provides an ingenious set of clues, which the reader is obliged to solve as the story unfolds. Ellen Raskin is considered one of the best writers of mystery and is a winner of the Edgar Allan Poe Special Award. (U)

Zia, written by Scott O'Dell. Boston: Houghton Mifflin, 1976. After *Island of the Blue Dolphins* won the Newbery Award, many readers asked Scott O'Dell questions about what happened to the Indian girl, Karana, in the years following her rescue from the island. In *Zia* he reveals those facts as far as they could be traced. Zia was the sister of Karana's dead mother and the person who cared for the Indian girl until she died. (U)

Bibliography

Allington, Richard L., and Michael Strange. "The Problem with Reading Games." *The Reading Teacher*, December 1977.

Blanchowicz, Camille L. Z. "Cloze Activities for Primary Readers." *The Reading Teacher*, December 1977.

Bloom, Benjamin S., ed. *Taxonomy of Educational Objectives: The Classification of Educational Goals Handbook I—Cognitive Domain*. New York: McKay, 1967.

Bormuth, John. "Comparable Cloze and Multiple-Choice Comprehension Test Scores." *Journal of Reading*, February 1967.

Culyer, Richard C. "Guidelines for Skill Development: Vocabulary." *The Reading Teacher*, December 1978.

Dewey, Godfrey. *Relative Frequency of English-Speech Sounds*. Cambridge, Mass.: Harvard University Press, 1923.

Ekwall, Eldon. *Diagnosis and Remediation of the Disabled Reader*. Boston: Allyn and Bacon, 1976.

Farr, Roger, and Nancy Roser. *Teaching a Child to Read*. New York: Harcourt Brace Jovanovich, 1979.

Fitzgerald, Gisela G. "Why Kids Can Read the Book but Not the Workbook." *The Reading Teacher*, May 1977.

Greathouse, Larry J., and Barbara J. Neal. "Letter Cloze Will Conquer Contractions." *The Reading Teacher*, November 1976.

Heilman, Arthur W. *Phonics in the Proper Perspective*. Columbus: Charles E. Merrill, 1976.

Huck, Charlotte. "Literature as the Content of Reading." *Theory into Practice*, December 1977.

Jongsma, Eugene. *The Cloze Procedure as a Teaching Technique*. Newark, Del.: International Reading Association, 1971.

Karlin, Robert. *Teaching Elementary Reading*, 3rd ed. New York: Harcourt Brace Jovanovich, Inc., 1980.

McCullough, Constance M. "Context Aids in Reading." *The Reading Teacher*, April 1958.

Robinson, Richard D. *An Introduction to the Cloze Procedure*. Newark, Del.: International Reading Association, 1972.

Ruddell, Robert B. *Reading—Language Instruction: Innovative Practices*. Englewood Cliffs, N.J.: Prentice-Hall, 1974.

Spache, George D., and Evelyn B. Spache. *Reading in the Elementary School*, 4th ed. Boston: Allyn and Bacon, 1977.

Chapter 11

When No Fire Can Warm You: Creating an Environment for Poetry

EMILY DICKINSON, one of the great American poets, wrote: "If I read a book and it makes my whole body so cold that no fire can ever warm me, I know that is poetry. If I feel physically as if the top of my head were taken *off*, I know that is poetry. These are the only ways I know it. Is there another way?"

Teachers are constantly being told that if the language arts program is to be successful, they must begin where the child is. Poetry is where the child is. Poetry can bring warmth; it can bring reassurance; and it can bring laughter to a child's life. To omit poetry from the language arts program would be like eliminating music: It would be taking away one of life's treasures.

When poetry is to be shared with elementary children, the experience should be carefully planned but at the same time spontaneous. The planned portion of the program consists of units organized by the teacher into daily activities and experiences. Such units may focus on individual poets and their work, on different poetic forms, or on individual topics in which poems serve as examples. The spontaneous portion of the program includes a daily fare of reading poems aloud, writing poetry, and collecting poetry to be used on special (and not so special) occasions.

Almost any classroom situation presents an appropriate opportunity for the teacher to share a poem with the class. The first snowfall of the year, for example, is a meaningful event to all elementary students and is worthy of celebration with the reading aloud of "Cynthia in the Snow" by Gwendolyn Brooks or "Snow in the City" by Rachel Field:

CYNTHIA IN THE SNOW[1]

IT SUSHES.
It hushes
The loudness in the road.

It flitter-twitters,
And laughs away from me.
It laughs a lovely whiteness,
And whitely whirs away,
To be
Some otherwhere,
Still white as milk or shirts.
So beautiful it hurts.
Gwendolyn Brooks

SNOW IN THE CITY[2]

Snow is out of fashion,
  But it still comes down,
To whiten all the buildings
  In our town;
To dull the noise of traffic;
  To dim each glaring light
With star-shaped feathers
  Of frosty white.
And not the tallest building
  Halfway up the sky;
Or the trains and buses,
  And taxis scudding by;
And not a million people,
  Not one of them all,
Can do a thing about the snow
  But let it fall!
Rachel Field

Poems may be effectively used to describe all kinds of people, faraway places, ridiculous situations, and fascinating topics that are a part of every child's daily life. Poems may be used for fun, for make-believe, or for simple relaxation. In the past several years there has been a resurgence of interest in poetry for children, and many verse forms are available. The use of poetry in the classroom makes children aware of some of the exciting and imaginative ways in which language can convey moods, emotions, and feelings.

In this chapter we will discuss the characteristics of an excellent poem, the types of poetry most preferred by children, as well as methods of presenting various kinds of poetry in the elementary classroom.

Poetry and Early Childhood

Attempting to define "poetry" for children is like trying to put a cloud into a jar, for poetry is indeed as elusive as a cloud. Eleanor Farjeon, like many other poets, has attempted a definition, but the mystery remains:

POETRY[3]

What is Poetry? Who knows?
Not the rose, but the scent of the rose;
Not the sky, but the light in the sky;
Not the fly, but the gleam of the fly;
Not the sea, but the sound of the sea;
Not myself, but what makes me
See, hear, and feel something that prose
Cannot: and what is it, who knows.

Eleanor Farjeon

Other writers have made similar attempts to say what poetry is:

An emotion has formed its thoughts; a thought has found its words.

—Robert Frost

Poetry is a spontaneous overflow of powerful feelings; it takes its origin from emotion recollected in tranquility.

—William Wordsworth

It is a sort of musical shorthand.

—Michael Lewis

It is a record of the best and happiest moments of the happiest and best minds.

—Percy Bysshe Shelley

The most effective way of saying things.

—Matthew Arnold

Poetry is speaking painting.

—Plutarch

Sutherland and Arbuthnot believe that attempts to define poetry are valueless to children but meaningful to adults because the definition will have an impact on the manner in which poems are presented.[4]

They maintain that children's taste in poetry will improve if they have repeated experiences with good poetry. Adults who share poems with them, therefore, must recognize qualities of excellence in poetry.

Perhaps the best definitions of poetry have been put forth by children themselves:

Poetry is magic words.

—Michael (age 7)

Poetry is words that rhyme.

—Cathy (age 8)

I think poetry is like music.

—Kevin (age 9)

I can't explain what it is, but I can tell you some.

—Leroy (age 10)

Poetry is kind of like songs but you don't sing them. . . . I like poems.

—Melanie (age 11)

Most children are born poets. They *move* with language when frolicking to the rhythmic refrain of verses. In their relaxed, unstructured play, children often recite verses that are hundreds of years old. During the short span of early childhood, older children succeed in passing on a tradition of poetry to younger children. As a result, children living thousands of miles apart enjoy many of the same merrymaking verses. Is it ever possible to forget jump-rope jingles such as

1, 2, 3, O'Lary
My first name is Mary.
Don't you think that I look cute
In my father's bathing suit?

---

[4]Zena Sutherland and May Hill Arbuthnot, *Children and Books*, 5th ed. (Glenview, Ill.: Scott, Foresman, 1977), p. 244.

When No Fire Can Warm You: Creating an Environment for Poetry 227

One of the most widely reprinted versions of Mother Goose rhymes is The Real Mother Goose by Blanche Fisher Wright, enjoyed here by a two-year-old girl. (Courtesy of Carol Nelson.)

Children are delighted when they can use words that have double meanings, when they are able to make riddles based on word play, and when they can put rhyming words together. Around the world, countless children have been guided toward improved facility with language by traditional play activities based on the rhythm of words and poetic refrains. Most people can easily recall the taunting and teasing rhymes they said as young children:

> Liar, liar
> Your pants are on fire
> Your nose is as long
> As a telephone wire.

What causes so many young children to enjoy poetry instinctively? First, they are at the right stage of language acquisition development. A child is full of fresh curiosity—questioning, exploring, and learning about the world. Anything important to a child's environment is exciting, and language is important. Second, the manner in which poetry is presented to young children ordinarily produces a positive response. Children usually encounter poetry first through nursery rhymes recited by parents or other significant adults in an atmosphere that is warm and intimate. The rhymes of early childhood "seem a natural part of living, even when the speaker is unskilled in the art of presentation."[5]

Poetry read aloud most often begins with the traditional rhymes of Mother Goose, which most people hear or sing during their preschool years. Primary grade teachers usually start the enjoyable process of extending children's appreciation of poetry by using as a point of departure the Mother Goose rhymes that boys and girls have learned at home.

Poetry in the Language Arts Program

With a little effort by the teacher, poetry will add a special touch to a personalized language arts program. Children in the primary grades almost instinctively respond to the rhythmic language of poetry read aloud. Besides encouraging the oral reading of poetry, successful programs motivate children to write their own poems, to keep records of poems they enjoy, and to collect poems from many sources. Some teachers schedule poetry at a specific time each day to make certain it is not slighted. They type poetry selections on cards and mount the cards on brightly colored construction paper. After the poems are read by the teacher, they are fastened to a wire called "A Line of Poetry."

Unfortunately, many children do not learn to enjoy poetry at all or lose interest in it as they

[5]Helen W. Painter, Poetry and Children (Newark, Del.: International Reading Association), 1970, p. 11.

At an attractive poetry corner in which many kinds of poetry books are available, students may take turns reading poems to each other. (Courtesy of Sandra Henderson.)

grow older. Ann Terry's research indicates that children's interest in poetry reaches a peak during the fourth grade and then begins to decline.[6] The reasons are varied but fall mainly into two categories. First, too few teachers read or use poetry in their classrooms on a regular basis. Research indicates that approximately 75 percent of the middle grade elementary teachers read poetry to the class only once a month or less.[7] One reason for this apparent lack of interest is that

many teachers had negative experiences with poetry when they were in college or high school. To many of them, poetry evokes unhappy thoughts of forced memorization and the required writing of interpretive essays. When such teachers reluctantly bring poetry into the classroom, their negative or lackadaisical attitude may diminish children's fondness for this special language form.

Another reason why many children do not enjoy or lose interest in poetry is that the selections chosen by the teacher are inappropriate for the elementary classroom. Terry believes that children have definite preferences in poetry and that

[6] Ann Terry, *Children's Poetry Preferences: National Survey of Upper Elementary Grades* (Urbana, Ill.: National Council of Teachers of English, 1974), p. 36.
[7] Ibid., p. 41.

their preferences are based not only on the content of the poem but also on the way in which the poem is presented. Studies conducted over the past fifty years indicate that children consistently enjoy three poetic elements: (1) rhyme, (2) rhythm, and (3) sound.

In selecting poems for reading aloud to children and in preparing them for oral presentations, the teacher needs to keep in mind the rhyme, rhythm, and sound of each poem.

Humorous poems remain the unsurpassed favorite, successfully combining those elements. The elementary teacher who is aware of children's preferences will be most likely to leave girls and boys with an abiding appreciation of verse and will "share poetry in a variety of ways as a natural part of the on-going language arts program."[8]

The long-term goal of poetry teaching is the development of a lifelong habit of reading and sharing good poetry. Language arts teachers can help children reach that goal by providing many different sources of poetry in the classroom—poems to be read aloud by the teacher and poems to be read by the children themselves.

Anthologies of verse are vital references for the elementary classroom. Most general anthologies provide a wide sampling of poems organized around interesting subjects and popular themes. The language arts teacher would do well to become acquainted with the topics contained in several of them. Many also include information about the poets, titles, and subjects as well as helpful teaching suggestions.

Specialized anthologies are more limited in scope. They are usually built around a single theme such as animals, monsters, seasons, holidays, or famous persons. Specialized anthologies may offer particular genres such as haiku, limericks, ballads, or narratives. Every language arts classroom should have on hand at least one general anthology and as many specialized collections as the budget will allow.

8Ibid., p. 50.

Another way for the teacher to become acquainted with excellent poetry for children is to learn who the leading poets for children are. Collections of their poems are always dependable and are certain to appeal to girls and boys. Some of the most popular poets are Dorothy Aldis, Harry Behn, Stephen Vincent Benét, Rosemary Carr Benét, Gwendolyn Brooks, Lewis Carroll, Marchette Chute, John Ciardi, Elizabeth Coatsworth, Walter de la Mare, Beatrice Schenk De Regniers, Eleanor Farjeon, Rachel Field, Aileen Fisher, Robert Frost, Kate Greenaway, Langston Hughes, Edward Lear, Myra Cohn Livingston, David McCord, Phyllis McGinley, Eve Merriam, A. A. Milne, Lillian Moore, Ogden Nash, Laura E. Richards, Robert Louis Stevenson, Carl Sandburg, Shel Silverstein, and Nancy Byrd Turner.

A splendid collection of poems by a single poet is *One at a Time* by David McCord. It contains, with one exception, all the poems first published in McCord's books *Far and Few, Take Sky, All Day Long, For Me to Say,* and *Away and Ago.* This magical volume marks the twenty-fifth anniversary of David McCord's poems in print. According to Clifton Fadiman, McCord is "both an acrobat of language and the authentic explorer of the child's world."

Characteristics of Poems for Classroom Use

Which poems should a teacher select for classroom use? When deciding which poems to share with children, the language arts teacher should carefully consider matters such as literary quality, the suitability of the work for oral reading, and the appropriateness of the work for its intended audience.

Literary Excellence

Poetry for children must meet high literary standards. The best poems are a unique blend of

A Profile of David McCord

SEVERAL YEARS AGO, David McCord wrote an introduction to himself: "David McCord was born in New York City, raised in Oregon, and spent (as he says) his gainful life at Harvard."[1] Although the information is accurate, it is hardly a just description of the man who is one of America's great essayists and poets.

McCord has been nominated for the National Book Award twice, and he has received many medals, citations, and honors over the years. In 1977 he became the first recipient of the Award for Excellence in Poetry for Children given by the National Council of Teachers of English. He was awarded the Golden Rose of the New England Poetry Club in 1941, the first William Rose Benét Award in 1951, and the Sarah Josepha Hale Medal in 1962. He is a former Guggenheim Fellow, Lowell Lecturer in Boston, and a Benjamin Franklin Fellow of the Royal Society of Arts in London. He has written or edited forty-four books in the fields of poetry, light verse, the essay, art, and medicine. Three libraries are named for him.

Born on November 15, 1897, near Greenwich Village in New York City, David McCord grew up on Long Island; in Princeton, New Jersey; and on a ranch in southern Oregon. He graduated in three years with highest honors from Lincoln High School in Portland in 1917. After serving in the field artillery in World War I, he received his A.B. degree at Harvard in 1921 and his master's degree in 1922. McCord now lives in Boston. He has spent over forty years at Harvard in many different capacities, including teacher of the advanced course in writing in the summer session. In 1956, he received Harvard's first honorary degree of Doctor of Humane Letters. He also holds honorary doctorates from nine other universities including Williams, Colby, Washington and Jefferson, and the Canadian University of New Brunswick.

Far and Few, David McCord's first book of verse for children, was published in 1952. It is in its seventeenth printing, and he still considers it one of his best:

> Without a doubt *Far and Few* is my favorite. It was more than 25 years in the making. The book contains "The Pickety Fence," surely my most anthologized poem. It took but a few minutes to write and 22 years to sell to *The Ladies Home Journal* for $6.00 a line.[2]

Poems by David McCord are featured in more than three hundred anthologies in the United States, Canada, the United Kingdom, and Australia. They have frequently been heard on radio station WGBH-FM in Boston and on the BBC. Readers have included Raymond Massey and the late Dame Sybil Thorndike. David A. Dillon has suggested that McCord's poems are held in high esteem by children because they capture "the essence of many common childhood experiences (a visit to the doctor or dentist, Christmas Eve, the loss of a pet), particularly children's

---

David McCord photo courtesy of Thomas Garland Tinsley.
[1] Information provided by McCord's publisher, Little, Brown and Company.
[2] Lee Bennett Hopkins, "Mother Goose's Sons and Daughters," *Teacher* (May–June 1978), p. 37.

encounters with nature (climbing a tree, observing the behavior of animals, noting subtle changes in the seasons)."[3] Myra Cohn Livingston, in a leading article in *Horn Book,* has also paid tribute to David McCord and his work:

> David McCord is a poet who has not only given to Cambridge, Boston, and academe his myriad talents but during the past twenty-six years has produced a body of work which ranks highest among all poetry written for children in this country. John Ciardi has put it well: "One is too few of him and there is, alas, no second."[4]

She goes on to say:

> He keeps abreast of the world of TV, laundromats, Little Leaguers, and Rapid Reading. He is alive to the current vernacular of "man alive," "natch," "the guy's name," "queer stinko stuff," "what's the diff?," "goshawful," and "real fast." An avowed admirer of the poet Elizabeth Madox Roberts for her ability to speak in the language of childhood, David McCord equals and often surpasses her. In "Wishful" the house is "flittery with bats." In "Bridges" he writes "the big one dizzies me." Nor is any reader likely to forget "The Star in the Pail," in which the reflection "silvered in the water."[5]

To grow up in the country, McCord believes, gives a person a sharpened sense of awareness and makes that person a careful observer of nature. And to him the ability to observe in detail is the greatest step toward becoming a poet. It saddens McCord that no youngster has ever been able to tell him the number of plates on a turtle's back: *always* thirteen. He tells aspiring writers:

> It was my upbringing in the Oregon woods, a then unvarnished frontier, that made me an observer of things, made me understand that botany runs to threes and fives in petals and leaves and that anatomy runs in twos and fours—two legs, four legs, two eyes, two ears, four spigots on a cow, and so on. The big exception: five fingers and five toes.[6]

In speaking of poetry for children, David McCord has said: "Poetry for children should delight; it really *has* to delight. Furthermore, poetry for children should keep reminding them, without any feeling on their part that they are being reminded, that the English language is a most marvelous instrument."[7] McCord warns teachers and parents of the risk involved in using poems of poor quality with children. He feels that they do more harm with one bad poem than they will do good with any six acceptable ones:

> One bad poem will leave a taste twice as bad in the mouth. As a boy I dipped a spoon into a rotten egg once, and I remember it was almost a year before I could think of eating another egg. If you dip your mind into a bad poem, you are going to remember that one, for some strange reason, rather than any number of good ones.[8]

Now in his eighties, David McCord continues to meet and talk with school children twice a week. "I must have talked to at least one hundred and fifty thousand of them from Boston to Milwaukee," he says, "to help in a small way to close the generation gap." When talking to the teachers of his young friends, McCord advises:

> Try to tell them, and make them believe, that writing a poem is one of the most wonderful kinds of discipline: discipline of language, and discipline of speech. Loving

---

[3]David A. Dillon, "Perspectives: David McCord," *Language Arts* (March 1978), p. 383.
[4]Myra Cohn Livingston, "David McCord: The Singer, the Song, and the Sung," *Horn Book* (February 1979), p. 25.
[5]Ibid., p. 33.
[6]Dillon, p. 383.
[7]Hopkins.
[8]Dillon, p. 383.

poetry and caring about it, learning some of it by heart, and reading it all their lives will enrich their lives in ways they can't, as children, readily understand. Try to discover how to make this understood.[9]

A critical article on David McCord in *Twentieth Century Children's Writers* concludes with these words: "McCord's ingenious and crisp inventions will doubtless go on pleasing readers for years to come. Might as well expect Edward Lear to move into oblivion."[10]

BOOKS OF VERSE FOR CHILDREN BY DAVID MC CORD

Far and Few, 1952
Take Sky, 1962
All Day Long, 1966
Every Time I Climb a Tree, 1967
For Me to Say, 1970
Pen, Paper, and Poem, 1971
Mr. Bidery's Spidery Garden, 1972
Away and Ago, 1975
The Star in the Pail, 1975
One at a Time, 1977

[9]Ibid., p. 387.
[10]Claudia Lewis, *Twentieth Century Children's Writers,* "David McCord," ed. D. L. Kirkpatrick (London: St. Martin's Press, 1978), p. 856. Copyright by the Macmillan Press, Ltd., 1978.

words that produce a special emotional appeal. Young children enjoy poetry mainly because of its rhythm and rhyme, but as they mature in their poetry awareness they will be able to appreciate other literary elements as well. Important characteristics to be found in outstanding poems for children include rhythm, rhyme, meter, alliteration, onomatopoeia, mood, and figurative language. We will discuss each of them briefly, in order to point out the many qualities present in excellent verse for children. We do not suggest that teachers formally teach children about each specific element. They should, however, look for such elements when they are selecting poems to use in the classroom, and they should subtly introduce them in the course of teaching.

Rhythm The regular recurrence of stressed and unstressed words or syllables gives a poem its rhythm, as in Eleanor Farjeon's "Mrs. Peck-Pigeon":

MRS. PECK-PIGEON[9]

Mrs. Peck-Pigeon
Is pecking for bread,
Bob-bob-bob
Goes her little round head.
Tame as a pussy-cat
In the street,
Step-step-step
Go her little red feet.
With her little red feet
And her little round head,
Mrs. Peck-Pigeon
Goes pecking for bread.
            Eleanor Farjeon

[9]Copyright 1933, © renewed 1961 by Eleanor Farjeon. From *Poems for Children.* Copyright 1951 by Eleanor Farjeon. Reprinted by permission of J. B. Lippincott Company.

ANDREW AIRPUMP asked his Aunt her Ailment:
Did Andrew Airpump ask his Aunt her Ailment?
If Andrew Airpump asked his Aunt her Ailment,
Where was the Ailment of Andrew Airpump's Aunt?

"Andrew Airpump" is an example of assonance, the repetition of vowel sounds. (Used by permission of Charles Scribner's Sons from Peter Piper's Alpha- *bet by Marcia Brown. Copyright © 1959 Marcia Brown.)*

Rhyme A correspondence in the final sounds of words or lines of verse is known as rhyme. It is the major source of poetry's appeal for very young children. One of the best-known Mother Goose poems is an excellent example of rhyme:

> Bye, baby bunting
> Father's gone a-hunting
> Mother's gone a-milking
> Sister's gone a-silking,
> And brother's gone to buy a skin
> To wrap the baby bunting in.

Meter The arrangement of words in lines having a regular pattern or rhythm is known as meter. Meter is usually identified by the position and number of stressed and unstressed syllables in each line. In formal analyses of poems, stressed syllables are usually marked with ╱ and unstressed syllables with ∪. For example:

$$\text{╱ ∪ ╱ ∪ ╱ ∪ ╱}$$
Jack and Jill went up the hill

One way to teach the concept of meter is to have girls and boys clap the beat of well-known poems, emphasizing the stressed syllables. A musical instrument such as a piano or guitar may also be used to accentuate the stressed syllables. Another technique is to have children pronounce words aloud, speaking the stressed syllables more strongly than the unstressed ones.

Alliteration The repetition of initial consonant sounds in two or more neighboring words is known as alliteration. It is a device frequently employed in children's poetry. Alliteration makes a poem appealing by tempting the listener to repeat the lines: "Peter Piper picked a peck of pickled peppers." "Sing a song of sixpence."

Assonance, the repetition of vowel sounds, is another type of repeated sound. An excellent book of poems that alternates examples of alliteration and assonance is *Peter Piper's Alphabet* by Marcia Brown. In it a nonsense rhyme illustrates each letter of the alphabet.

Onomatopoeia The use of words that sound like the thing or action they refer to is known as onomatopoeia. Words such as "hiss," "boom," "clang," "buzz," "crack," and "cuckoo" are onomatopoeic. David McCord has created an entire poem that imitates the sound of a stick hitting a picket fence:

THE PICKETY FENCE[10]

The pickety fence
The pickety fence
Give it a lick it's
The pickety fence
Give it a lick it's
A clickety fence
Give it a lick it's
A lickety fence
Give it a lick
Give it a lick
Give it a lick
With a rickety stick
Pickety
Pickety
Pickety
Pick
David McCord

Mood The state of mind or feeling that the poet conveys is said to be the mood of the poem. Works by the best poets may have a powerful impact on the reader or listener. A magnifi-

cent example of an evocative poem is "Fog" by Carl Sandburg:

FOG[11]

The fog comes
on little cat feet.

It sits looking
over the harbor and city
on silent haunches
and then moves on.
Carl Sandburg

Figurative Language Language compressed to create a vivid "word picture" is said to be figurative. Such language is apparent in "Fog" as well as in "City" by Langston Hughes:

CITY[12]

In the morning the city
Spreads its wings
Making a song
In stone that sings.

In the evening the city
Goes to bed
Hanging lights
About its head.
Langston Hughes

Oral Readability

Poetry should be read aloud. This statement is made in almost every book about poetry, but its importance cannot be overemphasized. At every grade level, teachers should read poetry aloud to their students. Children should also be encouraged to read poetry aloud and to interpret their own poetry orally. There is probably no better way to promote the writing of poetry than by encouraging students to read poetry aloud. Some poetry collections, such as John Ciardi's *You*

Read To Me; I'll Read to You, inspire teachers and students to read poetry together by combining adults' and children's poetry. Or poems may be paired by the teacher.

The mere realization that teachers should read poetry aloud to children is not sufficient. Poetry should be read *well* by teachers, or it should not be read at all. Reading poetry orally is a rewarding experience for both student and teacher, but it requires practice and skill. Children and teachers alike can have fun sharpening their own reading skills with this poem by Shel Silverstein:

SICK[13]

"I cannot go to school today,"
Said Little Peggy Ann McKay.
"I have the measles and the mumps,
A gash, a rash and purple bumps.
My mouth is wet, my throat is dry,
I'm going blind in my right eye.
My tonsils are as big as rocks,
I've counted sixteen chicken pox
And there's one more—that's seventeen,
And don't you think my face looks green?
My leg is cut, my eyes are blue—
It might be instamatic flu.
I cough and sneeze and gasp and choke,
I'm sure that my left leg is broke—
My hip hurts when I move my chin,
My belly button's caving in,
My back is wrenched, my ankle's sprained,
My 'pendix pains each time it rains.
My nose is cold, my toes are numb,
I have a sliver in my thumb.
My neck is stiff, my spine is weak,
I hardly whisper when I speak.
My tongue is filling up my mouth,
I think my hair is falling out.
My elbow's bent, my spine ain't straight,
My temperature is one-o-eight.
My brain is shrunk, I cannot hear,
There is a hole inside my ear.
I have a hangnail, and my heart is—what?

What's that? What's that you say?
You say today is . . . Saturday?
G'bye, I'm going out to play!"
            Shel Silverstein

Steps to be taken to prepare for reading poetry aloud are listed in Display 11.1.

Enjoyable to Children

Teachers trying to select appropriate poems for children should carefully consider their background, age, and their previous experiences with poetry. It is not always possible to predict which poems will be within the child's realm of understanding. This is not to say that poems with unfamiliar settings should never be used, however. Such poetry, with adequate explanation, is an excellent means of creating a vicarious experience for children. Films, filmstrips, and pictures may help the teacher provide the motivation necessary to "get into" such poems. A teacher in a rural area, for example, might have to review and preteach before reading "All Around the Town" by Phyllis McGinley:

ALL AROUND THE TOWN[14]

B's the Bus,
The bounding Bus,
    That bears a shopper store-ward.
It's fun to sit
In back of it
    But the seats are better forward.
Although it's big as buildings are
    And looks both bold and grand,
It has to stop obligingly
    If you but raise your hand.

E is the Escalator
    That gives an elegant ride.
You step on the stair
With an easy air

---

[13]"Sick" from *Where the Sidewalk Ends* by Shel Silverstein. Copyright © 1974 by Shel Silverstein. Used by permission of Harper & Row, Publishers, Inc.

[14]From *All Around the Town* by Phyllis McGinley. Copyright 1948, © renewed 1976 by Phyllis McGinley. Reprinted by permission of J. B. Lippincott Company.

1. Read the poem several times to become more familiar and comfortable with it.
2. Look up the meaning of all words that are not understood in context. It may be important to the meaning of the poem that a word origin or definition be checked. Be sure to check the pronunciation of individual words.
3. Look at the poem through the eyes of the poet to better understand what the poem is trying to say. Such understanding may then be translated into the spoken interpretation.
4. Notice the punctuation marks in the poem. Where is the best place to pause? To drop the voice? To raise the voice?
5. Read the poem aloud at a comfortable pace. Vary the rate as needed. Slow down to build suspense, to suggest slow movement, or to give an opportunity for the reader to react. Speed up to simulate action or suggest movement.
6. Vary the tone, pitch, or volume; voice dynamics is important to the reading of a poem. If the poem mentions a clock ticking or alludes to people shouting, for example, use the appropriate cadence or intonation.
7. Tape-record yourself reading the poem and evaluate your performance.
8. Listen to the poet or to professional actors read the poem. Cues for reading may then be taken from the performance of the actor or poet. Many companies have issued records or cassettes of poetry.

And up and up you glide.
It's nicer than scaling ladders
Or scrambling 'round a hill,
For you climb and climb
But all the time
You're really standing still.
Phyllis McGinley

Appeal to the Senses

Many poems are mediocre and dull. Poetry selected for children's enjoyment must be genuine and alive. A good poem will conjure up a mental image for children. According to Smith and Park, "The main intent of the [poet] is to tell a story, paint an image, provide enjoyment, create music. He aims to reach children and employs all the resources at hand to do so. He is a student of children and has retained many of their qualities."[15]

The sound, language, and content of poems selected for classroom use should work together to create an emotional response in the reader or listener. In an unusual and moving story, *The Bat Poet* by Randall Jarrell, a little brown bat discovers exciting activity going on during the daytime and tries to convince his friends and family to stay awake. They do not share his curiosity or poetic vision. He also writes poetry but finds it impossible to find a listener who appreciates it. Even his friend the mockingbird misunderstands. The combination of prose and poetry in *The Bat Poet* is a dramatic example of poetry that evokes strong emotional responses.

[15]James A. Smith and Dorothy M. Park, *Word Music and Word Magic* (Boston: Allyn and Bacon, 1977), p. 299.

One of the most touching poetry collections is the profound . . . *I Never Saw Another Butterfly,* a collection of drawings and poems created by Jewish children while they were imprisoned in the Terezin concentration camp during World War II. This revealing work shows the horrors of war through the eyes of the children. It should be shared only with students who are mature enough to handle such a tragic theme. Those who do read the poems and study the paintings will have a humanizing and rewarding experience.

Types of Poetry Enjoyed by Children

Poetry used in the classroom had best mirror children's likes and dislikes. Although some girls and boys seem to prefer one subject or form of poetry, most of their preferences will change with maturity and age. Fortunately, there is poetry for everyone. Obviously, some forms have more appeal than others and can well serve as bait for students reluctant to choose poetry as reading material. The five best-liked categories of poetry for children are nonsense poems, humorous poems, poems that tell a story, lyrical verse, and special verse forms such as couplets, quatrains, haiku, cinquain, and concrete poems. Each type of poetry will be discussed in the following paragraphs.

Nonsense Poems

One of the most exciting ways of introducing children to poetry is to provide them a lively encounter with nonsense verse. Preschool children may be introduced to nonsense verse through Mother Goose and other rhymes and rimbles of childhood play. They delight in cleverly constructed nonsense poetry that includes rhyming words, rhythmic language, and ludicrous events. One of the most popular writers of such verse is Laura E. Richards. Students are usually introduced to her poems in their basal language arts textbooks, and their favorite is "Eletelephony":

ELETELEPHONY[16]

Once there was an elephant,
Who tried to use the telephant—
No! no! I mean an elephone
Who tried to use the telephone—
(Dear me! I am not certain quite
That even now I've got it right.)

Howe'er it was, he got his trunk
Entangled in the telephunk;
The more he tried to get it free,
The louder buzzed the telephee—
(I fear I'd better drop the song
Of elephop and telephong!)
Laura E. Richards

Humorous Poems

It is sometimes difficult to determine where nonsense poetry ends and humorous poetry begins. Humorous poetry, however, usually deals with the amusing predicaments in which realistic characters find themselves. Quite often an animal with human qualities is used as the focal character in a slapstick situation or droll setting. Such humor is not only entertaining, but it is also motivating and serves as an effective tool for teaching concepts. It has a way of showing us our own wise and foolish behavior.

One of the most familiar writers of humorous poetry is A. A. Milne. His "Puppy and I" is excellent for reading aloud to children at all grade levels:

[16]Copyright 1930, 1932 by Laura E. Richards. From *Tirra Lirra* by Laura Richards. Reprinted by permission of Little, Brown and Co.

PUPPY AND I[17]

I met a Man as I went walking;
We got talking,
Man and I.
"Where are you going to, Man?" I said
  (I said to the Man as he went by).
"Down to the village, to get some bread.
  Will you come with me?" "No, not I."

I met a Horse as I went walking;
We got talking,
Horse and I.
"Where are you going to, Horse, today?"
  (I said to the Horse as he went by).
"Down to the village to get some hay.
  Will you come with me?" "No, not I."

I met a Woman as I went walking;
We got talking,
Woman and I.
"Where are you going to, Woman, so early?"
  (I said to the Woman as she went by).
"Down to the village to get some barley.
  Will you come with me?" "No, not I."

I met some Rabbits as I went walking;
We got talking,
Rabbits and I.
"Where are you going in your brown fur coats?"
  (I said to the Rabbits as they went by).
"Down to the village to get some oats.
  Will you come with us?" "No, not I."

I met a Puppy as I went walking;
We got talking,
Puppy and I.
"Where are you going this nice fine day?"
  (I said to the Puppy as he went by).
"Up in the hills to roll and play."
  "*I'll* come with you, Puppy," said I.
                                    A. A. Milne

Humorous poems are to be found in almost
every poetry collection. Poems by John Ciardi,
for example, are often reprinted because they

conjure up happy mental images for the reader
or listener:

THE MAN THAT LIVED IN A BOX[18]

I met a man that lived in a box
His wig was as red as the tail of a fox
His nose was as long as a fishing rod
(A small one, you know). He grinned like a cod,
And nodded his head and looked about
When he popped the lid and came jumping out.
And he winked a wink when I put him back
And shut the lid and said, "Goodnight, Jack!"
                                    John Ciardi

Story Poems

Once children accept humorous poetry and are
at ease with it, the teacher may wish to move to
somewhat longer poems that tell a story. Verses
that weave a tale are suitable both in specific
content areas and in the literature program. The
three major types of poem that tell a story are
ballads, narrative poems, and lyrical poems.

Ballads Ballads are stories or songs in poetic
form that have been handed down from generation to generation by word of mouth. Most popular ballads have no known author. A wide range
of topics and emotions are presented in them.

Ballads are frequently incorporated into the
middle grade program, where students most enjoy their plot and theme. Well-known ballads
that have been used by language arts teachers for
many years include "Get Up and Bar the Door,"
"Robin Hood and Allan-a-Dale," and "The Ballad of William Sycamore." Ballads typically include rhythm, rhyme, a refrain, and a story line.

Narrative Poems Narrative poems do not have
the songlike qualities of ballads, but they do

[17]From *When We Were Very Young* by A. A. Milne. Copy-
right 1924 by E. P. Dutton; renewed © 1952 by A. A.
Milne. Reprinted by permission of the publishers, E. P.
Dutton.

[18]From *I Met a Man* by John Ciardi. Copyright © 1961 by
John Ciardi. Reprinted by permission of Houghton Mifflin
Company.

"Some Little Things"
by Geren McCroskey
Grade 4

Some little pups,
Will fit into cups.

Some little kittens,
Will fit into mittens.

Some little rats,
Will fit into cats!

Some children prefer to write rhyming poetry, as illustrated by this trio of humorous couplets. (Courtesy of Geren McCroskey.)

relate a specific event or episode in verse. For the younger child, there are two masterpieces known throughout the world—"A Visit from St. Nicholas" by Clement C. Moore and "The Pied Piper of Hamelin" by Robert Browning. Moore's traditional Christmas poem introduced children to the image of Santa Claus in a red and white suit and to a sleigh pulled by eight reindeer. "The Pied Piper of Hamelin" was made popular by Kate Greenaway's illustrated edition and is often reprinted in language arts textbooks. Other narrative poems enjoyed by younger children include "The King's Breakfast" by A. A. Milne, "The Monkey and the Crocodile" by Laura E. Richards, "Custard the Dragon" by Ogden Nash, and "The Lost Zoo" by Countee Cullen.

For older students, there are numerous narrative poems that range from humorous to serious: "Paul Revere's Ride" by Henry Wadsworth Longfellow, "The Shooting of Dan McGrew" by Robert Service, "Abraham Lincoln" by Rosemary and Stephen Vincent Benét, and "Casey at the Bat" by Ernest Lawrence Thayer.

Lyrical Verse   Lyrical poetry, from the word "lyric" (meaning suitable for singing or set to music), sings its way into the mind of the reader or listener. A number of outstanding poets have written lyric poetry for children—Eve Merriam, Harry Behn, Walter de la Mare, Eleanor Farjeon. Lyric poetry need not be old or traditional, and it need not tell a story; it simply has a musical quality and a certain subjectivity that touches the reader or listener. Lyric poetry creates a more definite mood than narrative forms. Langston Hughes, in his poem "Snail," has created musical lines that elicit an emotional response:

SNAIL[19]

Little snail,
Dreaming you go.
Weather and rose
Is all you know.

Weather and rose
Is all you see,
Drinking
The dewdrop's
Mystery.

Langston Hughes

Special Verse Forms

Many genres are not only fascinating to children, but are also structured in such a way that the

[19]From *Selected Poems of Langston Hughes* by Langston Hughes. Copyright 1947 by Langston Hughes. Reprinted by permission of Alfred A. Knopf, Inc.

teacher can help individual students find a style to express their own ideas. Kenneth Koch, a highly creative teacher and poet, rejects some of the traditional ideas about writing poetry. He prefers to organize children's poetry around "formal devices which are more natural to children, more inspiring, easier to use."[20] According to Koch, procedures used to develop poetic writing should be appropriate to the maturity level of the child. Poetry writing should not impose constraints on children that prevent them from developing a feeling for such an intensely personal kind of writing. Special verse forms that children may use in their own personal writing are couplets, quatrains, haiku, cinquain, and concrete poetry.

Couplets Couplets, a basic form of rhymed verse, are two successive lines with the same meter and rhyme scheme. With the teacher's aid, the writing of couplets can both enhance children's language skills and remain a positive personal experience. David McCord's *Take Sky* contains many examples of the couplet; one is a couplet *on* couplets:

A couplet is two lines—two lines in rhyme
The first one comes easy, the second may take time.[21]

Quatrains A quatrain is four lines of verse. Quatrains are often used in the stanzas of songs and poems. They may be introduced in the primary grades as a sort of mathematical problem in which children try to identify the different rhyme scheme possibilities—*aabb, abab, abcd, aaba*, and so forth. Quatrains are especially appropriate for classroom writing experiences:

[20]Kenneth Koch, *Wishes, Lies, and Dreams: Teaching Children to Write Poetry* (New York: Vintage Books, 1971), p. 8.
[21]Copyright David McCord 1952. Used by permission.

MONDAY NIGHT

Meredith's decked out; (A)
His clean hair shines, (B)
And Cosell's about (A)
To deliver his lines. (B)

Haiku Haiku is a Japanese verse form. It is a lyric poem containing only three lines. Haiku is unrhymed and paints a small, vivid picture, usually of a scene in nature. Children, like other poets, enjoy writing haiku about the sun shining on a river, the crash of thunder, an industrious ant, a frog jumping into a silent pond, the first signs of summer—any experience in nature that has made an impression on them.

True Japanese haiku has exactly seventeen syllables arranged in the following pattern:

- 5 syllables in the first line
- 7 syllables in the second line
- 5 syllables in the third line

An old silent pond . . .
A frog jumps into the pond,
splash! Silence again.
Basho

This simple form is difficult to create. Teachers encouraging children to write haiku should not overemphasize the syllable count. It is more important that children be aware of the emotions, moods, and feelings of the stanza than that they crank out seventeen syllables.

With practice and experience, children usually come to treasure this poetry form. There are many beautifully illustrated books of haiku that might be included in the elementary library collection. They include works by the classical poets Basho, Issa, and Buson.

Here are two other examples of haiku, including one *about* haiku:

A dewdrop fades away:
It's dirty, this world and in it
There's no place for me
Issa

Good haiku need thought:
One simple statement followed
By poet's comment.
            David McCord[22]

Cinquain Cinquain is the American counterpart of haiku. It is a five-line unrhymed stanza containing twenty syllables arranged in the following pattern:

- 2 syllables in the first line
- 4 syllables in the second line
- 6 syllables in the third line
- 8 syllables in the fourth line
- 2 syllables in the fifth line

The first line in a cinquain poem forms the title. The second line contains two words that describe the title. The third line is three words that express the action of the poem's subject. The fourth line has four words that express feeling or emotion about the subject. For emphasis, the first letter of each line is capitalized. Here are two examples of cinquain written by children (notice that these lyric verses meet some but not all of the requirements of formal cinquain):

            Puppy
            Fluffy ball
            Frisking, wagging, jumping
            Partner and a pal
            Pet.

            Deer
            Sleek, graceful
            Running and leaping
            Happy to be free
            Buck.

Concrete Poetry Children seem to be very fond of concrete poetry. In concrete poems the words are arranged in the shape of the topic. Concrete poems have been "written" about such diverse topics as skyscrapers, pollution, trains, fire hy-

[22]Copyright David McCord 1952. Used by permission of Holt, Rinehart and Winston.

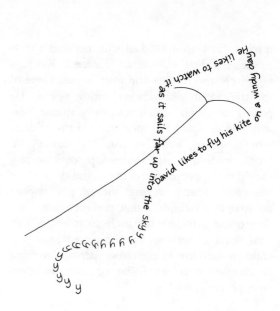

This concrete poem takes the shape of a kite "as it sails far up into the sky." (From Poems Make Pictures, *by Giose Rimanelli and Paul Pimsleur, illustrated by Ronni Solbert. Copyright © 1972 by Giose Rimanelli and Paul Pimsleur. Copyright © 1972 by Ronni Solbert. Reprinted by permission of Pantheon Books, a division of Random House, Inc.)*

drants, and windshield wipers. The literary merits of these poems may be dubious to some, but children enjoy them because they are fun to construct.

A word of caution: Children may become so involved with the picture that they forget about the words, feelings, and emotions. For this reason, the poem should be written before it is arranged into a "concrete" shape.

Using Poetry in the Classroom

Many teachers find it difficult to know how to organize a study of poetry, but as they become familiar with some of the most respected poets and with the types of verse enjoyed by most children, the prospect of teaching poetry becomes less daunting. Poetry programs may be organized in a variety of ways. We will discuss three general approaches, and then we will describe specific activities to be used in the classroom to lead children to have a positive attitude toward poetry.

Study Units

A poetry study unit is a two- or three-week block of time in the language arts program that concentrates on different verse forms, individual poets, or specific elements of poetry. The study unit usually includes a variety of activities ranging from choral reading to poetry writing. The unit should give the teacher and class members frequent opportunities to read poems aloud, to write their own poems, and to become involved in other interesting experiences with poetry and poets. It is suggested that every elementary language arts program contain at least one strong poetry study unit each year.

Mini-Units

Because poetry is so compressed, it is ideally suited for mini-units. Many elementary teachers periodically set aside a day or two for poetry-sharing activities. These brief sessions may be used to enrich a content area topic or to emphasize a special event such as a holiday or festival.

Since poetry study draws on all language arts skills, it may be used to complement any unit of study. The authors of most language arts textbooks for children incorporate poetry into at least one thematic unit of study. They also use poetry to promote other language activities such as creative writing or literature study. Thus, mini-units make possible a periodic exposure to poetry throughout the school year, even in programs that are predominantly textbook oriented.

The Daily Poetry Habit

Every elementary teacher should have poems available for occasions when the class completes an assignment earlier than expected, when a lesson plan goes astray, or when a spontaneous teaching situation arises.[23] At other times, a poem might be a good means of capturing the attention of the class or of setting a mood. Many teachers develop the "poetry habit" during their college years by starting a poetry file box. Such a file should be enlarged as the teacher becomes more knowledgeable about poetry for children.

Activities for Students

Activities carefully selected to enhance poetry can promote a wider reading and deeper appreciation of poetry. No experience should be allowed, however, that detracts from poetry or distorts the poems in any way. The following activities are examples of ways to enrich and enhance the poetry curriculum.

Making an Anthology of Verse Children may be motivated to read and listen to poetry by writing or collecting poems and grouping them in books that they make for themselves. The poems may be written by individual class members, gathered from the works of favorite poets, or both. The assembled poems are organized into a mimeographed booklet with construction paper covers.

Whenever such anthologies are created, they should be displayed in a prominent location for all to enjoy. Some teachers include them in the library collection to be checked out like any other book.

Poetry Pocket Charts The use of pocket charts made by the teacher may encourage each child

[23]Stephanie Gray, *Teaching Poetry Today* (Portland, Maine: J. Weston Walch Publishers, 1976), p. 3.

Beatrice Schenk de Regniers's line "Keep a poem in your pocket" is the title of this pocket chart. After reading a poem, the student places in the pocket a small card with the poem's title. (Courtesy of Dolly Wallace.)

to read poetry. Such charts ordinarily feature a motivating title or quotation and include a pocket to hold a card noting the poems each child has read. The title of each poem read by a student is written on the card and filed in the pocket. The filling of poetry pockets is an ongoing way to sustain interest in poetry and provides information that may be passed along to parents.

Choral Reading   The success of choral reading is directly related to the appropriateness of the selection and to the teacher's approach. Properly presented, choral reading is a creative and rewarding way to dramatize poetry with the entire class and share it with groups outside the classroom (see pages 267–272).

Listening to Recordings of Popular Poems   Poetry read aloud by well-known poets or other professionals is available on both records and cassette tapes. Children who have the opportunity to hear poets interpret their own poems are

bound to grow in their own understanding and appreciation of poetry.

Discovering Musical Versions of Poetry   Students are often amazed to discover that many songs are really poems set to music. In fact, some popular songs may be read aloud as a means to improve poetry awareness. The language arts teacher may also wish to select certain poems to be set to music.

Poet-of-the-Month Displays   Some language arts classrooms contain a number of poetry centers, one of which focuses on a different poet each month. The center should include a picture of the poet, a collection of the poet's books, and recordings of selected poems. The teacher may introduce the display each month with a discussion of the poet and an explanation of the various materials focusing on his or her life and work.

"Phoetry"   The term *phoetry* is a word coined from "photography" and "poetry."[24] It refers to a project in which children enliven their poetry with original photographs. Poems may be illustrated with Instamatic or Polaroid pictures and bound into a booklet made by students.

Inviting Poets to the Classroom   Almost every community has at least one person who writes poetry or records local lore in verse form. Such persons are usually willing to share their secrets about the craft of writing poetry. If the elementary school is located near a college or university, a faculty member trained in poetry reading might be invited to read favorite poems.

Ballad Maps   An interesting project for advanced students is the production of a ballad map. Groups of students may be challenged to produce a large map of a state, country, or continent and pinpoint the origin of folktales, songs,

[24]Julius F. Schillinger, "Phoetry," *Teacher* (March 1977), pp. 48–49.

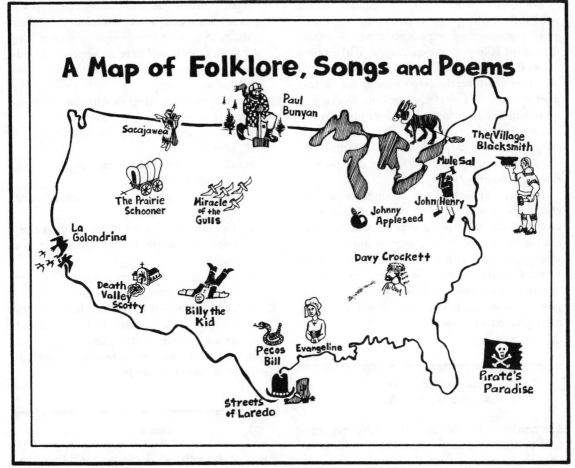

A Map of Folklore, Songs and Poems

Sacajawea

Paul Bunyan

The Village Blacksmith

Mule Sal

The Prairie Schooner

Miracle of the Gulls

John Henry

Johnny Appleseed

La Golondrina

Davy Crockett

Death Valley Scotty

Billy the Kid

Pecos Bill

Evangeline

Pirate's Paradise

Streets of Laredo

A sketch of a folktale map for the classroom bulletin board. Legends, tales, songs, and poems may be added near their place of origin as research and study reveal them to students. (Courtesy of Barbara Ellis.)

and poems. Expository paragraphs may accompany the map, which should be mounted at eye level in the library for passersby to read and enjoy.

Encouraging Children to Write Poetry

The writing of poetry by children is usually considered an integral part of the language arts program in the elementary classroom. It is safe to conclude, however, that one of the major barriers to a positive attitude toward poetry is the children's fear of failing in the difficult task of writing verse. Therefore, more important than the instructional approach used by the teacher is the classroom environment, which should not only promote poetry but invite children to develop some of their own.[25]

[25]Virginia Witucke, *Literature for Children: Poetry in the Elementary Classroom* (Dubuque, Iowa: Wm. C. Brown, 1970), p. 106.

Elementary students may be guided toward writing their own personal poetry by the use of *group* poetry-writing experiences, which reduce the risk of failure by the individual. If the poem is less than successful, it becomes a problem for the group to solve; the responsibility for success does not rest on a single girl or boy. Working in groups also causes children to share ideas and to interact with each other as they explore language, words, and poetic forms. It stimulates discussions in which every child can take pride in making a contribution.

Another way to help reduce students' anxiety about poetry writing is to have children write poems based on a specified pattern or formula. On the surface this may appear to diminish creativity, yet most poets do follow conventional forms. Children are more likely to appreciate the opportunity to write their own verse if they are given specific guidelines, and they are usually more pleased with the results.

Evaluating Poetry Written by Children

The teacher's method of evaluating poetry created by children directly affects their willingness to continue writing verse. Such evaluations constitute one of the most difficult tasks confronting the language arts teacher. The teacher seeks to sustain students' interest while at the same time improving their performance. John Warren Stewig has devised the following guidelines for evaluating poetry written by children:

1. Make no negative comments directly on the poems written by children. Instead, use a simple coding system indicating a plus sign next to those lines that are particularly effective and a question mark next to those lines that don't seem to fit.
2. Have students form into groups and ask them to critique their own poetry. This ap-

proach should be used when young poets have developed some confidence in their ability. Structure the groups in such a way that each poem will have some positive feedback, as well as the identification of problem areas.
3. Develop a series of questions that students can use to evaluate their own poetry
   a. Is the subject, topic, or theme appropriate?
   b. Do the words convey meaning, thought, or emotion?
   c. Is there insight into the object or event being described?
   d. Does the poem seem to follow the guidelines and directions established at the outset?
   e. Does the poem express sincere feelings from the writer?
4. Encourage students to publish their own poetry. This can be accomplished by means of a school newsletter to parents, a school newspaper, or mimeographed poetry anthologies collected by students.[26]

Summary

Poetry is a special kind of children's literature, and it should hold a special place in each elementary language arts classroom. The successful poetry program consists of both organized and spontaneous experiences with various verse forms. The organized portion of the poetry program consists of planned units and organized activities; the spontaneous part depends on the teacher's ability to present the right poem at the "teachable moment."

Poetry may be used to personalize the language arts program. Children are encouraged to

[26]John Warren Stewig, *Read to Write: Using Children's Literature as a Springboard to Writing* (New York: Hawthorn Books, 1975), pp. 214–215.

write their own poems, to read poetry aloud, and to participate in other poetry-related experiences that appeal to them personally and are at their level of readiness.

This chapter focused on elements of excellence in poetry, types of poetry enjoyed by children, and methods of using a variety of poems in the classroom. Many sources of poetry were listed and discussed including general anthologies, subject anthologies, and single poems. We think children should become acquainted not only with poetry, but also with creators of poetry and we discussed many fine poets from both the past and present. One section was devoted to ways in which children might be taught to write some poetry of their own. Specific guidelines were given for developing both long- and short-term poetry units.

Best Books for Children

The Bat Poet, written by Randall Jarrell and illustrated by Maurice Sendak. New York: Macmillan, 1967. The story of a little brown bat who couldn't sleep days and thus began to see the world differently. It is both a delightful animal fantasy and a commentary on the writing of poetry. Randall Jarrell's poems are as unusual and creative as the story itself. (P,M,U)

A Book of Americans, written by Rosemary and Stephen Vincent Benét and illustrated by Charles Child. New York: Holt, Rinehart and Winston, 1933. A collection of fifty-five narrative poems suitable for older elementary students. "Nancy Hanks" and "Abraham Lincoln" are traditional favorites; many others are useful in the social studies classroom. (M,U)

Chicken Soup with Rice, written and illustrated by Maurice Sendak. New York: Scholastic Book Services, 1962. A book of months written in verse form. Primary grade children anxiously await the first day of the new month when the teacher reads aloud the appropriate poem from Sendak's popular book. An interesting follow-up activity is the cooking of chicken soup with rice. (P)

The City . . . in Haiku, written by A. K. Roche. Englewood Cliffs, N.J.: Prentice-Hall, 1970. Emotional and sensitive photographs related to city life are carefully matched to classical haiku poetry. Such a unique collection of poems should appeal to the interests of older students. (M,U)

Favorite Poems by Dorothy Aldis, written by Dorothy Aldis. New York: Putnam, 1970. After the death of Dorothy Aldis, her publisher compiled some of her most popular poems. The poems center on everyday experiences and family relationships. (P,M)

Hailstones and Halibut Bones, written by Mary O'Neil and illustrated by Leonard Weisgard. Garden City, N.Y.: Doubleday, 1961. A book of color poems as well suited to science and art activities as to language arts instruction. Excellent for reading aloud. (P,M,U)

Hey, Bug! and Other Poems About Little Things, selected by Elizabeth Itse and illustrated by Susan Carlton Smith. New York: American Heritage Press, 1972. Thirty poems by well-known poets are included in a trade book that might be used as part of a science unit or simply read aloud at the appropriate time. The illustrations help to make this mini-anthology a classroom treasure. (P,M)

I Am the Darker Brother: An Anthology of Modern Poems by Black Americans, edited by Arnold Adoff and illustrated by Alvin Hollingsworth. New York: Macmillan, 1970. This anthology contains some of the best-known poems of Langston Hughes, Gwendolyn Brooks, Countee Cullen, and other talented black poets. The poems in this collection convey the feelings, moods, and attitudes of black Americans in a number of situations and settings. (M,U)

. . . I Never Saw Another Butterfly, written and illustrated by the children from the Terezin concentration camp between 1942 and 1944. New York: McGraw-Hill, 1964. The drawings and poems of children (all under the age of fifteen) portray the atrocities of war. In a combination of word and image, one sees not only the daily misery of these uprooted children but also the courage and optimism that is inherent in their faith. (U)

It Doesn't Always Have to Rhyme, written by Eve Merriam. New York: Atheneum, 1964. Eve Merriam uses her own poems to illustrate literary terms such as "simile," "homonym," "metaphor," "cliché," and "limerick." By using this popular book, students in the middle elementary grades can be guided toward the writing of verse. (M)

Now We Are Six, written by A. A. Milne and illustrated by Ernest Shepard. New York: Dutton, 1927. The two poetry books written by A. A. Milne, *When We Were Very Young* and *Now We Are Six,* continue to share an undiminished popularity with younger students. In this collection, Christopher Robin verbalizes the imaginative thoughts of children aged four to six. (P)

One at a Time, written by David McCord. Boston: Little, Brown, 1977. This anthology is the complete David McCord collection. All of the poems that were first published in *Far and Few, Take Sky, All Day Long, For Me to Say,* and *Away and Ago* are reprinted in this volume, which should be considered a necessity for every elementary school library and language arts classroom. (M,U)

Out Loud, written by Eve Merriam and illustrated by Harriet Sherman. New York: Atheneum, 1973. This unusual collection of modern poems about everyday objects and experiences emphasizes sound. The illustrations, line drawings, and titles give it a unique visual appeal to younger readers. (P,M)

Oxford Book of Poetry, compiled by Edward Blishen and illustrated by Brian Wildsmith. New York: Franklin Watts, 1963. Of the many anthologies for middle and upper elementary students, this collection is one of the most popular. It contains both traditional and contemporary poems that children enjoy, and the Wildsmith illustrations entice even the most reluctant poetry reader. (P,M,U)

Peter Piper's Alphabet, written and illustrated by Marcia Brown. New York: Scribner, 1979. Sounds of the alphabet are represented by famous old tonguetwister nursery rhymes. The pictures are filled with fun and foolishness to be enjoyed by children and adults alike. (P)

Poems, written by Rachel Field. New York: Macmillan, 1957. Primary grade children will instantly recognize the delightful imagery found in Rachel Field's poems. Her book includes selections from *The*

Pointed People (1924) and *Taxis and Toadstools* (1926). Familiar poems such as "Skyscrapers," "Taxis," "City Rain," and "Snow in the City" are contained in this collection. Many of the poems are known by teachers because of their frequent inclusion in language arts textbooks and poetry anthologies. (P,M)

Poems Children Will Sit Still For: A Selection for the Primary Grades, compiled by Beatrice Schenk de Regniers, Eva Moore, and Mary Michaels White. New York: Scholastic Book Services, 1969. Each of the 106 poems has been selected on the basis of the individual preferences of several well-known poets. The poems are grouped into categories such as fun, rhythm, numbers, and letters. For many of the poems, suggestions are offered for reading aloud, audience participation, and class discussion. (P)

Poems Make Pictures, Pictures Make Poems, written by Giose Rimanelli and Paul Pimsleur. New York: Pantheon, 1971. A marvelous picture book collection of simple poems arranged as visual puzzles. Words in the shape of objects such as an umbrella, a whale, and rain splattering on a house help to create the poetic image. This unique approach to the fun and pleasure of poetry might serve as an introduction to concrete poetry. (M,U)

Reflections on a Gift of Watermelon Pickle ... and Other Modern Verse, compiled by Stephen Dunning, Edward Lueders, and Hugh Smith. Glenview, Ill.: Scott, Foresman, 1966. Most of the poems in this anthology appeal to older students. This collection is illustrated by superb photographs, and it is available in paperback with an accompanying record. (U)

See My Lovely Poison Ivy: And Other Poems About Witches, Ghosts, and Things, written by Lillian Moore and illustrated by Diane Dawson. New York: Atheneum, 1975. A poetry anthology on a variety·of subjects that children enjoy is created by Lillian Moore's special talent. Children in the primary grades will enjoy these poems at Halloween time. (P,M)

Something Special, written by Beatrice Schenk de Regniers and illustrated by Irene Haas. New York: Harcourt Brace Jovanovich, 1958. A collection of original poems for children in the primary grades, including the popular "Keep a Poem in Your Pocket." (P,M)

Street Poems, written by Robert Froman. New York: McCall, 1971. Concrete poems are contained in this collection about street scenes—skyscrapers, vacant lots, street lamps, and billboards. Reluctant poetry readers will find these picture poems an inspiration to further reading and writing. (M,U)

Time for Poetry, 3d general edition, edited by May Hill Arbuthnot and Shelton L. Root, Jr., and illustrated by Arthur Paul. Glenview, Ill.: Scott, Foresman, 1968. With over seven hundred poems by poets ranging from Mother Goose to T. S. Eliot, this is probably the most comprehensive anthology of children's poetry available for the language arts classroom. Though somewhat dated, it contains many popular traditional and modern poems. The conclusion of the book contains some excellent suggestions for a classroom poetry program, and useful teaching notes are presented along with the individual poems. (P,M,U)

The Way Things Are and Other Poems, written by Myra Cohn Livingston and illustrated by Jenni Oliver. New York: Atheneum, 1974. Simple poems written from the perspective of a child are presented by a well-known poet. Not only has this talented writer edited children's poetry anthologies (*Listen Children, Listen* and *A Tune Beyond Us*), Myra Cohn Livingston makes it clear that she understands the poetry preferences of younger children. (P,M)

Where the Sidewalk Ends, written and illustrated by Shel Silverstein. New York: Harper & Row, 1974. Children of all ages enjoy the humorous poetry of Shel Silverstein. His poems tell stories of amusing animals and people who find themselves in the kind of absurd situations very familiar to children. (P,M,U)

You Read to Me, I'll Read to You, written by John Ciardi and illustrated by Edward Gorey. Philadelphia: Lippincott, 1962. Every other poem in this collection uses only a basic first-grade vocabulary. On the opposite page is a poem suitable for an adult to read to a child. For additional contrast, the poems are printed in two colors—one for the child and one for the adult. (P)

Bibliography

Arnstein, Flora. *Poetry in the Elementary Classroom.* New York: Appleton-Century-Crofts, 1962.

Boyd, Gertrude A. *Teaching Poetry in the Elementary School.* Columbus: Charles E. Merrill, 1973.

Gray, Stephanie. *Teaching Poetry Today.* Portland, Maine: J. Weston Walch, Publishers, 1976.

Hopkins, Lee Bennett. *Pass the Poetry Please!* New York: Citation Press, 1972.

Kimzey, Ardis. *To Defend a Form: The Romance of Administration and Teaching in a Poetry-in-the-Schools Program.* New York: Teachers & Writers, 1977.

Koch, Kenneth. *Rose, Where Did You Get That Red? Teaching Great Poetry to Children.* New York: Random House, 1973.

———. *Wishes, Lies, and Dreams: Teaching Children to Write Poetry.* New York: Vintage Books, 1971.

Larrick, Nancy, ed. *Somebody Turned on a Tap in These Kids: Poetry and Young People Today.* New York: Dell, 1972.

Livingston, Myra Cohn. *When You Are Alone It Keeps You Capone: An Approach to Creative Writing with Children.* New York: Atheneum, 1973.

Painter, Helen W. *Poetry and Children.* Newark, Del.: International Reading Association, 1970.

Schillinger, Julius F. "Phoetry." *Teacher,* March 1977.

Smith, James A., and Dorothy M. Park. *Word Music and Word Magic.* Boston: Allyn and Bacon, 1977.

Stewig, John Warren. *Read to Write: Using Children's Literature as a Springboard to Writing.* New York: Hawthorn Books, 1975.

Sutherland, Zena, and May Hill Arbuthnot. *Children and Books,* 5th ed. Glenview, Ill.: Scott, Foresman, 1977.

Terry, Ann. *Children's Poetry Preferences: National Survey of Upper Elementary Grades.* Urbana, Ill.: National Council of Teachers of English, 1974.

Witucke, Virginia. *Literature for Children: Poetry in the Elementary School.* Dubuque, Iowa: Wm. C. Brown, 1970.

Chapter 12

"Open Sez Me":
Creative Dramatics and Children's Books

OPEN SEZ ME, a play written by students, reveals many things about its young authors. Only girls and boys who have had the opportunity to participate in many creative dramatizations of literature are capable of devising or appreciating a satirical title of this kind. They have moved through several developmental stages of experiencing literature, progressing from being read to and having stories told them, to creating literature of their own—in this case by the retelling and updating of the classic tale "Ali Baba and the Forty Thieves." Their play reveals an understanding of both literature and play-acting that promises to bring them pleasure for many years to come.

In order to comprehend and fully appreciate the literature they read daily, children must be given opportunity and encouragement to respond to that literature in ways that have meaning for them *as children*. They need to talk about a story, write about it, depict it in art, act it out, and become involved in other activities that challenge them to interpret and synthesize. As a result of such responding, students internalize a story's mood and meaning, become acquainted with characters that often become lifelong friends, and move toward a deeper involvement with literature in general.

Dramatic interpretation of literature in the elementary classroom may be experienced in a wide variety of ways, four of which we will discuss in this chapter—story-acting, puppetry, readers theatre, and choral speaking. These four methods of dramatizing literature are practical and easy to stage; they communicate effectively with an audience of the performers' peers; and they require a minimum of props or costumes. They also happen to be dramatic activities highly favored by children.

Children's faces reveal how they feel about a well-performed dramatic presentation by their peers. (Courtesy of Lamar University.)

informal and spontaneous manner, there is a fair amount of structure in its planning and evaluation. Basically, there are eight sequential steps to be considered in the successful dramatization of a piece of literature:

1. The teacher selects a story that has lively action, several characters who speak and do things, imaginative use of language, and a phrase or passage that is repeated throughout.

2. The story is carefully prepared by the teacher for reading aloud or storytelling. On several different occasions it is shared with the students until they become well acquainted with its characterization, language, and plot.

3. In a follow-up discussion, the teacher uses provocative questions to clarify the story's concepts; to sharpen awareness of characterization, theme, and plot; and to emphasize the colorful language. Any procedure that aids comprehension of the story will in turn improve the quality of the dramatization.

4. Students either volunteer for the various parts, or they are assigned roles by the teacher. When the first dramatization of a

Story-acting

Although story-acting as a principal feature of children's creative dramatics is carried out in an

Children participating in creative dramatics may better understand and synthesize the meaning of literature. (Courtesy of Caldwood School, South Park Independent School District, Beaumont, Texas.)

tive evaluation with an eye toward improving succeeding productions. Generally, this appraisal is directed by the teacher, who is in a position to circumvent negative criticism that has a way of creating self-conscious performances in future attempts.

Many kinds of literature are suitable for story-acting, but nothing surpasses the folk tale. These familiar old stories have survived through the ages because they lend themselves well to an oral presentation. Storytellers have shortened, changed, improvised, and honed the tales until they have reached a nearly perfect state of compactness and simplicity, wasting not a single word. True folk tales are not only easy to read and easy to tell, but they are highly entertaining and perfect for dramatizing. The stories themselves, as well as the activities that relate to them, will be remembered when other school activities have long since been forgotten.

story is being cast, plans are made for repeat performances to include several new sets of actors.

5. The cast for the initial performance is given a brief period of time in which to organize scenes to be reenacted and to rehearse the action and dialogue. If the practice session can be held in private, the suspense is heightened and the play holds more enjoyment for its audience.

6. Time is provided for the cast or for a special crew to prepare simple props and costumes. The younger the children, the fewer the props that will be needed. A paper crown, a label pinned on, or a simple mask can transform a young child. On the other hand, older students prefer and can handle a more elaborate production.

7. The play is performed before an audience of the actors' peers, who are prepared to listen with attention, courtesy, and appreciation—fellow actors who anticipate their own roles in similar productions.

8. The performance is followed by a construc-

One of the most successful author-illustrators to rewrite folk tales for modern children is Margot Zemach. The humorous characters, lively action, and rollicking language have made her works favorites for storytelling, readers theatre, story-acting, puppetry, and other forms of drama. A collection of books by Margot Zemach, housed in the school or classroom library, will be a great asset to the teacher who routinely dramatizes literature as part of the language arts curriculum.

To Hilda for Helping, one of Margot Zemach's modern stories, is based on an incident in Zemach's own family. Hilda's father rewards her with a badge for helpfulness and good behavior. She wears it day and night, much to the annoyance of her sisters, who are not so helpful or well behaved. The only props needed to turn this story into a classroom production are some simple badges with suitable accolades printed on them. A dramatization of *To Hilda* could turn out to be the most enjoyable form of behavior modification a child ever encounters.

A Profile of Margot Zemach

IN EXPRESSING HER VIEWS on what it takes to make an effective book illustration for children, Margot Zemach has said:

> The modern trend of oversimplification is impossible; it's merely foisting the designer's ideas on children. Children are fascinated by detail. Take a child to the zoo and you may well find that amid all the exotic beasts, it's the pigeon walking around the child's feet that catches the attention. In the most elaborate picture, the chances are that what gives special delight is a little fly or a dropped glove.[1]

This basic understanding of what it takes to capture a child's imagination accounts for the intricate detail in Margot Zemach's illustrations and the lasting appeal her books hold for children.

Margot Zemach was born in 1931 in Los Angeles and spent her early childhood with her grandparents in Oklahoma City. Her stepfather, Benjamin Zemach, was a professional dancer and theatre director. He had come to America from Russia in 1927 with the famed Habima Hebrew Theatre Company. At age five Margot went to live with her mother, an actress, and her stepfather in New York City. For the next several years, her life was dominated by the theatrical activities of her parents. She fondly remembers going to museums, attending many plays and concert recitals, and playing with costumes from her stepfather's theatrical productions.

Because of her family's itinerant life-style, Zemach became something of a loner. Drawing caricatures was a favorite pastime. In them she portrayed the life around her: "The 'cartoons' were paintings and drawings of New York," she says. "Whatever I saw I drew, and I also made pictures to illustrate fairy tales I knew—which is probably how 'illustrators' begin, early in life with a need to make pictures of life, real and imagined."

In 1949, Zemach's stepfather took a position in Hollywood, and the family moved to the West Coast. The move to California during the 1950s had unpleasant ramifications for the Zemach family. It was the McCarthy era. Because of Benjamin Zemach's Russian birth and the notion of guilt by association, he was blacklisted in Hollywood. During those troubled times Margot Zemach began her professional art training at the Los Angeles County Art Institute and promptly lost her scholarship because she refused to take a loyalty oath.

In 1955 Margot Zemach reached an important milestone in her career and in her personal life. She won a Fulbright scholarship to study in Austria at the Vienna Academy of Fine Arts. On her first night in Vienna, she met Harve Fischtrom, "who," she recalls, "was a Fulbright student in the History of Ideas. . . . It didn't seem a very likely thing to either of us at the time, but from that day on, we spent the next eighteen years together."

Margot Zemach photo by Dan Robbin. (Courtesy of Farrar, Straus & Giroux, Inc.)
[1] A. L. Lloyd, "Margot Zemach," *Horn Book* (August 1974), p. 362.

On returning home from Vienna, Margot and Harve settled in Cambridge, Massachusetts, while Harve was a graduate student at Brandeis University. Their first child, Kaethe, was born in 1958, and during that same year Margot and Harve created their first children's book, *Small Boy Is Listening,* set in Vienna:

> We made our first children's book out of pure necessity and hope. Harve was a student and neither of us was well qualified for any but the poorest-paid jobs. I had already failed as a file clerk, messenger, salesgirl, and usherette—I was a receptionist who frowned. Now, in addition to being economically incompetent, we were parents; so we put together our first children's book, and luckily we sold it. This gave us a few hundred dollars, and it gave me unbounded faith that we could surely do it again and that in this way we could help to support a family which was growing.[2]

As a team Margot and Harve Zemach became highly successful in adapting and illustrating folk tales from many parts of the world—*The Speckled Hen* and *Salt* from Russia, *Nail Soup* from Sweden, *Too Much Nose* from Italy, and *Mommy, Buy Me a China Doll* and *Hush Little Baby* from the United States. In 1974, Margot won the Caldecott Medal for *Duffy and the Devil,* a Cornish tale retold by Harve and illustrated by Margot. It is a lively and humorous version of the Rumpelstiltskin story.

The Zemach team had completed fifteen books when Harve died in 1974. Margot and her four daughters now live in Berkeley, California, where she continues to write and illustrate children's books. She has never had a studio or a special place to paint, choosing instead to work in the living room with the children nearby giving her advice on how the characters should look. She considers her daughters her very best critics.

BOOKS ILLUSTRATED BY MARGOT ZEMACH

Small Boy Is Listening, 1958
Take a Giant Step, 1960
Can You Draw a Dog? A Hat with a Rose? 1961
The Three Sillies, 1963
Nail Soup, 1964
Salt: A Russian Tale, 1965
The Little Tiny Woman, 1965
The Question Box, 1965
The Tricks of Master Dabble, 1965
The Fisherman and His Wife, 1966
The King of the Hermits, 1966
Mommy, Buy Me a China Doll, 1966
The Speckled Hen: A Russian Nursery Rhyme, 1966
Mazel and Shlimazel or The Milk of a Lioness, 1967
Harlequin, 1968
When Shlemiel Went to Warsaw and Other Stories, 1968
The Judge, 1969
Fairy Tales Told in Denmark, 1970
Awake and Dreaming, 1970
Simon Boom Gives a Wedding, 1971
Alone in the Wild Forest, 1971

[2]Information provided by Zemach's publisher, Farrar, Strauss & Giroux, Inc.

Puppetry

One of the most famous books for children is the story of a puppet. First written in 1892 for the children of Italy, *Pinocchio* has long since been translated into all the major languages and is loved by boys and girls in every part of the world. Its author, Carlo Lorenzini, grew up in the rolling Tuscan hills of northern Italy. When he created the character of Pinocchio, he took as his *nom de plume* the name of the small village where his mother was born—Collodi.

To children, Pinocchio is more than a fictional character; he is a faithful friend with whom they can share their innermost feelings, their fears and hurts, their successes and failures. He experiences the same emotions as his readers, but with greater intensity. He helps children understand themselves. In the 1930s Paul Hazard, a children's literature scholar of world renown, wrote the following words in his small classic volume *Books, Children & Men:*

Young souls, still tender and unformed, in whom virtue is as yet only an instinct, in whom vices are as yet only faults, need help in asserting themselves. They are enraptured when they see and recognize themselves in a book. They see themselves as though in a mirror. Pinocchio is not bad; and if it were enough to have good intentions to be perfect, Pinocchio would be a paragon. But he is weak. He declares openly that we ought not to resist temptation because it is a waste of time. What he is forbidden to do is always a little more attractive than what he is ordered to do. Repentance follows close to sinning, but sinning follows close on repentance.[1]

Puppetry holds as much fascination for today's children as it did for their ancestors. When skillfully used in the classroom, it has the ability to entertain, teach, and inform. More importantly, it has a way of giving children insight into themselves and others.

No one knows who created the first puppet. In his book *The Art of the Puppet,* Bil Baird suggests that the first puppeteer may have been a priest who discovered that he could hinge the jaw of a religious mask and fool his peers into believing that the mask was alive. Another plausible explanation centers on the idea that someone observing a child at play with a doll had enough imagination to transform the toy into something more dramatic. At any rate, different cultures have created unique puppets for a vari-

[1]Paul Hazard, *Books, Children & Men* (Boston: *Horn Book,* 1944), p. 112. Used by permission.

Pinocchio has been translated into all the major languages of the world. Here it is shown in Greek and Italian, accompanied by a wooden replica from Collodi, Italy.

ety of reasons. For centuries, puppets have been used to entertain audiences, to educate people, and to make social commentary.

Small figures thought by archaeologists to be puppets have been found in Egyptian tombs that date back over three thousand years. Various stringed figures, thought to be the first mario-nettes, are mentioned in the writings of the ancient Greeks. Documents of some early Greek historians reveal that puppet shows were a form of entertainment as early as the fifth century B.C. Unfortunately, no written record has been preserved of the scripts from any of those first puppet performances. Even the early Christian church used puppetry in various religious rites.

The history of India, China, Japan, and other Asian countries suggests a penchant for puppetry. Japan still maintains an active classical puppet theatre near the city of Osaka. The origins of Japanese puppetry can be traced back to the *Rugutsu,* hunters who, during periods of rest, performed puppet shows from door to door.[2] This ancient form of puppetry became known as *Bunraku* (*bun* means "literature"; and *raku* means "pleasure"). The beauty and pageantry of traditional Japanese puppetry has made it a source of national pride in Japan.

[2]René Simmen, *The World of Puppets* (New York: Thomas Y. Crowell, 1972), pp. 72–74.

Each puppet representing a major character in a *Bunraku* puppet play is operated by three journeyman puppeteers. So much training is needed that twenty years of apprenticeship may pass before a puppeteer can become the main operator of a puppet. After attaining such high status, many puppeteers operate the same puppet for the rest of their lives.[3] Unlike American puppet performers, a *Bunraku* narrator tells the story and supplies all of the dialogue:

Making violent faces, expressing sorrow, the singer-narrator raises his voice as the drama requires. He cries along with the puppet, expressing the range of human feelings with incredible variety. Soon one gets the impression that these . . . emotions can almost enter the inanimate figure on the stage and that the human words come from the puppet's lips. It appears to talk and act humanly, in a mysterious and devilish manner.[4]

During the Middle Ages, puppetry became an important element of creative dramatics with its folk tales, stories of chivalry, and renditions of satirical comedy. The seeds of a puppeteering tradition were firmly planted; nearly every European country has a heritage of puppetry. Some of the best characterizations are *Punchinello* from Italy, *Petruchka* from Russia, *Kasper* from Germany, and *Punch and Judy* from England.

In parts of the world where television does not dominate people's entertainment, live theatrical productions continue to flourish in the form of opera, ballet, concert, theatre, and puppetry. America, unfortunately, has very few competent puppet performers who are associated with traveling companies. Even though their performances may be artistic and well appreciated by the small audiences who view them, traveling puppeteers in America are not well known. Only

A typical Sunday afternoon performance of Punchinello in Rome's Borghese Gardens. A widow in mourning joins the children as they watch the slapstick antics of Punch and his wife Judy.

those puppets who star in television productions become household names in the United States. The most widely known of this group include Edgar Bergen's Charlie McCarthy, Burr Tillstrom's Kuklapolitans, Shari Lewis's Lambchop, and Jim Henson's Muppets.

Types of Puppets

The word "puppet" embraces a wide variety of animated figures ranging from simple finger pup-

[3]Robert Ten Eyck Hanford, *The Complete Book of Puppets and Puppeteering* (New York: Drake Publishers, 1976), p. 18.
[4]Simmen, p. 73.

pets to complex marionettes. Children should participate in the creation of the simplest types before proceeding to the more complicated ones. In spite of literally hundreds of books and magazine articles about puppetry, the teacher may have trouble deciding which puppet form to use for a specific purpose with a particular class. We will briefly describe sixteen types suitable for classroom construction and use (see Figure 12.1).

Finger Puppets   A finger puppet is made by attaching facial features to a piece of construction paper, a bit of felt, or a strip of thin cardboard. The puppet is then placed on the index finger and held in position by means of a simple band or ring.

Fist Puppets   The bare hand can be used as the face of a puppet when the thumb is folded under the fingers and used as the movable lower jaw. The puppet's face is created by the imaginative use of washable colored markers or tempera paint.

Glove Puppets   To create a puppet on a glove, one or more of the fingertips of an inexpensive garden glove are decorated. To make the characteristics of the puppet interchangeable, a small piece of velcro may be attached to both the glove and the bodily feature. (Note: Any puppet that is placed over the hand or fist is considered to be a glove puppet. The most widely used glove puppet is the familiar sock puppet.)

Stick Puppets   Pictures of people, animals, toys, or other shapes may be collected from magazines and glued to a piece of oak tagboard. The stiffened shape is then taped or glued to a wooden stick or a plastic drinking straw.

Styrofoam Ball Puppets   The head of a puppet may be easily constructed by painting, pinning, or gluing objects on a ball of styrofoam. The completed head is fastened to a stick, and

Puppet Types

Figure 12.1   *Types of puppets. (Courtesy of Barbara Ellis.)*

clothes are made by draping a piece of cloth over the puppeteer's hand.

Rod Puppets   A rod puppet, similar to a stick puppet, has two or more parts that are attached to each other by means of a hinge, which allows freedom of movement. Animation is achieved by holding the puppet steady with one rod and manipulating the second for movement.

Box Puppets   Box puppets are made by fastening two small boxes together with a hinge in such a way that the openings of both boxes face toward the person holding them. The lower box becomes the mouth of the puppet, and the upper box becomes the head.

Paper Plate Puppets   A variation on the stick puppet is a paper plate decorated to become the

6. Rod Puppet

7. Box Puppet

8. Paper Plate Puppet

9. Sock Puppet

10. Paper Bag Puppet

11. Object Puppet

12. Mask Puppet

13. Board Puppet

14. String Puppet (Marionette)

15. Vegetable Puppet

face of a character. The decorated plate is attached to a stick or straw for handling.

Sock Puppets A sock puppet is created by inserting a folded piece of cardboard into the foot of a sock. When the puppeteer's hand is placed inside the sock, the mouth will open and close as the fingers are brought together over the cardboard.

Paper Bag Puppets A brown paper sack may be transformed into a person, animal, or book character by decorating the fold of the bag. Hair, eyes, clothing, and other features may be added by gluing to the sack colored pieces of construction paper, cloth, or other scrap materials.

Object Puppets A wide variety of objects may be transformed into puppets with a little imagi-

nation. Objects such as tin cans, egg cartons, or salt boxes can provide the starting point for many unique puppet forms.

Mask Puppets Practically any character from literature may be depicted by means of a mask. Students may make simple masks from cardboard painted appropriately and fastened around the head with a rubber band or string.

Board Puppets Board puppets, sometimes called "humanettes," are a variation of the comical puppets used years ago to entertain vaudeville audiences. The board puppet is a large cardboard cutout painted in the shape of a person, animal, or machine. Openings are left for the arms, legs, and face of the puppeteer.

String Puppets or Marionettes A marionette is

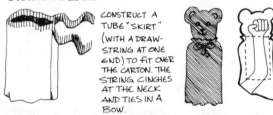

CUT EVENLY ALONG TOP EDGE OF CARTON. GOODWIN

MILK

PLACE INFLATED BALLOON SO THAT IT RESTS SOLIDLY ON THE CARTON'S CUT EDGE AND SECURE WITH MASKING TAPE.

APPLY 3 SOLID LAYERS OF PAPIER-MÂCHÉ STRIPS TO BALLOON AND CARTON TOP AND LET DRY. WHEN PASTE IS DRY, POP THE BALLOON AND CUT THE BOTTOM FROM THE CARTON.

APPLY FEATURES TO THE HEADS. DO THIS BY PAINTING FLAT FACES OR BUILDING DIMENSIONAL FEATURES WITH PAPIER-MÂCHÉ OVER CARDBOARD

CONSTRUCT A TUBE "SKIRT" (WITH A DRAW-STRING AT ONE END) TO FIT OVER THE CARTON. THE STRING CINCHES AT THE NECK AND TIES IN A BOW.

Figure 12.2 *Making papier-mâché puppets with milk cartons and balloons. (Courtesy of Barbara Ellis.)*

a complex figure with hinged body parts that are attached by strings to a control stick. This type of puppet requires both skill and practice to create and operate. It is usually considered too complicated for young children to operate, although they love marionette performances staged by older students.

Vegetable and Fruit Puppets Puppets may be made by impaling a piece of vegetable or fruit on a stick. Facial features for this perishable puppet may be made by inserting various objects into the vegetable or fruit or by attaching pieces of felt and yarn.

Papier-Mâché Puppets One of the easiest papier-mâché puppets to make has a large milk carton as its base (see Figure 12.2). The top is cut from the carton, and an inflated balloon is inserted. The balloon is covered with layers of paper strips dipped in paste. When dry, the balloon is popped, leaving a firm structure to be painted with tempera paint and turned into any storybook character. A drawstring slipcover forms the clothing or "fur." The milk carton puppet is large, and the full length of a child's arm may be used to manipulate it. This type of puppet is excellent for large audiences because it can be seen easily at a distance.

Stages for Puppet Shows

A stage is not absolutely necessary for the production of a successful puppet performance. Some puppet shows are enhanced, however, by the use of a stage. The main purpose of a puppet stage is to focus the attention of the audience on the puppets. The task is accomplished by simply masking off areas the puppeteer does not want the audience to see. We will briefly describe five stages easily constructed for use in the classroom (see Figure 12.3).

Table Stage A classroom table turned on its side makes a perfect stage for young puppeteers. The flat surface facing the audience becomes a fine backdrop. This simple stage is suitable for hiding the puppet operators, which is the main purpose of any puppet stage.

Doorway Stage A convenient stage may be created by draping a piece of cloth or a sheet over a rope stretched across a doorway (or draped over two chair backs). Such a stage is also an effective means to take a puppet show on the road—from classroom to classroom.

Puppets made from papier-mâché over inflated balloons. Photography by Michael Coody.

Chair Stage A cloth, sheet, or blanket may be draped over the handle of a broom placed across two chairs. The height of the stage can be easily adjusted by using chairs of different sizes.

Box Stage Cardboard boxes of various shapes and sizes are frequently used as puppet theatres in elementary classrooms. After appropriate openings are cut in the box, the imaginative use of tempera paint transforms a shipping container into a center for creative dramatics and puppetry. The box must be large enough to allow freedom of movement for the puppeteers.

Apron Stage The apron stage is the most professional of all puppet stages. Such stages are ordinarily constructed from plywood or chipboard in a three-part, folding-screen arrange-

ment. It is important to make the apron stage both portable and durable.

Scripts for Puppet Shows

The script should be carefully developed or selected before the puppets are made. All children enjoy making puppets and may spend too much time on their construction without giving the script adequate consideration. The language arts teacher may help students find a suitable published script, encourage students to write a script of their own, or help students adapt a story for use in a puppet show.

Published Scripts Scripts for classroom puppet shows may be found in professional magazines

Puppet Stages

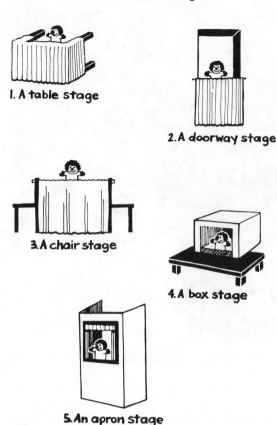

1. A table stage

2. A doorway stage

3. A chair stage

4. A box stage

5. An apron stage

Figure 12.3   Stages for puppet shows. (Courtesy of Barbara Ellis.)

and periodicals, basal language arts and reading textbooks, popular children's magazines, and books about creative dramatics or puppetry for the elementary classroom.

Scripts Written by Students   Boys and girls in the upper elementary grades are quite likely to express an interest in developing their own puppet scripts. This activity has the potential for reinforcing writing and other language arts skills. The teacher should carefully coordinate the writing of the script. The selection of the story to be used should be a joint teacher-student decision.

Time should be provided for individual thought, class discussion, and group participation. The class should prepare an outline of the action, decide where the climax is to come, and list the main events that must take place. The class should discuss how to divide the puppet show into scenes and what to dramatize in each scene. Students should be divided into groups, and each group should be responsible for some specific task in the preparation of the script. The groups should put the scenes together and correct flaws before performing in front of an audience.

The script may be fastened to construction paper, laminated, and the various parts underlined with a felt-tip marker for future use. Students should tape-record one or more versions of the final script. This step will give them the opportunity to evaluate their own performances and the quality of the script.

The teacher should arrange a class discussion about the strong and weak points of the complete puppetry project. For future reference, suggestions for improvement should be noted and filed. Force-field analysis (discussed in Chapter 5) could be used to resolve most problems.

Scripts Adapted from Children's Literature
Stories that contain an interesting plot with a lot of action and well-delineated characters with a great deal of dialogue are best suited to puppetry. It is probably best to begin with familiar stories and books.

As children gain experience in the use of puppetry, they often ask to help choose the story and to participate in the writing of the script. After an interesting story is selected, the dialogue usually needs to be reworked to make it more "speakable" and better suited to a puppet show. Before the puppet project is undertaken, however, the book or story should be read, discussed, and fully enjoyed. In the case of *Mr. Rabbit and the Lovely Present*, for example, it would be a shame for children to be deprived of the wonderful illustrations by Maurice Sendak.

Mr. Rabbit and the Lovely Present by Charlotte Zolotow is the sort of story that lends itself exceedingly well to a puppet performance. It contains a great deal of dialogue; colorful, rhythmic language; repetition; humor; action; and a satisfactory ending. In Display 12.1 we reproduce an adaptation for use by elementary students as a puppet performance.

Readers Theatre

Readers theatre is a form of creative dramatics in which two or more persons, through oral reading, help an audience to experience literature. Because it is done by more than one individual, it is sometimes called "group reading." Roy Beck has described it in this way: "Since one reader usually reads several parts, he merely *suggests* each character vocally, he does not characterize as an actor does. In oral interpretation, emphasis is placed on the literature, and *the readers communicate with the audience through the literature.*"[5]

Coger and White have pointed out that the best readers theatre performances have certain characteristics in common.[6] Scenery and costumes are not used or are only a minor part of the presentation. Action is merely suggested by the reader; the audience visualizes physical activity in their mind's eye. A narrator, speaking directly to the audience, establishes the basic situation or theme and links the various segments together. The narrator may also simplify the language if the story contains any hard-to-read material. A script is usually held by the reader or is at least in view of the reader. There is a continuing effort to develop and maintain a close personal relationship between performer and audience.

[5]Roy A. Beck, *Group Reading: Readers Theatre* (Skokie, Ill.: National Textbook, 1973), p. 2.
[6]Leslie Irene Coger and Melvin R. White, *Readers Theatre Handbook: A Dramatic Approach to Literature* (Glenview, Ill.: Scott, Foresman, 1967), p. 19.

The success of a readers theatre production depends on the oral aspects of the presentation rather than on acting skill or props. The reader uses facial expressions and tone of voice to convey the emotions, moods, and actions of the characters. Readers theatre omits stage properties, lights, and costumes so that nothing will divert the audience's attention from the characterization.

Readers theatre is often thought of as a performance by adults for other adults, but such is not the case. Children of all grade levels can enjoy and participate in this form of creative dramatics. In fact, the only prerequisites for a readers theatre production are that the performers know how to read and are willing to prepare the script so that it can be read fluently.

The development of a script requires two distinct steps: (1) selecting material with high literary value and strong dramatic appeal, (2) adapting the selection to bring about a positive audience response. Almost any piece of literature containing dialogue—poems, short stories, plays—may be used. Folk tales are especially good.

The story should require a minimum of rewriting. The characters should have compelling features and unique personalities. The language should be thought-provoking, rhythmic, and colorful. The plot should have an element of conflict and suspense. There should be much action—provocative, stirring, and intriguing. (The completed script may be made into a construction paper booklet. After the performance, the booklet may be placed in a learning center for students to enjoy as a free-time oral reading activity.)

For staging in the primary grades, the teacher is the most likely person to assume the role of narrator. Students in the upper elementary grades can stage their own performance; they may also write (or rewrite) some of the scripts.

Readers theatre provides a wide opportunity for creative thinking, practicing reading skills, oral expression, developing self-confidence, and

Display 12.1 Mr. Rabbit and the Lovely Present
by Charlotte Zolotow

(Revised as a Puppet Presentation)

L.G. = Little Girl
M.R. = Mr. Rabbit

L.G.: Mr. Rabbit, I want help.

M.R.: Help, little girl, I'll give you help if I can.

L.G.: Mr. Rabbit, it's about my mother.

M.R.: Your mother?

L.G.: It's her birthday.

M.R.: Happy birthday to her then. What are you giving her?

L.G.: That's just it. That's why I want help. I have nothing to give her.

M.R.: Nothing to give your mother on her birthday? Little girl, you really do want help.

L.G.: I would like to give her something that she likes.

M.R.: Something that she likes is a good present.

L.G.: But what?

M.R.: Yes, what?

L.G.: She likes red.

M.R.: Red. You can't give her red.

L.G.: Something red maybe.

M.R.: Oh, something red.

L.G.: What is red?

M.R.: Well, there's red underwear.

L.G.: No, I can't give her that.

M.R.: There are red roofs.

L.G.: No, we have a roof. I don't want to give her that.

M.R.: There are red birds, red cardinals.

L.G.: No, she likes birds in trees.

M.R.: There are red fire engines.

L.G.: No, she doesn't like fire engines.

M.R.: Well, there are apples.

L.G.: Good. That's good. She likes apples. But I need something else.

M.R.: What else does she like?

L.G.: Well, she likes yellow.

M.R.: Yellow. You can't give her yellow.

L.G.: Something yellow, maybe.

M.R.: Oh, something yellow.

L.G.: What is yellow?

M.R.: Well, there are yellow taxicabs.

L.G.: I'm sure she doesn't want a taxicab.

M.R.: The sun is yellow.

L.G.: But I can't give her the sun, though I would if I could.

M.R.: A canary bird is yellow.

L.G.: She likes birds in trees.

M.R.: That's right, you told me. Well, butter is yellow. Does she like butter?

L.G.: We have butter.

M.R.: Bananas are yellow.

L.G.: Oh, good. That's good. She likes bananas. I need something else though.

M.R.: What else does she like?

L.G.: She likes green.

M.R.: Green. You can't give her green.

L.G.: Something green, maybe.

M.R.: Emeralds. Emeralds make a lovely gift.

L.G.: I can't afford an emerald.

M.R.: Parrots are green, but she likes birds in trees.

L.G.: No, parrots won't do.

M.R.: Peas and spinach. Peas are green. Spinach is green.

L.G.: No. We have those for dinner all the time.

M.R.: Caterpillars. Some of them are very green.

L.G.: She doesn't care for caterpillars.

M.R.: How about pears? Bartlett pears?

L.G.: The very thing. That's the very thing. Now I have apples and bananas and pears, but I need something else.

M.R.: What else does she like?

L.G.: She likes blue.

M.R.: Blue. You can't give her blue.

L.G.: Something blue, maybe.

M.R.: Lakes are blue.

L.G.: But I can't give her a lake, you know.

M.R.: Stars are blue.

L.G.: I can't give her stars, but I would if I could.

M.R.: Sapphires make a lovely gift.

L.G.: But I can't afford sapphires, either.

M.R.: Bluebirds are blue, but she likes birds in trees.

L.G.: Right.

M.R.: How about blue grapes?

L.G.: Yes. That is good, very good. She likes grapes. Now I have apples and pears and bananas and grapes.

M.R.: That makes a good gift. All you need now is a basket.

L.G.: I have a basket. I will take my basket and fill it with the green pears and the yellow bananas and the red apples and the blue grapes. It makes a lovely present. Thank you for your help, Mr. Rabbit.

M.R.: Not at all. Very glad to help.

L.G.: Good-by, now.

M.R.: Good-by, and a happy birthday and a happy basket of fruit to your mother.

Puppets constructed for *Mr. Rabbit and the Lovely Present*. Photography by Michael Coody.
Adaptation of the text of *Mr. Rabbit and the Lovely Present* by Charlotte Zolotow. Copyright © 1962 by Charlotte Zolotow. By permission of the author and Harper & Row, Publishers, Inc.

teamwork to achieve common goals. It becomes a means to teach all four of the language arts skills: listening, speaking, reading, and writing. The most important benefit of readers theatre, however, is the satisfying experience of performing in front of an audience and the positive opportunity it provides for language arts students to have fun with literature.

"The Fisherman and His Wife" by the Brothers Grimm is an example of a traditional story that may be transformed into a readers theatre script. This prose selection, reproduced in Display 12.2, contains the essential elements for a readers theatre performance—lively dialogue, a humorous refrain, a rousing climax, and a gratifying conclusion.

Display 12.2 The Fisherman and His Wife
by Jakob and Wilhelm Grimm

N = Narrator   M = Man
F = Fish   W = Wife

N: Once long ago a fisherman and his wife lived in a tiny hovel close by the sea. Early every morning the fisherman would go down to the sea and fish. And he fished, and he fished. One day as he sat fishing, he felt a great tug on his line; and drawing it up he pulled a large flounder out of the sea. Much to the old man's surprise, the fish began to talk to him.

F: Old man, I beg you. Please let me live. I am not a fish but an enchanted prince. I will not be good to eat, so please let me go again.

M: Oh! You need not make so many words about it. I do not wish to eat a fish that can talk. So be off with you.

N: Then the fisherman took the flounder from the hook and threw him back into the water. The fish swam away leaving a long streak of blood behind him. When the fisherman went home that evening, he told his wife that he had caught a great flounder who talked with him—a fish who said he was an enchanted prince.

W: Did you not ask him for anything?

M: No, wife. Why should I ask him for anything?

W: Ah! Here we live in this dirty little hovel. You could have wished us a small cottage. Go back and tell the fish.

N: The fisherman was not happy at this command, but he did not want to go against his wife's wishes, and so he went to the sea. He stood at the water's edge and said:

M: O man, O man!—if man you be,
     Or flounder, flounder in the sea—
     Such a tiresome wife I've got,
     For she wants what I do not.

N: Soon the fish came swimming to him.

F: Well, what does your wife want?

M: Ah! My wife says I should have wished for something before I let you go again. She does not like living in our hovel. She wants a little cottage.

F: Go home, Old Man. She is in the cottage already.

N: So the man hurried home and found his wife standing in the door of the cottage.

W: Come in, husband. Come in. Is this cottage not much better than our hovel?

N: The man entered the cottage and was amazed to find a parlor, a bedchamber, and a kitchen all laid out in the nicest way. When he looked behind the cottage, he found a small garden with flowers and fruit, and a courtyard with chickens, ducks, and geese.

M: Ah! How happily we shall be able to live now.

W: We can try to live happily at least.

N: In a week or two the wife became restless and said:

W: Husband, our cottage is much too small and our garden also. I should like to live in a large stone castle. Go ask the fish to give us a castle.

M: Wife! Can't we be satisfied with the cottage? I should not go to the fish again. He will become angry.

W: Nonsense. If he can make a cottage, he can make a castle. Go along and ask him.

N: The man did not want to go to the fish, but he was afraid not to obey his wife's wishes; when he came to the sea it looked all blue and gloomy. He went to the edge of the water and said:

M: *Refrain*

F: What does she want now?

M: Ah, fish. My wife wants to live in a stone castle.

F: Go home, Old Man. She is in the stone castle already.

NARRATOR

Readers theatre staging of "The Fisherman and His Wife." (Courtesy of Barbara Ellis.)

N: So the fisherman went home and found his wife standing in the door of the stone castle.

W: See, husband. Is this not much better than our small cottage?

N: When the fisherman entered the castle, he found a great many servants there, and all the rooms were richly furnished. The table was filled with food and drink and in the courtyard were many sheep and goats.

M: Well, wife. Now we can live quite contentedly, can't we?

W: We can try to be contented at least.

N: The next morning the wife jostled her husband awake and said:

W: Husband! Get up! I want to be king of all this land.

M: Wife! Wife! What are you saying? I do not wish to be king.

W: But I do. Go and tell the fish.

M: Wife, the fish cannot make a king. He will become angry.

W: Nonsense. He can make a king. And he will do it quite gladly. Go along now.

Readers Theatre staging of "The Fisherman and His Wife." (Courtesy of Barbara Ellis.)

N: The man did not want to ask the fish, but he was afraid to go against his wife's wishes. He was heavy-hearted that his wife should want to be king. When he came to the water's edge he found the sea all dark gray in color with foam on the top and he cried out:

M: *Refrain*

F: Well, what does she want now?

M: Alas, fish. My wife wants to be king.

F: Go home, Old Man. She is king already.

N: Then the fisherman went home, and as he came close he saw a great palace surrounded by soldiers in uniform. He could hear the sound of drums and trumpets. When he entered the house, he saw his wife sitting on a high throne of gold and silver.

M: Well, wife, are you really a king now?

W: Yes, I am a king.

M: Ah, wife! It is a fine thing for you to be king and now there is nothing more you can wish for.

W: I don't know. I shall have to think about that. I begin to tire of being a king. I think I should like to be emperor.

M: Alas, wife! I do not wish to be emperor. The fish cannot make an emperor, and

I should not ask him.

W: Man! I am king and you are my slave. Go right now.

N: The man was sad and frightened, but he went to the sea, and the water was quite black and a great wind was blowing over it, but the fisherman cried out:

M: *Refrain*

F: What does she want now?

M: Oh! Fish. She wants to be emperor.

F: Go home, Old Man. She is emperor already.

N: So the fisherman went home again and found his wife sitting on a throne of solid gold and around her princes, earls, and dukes were her servants. The fisherman said to her,

M: Wife are you really emperor?

W: Yes, I am emperor.

M: Well, wife. It is fine to be emperor and you will be happy, for there is nothing else you can become.

W: Why should I stay an emperor when I could become pope.

M: Oh, wife! What are you saying? There is only one pope in all the world. The fish could never make a pope.

W: Husband, do what I say. I wish to be pope this very day. If the fish can make an emperor, he can make a pope.

N: So the man went again to the sea. As he came near it, the sea was all boiling and churning, and great waves were crashing against the shore. The man could hardly hear himself as he screamed out:

M: *Refrain*

F: Go home, Old Man. She is pope already.

N: And so the man went home and found his wife sitting on a throne that was one mile high, and she had three crowns of gold upon her head. A thousand candles were flaming around her.

M: Wife, are you really pope?

W: Yes, I am pope.

M: It is very good that you are pope and now we can live contentedly, for there is nothing else you can become.

W: Well, husband. I will have to think on *that*.

N: That night the wife could not sleep at all. She kept thinking and thinking about what else she could become. When morning came and she saw the sun rise she thought, "Could I not make that sun rise each morning? Could I not be God?" And so she poked her husband in the ribs and said:

W: Husband! Husband! Get up. I cannot stand to watch the sun come up each day without my help. Go and tell the fish that I want to be God.

N: Now the fisherman was sound asleep, but this frightened him so that he fell out of bed.

M: No! No! wife. Please be content to be pope. The fish cannot do what you ask. He cannot make you God.

W: What nonsense you speak, man. If he can make pope, he can make God. Go right now. I cannot stand it any longer. I must be God.

N: So the man started down to the sea and a great storm arose. The trees fell and rocks rolled down to the sea. The lightening flashed across the sky and thunder roared. The sea came up in great dark waves and the fisherman said:

M: *Refrain*

F: What does she want now?

M: Ah, fish. She wants to make the sun come up each morning and the moon rise each night. She wants to be God.

F: Go home, Old Man. She's back in the hovel again.

N: And there they live to this very day.

Adapted by Betty Coody for a readers theatre performance.

A Choral Reading Performance

Group A

Group B

Group C

Solo 1

Solo 2

Arrangement for a choral-speaking performance. (Courtesy of Barbara Ellis.)

Choral Speaking

Choral speaking, also known as "choral reading," "verse choirs," and "choric speaking," is a popular means of interpreting literature orally. Positive experiences with choral speaking add to children's enjoyment of both prose and poetry.

Although choral speaking is not strictly limited to the oral presentation of poetry, the two go together so beautifully that poems have often been used for choral-speaking activities.

The use of choral speaking can be traced back to the chants and songs of ancient peoples. In early religious services, many of the scriptures of the Old Testament were chanted as melodious refrains. Choral speaking as a form of dramatization, however, reached its peak in the tragedies of the ancient Greeks.

The choruses that performed in the Greek theatre were an integral part of the drama. They described details that were considered too shocking to show on stage, and they also commented on the actions of the major characters and echoed the reactions of the people who were witnessing the events.

During the Middle Ages, choral speaking as a means of interpreting literature was kept alive by troubadours and minstrels. These wandering storytellers traveled throughout Europe chanting traditional legends and improvising on the most recent lore. Many of the interpretations of life and the social commentary sung by these meandering chroniclers have become verses, choruses, and ballads known to generations of children and adults alike. A parent who sings Mother Goose rhymes to a child is continuing a tradition that can be traced back to the roving minstrels.

Choral speaking as a form of creative dramatics has the potential to be as popular with children of today as it was with their ancestors centuries ago. The most difficult aspect is getting it underway. The teacher must serve as the director to synchronize the rhythm, coordinate the dynamics, and orchestrate the intonation. In Display 12.3 we present a list of "dos" and don'ts" to help the teacher develop choral-speaking experiences that are both successful and enjoyable.

Choral speaking takes advantage of children's appreciation of rhythmic language and dramatic mood. It also provides excellent and satisfying experiences in performing with a group. Once choral speaking has been introduced in the primary grades, it should be used year after year as a means of furthering students' literary awareness.

Choral-speaking groups may be arranged in several ways, depending on the type of material that is to be used. Poetry that consists of stanzas followed by a refrain might be performed by solo speakers reciting each stanza and a group joining in with the refrain. Basic arrangements that have been used successfully by elementary teachers include stanza and refrain, antiphonal choirs, line-a-speaker, line-a-choir, and unison. We will discuss each arrangement on the following pages.

Stanza and Refrain

Verse consisting of stanzas and a refrain is frequently used for choral speaking. It has a two-part format consisting of a solo part (the stanza) and a choral part (the refrain). In this form of choral speaking, the teacher or a student recites the body of a poem and the rest of the class responds in unison to the chorus or refrain. The refrain may be repeated line for line, or it may vary as is often the case in an accumulative story. The use of the stanza and refrain arrangement is especially effective with younger elementary students; it is also the best choice for introducing girls and boys to choral speaking.

THE WIND

SOLOIST: I saw you toss the kites on high
         And blow the birds about the sky;
         And all around I heard you pass,
         Like ladies' skirts across the grass—

GROUP: O wind, a-blowing all day long,
         O wind, that sings so loud a song!

SOLOIST: I saw the different things you did,
         But always you yourself you hid.
         I felt you push, I heard you call,
         I could not see yourself at all—

GROUP: O wind, a-blowing all day long,
         O wind, that sings so loud a song!

SOLOIST: O you that are so strong and cold,
         O blower, are you young or old?
         Are you a beast of field and tree,
         Or just a stronger child than me?

GROUP: O wind, a-blowing all day long,
         O wind, that sings so loud a song!

—Robert Louis Stevenson

Antiphonal Choirs

Antiphonal, or responsive, choral speaking is a two-part arrangement used when the lines or stanzas may be divided on the basis of mood or plot. Selections that contain contrasts or unique characterization are especially well suited for antiphonal choral speaking. Most often the makeup of the "choirs" reflects the dualism of the poem—girls and boys, high voices and low voices, questioners and answerers. Antiphonal choral speaking is popular with children in the upper elementary grades and with others who have had some experience with choral speaking.

Display 12.3 The Dos and Don'ts of Choral Speaking

Dos	Don'ts
Choral speaking should be an enjoyable experience for both students and teacher alike.	It should not be approached as a routine classroom obligation.
Choral speaking should take place frequently and informally.	It should not be undertaken simply as a public performance for an audience.
Choral speaking should be guided initially by the teacher with the total involvement of the students.	It should not be overly structured; it needs to be experienced.
Choral speaking should involve only good poems carefully selected by the teacher with input from the students.	Selections should not be mediocre poems selected to correlate with science, social studies, or other content areas.
Choral speaking should focus on the natural rhythm of language variation within a poem.	It should not be allowed to take on a sing-song quality.
Choral speaking may involve appropriate dramatization that includes bodily gestures, facial expression, or choreography.	It should never be overdramatized; thoughtful delivery of the lines is more important than theatrics.
Choral speaking demands enunciation so clear that the audience can understand every word.	It should not allow unnecessary volume or words spoken too rapidly, both hazards that cause words to become unintelligible.
Choral speaking should emphasize the story or the idea of a poem.	It should not overemphasize the metrical beat, but neither should it be spoken in a monotone.

THE PIRATE DON DURK OF DOWDEE[7]

GROUP A: Ho, for the Pirate Don Durk of Dowdee!
He was as wicked as wicked could be,

GROUP B: But oh, he was perfectly gorgeous to see!
The Pirate Don Durk of Dowdee.

GROUP A: His conscience, of course, was as black as a bat,

But he had a floppety plume on his hat

GROUP B: And when he went walking it jiggled—like that!
The plume of the Pirate Dowdee.

GROUP A: His coat it was crimson and cut with a slash,
And often as ever he twirled his mustache

GROUP B: Deep down in the ocean the mermaids went splash,
Because of Don Durk of Dowdee.

GROUP A: Moreover, Dowdee had a purple tattoo,

[7]"The Pirate Don Durk of Dowdee" by Mildred Plew Meigs from *Child Life* (March 1923). Reprinted by permission of the estate of Marion Plew Ruckel.

And stuck in his belt where he buck-
led it through

GROUP B: Were a dagger, a dirk and a squiz-
zamaroo,
For fierce was the Pirate Dowdee.

GROUP A: So fearful he was he would shoot at a
puff,
And always at sea when the weather
grew rough

GROUP B: He drank from a bottle and wrote on
his cuff,
Did Pirate Don Durk of Dowdee.

GROUP A: Oh, he had a cutlass that swung at his
thigh
And he had a parrot called Pepperkin
Pye,

GROUP B: And a zigzaggy scar at the end of his
eye
Had Pirate Don Durk of Dowdee.

GROUP A: He kept in a cavern, this buccaneer
bold,
A curious chest that was covered with
mould,

GROUP B: And all of his pockets were jingly
with gold!
Oh jing! went the gold of Dowdee.

GROUP A: His conscience, of course, it was
crook'd like a squash,
But both of his boots made a slickery
slosh,

GROUP B: And he went through the world with
a wonderful swash,
Did Pirate Don Durk of Dowdee.

GROUP A: It's true he was wicked as wicked
could be,
His sins they outnumbered a hundred
and three,

GROUP B: But oh, he was perfectly gorgeous to
see,
The Pirate Don Durk of Dowdee.

—*Mildred Plew Meigs*

Line-a-Speaker

Line-a-speaker arrangements are similar to the
antiphonal setup but involve more than two
parts. Individual children or groups speak different lines or stanzas of the poem in sequence. The
sequence in which the parts are presented is repeated several times. Line-a-speaker is a popular
arrangement for older students as a means of interpreting, in a creative manner, traditional and
contemporary literature.

A SALUTE TO TREES[8]

GROUP A: Many a tree is found in the wood,
And every tree for its use is good.

GROUP B: Some for the strength of the gnarled
root,
Some for the sweetness of flower or
fruit,

GROUP C: Some for shelter against the storm,
And some to keep the hearthstone
warm,

GROUP A: Some for the roof, and some for the
beam,
And some for a boat to breast the
stream.

GROUP B: In the wealth of the wood since the
world began,
The trees have offered their gifts to
man.

GROUP C: I have camped in the whispering forest of pines,
I have slept in the shadow of olives
and vines;

GROUP A: In the knees of an oak, at the foot of
a palm,
I have found good rest and slumber's
balm.

[8]Used by permission of Charles Scribner's Sons from *Poems
of Henry Van Dyke* by Henry Van Dyke. Copyright 1911 by
Charles Scribner's Sons; renewal copyright 1939 by Tertius
Van Dyke.

GROUP B: And now, when the morning gilds the
boughs
Of the vaulted elm at the door of my
house,

GROUP C: I open the window and make a salute:
"God bless thy branches and feed thy
root!

ALL: Thou hast lived before, live after me,
Thou ancient, friendly, faithful tree!"

—Henry van Dyke

Line-a-Choir

The line-a-choir arrangement includes several
small groups of about four persons, each group
cast for a separate part. Some of the lines of the
poem are spoken by each of the small groups,
and some of the parts, such as the chorus or
refrain, are spoken by the groups together. Line-
a-choir makes possible the smooth integration of
the mood of the poem and the continuity of the
author's ideas. Experimentation with the line-a-
choir format can provide interesting results with
previously reluctant choral speakers. This form
of choral speaking is most successful when the
class is organized into several small groups and
various types of poetry are presented.

THE DUEL[9]

GROUP A: The gingham dog and the calico cat
Side by side on the table sat;

GROUP B: 'Twas half-past twelve, and (what
do you think!)
Nor one nor t'other had slept a wink!

GROUP C: The old Dutch clock and the Chi-
nese plate
Appeared to know as sure as fate
There was going to be a terrible spat.

[9]"The Duel" by Eugene Field from *Poems of Childhood* by
Eugene Field (New York: Charles Scribner's Sons, 1904).
Used by permission.

SOLO 1: *(I wasn't there; I simply state
What was told to me by the Chinese
plate!)*

GROUP A: The gingham dog went, "Bow-wow-
wow!"
And the calico cat replied, "Mee-ow!"

GROUP B: The air was littered, an hour or so,
With bits of gingham and calico,

GROUP C: While the old Dutch clock in the
chimney-place
Up with its hands before its face,
For it always dreaded a family row!

SOLO 2: *(Now mind: I'm only telling you
What the old Dutch clock declares is
true!)*

GROUP A: The Chinese plate looked very blue,
And wailed, "Oh, dear! what shall we
do!"

GROUP B: But the gingham dog and the calico
cat
Wallowed this way and tumbled that,

GROUP C: Employing every tooth and claw
In the awfullest way you ever
saw—
And, oh! how the gingham and calico
flew!

SOLO 3: *(Don't fancy I exaggerate—
I got my news from the Chinese
plate!)*

GROUP A: Next morning, where the two had sat
They found no trace of dog and cat;

GROUP B: And some folks think unto this day
That burglars stole that pair away!

GROUP C: But the truth about the cat and
pup
Is this: they ate each other up!
Now what do you really think of that!

ALL: *(The old Dutch clock, it told me so,
And that is how I came to know.)*

—Eugene Field

Unison

In a unison presentation all speakers recite the poem or story together; all voices speak the lines as one. This form of choral reading is sometimes difficult, however, because it may produce a "singsong" effect. A few manipulative devices (such as a puppet) or gestures will add variety and may improve the production.

Major responsibility for bringing about a successful performance rests with the director. If the director stresses the meaning, the semantics, and the plot of the story, a suitably expressive recitation will be more likely to result. The key to good unison speaking is much practice with a variety of selections. If the delivery is done in a singsong way, the group should be stopped at once and reminded to think of the meaning of the passage when they resume.

STOPPING BY WOODS ON A SNOWY EVENING[10]

ALL: Whose woods these are I think I know.
His house is in the village, though;
He will not see me stopping here
To watch his woods fill up with snow.

My little horse must think it queer
To stop without a farmhouse near
Between the woods and frozen lake
The darkest evening of the year.

He gives his harness bells a shake
To ask if there is some mistake.
The only other sound's the sweep
Of easy wind and downy flake.

The woods are lovely, dark, and deep,
But I have promises to keep,
And miles to go before I sleep,
And miles to go before I sleep.

—*Robert Frost*

[10]"Stopping by Woods on a Snowy Evening," from *The Poetry of Robert Frost* edited by Edward Connery Lathem. Copyright 1923, © 1969 by Holt, Rinehart and Winston, Inc. Copyright 1951 by Robert Frost. Reprinted by permission of Holt, Rinehart and Winston, Inc.

Summary

Creative dramatics helps children interpret and understand literature. Of the four types of creative dramatics discussed in this chapter, story-acting is the most informal and spontaneous. Very young children often begin dramatization from their earliest encounters with literature, and this behavior continues through the elementary grades as long as girls and boys continue to react to what they read. Folk tales are perhaps the most suitable literary genre for story-acting in the classroom.

Puppets come in all shapes and sizes, and they can be used to develop meaningful adventures with literature as well as to meet other objectives in the language arts program. Successful puppetry experiences promote good speaking habits, enlarge children's oral vocabulary, help children learn to develop ideas in a sequence, encourage creative thinking, motivate creative writing experiences, and provide an outlet for pent-up emotions and feelings.

Readers theatre is a staged program that allows the audience to create its own mental images while listening to skillful oral reading of literature. The players usually remain onstage or in a designated area throughout the performance. Readers use little or no movement; they suggest action with simple gestures, facial expression, and voice intonation. Readers theatre is only now coming into its own as an effective means of reinforcing the skills of oral reading.

Because poetry lends itself so well to group enjoyment, choral speaking is the perfect means to share it. Choral speaking is simply reading or reciting by individuals or groups under the direction of a leader. There are five basic arrangements in which a choral-speaking performance may be presented: (1) stanza and refrain, (2) antiphonal choirs, (3) line-a-speaker, (4) line-a-choir, and (5) unison. Choral speaking, like other forms of creative dramatics, provides a way for children to participate in the enjoyment of literature, which in turn strengthens basic language skills.

Best Books for Children

The Adventures of Pinocchio, written by C. Collodi and illustrated by Naiad Einsel. New York: Macmillan, 1966. Written in Italy in 1892, this is the original version, which has been translated into languages around the world and is a universal favorite of children. It is an edition that would be most appropriate for older readers who are familiar with the basic story. (M,U)

A Child's Garden of Verses, written by Robert Louis Stevenson and illustrated by Brian Wildsmith. New York: Franklin Watts, 1966. Robert Louis Stevenson was one of the first poets to write of childhood from a child's point of view. Originally published in 1885, this collection continues in popularity today. There are many classroom editions of *A Child's Garden of Verses*, ranging from Erik Blegvad's quaint pastel pictures to Brian Wildsmith's edition, which is a vivid kaleidoscope of color. All editions contain poems such as "The Wind" that are well suited for choral speaking. (P,M,U)

Drummer Hoff, written by Barbara Emberley and illustrated by Ed Emberley. Englewood Cliffs, N.J.: Prentice-Hall, 1967. This is an adaptation of an old folk rhyme in which many people bring parts to assemble a cannon. Events accumulate until the cannon is finally fired—"Drummer Hoff fired it off." The rhyme ends abruptly as the cannon is fired. The last picture leaves the reader with a feeling of peace. (P)

Duffy and the Devil, written by Harve Zemach and illustrated by Margot Zemach. New York: Farrar, Straus & Giroux, 1973. This 1974 Caldecott Award book is the story of Squire Lovel, who hires a local girl named Duffy to help with the spinning. A creature with horns and a long tail agrees to help Duffy with her spinning and knitting chores for three years, after which she must tell him his name. Both the language and the illustrations retain the characteristics of a Rumpelstiltskin story that children enjoy dramatizing. (P)

East of the Sun and West of the Moon and Other Tales, collected by P. C. Asbjornsen and illustrated by Jorgen E. Moe. New York: Macmillan, 1962. A classic collection of traditional Norwegian folk tales including the famous "The Three Billy Goats Gruff" and "The Blue Belt." Such a collection is a reminder that the folk tales found in one part of the world are similar to those found in other countries, though each retains its own national flavor. (P,M)

Eric Carle's Storybook: Seven Tales by the Brothers Grimm, retold and illustrated by Eric Carle. New York: Franklin Watts, 1976. It is difficult to imagine creative dramatics without the special enchantment of the fairy tale. Giants and dwarfs, monsters and magic fish, wise fools and wicked witches—these are the ingredients that have thrilled children in many lands. Eric Carle has captured the homely wisdom, fantasy, and humor of seven of the most popular tales from the Brothers Grimm, including "The Fisherman and His Wife." (M,U)

The Golden Treasury of Children's Literature, edited and selected by Bryna and Louis Untermeyer. New York: Golden Press, 1967. This collection of children's literature contains some of the finest and most enduring stories and legends. It includes time-tested classics, ancient myths, folk tales from distant lands, and some delightful modern stories. Many of the selections may be used as the basis for a puppet play, choral speaking, or a readers theatre production. (P,M,U)

Holiday Puppets, written and illustrated by Laura Ross. New York: Lathrop, Lee & Shepard, 1974. Included in this book are puppets for all seasons, made from wood, cloth, paper, cornstalks, styrofoam, and even dried apples. This original collection of puppets also contains puppet scripts to help children celebrate St. Valentine's Day, St. Patrick's Day, Purim, Easter, Columbus Day, Halloween, Thanksgiving, and Christmas. (P,M,U)

The Judge, adapted by Harve Zemach and illustrated by Margot Zemach. New York: Farrar, Straus & Giroux, 1969. This very funny story is told in verse and is perfect for classroom dramatization. Prisoner after prisoner appears before the judge, and each is accused of telling a fabricated tale. Every new witness adds one more detail to the horrible event about to occur. This Russian folk tale presents the plot for a lively farce that may be shared in the classroom. (M)

Mother, Mother, I Feel Sick, Send for the Doctor, Quick, Quick, Quick, adapted by Remy Charlip and Burton Supee and illustrated by Remy Charlip. New York: Parents' Magazine Press, 1966. This very old story is fun to do as a classroom play, a puppet show, or a readers theatre performance. It is a cumulative tale about a boy who has eaten too much. The humorous refrain and the hilarious sequence of events make it an excellent choice for dramatization. (P)

Mr. Rabbit and the Lovely Present, written by Charlotte Zolotow and illustrated by Maurice Sendak. New York: Harper & Row, 1962. A little girl with a problem of what to give her mother on her birthday receives help from a rabbit in finding the perfect gift. (P)

Nail Soup, adapted by Nils Djurklo and illustrated by Margot Zemach. New York: Follett, 1964. This story is the Swedish version of Stone Soup. An old man teaches a selfish woman how to make soup from a nail. An interesting dramatization could be presented as half of the students in the class perform *Nail Soup* and the other half portray the French version found in Marcia Brown's *Stone Soup.* (P)

Pinocchio, written by C. Collodi, adapted by Allen Chaffee, and illustrated by Lois Lenski. New York: Random House, 1946. One of the most popular of all children's stories, *Pinocchio* is the story of a mischievous puppet that Geppetto carves from a block of wood. When Pinocchio at last does something unselfish for someone else, he becomes a real boy. (P,M)

Salt: A Russian Tale, adapted by Harve Zemach and illustrated by Margot Zemach. New York: Follett, 1965. Ivan is a clever fool who becomes the hero in this Russian folk tale. A wealthy merchant gives each of his three sons a ship and a cargo to trade in foreign lands. Only Ivan "the fool" makes his fortune and wins the princess. Everyone is surprised with the unusual turn of events, especially Ivan's father. This is a typical "noodle" story. (P,M)

Seven Stories by Hans Christian Andersen, retold and illustrated by Eric Carle. New York: Franklin Watts, 1978. Seven stories, including "The Magic Boots" and "The Wild Swans," are included in this lavishly illus-

trated collection. Children in the middle grades will especially enjoy reading the various stories in a readers theatre presentation. (M,U)

Small Plays for Special Days, written by Sue Alexander and illustrated by Tom Huffman. New York: Seabury Press, 1977. The plays or skits each contain just two characters. This is intended to be an introduction to directed play-acting for middle grade students. With easily obtainable props, a minimum of costuming, and a few simple stage directions, children can be guided into the production of a simple play. (M)

The Tale of Peter Rabbit, written and illustrated by Beatrix Potter. New York: Scholastic Book Services, 1978. One of literature's most famous characters is Peter Rabbit, who was created in 1903. Since that time, generations of children have enjoyed reading and dramatizing the adventures of the well-loved Cottontail family. (P)

To Hilda for Helping, written and illustrated by Margot Zemach. New York: Farrar, Straus & Giroux, 1977. Hilda's father thinks she deserves a medal, and so he makes one for her out of the top of a tin can. The medal says "To Hilda for Helping." Hilda wears the medal day and night until her sister Gladys gets so mad she screams. Gladys conjures a fantasy of gloom and destruction for the medal, but Hilda doesn't see it that way. She looks on the brighter side. (P)

Bibliography

Bacon, Wallace. *The Art of Interpretation,* 2d ed. New York: Holt, Rinehart and Winston, 1972.

Baird, Bil. *The Art of the Puppet.* New York: Macmillan, 1965.

Beck, Roy A. *Group Reading: Readers Theatre.* Skokie, Ill.: National Textbook, 1973.

Bohmer, Gunter. *The Wonderful World of Puppets.* Boston: Plays, Inc., 1971.

Carlton, Lessie, and Robert H. Moore. *Reading, Self-Directive Dramatization and Self-Concept.* Columbus: Charles E. Merrill, 1968.

Coger, Leslie Irene, and Melvin R. White. *Readers Theatre Handbook: A Dramatic Approach to Literature.* Glenview, Ill.: Scott, Foresman, 1967.

Cullum, Albert. *Push Back the Desks.* New York: Citation Press, 1967.

Currell, David. *Puppetry for School Children.* Newton, Mass.: Charles T. Branford, 1970.

Fernandez, Thomas L. *Oral Interpretation and the Teaching of English.* Champaign, Ill.: National Council of Teachers of English, 1969.

Gilbert, Carolyn A. *Communicative Performance and Literature.* New York: Macmillan, 1977.

Gilles, Emily. *Creative Dramatics for All Children.* Washington, D.C.: Association for Childhood Education International, 1973.

Hanford, Robert Ten Eyck. *The Complete Book of Puppets and Puppeteering.* New York: Drake Publishers, 1976.

Hazard, Paul. *Books, Children & Men.* Boston: Horn Book, 1944.

Howard, Vernon. *Puppet and Pantomime Plays.* New York: Sterling, 1969.

Larson, Martha L. "Reader's Theatre: New Vitality for Oral Reading." *The Reading Teacher,* January 1976.

Lee, Charlotte I., and Frank Galati. *Oral Interpretation,* 5th ed. Boston: Houghton Mifflin, 1977.

Long, Beverley Whitaker; Lee Hudson; and Phillis Rienstra Jeffrey. *Group Performance of Literature.* Englewood Cliffs, N.J.: Prentice-Hall, 1977.

McCaslin, Nellie. *Act Now!* New York: S. G. Phillips, 1975.

———. *Children and Drama.* New York: McKay, 1975.

———. *Creative Dramatics in the Classroom.* New York: McKay, 1974.

———. *Theatre for Young Audiences.* New York: Longman, 1978.

McIntyre, Barbara M. *Creative Dramatics in the Elementary School.* Itasca, Ill.: F. E. Peacock, 1974.

McPharlin, Paul. *The Puppet Theatre.* Boston: Plays, Inc., 1969.

Mattingly, Alethea Smith, and Wilma H. Grimes. *Interpretation: Writer, Reader, Audience,* 2d ed. Belmont, Calif.: Wadsworth, 1970.

Post, Robert M. "Children's Readers Theatre." *Language Arts,* March 1979.

Sandifer, C. M. "From Print to Rehearsal: A Study of Principles for Adapting Literature to Reader's Theatre." *Speech Teacher,* March 1971.

Siks, Geraldine Brain. *Children's Literature for Dramatization.* New York: Harper & Row, 1964.

Simmen, René. *The World of Puppets.* New York: Thomas Y. Crowell, 1972.

Smith, James A., and Dorothy M. Park. *Word Music and Word Magic.* Boston: Allyn and Bacon, 1977.

Sutherland, Zena, ed. *The Arbuthnot Anthology of Children's Literature,* 4th ed. Glenview, Ill.: Scott, Foresman, 1976.

Taylor, Loren E. *Informal Dramatics for Young Children.* Minneapolis: Burgess, 1965.

———. *Pantomime and Pantomime Games.* Minneapolis: Burgess, 1965.

Chapter 13

Making the Most of Media:
Books and Nonbook Materials in Partnership

TEACHING A CHILD how to read is only one of the teacher's tasks. The teacher also has an obligation to develop within a child a lasting desire to read. The latter is a more difficult undertaking.

The most promising place for a lifelong reading habit to begin is in a well-stocked elementary school library. Textbooks, workbooks, and programmed materials may be the basis of instruction in the classroom, but the library provides interesting, challenging, enriching, and entertaining material that creates the will to read. For this reason, it is important for the teacher and the librarian to work together as a team to create interest in the library and to teach the skills needed for efficient use of the library's abundant resources.

The classroom teacher deliberately plans activities, projects, and reports that are meant to get children into the library. At the same time, the librarian cooperates with the teacher and coordinates the library work in such a way that it reinforces and enhances classroom instruction. The library program is an important extension of the language arts curriculum.

In this chapter we will suggest ways to stimulate interest in library books and book-related media and to teach some of the basic library skills needed by elementary students.

Library Skills for Children in the Primary Grades

On entering school, kindergarten and primary children become pleasantly acquainted with the school library as the teacher and the librarian share responsibility for reading aloud to them from picture books, for telling them stories with felt board and puppets, for playing recordings of poetry and drama, and for showing them films and filmstrips related to books. Eventually, the children are shown how to locate books by title and appearance on library shelves. For the convenience of beginning readers, most libraries provide a special shelf of easy-to-read books labeled with an E. Respect for books, the parts of a book, and book care are a subtle part of all library experiences for young children.

At the upper primary level, most children begin using the card catalog with a great deal of help from the teacher and librarian. Since the subject catalog seems easier for most beginners to manage, it is introduced first. Later, the title and author catalogs are introduced. Young students soon come to understand that books are shelved in a library in a systematic arrangement solely for the reader's benefit.

Library Skills for Children in the Intermediate Grades

Students in the intermediate grades become more and more independent in locating books in the school library. As they learn the ten major classifications of the Dewey Decimal System, they refine their skills in using the card catalog and thus require less assistance.

Using the Card Catalog

The card catalog provides an index to all the books in a library. Each book is usually represented in the catalog by three cards, identifying the work by author, title, and subject (see Display 13.1). All three cards contain the same basic information about the book—the name of the author, the book title, the name of the publisher and year of publication, the number of pages, the presence of illustrations, the call number assigned to the book. At the top of the author card is the author's name; at the top of the title card is the book title; at the top of the subject card is the subject of the book. The cards are placed in the card catalog in alphabetical order.

Display 13.1 Explaining Author, Title, and Subject Cards

A cube made from two half-gallon milk cartons will help to acquaint students with title, subject, and author cards. Three sides should be replicas of real cards. The other three sides should contain the call number, a definition of the book type, and a representative symbol. Cubes should be made for each of the ten Dewey classifications.

Courtesy of Barbara Ellis.

Understanding the Dewey Decimal System

Melvil Dewey, probably more than any other person, was responsible for the sound development of library science in the United States. He was one of the founders of the American Library Association and a founder and editor of the *Library Journal*. Most people know him, however, as the originator of the Dewey Decimal System, a method of classifying all books (except fiction) into ten groups:

000–099 General Works (reference books)

100–199 Philosophy (psychology, ethics)

200–299 Religion (Bible, myths)

300–399 Social Sciences (sociology, economics, political science, etiquette)

400–499 Grammar and Language (dictionaries)

500–599 Science (mathematics, astronomy, chemistry, birds)

600–699 Useful Arts (agriculture, aeronautics, radio)

700–799 Fine Arts (photography, painting, music)

800–899 Literature (stories, poems, essays)

900–999 History (travel, biography)

Steps in Checking Out a Book

1. Locate the book to be checked out.

2. Find the book card.

3. Sign your name on the card.

4. Have the date due stamped in your book.

Due

FEB 6 1979

5. Read and enjoy your book!

The main steps to be taken in checking out a book are shown here in comic strip style. The cartoons may be enlarged to form a teaching poster for the classroom or library. (Courtesy of Barbara Ellis.)

Dewey's purpose was to simplify the organizing and shelving of large collections and to make it easy for library users to locate books. He decided on the ten main groups by imagining himself a prehistoric man and then posing to himself questions he guessed a prehistoric man might have asked about himself and the world around him (see Figure 13.1).

Each of Dewey's ten groups is subdivided. The main number, listed first on the spine of the book, is followed by a decimal point and the number of the appropriate subgroup. Once the number of a nonfiction book is located in the card catalog, the reader goes to the indicated section of the library to find books arranged by the main Dewey group number, the subgroup number, the first letter of the author's surname, and the book title (see Figure 13.2).

Fiction is arranged in a special section of the library, alphabetically by the author's last name. In the case of two books by the same author, the books are arranged in alphabetical order by title (see Figure 13.3).

The Dewey Decimal System is the most widely used classifying procedure and is used almost exclusively in elementary school libraries. It

THE DEWEY DECIMAL SYSTEM

WHO AM I?
100-199

WHO MADE ME?
200-299

WHO IS THE MAN IN THE NEXT CAVE?
300-399

HOW CAN I MAKE THAT MAN UNDERSTAND ME?
400-499

WHAT MAKES THINGS HAPPEN IN THE WORLD AROUND ME? 500-599

HOW CAN I CONTROL NATURE?
600-699

HOW CAN I ENJOY MY SPARE TIME?
700-799

WHAT ARE THE STORIES OF MAN'S GREAT THOUGHTS AND DEEDS?
800-899

HOW CAN I RECORD WHAT MAN HAS DONE?
900-999

HOW CAN I STORE FACTS IN BOOKS?
000-099

Figure 13.1   *The Dewey Decimal System (Courtesy of Barbara Ellis.)*

INTRODUCING THE EARTH: GEOLOGY, ENVIRONMENT, AND MAN

Matthews,W.H.
550
M

The Look-it-up Book of the Earth

Simon,S.
550
S

The Wonders of Geology

Collins,Henry
551
C

THE EARTH'S CRUST

Matthews,W.H.
551
M

Rocks, Rivers and the Changing Earth

Schneider,H.
551
S

WHY THE EARTH QUAKES

May, Julian
551.2
M

VOLCANO!

Buehr,Walter
551.21
B

Figure 13.2 Students should be taught that informational books are shelved in a systematic way according to the Dewey Decimal classification. (Courtesy of Barbara Ellis.)

should be mentioned, however, that very few schools use a "pure" Dewey system. Most adapt and modify it to fit their own purposes. Librarians and teachers know that the simpler the method of classification, the easier it will be for children to find the books they need.

Providing Information About Authors, Illustrators, and Publishers

Children actively involved in a daily program of literature will be interested in news and information about authors and illustrators of their favorite books. Classroom activities to take advantage of this interest include preparing biographical sketches, comparing several books by the same author, or studying an artist's style and technique. As a supplement to traditional reference books that contain information on authors and illustrators, the teacher or librarian will do well to keep a file of newspaper and magazine clippings, book jackets, publishers' newsletters, and other such material for students to use. Photographs and biographical sketches of authors, poets, and illustrators are especially enjoyed.

Elementary school children may also be interested in learning something about the publisher of a book. The name of the publishing company

The Story of Sera Pina
Anne H. White
j
W

On Your Own Two Feet
Bessie F. White
j
W

Charlotte's Web
E.B. White
j
W

Stuart Little
E.B. White
j
W

The Trumpet of the Swan
E.B. White
j
W

I, the Autobiography of a Cat
Eliza O. White
j
W

Up Periscope
Robb White
j
W

Figure 13.3 *Fictional books are shelved systematically by the author's last name. (Courtesy of Barbara Ellis.)*

printed on the jacket, cover, title page, and copyright page may be pointed out to them. The function of the publisher as manufacturer, advertiser, and bookseller will be better understood if the class is permitted to select a book from a catalog and then order it directly from the publisher.

Teaching the Parts of a Book

Children's interest in the way a book is put together may be stimulated by means of a bulletin board display, overhead transparencies, or slide or filmstrip presentations. Selected books may then be examined and discussed informally. A follow-up activity in which students write, illustrate, and bind their own books is one effective way to show each part of a book and explain its unique function.

The parts of a book to be pointed out to children are the jacket, cover, and spine; the endpapers; the title and copyright pages; the table of contents and preface; the main text; and the appendix and index. Of course, not all books will have every part.

Jacket, Cover, and Spine

The jacket is the colorful paper cover that folds around the outside of a hardcover book. It provides eye appeal to the prospective reader as well as protection for the book. The flaps are parts of the jacket that fold inside the front and back covers. The front flap usually contains a brief summary of the book's contents. The back flap usually contains essential information about the author and illustrator.

The pages of a book are enclosed by a covering made of heavy cardboard covered by paper or cloth (in the case of a hardcover book) or made of flexible paper (in the case of a softcover book).

The spine is the part of a book that is visible when the book is upright on a shelf. It is the central support or "backbone" of a book. The spine usually carries the title of the book, the surname of the author, and the name of the publisher. The spine and cover are known as the "binding."

Endpapers

Endpapers are heavy sheets of paper pasted inside the front and back covers to conceal the rough edges of the binding. The endpapers are often decorated in such a way as to offer a glimpse into the contents of the book.

Title Page and Copyright Page

The title page tells the title of the book, the author, the name and place of the publishing company, and if the book is illustrated, the name of the artist.

The copyright page identifies the individual or organization that controls the right to publish or reprint the material. It also includes the copyright date, which is almost always the year in which the book was published.

Table of Contents and Preface

The table of contents lists the chapter titles and subheadings that appear in the main text and gives the numbers of the pages on which they occur.

The preface contains remarks by the author discussing the purpose and content of the book. It sometimes acknowledges individuals who have helped in the preparation of the project.

Main Text

The main text is the body of the book. It follows all the introductory pages.

Appendix and Index

The appendix contains items such as explanatory notes, tables, lists, and other supplementary material.

The index is an alphabetized list of topics and names mentioned in the main text and the page numbers on which each item is found.

Activities to Promote Library Skills

Students at all grade levels should participate in a variety of activities and exercises planned jointly by the teacher and the librarian. Such activities are designed to promote library skills by means of systematic instruction and practice.

The following procedures are suggested to strengthen specific library skills and to build appreciation for books:

COLORFUL CLASSIFICATIONS

Read a book. For each book you read, color one section on the proper shelf.

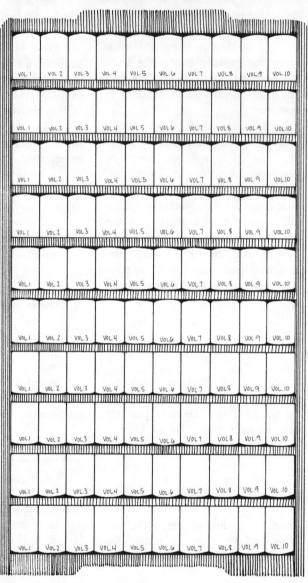

Biography

Drama

Fiction

Historical Fiction

Informational

Jokes and Riddles

Poetry

Romance and Adventure

Science Fiction

Travel

Students might use a decorative bar graph to keep track of the number and type of books they read during a school year. (Courtesy of Barbara Ellis.)

MYTHOLOGY

IF YOU LIKE THESE CHARACTERS.

YOU'LL LOVE THESE!

IRIS	AJAX
HERA	HERMES
ATHENA	PERSEUS
DEMETER	ACHILLES
ARIADNE	HERCULES
PERSEPHONE	PROMETHEUS

An attractive library bulletin board and exhibit with a popular modern theme. (Courtesy of Jan Burns.)

- Enlist student volunteers to make bookmarks and posters that advertise books, reading, and library services.

- Plan library sponsored programs on children's books for newspapers, radio, television, and school assemblies.

- Devise a record system in which each student keeps a personal account of self-selected reading. At the end of a semester, send the list or display home to give parents an indication of their child's achievement.

- Create a series of bulletin boards emphasizing a literary genre—mythology, tall tales, folktales, etc.

- Encourage prompt return of books by awarding a prize to the class that has the best record. Display individual and classroom successes in a prominent place in the library.

- Color code the Caldecott and Newbery award winning books and display Newbery and Caldecott posters.

- Create a library scrapbook. The book could be made as an annual project and could contain photographs, projects, letters, illustrations, etc.

- Make library displays around themes such as: favorite authors, new books, or special holidays. Such displays should be changed fre-

When overdue books become a problem, a schoolwide contest initiated by the librarian might improve the situation. *(Courtesy of Sam Houston Elementary School, Port Arthur, Texas.)*

quently and could be made as part of an ongoing class activity.

- Produce a spinner of book categories for students who have difficulty in deciding on a book. Such a device may be divided into twelve reading categories (see dial-a-book) and used to motivate reluctant readers to read widely.

- Acquire a collection of children's books that teach *about* the library. The list below contains some suitable ones:

ABC for the Library by Mary Little. New York: Atheneum, 1975.

I Know a Librarian by Virginia Voight. New York: Putnam, 1967.

I Want to Be a Librarian by Carla Greene. Chicago: Children's Press, 1960.

Let's Find Out About a Book by Mildred L. Nickel. New York: Franklin Watts, 1971.

Let's Go to the Library by Naomi Buchkeimer. New York: Putnam, 1957.

Libraries: A Book to Begin On by Susan Bartlett. New York: Holt, Rinehart and Winston, 1964.

Through Library Doors by Linda Beek. Englewood Cliffs, N.J.: Scholastic Book Services, 1968.

Using Children's Art in the Library Program

When children's artwork is viewed as a means of self-expression and a mode of communication, it becomes a perfect accompaniment to literature and a vehicle for luring children into the library and keeping them there. A variety of art activities may be inspired by lively storytelling and reading-aloud sessions and by students' personal encounters with books. Art projects may be group or individual efforts. They may be supervised by the classroom teacher or by the librarian and displayed in either the classroom or the library.

Three art-literature projects that have been used by teachers and librarians to help promote books, reading, and library services are the creation of murals, friezes, and collages.

Murals

Large wall paintings known as murals go back to the time when prehistoric people scratched outline pictures on the walls of their caves. Murals in the elementary school are made by applying tempera paint with large brushes to a strip of white wrapping paper spread on the floor. The completed mural is fastened to the wall and finished off with a caption.

Opportunities to use literature as the basis of mural composition are almost limitless if students are given free rein to interpret books, stories, and poems in their own way. Books that give rise to strong mental images of the beauty in nature are excellent for murals. Such books include *The Happy Owls* by Celestino Piatti; *Time of Wonder* by Robert McCloskey; *White Snow, Bright Snow* by Roger Duvoisin; *Little House on the Prairie* by Laura Ingalls Wilder; *The Magic Bone* by William Steig; *Island of the Blue Dolphins* by Scott O'Dell; and *Call It Courage* by Armstrong Sperry.

Friezes

A frieze is a long, narrow, horizontal band or border used for decorative purposes. In ancient

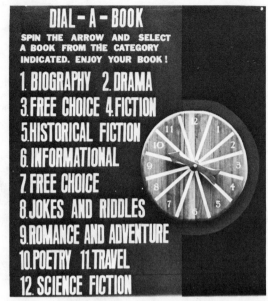

Indecisive girls and boys may enjoy using a wooden wheel with numerals and a spinner to select a book category. The list of categories may be changed to coincide with age-level interests. (Courtesy of Dan Coody and Peggy Flynn.)

A fourth-grade teacher tells the story of "Burt Dow, Deep Water Man," for which her students have created paper sculpture whales to illustrate it. Notice the bandage on the tail of each fish. (Courtesy of Maria Harmon, St. Catherine's Elementary School, Port Arthur, Texas.)

Committees of second-grade students prepare collage friezes based on picture books by Ezra Jack Keats. Completed friezes were placed in the school library for other students to enjoy. (Courtesy of Gloria Turner and Janna Bonura, Roy Guess Elementary School, Beaumont, Texas.)

Greek architecture, the frieze was a band of low-relief sculpture usually located at the top of the outer wall of the temple. When made by school children, a frieze consists of objects or shapes pasted on a long band of paper.

Any story of the accumulative type is excellent as a springboard for frieze making. Since repetition is the mode of such stories, students may add as many pieces to the frieze as they wish. Some books well suited to frieze making are *Millions of Cats* by Wanda Gag, *Alligators All Around* by Maurice Sendak, *A Sky Full of Dragons* by Mildred Whatley Wright, *The Five Hundred Hats of Bartholomew Cubbins* by Theodor Seuss Geisel, and *Mr. Popper's Penguins* by Florence and Richard Atwater.

Collage

A collage is made by pasting different shapes and textures of materials to a flat surface. Collage material may include fabrics and papers of varying textures and colors, soft wire, ribbon, yarn, seeds, macaroni, and other materials that are interesting in pattern, texture, color, and shape.

The children's author and illustrator who has made the most effective use of collage is Ezra Jack Keats. Barbara Bader has compared his cutout work with that of Matisse:

Keats's work has a simplicity of line and a broadness of form foreign ordinarily to paint or pen. It seems likely, moreover, that Matisse is somewhere behind that wild wallpaper, the brilliant pink and orange and yellow buildings outside (under a violet sky); and that the very making of cutouts, the play factor, frees the artist to play as well with color and pattern.[1]

Children are captivated by the stories of Peter, the central character in six of Keats's books. They see their behavior reflected in his, and the cutout work used by Keats to silhouette Peter makes them want to try their hand at collage.

Using Nonbook Media with Books

The use of names such as "instructional media center" and "instructional materials center" for what has traditionally been called the "library" reflects the expansion of materials and services that are now integral parts of most school programs. Until recently, an elementary school was considered fortunate if it had a room to house its book collection and a certified librarian to work with children. Today, many schools have a "media center" containing—in addition to books—nonbook media such as projection equipment, films, filmstrips, tapes, recording devices, slides, art prints, cameras, duplicating machines, production equipment, artifacts, and perhaps even live animals.

[1]Barbara Bader, *American Picturebooks: From Noah's Ark to the Beast Within* (New York: Macmillan, 1976), p. 379.

The widespread use of audiovisual and other nonbook materials in the elementary school resulted from a report issued in 1960 by the American Association of School Librarians. Entitled *Standards for School Library Programs*, the document outlined the need for libraries to supplement their book collections with nonbook teaching materials. The 1965 Elementary and Secondary Education Act provided money as an incentive to increase the availability of audiovisual resources in the classroom. The aim of the act was "to strengthen and improve educational quality and educational opportunities in the nation's elementary and secondary schools." With the subsequent infusion of federal money, school libraries increased their book collections and developed media centers for instructional improvement.

Unfortunately, a sequence of unforeseen events has impeded the efficient instructional use of audiovisual materials. Teacher education programs have not made full use of such equipment in their efforts to train school personnel. Some administrators and teachers have not fully realized the educational potential of audiovisual materials and often consider them unnecessary frills. Because many commercial producers of instructional products were eager to cash in on the federally funded bonanza, the content of many of the earliest materials was unsatisfactory and the technical quality was often poor. With inflation in the 1970s and 1980s have come a growing apprehension about the cost of educational services and a major decline in the amount of money available for instructional materials. In recent years, however, the quality of audiovisual products has sharply improved as teachers have become more selective. A major responsibility of the language arts teacher is to become acquainted with the nonbook media on hand and learn how to use them wisely.

In 1975 the American Library Association recommended that schools provide all children with a variety of instructional nonbook materials. According to the ALA guidelines, schools with 500

A Profile of Ezra Jack Keats

EZRA JACK KEATS received the Caldecott Medal in 1963 for *The Snowy Day,* the first book he both wrote and illustrated. A movie adaptation of the book later won a prize at the Venice Film Festival, and Peter, the central character, reappeared in five subsequent Keats books.

In commenting on *The Snowy Day* and the impact it has made on his work, Keats tells his readers:

> For 10 years I had been illustrating other people's books and there was never a black child in those books as the hero. So I resolved that when I had the confidence to do my own book, my hero would be a black child. I felt I was ready to try writing.

The result was *The Snowy Day.*[1]

Once Keats decided that his hero would be a black child, he made many sketches and studies of black children, "so that Peter would not be a white kid colored brown." He wanted Peter to be in the book on his own, not through the benevolence of white children or anyone else.

The idea for *The Snowy Day* was born one evening as Keats and some friends were reminiscing about the things they did as children when the snow fell and transformed their dingy neighborhood into a wonderland. "The city would become magical," Keats recalls. "All the dirt would disappear, everything seemed enchanted, and I felt as if I were on another planet. It was just beautiful!"

Many good things have happened to Ezra Jack Keats since publication of his famous snow story, not the least of which is the satisfaction of knowing that Peter and his friends are internationally known and loved:

> One of the nicest things that has happened is that my books now appear in countries all over the world. When I want to, I can hear Peter walking through the snow in many languages: *Crunch, crunch, crunch* in England; *knaar, knaar* in Sweden; *krunsj, krunsj* in Norway; *narskun, narskun* in Finland; *knirk, knirk* in Denmark; *kyu, kyu* in Japan.[2]

Before he began writing and illustrating books for children, Keats was a painter, and his work can be seen in some of the finest art collections in America. In 1965 he was selected as a contributing artist for UNICEF Christmas cards. In 1973, the children's reading room of the Warrensville Public Library in Ohio was named for him. In 1974, Keats was the guest of honor in Tokyo, Japan, at the opening of a children's roller-skating rink, which has a plaque bearing his name. The rink was built as a result of an enthusiasm for roller-skating sparked by his book *Skates!*

Keats has said about his art and writing: "What I want to show in all my books is that it doesn't matter where a child lives, that I want him to know that he's there and he's important, that there's hope and that he's got the resourcefulness to make it."

Ezra Jack Keats photo is used by permission.
[1] Information provided by Weston Woods, Weston, Connecticut, and Viking Press.
[2] Ezra Jack Keats, "Dear Mr. Keats . . . ," *Horn Book* (June 1972), p. 310.

BOOKS BY EZRA JACK KEATS

The Snowy Day, 1962
Whistle for Willie, 1964
John Henry: An American Legend, 1965
Jennie's Hat, 1966
Peter's Chair, 1967
Letter to Amy, 1968
Little Drummer Boy, 1968
Hi, Cat! 1969
Goggles, 1969
Apt. 3, 1971
Pet Show, 1972
Psst Doggie, 1973
Skates! 1973
Kitten for a Day, 1974
Dreams, 1974
Louie, 1975
The Trip, 1978

students or less would have a collection of instructional media totaling at least 20,000 items, or about 40 items per student. By ALA standards, the *ideal* media center would contain

- Books: 8,000 to 12,000 volumes (16 to 24 per student)
- Periodicals: 50 to 175 titles
- Films: access to 3,000 titles of 16mm films and 500 to 1,000 titles of 8mm films
- Filmstrips: 500 to 2,000 (1 to 4 per student)
- Slides and transparencies: 2,000 to 6,000 items (4 to 12 per student)
- Tapes, cassettes, records, and audio cards: 1,500 to 2,000 items (3 to 4 per student)
- Games and toys: 400 to 750 items
- Specimens: 200 to 400 items
- Models and sculpture: 200 to 500 items

The ALA also suggested that the media center be staffed by one full-time qualified specialist for every 250 students and a support staff of at least one media aide per specialist. Such a design represents the ideal support system for a school's instructional program and is certainly a worthy goal toward which to strive.

Using Nonbook Media to Teach

A collection of quality instructional media resources is essential for extending the language arts program. Filmstrips, films, video cassettes, records, cassette tapes, and slides may be used to introduce a poem, to explain different parts of speech, or to provide background for a piece of children's literature. The school's library learning center may not meet the ALA guidelines; nevertheless, as many media materials as the budget will allow should be made available to both teachers and students.

Television

It was through the eye of a television camera that the world watched American astronauts plant a flag on the barren soil of the moon. Television has remained unsurpassed for attracting and holding mass audience. Events are now routinely televised as they occur, imaginative productions are dramatically portrayed, and various programs are conveniently recorded and stored for personal viewing. With all of this technological sophistication, however, television remains a social paradox.

Television poses two interrelated problems for parents and teachers: (1) the excessive amount of time that many children spend watching it, (2) the disappointing quality of much television programming. It has been estimated that by the time children are eighteen years of age, they have spent more time watching television (16,000 hours) than attending school (11,000 hours). Girls and boys spend an average of three hours per day watching television, and many log six or more hours in front of a television screen. According to Charlotte Huck, "Children reach their peak period of viewing at ages 10 to 12; the very time when they used to reach their peak of reading."[2]

A number of research studies have consistently found that good readers spend less time watching television than do poor readers. Parents, of course, are the primary adults to monitor the amount of time their children spend watching television. However, the language arts teacher who provides exciting language activities and rich book experiences may have a pronounced effect on the child's taste in viewing as well as on the amount of time spent in viewing. Many language arts teachers use suitable television programs to enhance regular classroom activities. Once an outstanding program has aired,

[2]Charlotte Huck, *Children's Literature in the Elementary School*, 3d ed. (New York: Holt, Rinehart and Winston, 1979), p. 615.

The Ingalls family of NBC-TV's "Little House on the Prairie." Left to right, Melissa Gilbert, Michael Landon, Karen Grassle holding Wendy Turnbeaugh, and Melissa Sue Anderson with arms around Lindsay Greenbush. The dog's name is Bandit. (Photo courtesy of the National Broadcasting Company, Inc.)

the teacher has a perfect opportunity to read a related story, to stage a puppet play, or to teach a creative writing lesson on characterization. For example, each winter one network broadcasts "The Wizard of Oz." This show has been enjoyed by generations of children and consistently provides inspiration for further reading of Frank Baum's books.

In addition to concern over time spent in watching television, there is growing discontent about the quality of television programming. It is because of television's lowest common denominators—vulgarity and suggestiveness, violence,

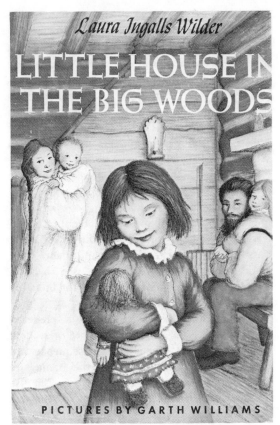

Laura Ingalls Wilder

LITTLE HOUSE IN THE BIG WOODS

PICTURES BY GARTH WILLIAMS

Garth Williams's impression of the Ingalls family from the 1953 edition of the Little House in the Big Woods.

One of the longest running and most popular of such shows is based on some of the finest contemporary literature for children—the Little House books by Laura Ingalls Wilder. Long-time lovers of the Little House books were dismayed at the prospect of having them rewritten for television, and many watched the pilot program with no small amount of trepidation. But most of the same people have since acknowledged that the series has caused more children and adults to know and appreciate the books than the author could ever have imagined in her lifetime.

It is only natural that people living in a highly technological and mechanized society would be drawn toward a quieter and simpler time—to a time when a family could pack up and move when things got too crowded. Legend has it that at one time in Wisconsin the forest was so dense that a squirrel could hop from limb to limb for a thousand miles without ever touching the ground. It was in those woods that Laura's Pa made a clearing to build the little house for his family. Laura was later to describe her childhood impression of the big woods:

So far as the little girl could see, there was only the one little house where she lived with her Father and Mother, her sister Mary and baby sister Carrie. A wagon track ran before the house, turning and twisting out of sight in the woods where the wild animals lived, but the little girl did not know where it went, nor what might be at the end of it.[4]

Without a doubt, the major reason why both the books and the television show hold so much appeal for people of all ages is that Laura Ingalls Wilder was a remarkably gifted writer who had the ability to transport her readers to her own time and place. The television shows, even though many of the episodes are radical departures from the original story, have remained surprisingly faithful in showing her philosophy: . . . "the real things haven't changed. It is still

and commercialism—that fears have emerged.[3] Many behavioral scientists are convinced that continued exposure to models of negative behavior, such as those often featured on television, has a significantly adverse impact on the psychological development of certain children. The research findings are conflicting; nevertheless, they have caused the networks to upgrade the quality of programs available during the "family hour."

[3]Gerald H. Maring, "Books to Counter TV Violence," *The Reading Teacher* (May 1979), pp. 916–920.

[4]Laura Ingalls Wilder, *Little House in the Big Woods.* New York: Harper & Row, Publishers, Inc., 1932, p. 2.

best to be honest and truthful; to make the most of what we have; to be happy with simple pleasures; and to be cheerful and have courage where things go wrong."[5]

Whatever its shortcomings, the television version of "Little House on the Prairie" deserves to be cited as an excellent example of the medium's capacity for enhancing and extending children's experiences with literature.[6] Language arts teachers and elementary school librarians have taken advantage of the show's success to promote a variety of reading experiences.

Filmstrips

A filmstrip is a sequence of related pictures, or frames, processed on 35mm film and placed on a continuous strip. The number of frames varies according to the complexity and length of the subject matter. Each frame contains a color picture of a photograph, cartoon, drawing, or graph. Filmstrips usually fall into one of two categories. Some have printed subtitles and no sound. Some are accompanied by a recording or cassette tape that describes each frame.

The advantages of using filmstrips in the elementary language arts classroom are numerous. Children find it easy to focus their attention on the visual (and auditory) information presented in a filmstrip containing a single concept. Filmstrips enable a large group of children to see the same picture at the same time. Individualized viewing is also possible if the projector is placed in a learning center or study carrel.

The use of filmstrips requires a minimum of mechanical know-how. Even a young elementary school child can easily use this versatile learning aid. Filmstrips are relatively inexpensive. They also have the important qualities of durability and versatility, two important aspects to be considered in budgeting. Individual filmstrips in their metal or plastic containers require little storage space and are easily organized in the library. They may be arranged in a sequential manner so that children may easily locate them. Usually a drawer or tray is used to shelve a variety of filmstrips from which students are allowed to select.

An estimated half-million titles are available for classroom use. There are appropriate filmstrips for all aspects of the language arts program—from parts of speech to literature appreciation.[7] A host of good filmstrips about outstanding books for both younger and older readers is available. They may be used to introduce a book to the entire class or for literature study by an individual student.[8]

Every filmstrip is developed in a predetermined order. As a result, the teacher or student can be certain of proper content sequence and may control the pace at which the frames are introduced. The language arts teacher can use filmstrips to introduce, to teach, or to reinforce almost any language arts skill. Filmstrips provide a graphic means to portray language arts concepts, ideas, and examples to individual students or the entire class.

Cassette Tape Recorders

The tape recorder and its accompanying cassette tapes are easy to use, inexpensive, and versatile. According to Polette and Hamlin, "Tape recording has become to the students' ears what chalkboards have been to the eyes. Students and teachers are able to hear themselves as they are

---

[5]Excerpted from a letter Laura Ingalls Wilder wrote to some of her young readers. Courtesy Harper & Row, Publishers, Inc.

[6]For a complete correlated unit on the *Little House* books, see Chapter 3.

[7]A practical guide on how to produce a classroom filmstrip may be found in the March 1967 issue of *Instructor* magazine.

[8]Ethel L. Heins, "Literature Bedeviled: A Searching Look at Filmstrips," *Horn Book* (June 1974), pp. 306–313.

---

heard by others."[9] Compact cassette tape recorders are now present in almost every language arts classroom. They have great potential as a learning tool in the often neglected areas of listening and speaking.

The tape recorder may be used in a variety of ways in the elementary classroom.

Mini-Lessons The teacher may tape-record mini-lessons, which present content information and give practice in listening and following directions. When boys and girls have completed the directed lesson, they are asked to respond to questions on the tape by placing their answers on a laminated answer sheet, or they are asked to perform a follow-up activity such as creative writing. A tape-recorded learning activity may be entirely self-contained by including materials necessary for reading or writing, directions for completing the lesson, and procedures for student self-evaluation.

Spelling Tapes Individualized spelling tapes that correlate with the basal spelling program may be easily produced. After the weekly spelling routine is completed, the final spelling test is taped and students are asked to write their words on an answer sheet. This activity offers children the opportunity to work on individualized spelling lessons.

Tape Pals After writing a creative story or report, the language arts teacher might suggest that students record their work on a cassette tape. The tapes may be shared or exchanged with members of another class.

An extension of this idea is to have the class find "tape pals" by exchanging the recorded tapes with students in other parts of the country. The names and addresses of teachers who wish to correspond and exchange various learning experiences are often listed in professional magazines and journals.

Cross-Age Tutoring Many schools encourage cross-age tutoring—older students working with younger children. Such programs promote individualized instruction and extend students' learning. Because tutoring time is often limited, many effective activities may be tape-recorded in advance. For example, the older student may tape a story or other written material with appropriate follow-up questions, and the younger child might record the answers directly on the cassette tape. The completed recording may then be used as the basis for a discussion at the next tutoring session.

Author-of-the-Month Centers The language arts teacher might create an author-of-the-month learning center. Such a center usually features a picture of the author, books, copies of his or her recorded versions of the stories, and filmstrips of the books. The teacher may wish to include a blank tape and a cassette tape recorder so that students may record their own comments and reactions to the author's books. In this way girls and boys will have an opportunity to hear the reactions of other readers and to express their own point of view.

Photography

The availability of Polaroid and Instamatic cameras has brought about an interest in photography as a means of widening the traditional boundaries of the elementary classroom. While taking pictures of their own experiences, students are learning to view the world in a more comprehensive way. The camera becomes a source of personal satisfaction as children share their experiences with others.

The two most popular photographic media for use in the elementary classroom are prints

[9] Nancy Polette and Marjorie Hamlin, *Reading Guidance in a Media Age* (Metuchen, N.J.: Scarecrow Press, 1975), p. 213.

A school principal and two students reflect on the year's activities. Displayed in a prominent place, the photographic scrapbook becomes a focal point of the library. *(Courtesy of Dorothy Nell Garren, Sam Houston Elementary School, Port Arthur, Texas.)*

and slides.[10] Color prints may be created on the spot with a Polaroid camera or in a more traditional way with an Instamatic camera and commercial film processing. Both approaches offer the language arts teacher a means of helping children to observe, to question, to differentiate, to value, and to learn. Photographic prints may be used in the language arts classroom to illustrate language-experience charts, creative writing, holiday books, concepts being taught (for example, near, far; over, under), personal or group scrapbooks, accounts of field trips and creative dramatics activities, poetry books, sequence stories, bulletin boards, and picture dictionaries.

Commercially processed slides are the most economical and adaptable of all photographic media. Slides may be projected to a very large

[10]For more information about photography in the classroom, write to Eastman Kodak Company, Motion Picture and Educational Products Division, Rochester, New York 14650.

group or used by individual children in a learning center. Dramatic productions, bulletin boards, learning activities, and classroom presentations are all excellent subjects for a slide presentation.

Some teachers photograph material from books and create caption slides to reinforce cognitive learning.[11] This procedure gives teachers the opportunity to present information to the entire class by enlarging some of the visual material from the textbook. By showing a slide of an important graph, chart, or illustration, the teacher may improve children's visual literacy by teaching them how to "read" graphic information. Slides may also be made in the classroom, without the use of a camera, according to the directions given below.

Directions for Making Slides

1. Cut a picture from a glossy or high quality paper to a size of 2 inches by 2 inches (or smaller).
2. Cut a piece of clear contact paper to the size of 2 inches by 2 inches and peel off the paper backing.
3. Place the contact paper on the picture, sticky side down.
4. Rub a coin over the plastic to remove air bubbles.
5. Soak the picture in soapy water for two minutes.
6. Remove the picture and peal the contact paper from the picture. (The ink will adhere to the contact paper.)
7. Mount the contact paper in a 2 inch by 2 inch plastic slide mount.
8. Place the completed slide in a projector for viewing.

[11]Before duplicating material from books, copyright regulations should be checked or permission requested from the publisher.

Bulletin Boards

A good bulletin board invites and encourages creative thinking by children; it stimulates them to further activity and investigation; and most important of all, the display can help to integrate the life and learning of the classroom.[12] Essentially a bulletin board has two main functions. It is a medium for students to display their work and learning experiences, and it allows the teacher to present new facts, ideas, or events.

An effective bulletin board calls for organization and planning. In fact, the teacher would be wise to plan bulletin boards for an entire year on the basis of the major instructional units to be taught. Each bulletin board will require a title or topic, materials to display, lettering for a caption, and an attractive arrangement.

The best bulletin boards always focus attention on a single subject or theme. The title should immediately convey the central thought or message; it ought to be simple, direct, and appropriate to grade level.

Many ideas for language arts bulletin boards and classroom displays may be found in commercially produced materials and publications for teachers. The best source of innovative ideas, however, will be the classroom teacher who creates and adapts materials to specific classroom situations and students who are permitted to create bulletin board materials reflecting their own interests.

Materials such as construction paper, wallpaper, cloth, burlap, and corrugated paper will be needed for the background. Actual objects, drawings and pictures, cartoons, stick figures, and so on may be collected for the display. Creating an effective bulletin board will be easier if a file of display materials is maintained on a year-round basis.

[12]Edgar Dale. *Audiovisual Methods in Teaching*, 3d ed. (Hinsdale, Ill.: Dryden Press, 1969), p. 330.

Whether the bulletin board is to be used for instruction or for displaying students' work, the teacher should keep the following guidelines in mind:

1. Arrange the captions and displayed materials to follow a left-to-right progression.
2. Direct attention to a focal point. Avoid cluttered arrangements that draw attention away from the central feature of the display.
3. Place captions at the bottom of the board only when it is above or at eye level.
4. Use a string or lines to help children follow a message, a sequence, or a progression of events.
5. Give bulletin boards a feeling of completeness by placing a border or frame around the display.

The caption focuses attention, presents a theme, and communicates an idea; thus the lettering should balance the display, not dominate the viewer's perception. Upper-case letters look important and forceful; they should be used only for short words or phrases. Printed letters bring a feeling of informality and friendliness. They are commonly used for longer words and sentences. Cursive writing gives an impression of formality and delicacy. It should be used only in the upper elementary grades. Textured letters attract attention and can be used to emphasize key words. They are appropriate only if they are an integral part of the overall message.

Summary

The success of any language arts program depends largely on an ample collection of library books, carefully selected, efficiently organized, and attractively displayed. Another vital part of the success equation is the teacher-librarian relationship. Both share the responsibility of teaching library skills and creating a lasting interest in books. Every instructional unit taught in the classroom should be calculated to get children into the library. At the same time, library activities should reinforce and enhance classroom work. To make it as easy as possible for all students (including kindergarteners) to locate and check out suitable books should be the goal of both the teacher and the librarian.

Some of the library skills needed by elementary school students are understanding the basic Dewey Decimal System, using the card catalog, being able to locate books on the shelves. Once they become involved with books, students enjoy knowing how a book is put together and something about the people who create a book.

In making the library appealing to students, the teacher and librarian may wish to use book-related art activities, displays, and contests. Children enjoy a wide variety of library games and find them helpful in learning library skills.

The use of nonbook media such as television, filmstrips, tapes, photography, and transparencies may enhance children's experiences with books. No material, of course, should be used at the expense of books or to replace books. On the contrary, every activity should lead to more and better reading.

Best Books for Children

Abel's Island, written and illustrated by William Steig. New York: Farrar, Straus & Giroux, 1976. A spoiled and pampered mouse is deposited by floodwater onto a deserted island. He is forced for the first time to survive by his own energy and intelligence. (P,M)

The Amazing Bone, written and illustrated by William Steig. New York: Farrar, Straus & Giroux, 1976. Pearl, a charming little pig in a pink dress with sunbonnet to match, is walking home from school on a beautiful spring day. As fate will have it, she finds a magic bone that speaks not only in Pearl's language but in *any* language. The two become good friends and save each other from many dangers. Pearl takes the bone home to provide conversation and music for her family. (P)

The Anti-Coloring Book, written and illustrated by Susan Striker and Edward Kimmel. New York: Holt, Rinehart and Winston, 1978. The authors tell us they did not write this book for those fortunate children whose art remains untouched by adult interference. This book is designed to counteract the negative effects that coloring books have on a child's creativity. (M,U)

Big Red, written by Jim Kjelgaard and illustrated by Bob Kuhn. New York: Bantam Press, 1976. A classic story of a boy and his faithful Irish setter. Adventure and loyalty are the key ingredients. (M)

Caleb & Kate, written and illustrated by William Steig. New York: Farrar, Straus & Giroux, 1977. While Caleb the carpenter dozes in the forest, the witch Yedida turns him into a dog. He hurries home to his wife Kate, who is weeping for her lost husband. She falls in love with the dog, who somehow reminds her of Caleb. He comforts Kate while she continues to mourn for Caleb. Eventually, a miracle turns Caleb back into a man. (P)

Emma's Dilemma, written by Gen LeRoy. New York: Harper & Row, 1975. A crisis arises when thirteen-year-old Emma's grandmother becomes allergic to Emma's beloved dog, Pearl. The plot is built around solving the problem. (P)

The Friendly Woods, written by Charles House. New York: Four Winds Press, 1973. A boy overcomes his neurotic fear of the woods by making a study of animal tracks and signs. A useful tracking guide is included. (P,M)

The Genie of Sutton Place, written by George Selden. New York: Farrar, Strauss & Giroux, 1973. A master storyteller spins another great tale. Tim, an unhappy orphan, is given the services of an Arabian genie, and his life immediately takes on a brighter look. (P,M)

The Golden Circle, written by Hal Borland and illustrated by Anne Ophilia Dowden. New York: Thomas Y. Crowell, 1977. This "book of months" is the creation of two fine artists who paint the natural world of trees, flowers, vines, birds, butterflies, and frogs to show the beauty of the changing seasons. A brief discussion accompanies each illustration. (M,U)

The Hiding Game, written and illustrated by Ben Schecter. New York: Parents' Magazine Press, 1977. Henri and Pierre are two young hippopotamus friends who decide to play a game of hide and seek. When they hide themselves so well that they have to spend the day and half the night looking for each other, they decide to go swimming instead. The background is beautiful woodland scenery done in watercolor. (P)

In the Night Kitchen, written and illustrated by Maurice Sendak. New York: Harper & Row, 1970. A dream fantasy based on the television commercial idea of "baked while you sleep." Mickey falls out of bed and into a batter where three jolly bakers stir and sing, "Milk in the batter! Milk in the batter! Stir it! Scrape it! Make it! Bake it!" A popular story with young children. (P)

To Hilda for Helping, written and illustrated by Margot Zemach. New York: Farrar, Straus & Giroux, 1977. Because Hilda is so faithful in setting the table every night while her sisters find other things to do, her father gives her a medal inscribed "To Hilda for Helping." She wears it day and night, and the sisters get madder and madder. They predict that the medal will bring doom to Hilda, but she counteracts their forecast with one of her own. (P)

A Tree Hurts Too, written and illustrated by the U.S. Forest Service, 1975. Beautiful, realistic watercolor paintings lead the reader through the life cycle of a tree. Emphasizes the importance of conservation. (P)

The Trenton Pickle Ordinance and Other Bonehead Legislation, written by Dick Hyman. New York: Longmans, Green, 1976. A collection of six hundred pieces of foolish legislation still on the books. Excellent for helping students appreciate satire and irony. (M,U)

The Turtle's Picnic, adapted by Terry Berger and illustrated by Erkki Alanen. New York: Crown, 1977. Three completely nonsensical short stories about animals. Easy enough for beginning readers to read for themselves. (P)

The Twenty-Elephant Restaurant, written by Russell Hoban and illustrated by Emily Arnold McCully. New York: Atheneum, 1978. An old man and an old woman have lived together happily for fifty years. Their only problem has been a wobbly table. "It's all right for a man to wear out a table, but a table shouldn't wear out a man." They decide to build a new table—one strong enough to hold an elephant. Because the work makes them feel so young, they decide to build twenty tables and advertise for elephants. (P,M)

Ultra-Violet Catastrophe, written by Margaret Mahy and illustrated by Brian Froud. New York: Parents' Magazine Press, 1975. Sally expects to waste a good day when she has to visit Aunt Anne. "She doesn't like me even to *breathe.* She fusses and fusses all the time." But things take a turn for the better when Sally and Great Uncle Magnus have adventures that leave them "wet and muddy and stained and torn." (P,M)

Up Day Down Day, written and illustrated by Jacquie Hann. New York: Four Winds Press, 1978. Two boys who are best friends share everything including good and bad happenings. They have "up" days and "down" days, but they spend them together making the bad ones tolerable and the good ones even better. Easy enough for beginning readers. (P)

Whistle for Willie, written and illustrated by Ezra Jack Keats. New York: Viking Press, 1964. Peter, a small black boy, accomplishes the important task of learning to whistle. Now he is able is call his dog, Willie. A realistic story of patient effort and achievement. (P)

Bibliography

Bader, Barbara. *American Picturebooks: From Noah's Ark to the Beast Within.* New York: Macmillan, 1976.

Cheyney, Arnold B. *Teaching Reading Skills Through the Newspaper.* Newark, Del.: International Reading Association, 1971.

Dale, Edgar. *Audiovisual Methods in Teaching,* 3d ed. Hinsdale, Ill.: Dryden Press, 1969.

Debes, John, and Clarence Williams. "The Power of Visuals." *Instructor,* December 1974.

Flynn, Peggy. "What's Black and White and Spread All Over? The Newspaper." *Journal of Reading,* May 1978.

Green, Ellin, and Madalynne Schoenfeld. *A Multimedia Approach to Children's Literature,* 2d ed. Chicago: American Library Association, 1977.

Heins, Ethel L. "Literature Bedeviled: A Searching Look at Filmstrips." *Horn Book,* June 1974.

Huck, Charlotte. *Children's Literature in the Elementary School,* 3d ed. New York: Holt, Rinehart and Winston, 1979.

Larrick, Nancy. *A Parent's Guide to Children's Reading,* 4th ed. New York: Doubleday, 1975.

McCracken, Robert, and Marlene McCracken. *Reading Is Only the Tiger's Tail.* San Rafael, Calif.: Leswing, 1972.

Maring, Gerald H. "Books to Counter TV Violence." *The Reading Teacher,* May 1979.

May, Jill P. "How to Sell Doughnuts: Media and Children's Literature." *Language Arts,* April 1979.

Paine, Carolyn A. "The Great Picture Lift." *Learning,* April 1974.

Pett, Dennis W. "Visual Literacy." *Classroom-Relevant Research in the Language Arts.* Washington, D.C.: Association for Supervision and Curriculum Development, 1978.

Polette, Nancy, and Marjorie Hamlin. *Reading Guidance in a Media Age.* Metuchen, N.J.: Scarecrow Press, 1975.

Rice, Susan. *Films Kids Like.* Chicago: American Library Association, 1973.

———. *Standards for School Library Programs.* Chicago: American Association of School Librarians, 1960.

Stewig, John Warren. "Book Illustrations: Key to Visual and Verbal Literacy." *Using Literature in the Elementary Classroom.* Urbana, Ill.: National Council of Teachers of English, 1978.

Winn, Marie. *The Plug-In Drug: Television, Children and the Family.* New York: Viking Press, 1977.

Chapter 14

A Medicine Chest for the Soul:
Using Books to Help Children Cope with Problems

BOOKS MAKE A DIFFERENCE. There is little doubt that by empathizing with believable book characters, whether of the animal or human variety, readers may be better able to understand themselves and others. When children read about a character whose behavior has brought about failure or success, they may recognize aspects of their own personalities and make whatever adjustments are appropriate. Obviously, the vicarious experiences of reading are less threatening to one's ego than the reality of everyday life. Moreover, they are reversible. If readers decide that they do not want to follow the course of action taken by a certain character, no third person will be able to sit in judgment of that decision.[1]

The classroom teacher is the logical person to bring books and children together in unobtrusive ways that will meet children's needs. The teacher is in a much better position than the school counselor or psychologist, for example, to observe each child closely over a period of time and to recognize unique needs and interests. Most children will never see a professional counselor. Nevertheless, they have basic psychological needs that may be partially satisfied with well-written, beautifully illustrated books. The language arts or reading teacher, working closely with the school librarian, has the best opportunity to make available on a day-to-day basis books that can make a difference in children's lives.

Printed in a child's handwriting on the title page of a copy of *Charlotte's Web*, for example, were the words "So dear to my heart." That inscription was one young reader's tribute to Wilbur and Charlotte. A book that evokes such an expression of emotion has undoubtedly given the child a new insight into self. Such personal and profound interaction between a reader and literature is a form of bibliotherapy—the relief of personal problems and inner conflicts by means of books and reading.

[1]Tony Shepherd and Lynn B. Iles, "What Is Bibliotherapy?" *Language Arts* (May 1976), p. 569.

In contrast to bibliotherapy is didacticism— the use of writing to teach, preach, and moralize. Didactic literature sets out to change the reader's attitudes or behavior. It often promises entertainment but fails to deliver much enjoyment because its heavy-handed moralizing usually leaves the reader with an overdose of guilt.

Unfortunately, the number of didactic trade books and stories being published for children is increasing. Many adults, mistaking didactic works for those that lead young readers to new awareness about themselves and others, think that didacticism is exactly what girls and boys need. It is therefore essential that the beginning teacher recognize the difference between the two types of literature and acquaint students with writing that seeks to do more than preach citizenship and morality.

In this chapter we will contrast the didactic approach of school books used by generations of Americans with bibliotherapy, a new term for a venerable concept. We will explain how the language arts teacher can use books to help children satisfy the basic needs identified by psychologist Abraham Maslow.

The Didactic Approach

For more than two centuries, teachers in America have used reading matter to inculcate moral values and religious beliefs. The first real textbook used in colonial schools was the *New England Primer*. This small book covered with two thin layers of wood contained the alphabet, a list of "easie syllables for children," and lists of words grouped by the number of syllables they contained. This material was followed by verses and sentences accompanied by woodcuts to illustrate each letter of the alphabet. The little pictures reflected a strong religious emphasis. Indeed, the primary aim of the primer was to teach children to read so that they could read the Bible.

In 1783, Noah Webster's *American Spelling Book* replaced the *New England Primer* as the

Rhymed alphabet pages in the New England Primer *(1727).*

A	In *Adam's* Fall We Sinned all.
B	Thy Life to Mend This *Book* Attend.
C	The *Cat* doth play And after flay.
D	A *Dog* will bite A Thief at night.
E	An *Eagles* flight Is out of fight.
F	The Idle *Fool* Is whipt at School.
N	*Nightingales* fing In Time of Spring.
O	The *Royal Oak* it was the Tree That fav'd His Royal Majeftie.
P	*Peter* denies His Lord and cries.
Q	Queen *Efther* comes in Royal State To Save the JEWS from difmal Fate
R	*Rachol* doth mour. For her firft born.
S	*Samuel* anoints Whom God appoint.

most widely used "language arts" textbook. Webster, as a teacher, had become dissatisfied with the textbooks available to children. He wanted to write books that would instill American culture and values while teaching girls and boys to write, spell, and read.

The speller was a small book, about 4 inches by 6½ inches. Its cover, two thin sheets of wood covered with light blue paper, gave it its well-known nickname—the blue-backed speller. The book contained lists of words divided into syllables for spelling and short moralistic stories for reading. It was a combination of speller, reader, and moral guide. Few would question the worthiness of Webster's goals, but his enthusiasm for morality and patriotism resulted in some highly didactic writing.

Webster's spelling book was used widely for more than a hundred years, and to the present time it has never been out of print. Its wide popularity has had some interesting sidelights. In 1786, some unscrupulous publishers pirated the speller and started Webster on a vigorous campaign for copyright laws. He wrote letters, lectured, and lobbied until Congress, influenced by his arguments, enacted the first national copyright legislation in 1790. The blue-backed speller is said to have sold more than 100 million copies. The royalties supported Webster while he prepared the famous dictionary that bears his name.

The school textbook as we know it today was born during the rapid expansion of public education in the nineteenth century. Many publishers introduced a reader or a series of readers to American schools, but William McGuffey, a young college professor from Ohio, developed a set of readers that surpassed them all. His readers

The following is a page reproduced from Noah Webster's speller:

28 | THE ELEMENTARY | | |

BĀR, LĂST, CÂRE, F4LL, WH4T; HĔR, PRĔY, THÊRE; ĜET; BĬRD, MARĪNE; LĬŊK;

No. 32.--XXXII.

WORDS OF TWO SYLLABLES, ACCENTED ON THE SECOND.

a bāse'	re elāim'	un sāy'	ben zoin'
de base	pro elaim	as say	a void
in ease	dis elaim	a way	a droit
a bate	ex elaim	o bey	ex ploit
de bate	de mēan	eon vey	de eoy
se date	be mōan	pur vey	en joy
ere ate	re tāin	sur vey	al loy
ob late	re main	de fȳ	em ploy
re late	en grōss	af fȳ	an noy
in flate	dis ereet	de nȳ	de stroy
eol late	al lāy	de erȳ	eon voy
trans late	de lay	re boil	es pouse
mis state	re lay	de spoil	ea rouse
re plēte	in lay	em broil	de vour
eom plete	mis lay	re eoil	re dound
se erete	dis play	sub join	de vout
re çīte	de eay	ad join	a mount
in çite	dis may	re join	sur mount
po lite	de fray	en join	dis mount
ig nite	ar ray	eon join	re eount
re deem	be tray	dis join	re nown
es teem	pōr tray	mis join	en dow
de elāim	a stray	pur loin	a vow

Strong drink will debase a man.

Hard shells incase clams and oysters.

Men inflate balloons with gas, which is lighter than common air.

Teachers like to see their pupils polite to each other.

Idle men often delay till to-morrow things that should be done to-day.

A page from Noah Webster's American Spelling Book. *Notice the moral advice in the form of proverbs that contain words in the list above.*

were "graded"; they contained easy material for beginning students and more difficult material for advanced ones. This was a new idea in textbooks.

Like Webster's blue-backed speller, McGuffey's readers were extremely popular, selling over 122 million copies between 1836 and 1920. They have been criticized for their mercenary themes.

In the stories, virtue is seldom its own reward. Rather, a child would perform a kind deed for a stranger who typically turned out to be a wealthy relative who later left the Good Samaritan a fortune. The lesson was often so obvious that it offended the sensibilities of children. Nevertheless, the books did provide a certain amount of entertainment to children at a time when there was little of that ingredient to be found in any literature.

Well into the 1920s, many elementary schools were still using books written and illustrated for the purpose of changing attitudes and improving behavior. *Slovenly Peter,* for example, contained stories designed to correct almost any bad habit a child might have, from lying and cheating to sloppiness and thumb-sucking.

During the past fifty years, basal language arts and reading textbooks have evolved, changed, and improved. Much less emphasis is placed on moralizing, and a great deal more attention is given to the storyline. In spite of the improvements, however, an avalanche of criticism descended on textbook publishers during the 1960s. Critics attacked the narrow instructional approach of the books, their overemphasis on white, middle-class society, and their stereotyped portrayals of women and girls. As a result of the controversy, Dick and Jane, two of the most famous and long-lived textbook characters were laid to rest.

Publishers responded to the criticism by trying to combine instruction in the skills necessary for effective communication with a more realistic and balanced portrayal of ethnic groups and women. Even at that, some publishers were accused of "sticking in" minority characters without giving them a vital and relevant part in the story's happenings.

A promising change in textbooks has come about recently: More attention is being given to students' interests and needs. The story itself is given primary consideration; it is often taken from the writings of outstanding authors and is used as a sampler in the textbook. The new material is much less didactic, because the best writers for students, whether they are writing a school text or a trade book, do not assume that all children need preachment.

The Bibliotherapy Approach

Bibliotherapy, the use of books to help people understand and cope with the problems of everyday life, has been actively practiced since the time of Aristotle, when the libraries of ancient Greece carried these inscriptions: "The Healing Place of the Soul" and "The Medicine Chest for the Soul."[2] In 1916, the concept of bibliotherapy was formally introduced by Samuel McChord Crothers in an article in the *Atlantic Monthly*. The term "bibliotherapy" was first defined professionally, however, in 1941 in *Dorland's Illustrated Medical Dictionary*, as "the employment of books and the reading of them in the treatment of nervous disorders."[3] In 1962, *Library Trends* devoted an entire issue to the topic of bibliotherapy. In it Ruth Tews presented the results of her thorough study. She wrote, "Bibliotherapy is a program of selected activity involving reading materials, planned, conducted, and controlled as treatment under the guidance of the physician for emotional and other problems."[4]

During the past few years, best-seller lists for adult readers have consistently reflected an interest in psychological and self-help material. Millions of copies of books such as *I'm OK, You're OK; Looking Out for Number One; How to Be Your Own Best Friend;* and *Your Erroneous*

[2]Mildred T. Moody and Hilda Limper, *Bibliotherapy: Methods and Materials* (Chicago: American Library Association, 1971), p. 3.
[3]Ibid., p. 7.
[4]Ruth Tews, "Introduction," *Library Trends* (October 1962), pp. 97–105.

ECLECTIC SERIES.

NOTES.—5. *Cedars of Lebanon.* A species of cedar, of great magnificence, formerly abundant in Mt. Lebanon and the Taurus Range in Asia Minor, but now almost entirely destroyed. The wood is durable and fragrant, and was used in the construction of costly buildings, such as the palace of David and Solomon's Temple.

7. *Leviathan.* This name is applied in the Old Testament to some huge water animal. In some cases it appears to mean the crocodile, but in others the whale or a large sea-serpent,

---

LII. MY MOTHER.

1. OFTEN into folly straying,
   O, my mother! how I've grieved her!
   Oft I've heard her for me praying,
   Till the gushing tears relieved her;
   And she gently rose and smiled,
   Whispering, "God will keep my child."

2. She was youthful then, and sprightly,
   Fondly on my father leaning,
   Sweet she spoke, her eyes shone brightly,
   And her words were full of meaning;
   Now, an Autumn leaf decayed;
   I, perhaps, have made it fade.

3. But, whatever ills betide thee,
   Mother, in them all I share;
   In thy sickness watch beside thee,
   And beside thee kneel in prayer.
   Best of mothers! on my breast
   Lean thy head, and sink to rest.

A page from McGuffey's Fifth Eclectic Reader, *a textbook read by five generations of American school children.*

Zones have been sold. If such books have so much appeal for adults, it follows that children could benefit from books of a similar nature presented at their level of interest and readability—books they could choose at will. As a matter of fact, Abraham Maslow, the eminent psychologist, recommended that there should be bookstores dedicated to handling and promoting bibliotherapeutic materials—"shelves stocked with

THE STORY OF LITTLE SUCK-A-THUMB

One day, Mamma said, "Conrad dear,
I must go out and leave you here.
But mind now, Conrad, what I say,
Don't suck your thumb while I'm
    away.
The great tall tailor always comes
To little boys that suck their thumbs;
And ere they dream what he's about,
He takes his great sharp scissors out
And cuts their thumbs clean off,—and
    then
You know, they never grow again."

Mamma had scarcely turn'd her back,
The thumb was in, alack! alack!

A didactic story from Slovenly Peter.

The door flew open, in he ran,
The great, long, red-legged scissor-
man.
Oh! children, see! the tailor's come
And caught our little Suck-a-Thumb.
Snip! Snap! Snip! the scissors go;
And Conrad cries out—Oh! Oh! Oh!
Snip! Snap! Snip! They go so fast;
That both his thumbs are off at last.

Mamma comes home; there Conrad stands,
And looks quite sad, and shows his hands;—
"Ah!" said Mamma, "I knew he'd come
To naughty little Suck-a-Thumb."

humanistic books, journals, and pamphlets."[5] Even though bookstores like those Maslow advocated may not yet exist, many excellent books do portray real people solving and adjusting to problems of personal appearance, physical disability, social acceptance, neglect and deprivation, poverty, war, prejudice, and other circumstances that may affect the lives of children.

At the present, bibliotherapy in the classroom consists of using literature to enrich the lives of all children and to give them the inner resources they need to solve personal problems. As defined by Savage and Mooney, bibliotherapy is a "dynamic interaction through which a person finds solutions to personal problems in the stories s/he reads."[6] The teacher trying to decide which books are appropriate for bibliotherapy should keep in mind certain criteria. In the words of Charlotte Huck:

A book may be considered as suitable for bibliotherapy if it tells an interesting story and yet has the power to help a reader (1) acquire information and knowledge about the psychology and physiology of human behavior, (2) learn what it means to "know thyself," (3) find an interest outside himself, (4) relieve conscious problems in a controlled manner, (5) utilize an opportunity for identification and compensation, and (6) illuminate difficulties and acquire insight into his own behavior.[7]

In classrooms where bibliotherapy is being used, certain practices, behaviors, and attitudes can be observed. A plentiful supply of books is available at the fingertips of students. Books in the classroom are of excellent quality and have been selected for their therapeutic as well as literary value. Time is provided for students to browse among the books and to read them independently.

It is evident that the teacher knows the students well, is alert to their problems, and is able to recommend helpful books in subtle and unobtrusive ways. In such an atmosphere, students learn to go to books not only for entertainment and information, but also for comfort, reassurance, and inspiration.

Although bibliotherapy is usually a private affair between book and reader, there are times when a book might be helpful to an entire group. In times of crisis, it is a sensitive teacher who reads aloud a sustaining book—a teacher who believes in the importance of bibliotherapy.

Perhaps the best reason to bring children and books together for beneficial purposes is to satisfy what Abraham Maslow has termed "life's basic needs."

Satisfying Basic Needs by Reading

Meeting basic needs is a goal toward which all normal persons strive from birth to death. Initially, a young child's needs are narrow and self-centered. The primary needs are usually fulfilled by the love and protection found in the immediate family. As the child matures, however, attitudes and feelings are extended and directed toward others. With maturation come the pursuit of meaningful tasks and the feeling of confidence that results from being able to accomplish them. The classroom teacher who is knowledgeable about needs theory realizes that the behavior of children does not just happen; it is caused by the struggle to satisfy certain needs.

Abraham Maslow defined seven basic needs and ranked them in a hierarchy. He grouped needs into the following categories: (1) physiological, (2) safety, (3) love and belonging, (4) esteem, (5) knowledge and understanding,

[5]Abraham Maslow, *Toward a Psychology of Being* (Princeton, N.J.: Van Nostrand, 1968), p. 240.
[6]John F. Savage and Jean F. Mooney, *Teaching Reading to Children with Special Needs* (Boston: Allyn and Bacon, 1979), p. 378.
[7]Charlotte Huck, *Children's Literature in the Elementary School*, 3d ed. (New York: Holt, Rinehart and Winston, 1976), p. 264.

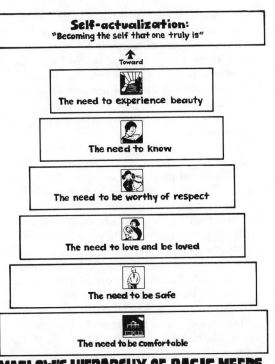

Figure 14.1 Maslow's Hierarchy of Basic Needs (Courtesy of Barbara Ellis.)

(6) aesthetic, and (7) self-actualization (see Figure 14.1).

Once teachers understand their students' needs, it is easier to provide books and stories that help to satisfy those needs. It then becomes a matter of leading a child to the right book at the right time. There are no guarantees in bibliotherapy; a chosen book might not help a child at all. On the other hand, many of us can pinpoint a date in our lives when a book made a great difference.

Physiological Needs: The Need to Be Comfortable

Satisfaction of the need for food, drink, shelter, and freedom from pain is fundamental for human survival. Children are almost entirely dependent on other people for their physical well-being and security. The child's sense of physiological comfort begins with parental love and depends on the necessities of proper nourishment, ample rest, and adequate shelter. Regrettably, some boys and girls spend much of their childhood unsure of whether their basic needs will be met.

Books cannot provide nourishment for a hungry child or give warmth to a child suffering from the cold. Literature, however, can portray the timeless struggle to satisfy physiological needs. It can show the effect that such a quest has on all human beings. In *M. C. Higgins, the Great*, Virginia Hamilton's 1975 Newbery Award book, Mayo Cornelius Higgins sits atop a gleaming forty-foot steel pole overlooking his home on Sarah's Mountain. From his perch, M. C. is able to observe the remains of a once picturesque valley and the wounds inflicted on the environment by the strip-mining of coal. M. C. fears that the monstrous pile of trees and dirt will wash down the mountain and destroy not only his home but his very way of life:

To the north and east had been ranges of hills with farmhouses nestled in draws and lower valleys. But now the hills looked as if some gray-brown snake had curled itself along their ridges. The snake loops were mining cuts just like the one across Sarah's Mountain only they were a continuous gash. They went on and on, following fifty miles of a coal seam. As far as M. C.'s eyes could see, the summits of hills had been shredded away into rock and ruin which spilled down into croplands at the base of the hills.[8]

Many children in this country face similar assaults on their surroundings. Practically every newscast reports such threats. To read about M. C. Higgins, and his struggle to cope with a problem completely beyond his control, can help

[8]Virginia Hamilton, *M. C. Higgins, the Great* (New York: Macmillan, 1974), pp. 36–37.

children face their own fears in a rational manner and to live with anxiety without being overwhelmed by it.

Safety Needs: The Need to Be Safe

All people need to exist in a predictable, stable, and nonthreatening physical environment. A child's sense of safety may be disrupted by almost any situation that is perceived as a threat. To the child, the source of the threat makes little difference. The elementary teacher who promotes a wholesome, familiar routine will create a sense of physical well-being that is needed by all children. Systematic experiences with literature should play a large part in that routine.

Children of elementary school age are frightened by the specter of crime, disease, poverty, and war. Some undergo very real threats to their physical welfare from abusive parents or bullying siblings or schoolmates. Teachers cannot always shield children from danger or from the emotion of fear, but they can give them inner strength to deal with some of life's hazards. One way to help them cope with fear and anxiety is to acquaint them with strong book characters who find ways to deal successfully with similar problems.

The book *Benjie on His Own* gives a realistic picture of a young boy effectively coping with problems that often occur in an insensitive urban environment. One scene shows six-year-old Benjie's nervousness when Granny is not waiting to walk him home after school. He asks an older friend to take him home, but his friend wants to stay at school and play basketball. Benjie, anxious to get home and see if Granny is all right, goes on alone. His worst fears are confirmed when some older boys ask him for money:

A few big boys were down the street. They looked at him in a way he didn't like. He started to cross the street. But he didn't have a chance. The boys were all around him. "Going to the store for your mother, boy?" a tall boy in dark glasses asked.

He wanted to say, "What's it to you?" Or, "You let me be." Or, "Don't call me boy like that."

There were a lot of sayings in his mind, but he didn't let them out. The thing he cared most about was getting home fast to see how Granny was.

Benjie looked down at his feet and shook his head. "I'm going home from school," he said.

A boy with striped pants said, "He hasn't got any money."

"Make him turn his pockets out," the tall boy said.

Benjie turned his pockets inside out. They could see he didn't have any money. They looked at his arm to see if he had a watch.

Benjie tried not to think how scared he was so he wouldn't cry or try to run. He knew he couldn't run as fast as these big boys.

"What shall we do with him?" a fat boy asked.

Benjie looked at him. "Let me go home, please," he said. "I think my grandmother is sick."

"Baby wants his grandmother," the tall boy said.

"Oh, shut up!" said the boy with the striped pants. "Maybe his grandmother is sick. Go on home, kid."

"Next time you come around here, have some money with you," the fat boy said.

Benjie ran. At the corner he turned and looked back. They weren't coming after him. He was safe.[9]

Unfortunately, all children at some point in their lives experience cruelty, injustice, and abuse. Benjie kept his wits about him and used good sense to survive a serious threat to his safety and well-being. To young readers who understand his plight all too well, Benjie becomes an heroic character who gives them a bit of his courage.

Love and Belonging Needs: The Need to Love and Be Loved

People need to develop relationships based on reciprocated affection. For many years songwrit-

[9]From *Benjie on His Own* by Joan M. Lexau, 1970, The Dial Press.

ers have verbalized the basic need to love and be loved in return. Teachers who realize that a child's need for love is pervasive and continuous will be motivated to provide opportunities for children to experience love and belonging in many ways and at all stages of their development.

The family unit is usually the primary source of affection and attachment for children. Feelings of love and belonging, however, are absent in many homes. For children in such situations, the school may be a refuge where affectionate relationships with adults can partially compensate for the feelings of love and belonging that are missing in the home. Adults who work with children should be prepared not only to provide the warmth and understanding that is needed by all boys and girls but also to meet the special and unique needs of some individuals.

In addition to positive interpersonal relationships in the classroom, children also need vicarious experiences with warm and sensitive book characters. A classic case of love and friendship is described in a heartfelt way by Kenneth Grahame in his mock epic *The Wind in the Willows*. Rat and Mole miss their beloved riverbank and long to be home where there is peace and security, but their friend Toad, irresponsible and selfish as usual, must have someone to look after him in his latest escapade:

At last they turned into their little bunks in the cart; and Toad, kicking out his legs, sleepily said, 'Well, goodnight you fellows!

'This is the real life for a gentleman! Talk about your old river!'

'I don't talk about my river,' replied the patient Rat. 'You know I don't, Toad. But I think about it,' he added pathetically, in a lower tone: 'I think about it—all the time!'

The Mole reached out from under his blanket, felt for the Rat's paw in the darkness, and gave it a squeeze. 'I'll do whatever you like, Ratty,' he whispered. 'Shall we run away tomorrow morning, quite early—very early—and go back to our dear old hole on the river?'

'No, no, we'll see it out,' whispered back the Rat. 'Thanks awfully, but I ought to stick by Toad till this trip is ended. It wouldn't be safe for him to be left to himself. It won't take very long. His fads never do. Good night!'[10]

The close friendship between Ratty and Mole endears the two small creatures to children. To read about such a satisfying companionship between two book characters helps them learn the art of being a friend, and helps them appreciate what it means to have a friend.

Esteem Needs: The Need to Be Worthy of Respect

Within every person is the desire to take pride in oneself and to be held in high esteem by others. The need to be worthy of respect is satisfied initially in the immediate family. Elementary schools often provide the first formal learning environment in which a child may be respected as a unique individual outside the family.

Teachers, recognizing children's need for esteem, can provide wholesome experiences that make girls and boys feel good about themselves and proud of each other. Children should be permitted to set for themselves goals that are within their ability to attain. The teacher should help them to pursue realistic goals, providing them with the necessary means to achieve goals that will promote a positive self-concept. Children who achieve their goals should be sincerely praised; their parents and other appropriate individuals should be notified.

As children mature, they learn how to control their own behavior and thus are able to manage their own environment to some extent. Moreover, they gradually develop a self-concept that parallels the image other people have of them. Because of the negative treatment some children

[10]Kenneth Grahame, *The Wind in the Willows* (New York: Scribner, 1954), pp. 33–34. Used by permission.

experience at the hands of adults and peers, they develop a low opinion of themselves. A book like *Call It Courage* can bring hope and encouragement to students who hear it read aloud by a respected teacher.

Mafatu, in Armstrong Sperry's 1941 Newbery Award book *Call It Courage,* is labeled a coward by the men, women, and children of his village. His name means "Boy Who Was Afraid." Mafatu, a South Sea Islander, is terrified of the sea, and since his people spend their days on the sea and their nights near the sea, he becomes an outcast. In a rite of passage from boyhood to adult status, he forces himself to set out alone on a small raft with only his dog Uri for company. He sails toward a mysterious island in the distance. Years later when he returns home, a boar's tooth necklace shining around his chest is a symbol of his successful struggle to overcome the stigma of cowardice:

"My father," Mafatu cried thickly, "I have come home."

The Great Chief's face was transformed with joy. This brave figure, so thin and straight, with the fine necklace and the flashing spear and courage blazing from his eyes—his son? The man could only stand and stare and stare, as if he could not believe his senses. And then a small yellow dog pulled himself over the gunwale of the canoe, fell at his master's feet. Uri. . . . Far overhead an albatross caught a light of gold on its wings. Then Tavana Nui turned to his people and cried: "Here is my son come home from the sea. Mafatu, Stout Heart. A brave name for a brave boy!"[11]

Mafatu's struggles to become a person of worth and dignity are the dilemmas faced by adolescents everywhere. The satisfying outcome gives them faith that they too will eventually triumph, and in the long run win the much-needed admiration of family and friends.

Knowledge and Understanding Needs: The Need to Know

All children seem to possess natural curiosity. For younger children, the question "Why?" is an integral part of growth and development. In the elementary classroom, it is the teacher's responsibility to stimulate and encourage this natural desire to secure answers to questions and solutions to problems. The need to know is partially met by textbooks that teach needed skills in a sequential manner. Informational trade books are another important means of satisfying the curiosity of children. Such books can be used to answer specific questions or to fulfill the need for broader knowledge.

The variety of informational books for children in elementary schools is immense, ranging from simple concept books for younger children to books on very specific topics for older readers. According to Sutherland and Arbuthnot, "The best informational books are written by authors who know their subjects well, and who write about them imaginatively, with an understanding of the needs and limitations of their audience."[12]

The quest for knowledge and solutions to problems is dramatically portrayed in books. Fiction provides excellent models of strong characters seeking answers to questions about the meaning of life. One example is *Sounder,* the 1970 Newbery Award book by William H. Armstrong. Except for a dog named Sounder, none of the characters has a name. They are simply called "the boy," "the mother," and "the father," thus universalizing their suffering and resistance to injustice. The sharecropper family endures pain and suffering after the father is imprisoned for stealing a ham to feed his hungry family. For

[11]Armstrong Sperry, *Call It Courage* (New York: Macmillan, 1940), p. 94. Used by permission.

[12]Zena Sutherland and May Hill Arbuthnot, *Children and Books,* 5th ed. (Glenview, Ill.: Scott, Foresman, 1977), p. 444.

many years the boy searches for his father and for someone to teach him to read and write:

The boy was trying to read aloud, for he could understand better if he heard the words. But now he stopped. He did not understand what it said; the words were too new and strange. He was sad. He thought books would have words like the ones he had learned to read in the store signs, words like his mother used when she told him stories of the Lord and Joseph and David. All his life he had wanted a book. Now he held one in his hands, and it was only making his bruised fingers hurt more. He would carry it with him anyway.[13]

At the age when students are likely to read a book like *Sounder*, they are expending a great deal of time and energy in learning to read and write effectively. Furthermore, they have been at it for a good portion of their lives. The young boy in *Sounder*, who wants desperately to learn to read and write, can help them to appreciate their remarkable achievement in becoming a literate person.

Aesthetic Needs: The Need to Experience Beauty

The frantic pace of adult life and the quest for economic success make it impossible for many people to perceive beauty. By the same token, the overscheduled and programmed lives of some children deprive them of time to look for beauty and to contemplate loveliness when they find it.

Unless both teachers and parents take seriously a child's need for beauty, for aesthetic satisfaction, the curriculum will probably become even more fragmented and categorized than it is now. Children will spend many more hours in basic skill-building exercises of the recognition and recall type. Art, music, and creative physical education will be the losers. An awareness of this "hurried child" syndrome makes it imperative that the classroom become a sanctuary where time is provided for dreaming and imagining, for wandering down unknown paths to find secret treasures.

In the search for beauty and order, books are essential—books that realistically portray people whose aesthetic needs are being met. In *Blue Willow* by Doris Gates, the only object of beauty and value owned by a migrant family of the Depression era is a blue willow plate. Janey Larkin's mother promises her that when they have their own home, they will take the plate out of the trunk and give it a place of honor. In the meantime, Janey is allowed to unpack the plate on occasion and look at it:

. . . the willow plate was the only beautiful thing the Larkins owned. It was a blue willow plate, and in its pattern of birds and willows and human figures it held a story that for Janey never grew old. Its color, deep and unchanging, brought to her the promise of blue skies even on the grayest days and of blue oceans even in an arid wasteland. She never grew tired of looking at it.[14]

Only with guidance and experience can children grow to see beauty, to find it in unexpected places, and to fully appreciate its impact. Doris Gates describes in eloquent terms Janey's feelings about the beautiful plate.

Self-Actualization Needs: Becoming the Self That One Truly Is

In his studies of psychological health, Maslow arrived at the conclusion that the characteristics

---

[13]Excerpt from *Sounder* by William H. Armstrong. Text copyright © 1969 by William H. Armstrong. By permission of Harper & Row, Publishers, Inc.

[14]Doris Gates, *Blue Willow* (New York: Viking Press, © 1940). Used by permission. Renewed © 1968 by Doris Gates.

of self-actualization that he found in older people did not exist in young, developing persons. (Those characteristics are described in Display 14.1.) Maslow surmised that societal factors kept them from achieving self-actualization at an earlier age. He believed that the best we can expect and hope for in young people is a "growing well" situation in which we see them make full use of their talents, capacities, and potentialities. Young people moving toward self-actualization are those who are doing what they are capable of doing or, in Nietzsche's words, "becoming what thou art!"

As Maslow's studies progressed, he developed profiles of several public and historical figures in an effort to evaluate their psychological health. He found two people, Abraham Lincoln and Thomas Jefferson, whom he considered to have achieved as much self-actualization as it is possible to attain. Seven other figures he considered "highly probable" were Albert Einstein, Eleanor Roosevelt, Jane Addams, William James, Albert Schweitzer, Aldous Huxley, and Spinoza.[15]

In the course of his search for subjects whose psychological health could be studied, Maslow turned to literature, hoping to find self-actualized people among the fictional characters created by novelists and dramatists. He was unable to find any suitable examples. (He always considered this failure a thought-provoking discovery.)

We might speculate about why Maslow was unable to find self-fulfilled characters in literature. Perhaps writers who are not self-actualized cannot portray characters who are. Another possibility is that writers are not interested in creating self-actualized characters.

Recognizing the risk involved in attempting to take up a task that Maslow abandoned, we will nevertheless examine a fictional character who appears to have been quite successful in meeting the basic needs of life. The character was created

over two centuries ago but is familiar to all modern children: Robinson Crusoe.

It is immaterial whether Daniel Defoe was aware when he created Crusoe that all human beings have various needs that must be satisfied if they are to attain full mental health and happiness. What is significant is that Defoe was able to endow Crusoe with the qualities of good psychological health. Every task Robinson Crusoe performs, every behavioral stance he assumes, shows a man striving toward self-fulfillment and happiness. On his lonely island, he constructs a shelter inside a cave and makes it weatherproof and comfortable, adding a crudely built table and chair and a shelf for his belongings. Around all this he builds a fortress to protect himself from dangers both real and imagined.

To feed himself, Crusoe hunts game, collects eggs and fruit, and plants and harvests corn. He finds ingenious ways to preserve and store food for his future needs. He strolls his island in a suit made of animal skins to keep him cool from the tropical sun. A pointed fur cap sheds the rain.

For love and companionship, he tames a parrot and painstakingly teaches it to say his name. From the wrecked ship he carries two cats to the island, and he coaxes the ship's dog to swim ashore behind him. Of the dog he tells us, "I wanted nothing that he could fetch me; I only wanted to have him talk to me."

In his need to learn, to know, and to comprehend, Crusoe salvages charts, logs, Bibles, and books. He studies the tides, the stars and clouds, plants and animals of the island, keeping a diary of his discoveries. He devises a calendar to keep an accurate record of time and is bothered that somewhere in his reckoning he has lost a day.

Beauty is a vital part of Crusoe's life. He weaves baskets to hold his food and molds clay pots in which to cook it. He systematically hangs his hunting gear on hooks and places his utensils on the shelf in an attractive and efficient manner: "It gives me pleasure to see my goods in order." A beautiful and serene grove of trees on a high

[15]Abraham Maslow, *Motivation and Personality*, 2d ed. (New York: Harper & Row, 1970), p. 152.

Display 14.1 Common Characteristics of Maslow's Self-Actualized Individual

Maslow described fifteen common characteristics of what he calls the "self-actualized individual." He conceived of these characteristics as providing a composite picture of a well-adjusted individual who could serve as a goal toward which all people might strive.

1. *Efficient perception of reality and comfortable relations with it.* Excellent judges of character, self-actualized individuals can distinguish sincerity from falseness better than most. In addition, they do not have a pressing need to mold reality into neat categories but rather accept it with all its complexities.

2. *Acceptance of self and of others.* They are not defensive about themselves or their beliefs. They have nothing to hide and nothing to protect and are therefore open to and accepting of others.

3. *Spontaneity.* They are not concerned with impressing others; they feel free to think and act spontaneously. They are, however, careful not to intentionally distress other people.

4. *Problem centering.* These individuals approach problems with no personal biases. Self-interest does not sway them from a clear-sighted perception of the facts.

5. *Detachment; the need for privacy.* Their lack of rigid attachment to any set of particular ideas allows these individuals to be relatively objective in their judgments. Although they are not antisocial, they do value the time they spend alone.

6. *Autonomy; independence of culture and environment.* They are not rigidly tied down to the culture in which they reside.

7. *Continued freshness of appreciation.* They have a real sense of joy in experiencing all aspects of life.

8. *Mystic experience or the "oceanic" feeling.* Self-actualized individuals have "feelings of limitless horizons opening up to the vision, the feeling of being simultaneously more powerful and also more helpless than one ever was before, the feeling of great ecstasy and wonder and awe, the loss of placement in time and space, with, finally, the conviction that something extremely important and valuable had happened."

9. *Social interest.* The self-actualized person has a strong sense of unity and brotherhood among all human beings.

10. *Interpersonal relations.* They usually have a small number of very deep and rich relationships with both men and women.

11. *Democratic character structure.* They are relatively free from prejudice and jealousy.

12. *Discrimination between means and ends.* They are, for the most part, patient people. They often enjoy the work involved in achieving a goal as much as the achievement of the goal itself.

13. *Sense of humor.* Their humor is constructive rather than destructive; it is not aimed at hurting or putting people down.

14. *Creativeness.* In their everyday lives they tend to be original and inventive.

15. *Resistance to enculturation.* They can appreciate views very different from their own.

From *Toward a Psychology of Being*, 2d ed., by Abraham H. Maslow. © 1968 by Litton Educational Publishing, Inc. Reprinted by permission of Van Nostrand Reinhold Company.

hill becomes his refuge, his "Bower" where he sits daily and looks out to sea.

In observing Robinson Crusoe as he struggles to meet his needs, it might appear that the need for self-esteem is not involved, that his motives are toward survival and self-preservation. Yet, when a ship arrives to rescue him after some thirty years on the island, and the captain and two sailors come ashore, Crusoe invites them to his lodging, "Where I refreshed them with such provisions as I had, and showed them all the contrivances I had made during my long, long inhabiting of that place. All I showed them, all I said to them, was perfectly amazing." We find after all that he did need to accomplish something worthy of respect. It was not enough merely to survive; he needed other people to appreciate his remarkable achievement.

The story of Robinson Crusoe is complete and satisfying. It is a blueprint for making order out of chaos. The young person who reads it will be influenced by its meaning from that time on and may find it a bit easier to "live well" on the way to self-fulfillment.

In a well-stocked attic, Laura and Mary play with their dolls. Illustration by Garth Williams from Little House in the Big Woods by Laura Ingalls Wilder. Copyright 1953, as to pictures, by Garth Williams. By permission of Harper & Row, Publishers, Inc.

The Role of Illustrations in Bibliotherapy

In considering the use of literature to help students meet developmental needs and solve personal problems, illustrations have been almost totally ignored as having any therapeutic value for the reader. Researchers and practitioners who have ventured into the realm of art as therapy have focused mainly on the child's own art work and the creative process itself as having "healing" value. There is no question that children do benefit from self-expression with many kinds of art materials. Creative acts such as drawing, painting, cutting, pasting, and modeling are deeply satisfying to children. Some of the same positive values are also offered by looking at pictures.

Many of the finest artists in the United States and in other countries have dedicated themselves to illustrating books with pictures that nourish children's imagination and spark their curiosity. Robert Lawson once said, "You find yourself constantly striving to bring your work up to the level of children."

During the elementary school years, children need many experiences with illustrations in books. Most exposures will be (and ought to be) informal, but some activities need to be planned by the teacher if students are to develop visual literacy skills and a sensitivity to art as communication. In *Using Literature in the Elementary Classroom*, Sam Sebesta tells teachers: "We must

Illustration from Where the Wild Things Are *by Maurice Sendak. Copyright © 1963 by Maurice Sendak. By permission of Harper & Row, Publishers, Inc.*

develop ways to encourage children to interact with the illustrations, so that the artist can then provide additional content and comment, adding richly to the readers' understanding and enjoyment of the story."[16]

Robert Lawson was once asked what features he put into his illustrations to make them so appealing to children. His thoughtful response was

to describe the impact a picture can have on the life of a child: "No one can possibly tell what tiny detail of a drawing or what seemingly trivial phrase in a story will be the spark that sets off a great flash in the mind of some child, a flash that will leave a glow there until the day he dies."[17]

To meet the basic needs of life is a constant struggle depicted over and over again in stories written for children, and the same struggle is re-

[16]John Warren Stewig and Sam L. Sebesta, eds., *Using Literature in the Elementary Classroom* (Urbana, Ill.: National Council of Teachers of English, 1978), p. 35.

[17]Robert Lawson, "The Caldecott Medal Acceptance," *Horn Book* (July 1941), p. 277.

Frog and Toad enjoy friendly companionship as they watch their garden grow. Illustration from Frog and Toad Are Friends *by Arnold Lobel.*

flected in illustrations. We see Laura and Mary basking in the warmth of an attic filled with slabs of bacon, smoked hams, pumpkins, onions, and potatoes—all stored there by responsible parents as security against the ravages of a long winter. Garth Williams was just as effective in illustrating the scene as was Laura Ingalls Wilder in writing it many years earlier.

In *Where the Wild Things Are*, Maurice Sendak retrieves Max from a dream fantasy and returns him safely to his own familiar room where a warm supper is waiting for him. The element of danger and risk is behind him, and contentment prevails again. The last illustration in the book helps young children to feel what

Max felt and helps to satisfy their innate longing to be safe.

It would be impossible to enumerate all the books that portray the need for love and belonging as a theme. For young readers, however, *Frog and Toad Are Friends* by Arnold Lobel is one of the best examples. It is a series of low-key stories reminiscent of *Wind in the Willows*. The delicate illustrations are a perfect complement to the text and help readers better understand their own great need for loving relationships with a best friend.

The artist Taro Yashima has always been concerned with giving children the inner strength they need to cope with problems they all have to

Soon after that came graduation day.

Chibi was the only one in our class honored for perfect attendance through all the six years.

A Profile of Taro Yashima

JUM IWAMATSU, better known by his pseudonym Taro Yashima, was born in 1908, the last of three sons of a country doctor in a small village on Kyushu Island, Japan. His father was also a collector of Oriental art and believed that art is as important to humanity as medicine. When Yashima as a small boy announced his decision to become an artist, his father quickly gave him money to buy a box of oil paints. Of his father's influence Taro Yashima said later, "When I decided to be an artist, my father was still alive and gave me encouragement and left me word in his will not to give up my first decision."

After graduation from high school, Taro Yashima became an art student at the Imperial Art Academy of Tokyo and gradually moved into the world of professional artists. His opposition to the Japanese government's militaristic policies resulted in his imprisonment, but in 1939 he and his wife Mitsu, also an artist, escaped to the United States, leaving their young son Mako behind to stay with his grandparents. In New York, the Yashimas enrolled in the Art Students' League and continued their painting. When war was declared between Japan and the United States, Yashima joined the U.S. Army and served in the Office of War Information and in the Office of Strategic Services.

Two years after the end of World War II, the Yashimas' son, then fifteen, joined them. At about the same time, their daughter Momo was born. Unfortunately (or perhaps fortunately), Taro Yashima was stricken by a painful ulcer that kept him bedridden for the next four years. He explains that during that time it was inevitable that he would check over his life experiences and re-form himself and his art from the beginning:

> And, very fortunately and unexpectedly, this struggle was helped by the fact that I was able to live with our newborn daughter so intimately. I was able not only to observe every moment of our daughter's growth but also to root out a certain prejudice toward women that had existed in me more or less as a result of my upbringing in Japan. Our daughter, who was two years old or so, used to put her cheek on mine whenever I had an ulcer pain. If it were not for my illness I never would have known that such a gentle human being could exist in such a little helpless baby.[1]

Because he wanted to thank his little girl for the comfort she had brought to him during his long illness, Yashima began to create stories from his childhood in Japan. Out of that period in his life came *The Village Tree* and *Plenty to Watch*, his first two picture books for children. A *New York Times* critic wrote of these two works: "The work of Taro Yashima leaves this reviewer with a strong feeling that here is an artist-writer who knows children, respects and loves them deeply. With

Taro Yashima photo is used by permission.
[1]Taro Yashima, "On Making a Book for a Child," *Horn Book* (February 1955), pp. 23–24. Copyright 1955 by The Horn Book, Inc. Used by permission.

both words and pastel-and-ink strokes he has captured their simplicity, gaiety, and sense of wonder."

Over the years, Taro Yashima has had one-man shows of his paintings in New York; Washington, D.C.; Los Angeles; and Pasadena. His works are in numerous public and private collections, and his illustrations have appeared in many magazines, including *Vogue, Fortune,* and *Harper's.* He and Mitsu collaborated on *Plenty to Watch* and *Momo's Kitten.*

Most people consider *Crow Boy* Yashima's masterpiece—a picture book that makes a social and psychological statement about acceptance of a person who is seen as "different." *Crow Boy* is a profound book and at the same time artistically beautiful. Nicolas Mordvinoff has described it in this way:

> The design is unusual. This large book seems even bigger than it is, yet not big enough for the colorful compositions that make the space surrounding them gleam magically more white than white. The sweeping rhythm of the pictures carries one through endless surprises. . . . The bold expressionism with a touch of humor tempered by an oriental delicacy, blends in a rare poetic mood and carries through from the first to the last—not to ignore the endpapers, which are among the most beautiful designs.[2]

Crow Boy was named a Caldecott Honor Book, as were *Umbrella* and *Seashore Story.*

All of Yashima's books reflect his desire to contribute his best for the growth of the younger generation: "I would like to continue publishing picture books for children until my life ends. The theme for all those should be, needless to say, 'Let children enjoy living on this earth, let children be strong enough not to be beaten or twisted by evil on this earth.'"[3]

Today Mako and Momo Yashima are both actors; he was nominated for an Academy Award for his performance in the movie *Sand Pebbles.* Taro Yashima lives in Los Angeles, California.

BOOKS BY TARO YASHIMA

Plenty to Watch, 1954
Crow Boy, 1955
Umbrella, 1958
Youngest One, 1962
Seashore Story, 1967
The Village Tree, 1972
Momo's Kitten (written with Mitsu Yashima), 1977

[2]Nicolas Mordvinoff, "Artist's Choice: Crow Boy," *Horn Book* (December 1956), pp. 429–430.
[3]Muriel Fuller, ed., *More Junior Authors* (New York: H. W. Wilson, 1963), p. 231.

face. As a buttress against the debilitating effects of failure and disappointment, Yashima helps his characters to accomplish a task that earns for them the respect and admiration of others. In turn, they gain a bit more respect for themselves. Crow Boy, for example, is superior in two ways: He is honored for six years of perfect attendance in school, and he can imitate the voices of crows. Yashima illustrates the scene by showing Crow Boy with a certificate—an age-old symbol of success.

The time children spend poring over picture books is one manifestation of their need for aesthetic satisfaction. Each of the Caldecott Award books contains illustrations that linger in a person's consciousness long after the book has been

Carl chose first. He picked out an egg with a picture of a fine galloping horse on it. Katy chose an egg with a lovely bird sitting on a branch.

Katy held up her egg and looked at it closely. She turned it round and round to see all the bright colors.

(Reprinted with the permission of Charles Scribner's Sons from The Egg Tree *by Katherine Milhous. Copyright 1950 by Katherine Milhous.)*

This illustration is filled with many small details that intrigue young readers and assist them in comprehending the story. (Illustration from Abraham Lincoln, *by Ingri and Edgar Parin d'Aulaire. Copyright 1939 by Doubleday & Company, Inc. Reprinted by permission of the publisher.)*

put aside. An example that comes to mind at once is *The Egg Tree* by Katherine Milhous. In a story format she describes the folk art of a region and then enhances and illuminates the story with authentic designs that have been handed down from one generation to the next.

The need to know manifests itself in many ways. Book characters are often shown in a search for information and insight. Most children are familiar with the story of young Abraham Lincoln studying by the light of an open fire. He was later to tell the story to his own children. The incident was depicted by Ingri and Edgar d'Aulaire in their biography for young readers. It is quite conceivable that Lincoln himself would have liked their rendering of that memorable experience from his childhood.

As children move toward self-actualization, it is reassuring for them to read about others who are striving to become "that person one truly is." To finally realize that the quest itself can bring happiness is one of life's important discoveries. Unfortunately, many people never reach that understanding. Celestino Piatti, in *The Happy Owls*, uses "people in feathers" to make this point. The owls are not able to share their happiness with the barnyard fowl no matter how they try. The chickens, ducks, and geese simply have no con-

The owls have found the secret to true happiness and Piatti's illustrations help to convey their message. (From The Happy Owls *by Celestino Piatti. Copyright © by Artemis Verlag, Zurich, Swit-* zerland. *First U.S. edition 1964 by Atheneum Publishers. Used by permission of Atheneum Publishers.)*

cept of what they must do or what they must look for to be happy. Piatti's poster-like paintings illustrate the deep companionship and understanding between the two owls: "But the owls snuggled still closer to one another, blinked their big round eyes, and went on thinking their wise thoughts."

Summary

Meeting the special needs of every elementary child is a goal toward which all language arts teachers must constantly strive. Children's needs range from emotional support in the resolution of personal problems to appropriate instructional strategies. For over two centuries, teachers in the United States have relied on literature as a major resource to fulfill this goal.

Many of the earliest trade books and textbooks are now considered didactic literature—writing that aims to teach, preach, or moralize. Didacticism was a staple of early schoolbooks such as the *New England Primer,* Webster's *American Spelling Book,* and McGuffey's *Eclectic Readers.* During the past fifty years, significant changes have occurred in textbooks and trade books. Minority groups are more realistically portrayed; girls and women are now shown in nonstereotyped roles; and themes of contemporary living are presented in realistic ways.

"Bibliotherapy" is a rather new term for the old practice of using literature to help individuals resolve personal problems and inner conflict. Bibliotherapy in the classroom is marked by the use of literature to enrich the lives of all children and to give them the resources to find solutions to the dilemmas they will face in the course of growing up. The aim of bibliotherapy is to satisfy what Abraham Maslow calls "life's basic needs." Maslow arranged these needs in a hierarchy; they are physiological needs, safety needs, love and belonging needs, esteem needs, knowledge and understanding needs, aesthetic needs, and at the highest level of Maslow's hierarchy, self-actualization needs—the need to become whatever one is capable of becoming. Few persons attain the highest level, but the quest itself can bring happiness.

Literature can help children "live well" on the way to self-actualization. Not only the text of a book but the illustrations as well may have therapeutic value for children, especially if they are encouraged to respond to the pictures and if the art work is of excellent quality and carefully coordinated with the text.

Best Books for Children

Abraham Lincoln, written and illustrated by Ingri and Edgar Parin d'Aulaire. New York: Doubleday, 1939. This was the first biography to receive the Caldecott Award. The colors in the book are rich, and the pictures are filled with accurate historical details. The authors purposely portray Lincoln as he lived, not as he died. An excellent informational book for younger readers. (P,M)

. . . and Now Miguel, written by Joseph Krumgold and illustrated by Jean Charlot. New York: Crowell, 1953. The members of Miguel's family have been shepherds for generations. Young Miguel struggles to prove to his father that he is as mature and competent as his brother. The story centers on the desire for acceptance and responsibility. This book could be used with a child who resents being the middle sibling. (M,U)

Benjie on His Own, written by Joan M. Lexau and illustrated by Don Bolognese. New York: Dial Press, 1970. Benjie, a young child, becomes worried when his Granny is not waiting to walk him home after school. On his way home by himself, Benjie is chased by an unfriendly dog and is frightened by a group of older boys who search him for money. This sequel to *Benjie* realistically portrays the plight of a young child in an insensitive urban environment. Benjie is called on to use his wits and resourcefulness to survive. (P)

Blue Willow, written by Doris Gates. New York: Viking Press, 1940. *Blue Willow*, a child's version of *The Grapes of Wrath*, deals with the issue of poverty in a forthright way. It gives a realistic picture of the problems faced by migrant agricultural workers. Janey Larkin, a preadolescent girl, is the leading character and one of the most memorable characters to be found in children's books. (M,U)

Bridge to Terabithia, written by Katherine Paterson and illustrated by Donna Diamond. New York: Crowell, 1977. Katherine Paterson's 1978 Newbery Award book is the story of a developing friendship between two nonconformists. The two children invent a fantasy kingdom named Terabithia that is also a private hideout in the woods. A gentle spring creek near Terabithia turns into a torrent, and the girl drowns. The boy struggles with his feelings about death and gains a greater appreciation for life. (U)

Call It Courage, written by Armstrong Sperry. New York: Macmillan, 1940. Fifteen-year-old Mafatu, a South Sea Islander, grows up with a fear of water after his mother dies in the sea when he is young. The men of the tribe ridicule the boy for his fear. Mafatu conquers his fright by setting sail for another island and, with considerable resourcefulness, provides himself with the necessities of life. Mafatu finally returns home as a socially acceptable person and one who has a higher opinion of himself. (M,U)

Crow Boy, written and illustrated by Taro Yashima. New York: Viking Press, 1955. Chibi, a young Japanese student, portrays the quest for knowledge by "leaving his home for school at sunrise every day for six long years." He is the only student in class to be honored for perfect attendance. Chibi is treated as an outsider by his classmates until an understanding teacher discovers he can imitate the voices of crows—a rare talent that brings him respect and a new name. (P)

Down, Down the Mountain, written and illustrated by Ellis Credle. New York: Thomas Nelson, 1934. Hetty and Hank, who live in a little log cabin in the Blue Ridge Mountains, both want new shoes to wear to church. Their granny encourages them to plant turnip seeds and to sell the turnips for new shoes. Hetty and Hank eventually take their turnips down to the town at the foot of the mountain. The last scene shows them going down the aisle of the church wearing squeaky new shoes. (P,M)

The Egg Tree, written and illustrated by Katherine Milhous. New York: Scribner, 1950. The traditions of Easter in a Pennsylvania Dutch family are the theme of this book. It is a delightful story of cooking, decorating, hiding, hunting, and eating Easter eggs. This story is not only one of excitement; it is also one that encourages aesthetic appreciation. Directions are given for making the lovely Easter egg tree. (P)

Frog and Toad Are Friends, written and illustrated by Arnold Lobel. New York: Harper & Row, 1970. A 1971 Caldecott runner-up that portrays the strength of the warm friendship between Frog and Toad. The text describes their friendship, and pastel shades of spring make a nice background for their activities. (P)

The Happy Owls, written and illustrated by Celestino Piatti. New York: Atheneum, 1964. The fowl in the barnyard do nothing but argue and fight all day; in contrast, the owls seem peaceful and content. The owls try to explain how they are able to live together in harmony, but the fowl cannot understand. The story, beautifully illustrated, explores the meaning of contentment and its elusiveness. (P)

The Hundred Dresses, written by Eleanor Estes and illustrated by Louis Slobodkin. New York: Harcourt Brace Jovanovich, 1944. Wanda Petronski is a shy ten-year-old girl who wears the same faded dress to school every day. She tells her classmates that she has one hundred dresses at home. Wanda's classmates, Peggy and Maddie, tease her about the dresses un-

til Wanda and her family move to another city and the two girls are made aware of the cruelty of their teasing. (M)

M. C. Higgins, the Great, written by Virginia Hamilton. New York: Macmillan, 1974. Mayo Cornelius Higgins sits on his gleaming forty-foot pole, towering over his home on Sarah's Mountain and thinks about the meaning of life—his own life and that of his family. The modern theme of environmental ravage is well suited to the adolescent reader. (U)

Seashore Story, written and illustrated by Taro Yashima. New York: Viking Press, 1967. Children playing at the seashore are reminded of an ancient legend: "It could have happened here, in such a place," they said. And so begins the story of Urashima, an old fisherman who stayed away so long that his loved ones forgot him. A Caldecott Honor Book. (P)

The Secret Garden, written by Francis Hodgson Burnett and illustrated by Tasha Tudor. Philadelphia: Lippincott, 1911. Mary Lennox is sent to live with a reclusive uncle in England, where she meets her cousin Colin, a bedridden man prone to temper tantrums. Long confined to a wheelchair, Colin discovers that his legs are weak but not paralyzed; he learns to walk again. This story encourages children to reach out to others. (P,M)

Sounder, written by William H. Armstrong. New York: Harper & Row, 1969. A young black boy's mother offers quiet strength and encouragement as he searches for his father who has been imprisoned for stealing food. The story would be one of despair but for an understanding schoolmaster who offers the boy hope for the future. (U)

Umbrella, written and illustrated by Taro Yashima. New York: Viking Press, 1958. Momo is too grown up to remember the new rainboots and umbrella given her on her third birthday, but whether she remembers or not, the first day she wore the boots and carried the umbrella was the first day in her life that she walked alone, "without holding either her mother's or her father's hand." (P)

The Wind in the Willows, written by Kenneth Grahame. New York: Scribner, originally published in 1908. An ageless tale that describes the adventures of four friends: Mole, Water Rat, Badger, and Toad. Their deep friendship endures despite the strain placed on the relationship by the overbearing Toad. It contains a great deal of provocative conversation among the animals. (M,U)

Youngest One, written and illustrated by Taro Yashima. New York: Viking Press, 1962. Step by step, Youngest One overcomes his shyness to begin a friendship with Momo. When he finds courage enough to keep his eyes open and to look at her, he finds, "Sure enough, right there, smiling eyes in Momo's face were looking straight at him! AND Bobby smiled right back." (P)

Bibliography

Ashley, L. F. "Bibliotherapy, etc." *Language Arts*, April 1978.

Cullinan, Bernice E. *Literature and the Child*. New York: Harcourt Brace Jovanovich, 1981.

Dreyer, Sharon Spredemann. *The Book Finder*. Circle Pines, Minn.: American Guidance Service, 1977.

Gibson, Janice T. *Psychology for the Classroom*. Englewood Cliffs, N.J.: Prentice-Hall, 1976.

Hoagland, Joan. "Bibliotherapy: Aiding Children in Personality Development." *Elementary English*, July 1972.

Huck, Charlotte. *Children's Literature in the Elementary School*, 3d ed. New York: Holt, Rinehart and Winston, 1976.

Kantrowicz, Viola. "Bibliotherapy with Retarded Readers." *Journal of Reading*, December 1967.

Kimmel, Eric. "Can Children's Books Change Children's Values?" *Educational Leadership*, November 1970.

Kramer, Edith. *Art as Therapy with Children*. New York: Schocken Books, 1971.

Maslow, Abraham. *Motivation and Personality*, 2d ed. New York: Harper & Row, 1970.

———. *Toward a Psychology of Being*. Princeton, N.J.: Van Nostrand, 1968.

Moody, Mildred T., and Hilda Limper. *Bibliotherapy: Methods and Materials*. Chicago: American Library Association, 1971.

O'Bruba, William S. "Bibliotherapy: Solving Problems Through Reading." *Reading Horizons*, Spring 1978.

Savage, John F., and Jean F. Mooney. *Teaching Reading to Children with Special Needs*. Boston: Allyn and Bacon, 1979.

Shepherd, Tony, and Lynn B. Iles. "What Is Bibliotherapy?" *Language Arts*, May 1976.

Spache, George D. *Good Reading for Poor Readers*. Champaign, Ill.: Garrard, 1974.

Stewig, John Warren, and Sam L. Sebesta, eds. *Using Literature in the Elementary Classroom*. Urbana, Ill.: National Council of Teachers of English, 1978.

Sutherland, Zena, and May Hill Arbuthnot. *Children and Books*, 5th ed. Glenview, Ill.: Scott, Foresman, 1977.

Tews, Ruth. "Introduction." *Library Trends*, October 1962.

Chapter 15

More Alike Than Different:
Meeting the Special Needs of Children

UNTIL QUITE RECENTLY, children who differed greatly from the "norm" were excluded from the regular school program. Some of them were isolated in special education classes; others were simply hidden away at home or in institutions. A more enlightened attitude has resulted in better educational opportunities for these children. In studying the needs of retarded and handicapped children, an awareness emerged that many children have difficulty learning to read and write for various reasons and at varying levels of disability. Subsequently, the modern language arts curriculum, with its emphasis on individualized instruction, has emerged to better meet the needs of all students.

Traditionally, children with special needs were grouped together on the basis of their ability, handicapping condition, or some other factor. They were not taught in the regular classroom. In recent years, this educational policy has been changing. More accepting social attitudes, improved research into children's growth and development, and the impact of state and federal legislation on local schools have been responsible for the change.

As a result, a common sense system of services for children with physical, emotional, or mental problems has emerged. This program is called "mainstreaming." Mainstreaming is a term applied to the process of integrating handicapped children, whenever possible, into regular educational programs. It does not mean that all handicapped students will be placed in regular classrooms. Rather, mainstreaming refers to a broad range of services afforded special education students and calls for placement in the "least restrictive environment;" in other words, the climate most suitable to a child's capability. Under this plan, the instructional setting closest to regular education will be provided. For some children, a separate program is needed; for others, partial or full-time placement in the regular classroom is suitable. The underlying philosophy of mainstreaming is educational flexibility and personalized instruction for each child.

The integration of the special-needs children into the regular classroom requires acceptance and accommodation from the teacher. Since the needs of such children are diverse, there is no one best way to organize the class for effective instruction. In this chapter we will suggest several teaching strategies to meet the dissimilar needs of special students in the regular classroom.

Teaching Children with Physical, Emotional, or Mental Problems

When Paul Jockimo was born, something was wrong. On his right hand, where there should have been five fingers, there was only the stump of a flexible wrist. On his right foot, where there should have been five toes, there was only the stump of a flexible heel. On his left hand, there was an enlarged thumb and a webbing-together of two fingers, and on his left foot, there was only the heel and the big toe. What went wrong? Not even the medical experts can say. Who was to blame? No one. Nevertheless, Paul is handicapped and has had to learn to live in a world made for people without physical handicaps.[1]

This passage is from *Don't Feel Sorry for Paul* by Bernard Wolf. At first glance, some readers might consider Paul Jockimo just a severely handicapped boy, but after reading the first few pages of Paul's story, they will perceive the meaning of the book's title. Paul is one of America's 7 million school-age children who are emotionally, physically, or mentally handicapped.[2] The book's message is straightforward: Paul (and, by extension, other handicapped people) succeed in their own way; they do not need or want pity.

[1]Excerpt from *Don't Feel Sorry for Paul,* written and photographed by Bernard Wolf. Courtesy of J. B. Lippincott Publishers.
[2]According to the U.S. Office of Education, this number represents about 12 percent of the girls and boys between the ages of six and nineteen.

Special Education for the Handicapped

Over the years, the awareness of parents and teachers that some girls and boys have needs that are significantly different from the needs of most other children has resulted in the creation of special learning environments and the development of unique teaching procedures. So-called special education programs have been established to help handicapped children develop their abilities to the fullest extent.

Classroom teachers do not assume sole responsibility for the instructional program of the special education student. There are many professional persons and a wide variety of teaching aids to support the language arts teacher. Although each school has its own philosophy, federal legislation now requires that all districts provide adequate services for special education students ages three to twenty-one. Such services usually include: (1) professional diagnosticians, (2) individualized education, (3) tutorial programs, (4) special learning devices, (5) itinerent teachers, (6) resource classrooms, and (7) special education classes.

It is important for language arts (and other) teachers to be aware of several problems associated with the concept of special education. First, identifying the children who should participate and enrolling them in special programs is no routine matter. Teachers often become frustrated because the screening process for special education is a time-consuming procedure. Children with special needs may remain in a regular classroom for almost the entire year while diagnosticians and other specialists test and prescribe for them. Second, many children are classified as "borderline handicapped" and, as a result, may not have the opportunity to participate in special education programs. In such cases the regular classroom teacher retains the primary responsibility for meeting the children's special needs. Third, mainstreaming—removing handicapped children from special education classes and placing them in the mainstream of regular classrooms where they are integrated with their nonhandicapped peers—has become a reality.

Special education is, therefore, that part of public education that provides all handicapped children full educational opportunities. Through such services, handicapped students are now guaranteed an equal opportunity for a free appropriate education. To the extent that they will benefit, handicapped students are educated with their nonhandicapped peers. The comprehensive design for the education of handicapped students was mandated in 1975 with the passage of Public Law 94-142.

The Education for All Handicapped Children Act

In recent years ideas about how to best meet the needs of special students have been changing. During the past decade, court decisions and state laws have consistently declared that handicapped children have the same educational rights as other children and are entitled to instruction geared to their needs, whether in special or regular classes or in both. In 1975, the passage of the Education for All Handicapped Children Act, Public Law 94-142, strengthened the movement for educational equality for all children. Its essential features are similar to the requirements that some state courts and legislatures had previously set forth to ensure that each handicapped child would receive a free, appropriate public education.[3] Public Law 94-142, however, brought some badly needed uniformity and consistency to disparate state laws.

According to Public Law 94-142, neither the government nor the school can charge parents for the expense of special education. A combination of local, state, and federal funding must pay for the handicapped child's education. The law

[3]Nevertheless, it has been estimated that only slightly more than half of the handicapped students receive the kind of educational program they need, either in special or in regular classes.

obliges schools to provide all handicapped children an opportunity to achieve their potential in the "least restrictive environment." For some, this might mean short-term integration with nonhandicapped students for nonacademic work such as physical education. For others, it might mean mainstreaming—assignment to a regular classroom with appropriate special instruction as needed. The law requires handicapped and nonhandicapped children to be educated together whenever possible.

The Education for All Handicapped Children Act is part of an ongoing movement toward the development of programs designed to meet the unique educational needs of each individual child. When needs are adequately met, the handicapped boy or girl has a chance to become all that he or she is capable of becoming.

The Problem of Matching the Program to the Child

The concept of mainstreaming tends to preclude grouping girls and boys on the basis of their disabilities. Writers and supporters of Public Law 94-142 make the point that, although there are many classes and types of handicaps, children with and without disabilities are more alike than different, and the attempt to label and classify every disability will prevent a child's full integration with nonhandicapped peers.

To identify and count handicapped children for formula funding, federal and state laws tend to use diagnostic labels such as autism, deafness, or neurological impairment. This manner of definition is inefficient because children labeled in different ways may have identical learning or behavioral problems. A better procedure would be to base classification and educational programs on terms such as "high incidence," "low incidence," and "sensory-impaired/physically handicapped." Children who are mildly or moderately mentally handicapped, language or learning disabled, or behaviorally disordered manifest similar school-related behaviors. They would be classified as high-incidence handicapped because their disabilities make up the largest percentage of handicapping conditions. Children in this group have the least severe learning problems and are most easily afforded the mainstreaming option.

The federal law establishes priorities for special educational services to handicapped children not served by existing programs and to handicapped children with severe learning impairment. Most of the "priority" children would be in the second category, low-incidence handicapped, meaning that they are severely or profoundly mentally handicapped or emotionally disturbed. Low-incidence handicapped children are relatively few in number and may be clustered because of the severity of their disability. The major difference between the high- and low-incidence groups is in the degree or severity of learning or behavioral problems. As a result, low-incidence children are not usually afforded the mainstreaming option and will probably remain in self-contained special education units or classrooms.

Children classified as sensory-impaired/physically handicapped have auditory, visual, or orthopedic handicaps. Their needs are much more obvious than those of high-incidence children. Their impairments typically involve the inability to receive information in the usual manner rather than learning or behavioral problems. As a result, learning opportunities and teaching modifications for them are possible within the regular classroom; many of these children will be able to function in the mainstream.

Shaping the Curriculum to Accommodate the Mainstreamed Child

There is a consensus among professional educators that a curriculum for the handicapped should not differ in content from a curriculum

This young child has learned to appreciate the ritual of looking at a favorite picture book while sitting in a bamboo swing surrounded by toys she associates with the book. (Courtesy of Steve and Kathy Crain.)

for the nonhandicapped. The differences between educational programs for special and nonhandicapped children should be in teaching technique and emphasis. The teacher of special-needs children should modify the way in which the content is presented, the way in which the child is asked to respond to the content, or the position of the child in the content sequence.

Cawley and others have developed a comprehensive plan for relating teaching technique and learner response in mathematics instruction.[4] Its utility is apparent for the language arts teacher. According to their model, the teacher can present material in one of four ways: (1) by gestur-

ing or constructing something, (2) by presenting pictures, (3) by stating words, or (4) by writing words. The learner can respond to material in one of four ways: (1) by gesturing or constructing, (2) by identifying pictures or objects within choices, (3) by stating words, or (4) by writing words. Each teaching strategy can be used with a different method of student response, thereby producing sixteen possible instructional interactions for any content objective. If a handicapped child cannot acquire information in one interaction, the teacher has many other options to fall back on.

It is imperative that the language arts teacher locate in the developmental sequence the level at which the handicapped child can perform. If a child cannot meet curriculum expectations at one level, the teacher must place the child at a different level. It is probable that the teacher will have to adapt the presentation of content and the expected response by the learner once the appropriate level has been determined.

It is critical for every language arts teacher to understand and apply these instructional principles to meet the needs of handicapped children. The personalized instruction described in Chapter 3 is also appropriate for the mainstreamed child. Guidelines for individualizing instruction to meet the needs of mainstreamed boys and girls are listed in Display 15.1.

The Use of Literature in the Mainstream

Good books involving handicapped persons serve two important purposes. In the words of Charlotte Huck: "They provide images with which disabled youngsters may identify, and they help physically [and emotionally] normal children develop an intelligent understanding of some of the problems which disabled persons face."[5] For

[4] J. Cawley, A. Fitzmaurice, M. Goodstein, A. Lepore, R. Sedlak, and V. Althaus, *Project MATH* (Tulsa: Educational Progress, 1976).

[5] Charlotte Huck, *Children's Literature in the Elementary School*, 3d ed. (New York: Holt, Rinehart and Winston, 1979), p. 422.

Display 15.1 Strategy for Individualizing the Teaching of Mainstreamed Children

1. Develop short-term instructional goals to meet the child's special needs.

2. Prepare specific and realistic objectives that comply with the program requirements of the child.

3. Tell the child what is expected to successfully complete a particular learning objective. This can be accomplished by stating clear directions in different ways.

4. Teach content information in small, meaningful units. To do this, the teacher may have to use special instructional materials and may need to elicit a different type of response from the student.

5. Provide opportunities for the student to receive recognition for accomplishments. This can be done through the use of record charts, performance graphs, and sincere verbal praise.

6. Encourage the child to compete with self rather than with peers. The importance of grades should be minimized and the significance of progress emphasized. The child's success should be communicated to the child and to appropriate adults.

7. Create an organized and systematic instructional plan. The accomplishment of this difficult task will require ongoing communication with appropriate persons, orderly school records, and frequent revision of the instructional program.

8. Remain patient and understanding when dealing with disruptive behavior from the mainstreamed child. Although this may be an arduous task at times, consistent and calm behavior by the teacher is likely to achieve positive results.

9. Make nonhandicapped children sensitive to their special role in maintaining classroom stability for the child with special needs. The teacher should make the nonhandicapped children aware of the learning and behavioral problems, as well as the strengths, of the mainstreamed child.

10. Promote the wide use of different kinds of reading material. This should be done with both content area subjects and bibliotherapeutic materials.

---

an author to portray authentically the problems faced by the handicapped, the story must be sensitive without being maudlin, realistic without being melodramatic, accurate without being patronizing. Monson and Shurtleff have stated this idea in a succinct way, "Carefully selected literature can help to prepare the nonhandicapped children for the experience of knowing children with physical disabilities."[6]

[6]Dianne Monson and Cynthia Shurtleff, "Altering Attitudes Toward the Physically Handicapped Through Print and Non-Print Media," *Language Arts* (February 1979), p. 167.

Well-written literature for children or adults is a mirror of life. One of the major characters in Harper Lee's classic *To Kill a Mockingbird* is neither seen nor heard. All know about the retarded man, yet they pretend he does not exist. This situation reflects the attitude of many individuals toward people with physical or psychological problems.

Much recent literature attempts to portray realistically the problems faced by both handicapped and nonhandicapped persons. An example is Betsy Byars's Newbery Award winning book *The Summer of the Swans*, the story of a teen-age girl and her retarded brother Charlie. Feeling sorry for herself, Sara cries about her stubby fingers, big feet, and skinny legs. Her problems become inconsequential when she discovers that Charlie has disappeared. Love and concern for her brother's welfare helps to transform Sara's self-image from that of an adolescent ugly duckling to an emotionally mature swan:

She walked along the edge of the ravine, circling the large boulders and trees. Then she looked down into the ravine where the shadows lay, and she felt as if something had turned over inside her because she saw Charlie.

He was standing in his torn pajamas, face turned upward, hands raised, shouting with all his might. His eyes were shut tight. His face was streaked with dirt and tears. His pajama jacket hung in shreds about his scratched chest.

He opened his eyes and as he saw Sara a strange expression came over his face, an expression of wonder and joy and disbelief, and Sara knew that if she lived to be a hundred no one would ever look at her quite that way again.

She paused, looked down at him, and then, sliding on the seat of her pants, went down the bank and took him in her arms.

"Oh, Charlie."

His arms gripped her like steel.

"Oh, Charlie."

She could feel his fingers digging into her back as he clutched her shirt. "It's all right now, Charlie, I'm here and we're going home." His face was buried in her shirt and she patted his head, said again, "It's all right now. Everything's fine."[7]

It is the professional obligation of language arts and other teachers to help children with special needs make full use of their unique abilities and talents. Reading aloud from books like *The Summer of the Swans* and encouraging children to read books of this type on their own is one of the most effective ways to accomplish this task.

[7]From *The Summer of the Swans* by Betsy Byars, illustrated by Ted CoConis. Copyright © 1970 by Betsy Byars. Reprinted by permission of Viking Penguin, Inc.

Summer of the Swans *by Betsy Byars portrays a sensitive concern of a sister for her retarded brother. From* The Summer of the Swans *by Betsy Byars, illustrated by Ted CoConis. Copyright © 1970 by Betsy Byars. Reprinted by permission of Viking Penguin Inc.*

Teaching Children with Special Language Needs

The goal of American education has always been to provide learning opportunities for personal growth while teaching the skills needed for literacy. For thousands of children who are unable to speak standard English for one reason or another, attending school has often been a frustrating experience, and the attainment of educational goals has been difficult if not impossible.

Educators often use the terms "speakers of non-standard English" and "speakers for whom English is a second language" to describe children who have difficulty achieving in school because of inadequate grounding in the English language. Speakers of non-standard English speak a version of English that is uniquely different from the standard English spoken by most people. Speakers for whom English is a second language speak a language other than English as their first language. The language barrier imposes a severe restriction on the social development, vocational opportunity, and academic achievement of such children.

Language instruction for them is often slow and difficult. Costly commercial programs promising immediate, monumental, and miraculous results have failed to live up to their claims. Successful language arts teachers, however, have long understood that sound teaching practices and personalized instruction are more beneficial than complicated or expensive learning procedures. In other words, children with special language needs will profit from the same kind of teaching excellence that benefits all other students.

Culturally Disadvantaged Children

Language may be defined as the systematic arrangement of speech sounds that people make to convey meaning. Individuals who make the same or nearly the same sounds and are able to communicate effectively with each other are considered to be speaking the same language. Meaningful communication is adversely affected when the sounds uttered by one individual or group differ greatly from those made by most speakers. Oral communication difficulties may result from a dialect that diverges greatly from standard English. Children who use such a dialect will have trouble making themselves understood orally and in writing.

The culturally disadvantaged child trying to learn to read faces two major obstacles. First, the child is expected to make sense of written symbols representing a version of language that may be unfamiliar in sound, vocabulary, and grammar. As a result of this unfamiliarity, the child will find it difficult to grasp meaning while struggling to decode individual speech sounds. Second, the child is caught up in a curriculum that assumes mastery of the fundamentals of the oral form of standard English in the preschool years. The culturally disadvantaged child has mastered the dialect of a particular speech community; thus his or her English will probably be nonstandard and very different from the oral language used in the typical curriculum based on standard English.

These problems are compounded by the fact that many people, including some professionals, convey the attitude that nonstandard English is "bad" English. Tragically, some go farther and claim that somehow "bad language is the same as bad people."[8] This notion is absurd, of course; a person's language system has nothing to do with a person's worth. Furthermore, nonstandard English is no less systematic or "grammatical" than standard English. In fact, nonstandard English is simply one of many varieties of English.

Two factors strongly influencing the degree of success culturally disadvantaged children have in learning standard English are the teacher's attitude and the instructional program itself. If the teacher believes a child's language is inferior and conveys that belief to the student, instruction will most likely consist of continual correction and reprimand by the teacher. To the child, the message being sent out by the teacher will be clear: "I don't like your language. I don't like your culture. I don't like your family. I don't like you." The accuracy of this statement is borne out by the fact that a disproportionate number of

[8]Kenneth R. Johnson, *Teaching the Culturally Disadvantaged* (Palo Alto, Calif.: Science Research Associates, 1970), p. 145.

Display 15.2 Strategy for Teaching Speakers of Nonstandard English

1. Refrain from making negative judgments about the child's language.
2. Teach standard English as an oral language before attempting to provide instruction in reading or writing.
3. Describe the practical benefits of learning standard English.
4. By example, indicate differences between the child's language system and standard English. Children need to hear language differences before they can act on them.
5. Emphasize only major language differences, not the fine points of English grammar.
6. Tape-record children's speech frequently. Have children evaluate themselves on specific items that have been previously taught.
7. Arrange the classroom so that effective oral language is encouraged.
8. Use the language-experience approach to promote reading and writing instruction based on children's natural oral language.
9. Make a concerted attempt to understand the child's cultural background.
10. Commend students on a regular basis for effort and improvement.

---

culturally disadvantaged students drop out of school carrying deep within them feelings of inferiority, hostility, and frustration.

Writers and illustrators are now creating literature that has the power to help children deal with many of the limiting and negative experiences they have to face. Virginia Hamilton, for example, knows instinctively how to write for culturally disadvantaged children, whether black or white:

When I decide to write a story, I don't say to myself, now I'm going to write a Black story. But it happens that I know Black people better than any other people because I am one of them and I grew up knowing what it is we are about. I am at ease with being Black. More than anything, I write about emotions, which are part of all people.[9]

A successful language arts teacher consistently works to resolve the differences between the child's dialect and standard English. Guidelines

[9]Virginia Hamilton, "Writing the Source: In Other Words," *Horn Book* (December 1978), p. 618

for providing such instruction are listed in Display 15.2.

The English problems of the culturally disadvantaged child are almost always more complex than those of the child who enters school knowing how to speak standard English. Nevertheless, with sensitivity to students' individual needs and feelings, as well as a willingness to use existing materials and methodologies in nontraditional ways, the language arts teacher will be able to help. The teacher should adopt a low-key approach that includes fun and humor so that good talk can flourish in an accepting environment. This tactic may be successfully used in a classroom that features storytelling and reading aloud by the teacher on a daily basis.

Linguistically Disadvantaged Children

Linguistically disadvantaged children speak a language other than English as their first language. Their knowledge, background, and experiences with a foreign language are likely to cause a major problem when they try to learn English. As a result, such children are often classified according to their proficiency in spoken English. Boys and girls who may require special help include

1. Children who speak English more often than they speak a foreign language. (English is the primary language of children in this group; many of them speak only English.)
2. Children who speak a foreign language more often than they speak English. (The first language of children in this group is not English.)
3. Children who speak English half of the time and a foreign language the other half. (Some of these children speak a hodgepodge, such as "Spanglish," which Mexican-Americans call *pocho*.)
4. Children who speak only a foreign language. (Children in this group speak no English.)[10]

In general, non-English-speaking students have failed to achieve their potential in American public schools. This is particularly true of those whose primary language is Spanish. In many instances, neither the curriculum nor the teacher is adequately prepared to deal with the unique needs of such students. Few teacher preparation programs require prospective teachers to demonstrate proficiency in a foreign language. Consequently, many college students have not had the opportunity to learn about the culture of another country and gain background information that would help them to assist children coping with English as a foreign language. Effective instruction of girls and boys who do not speak English depends on the willingness of the teacher to learn about the culture of linguistically disadvantaged students.

The most frequently spoken foreign language in the United States is Spanish. According to the U.S. Bureau of the Census there are over 11 mil-

Students with limited ability to speak English began with simple charts and eventually created a complex story based on a unit of study. (Courtesy of Monteel Copple, Edison Junior High School, Port Arthur Independent School District, Port Arthur, Texas.)

lion Hispanics in the United States; nearly one out of twenty persons is of Hispanic birth or ancestry.[11] Can monolingual teachers be expected to effectively teach Spanish-speaking children and other children whose first language is not English? The answer is a resounding *yes*, though with certain strategies.

Teaching Strategies

Throughout this text we have described procedures for successfully teaching the language arts. Culturally and linguistically disadvantaged children will benefit from many of the techniques already presented. Three approaches particularly well suited to their needs are the language-experience approach, the teaching of English as a second language, and individualized instruction.

---

[10]Johnson, p. 171.

[11]Samuel A. Perez, "How to Effectively Teach Spanish-Speaking Children, Even If You Are Not Bilingual," *Language Arts* (February 1979), pp. 159–162.

A Profile of Virginia Hamilton

TO BE AWARDED the Newbery Medal is no small accomplishment for any writer at any time, but when Virginia Hamilton won it in 1975 for *M. C. Higgins, the Great,* the event was more noteworthy than usual. She was the first black woman and black writer to be so honored. To her fans, the award came as no surprise. They had already come to know her as a master storyteller—a spinner of good yarns.

She tells her readers that stories and folk tales were an important part of her own growing up: "My Uncle King told the best tall tales; my Aunt Leanna sang the finest sorrowful songs. My own mother could take a slice of fiction floating around the family and polish it into a saga. So could my father."

Virginia Hamilton claims to have inherited a storytelling trait from her ancestors, and a brief anecdote from her Newbery acceptance speech bears out that she too could take a small happening and polish it into a saga. Here is Hamilton's version of a dialogue that took place between her and her editor when the writing of *M. C. Higgins, the Great* had bogged down for lack of direction:

... I slumped back, glumly eyeing Hirschman, the smell of defeat as unsavory as wild onion in my nostrils.

She stared back rather unsympathetically, I thought at the time, and totally uninterested in my fading confidence.

"What about the pole?" she asked.

"What about it?"

"What's it a symbol of?"

"It's ... just what the kid sits on?" I asked tentatively.

"But why doesn't he 'just' sit on the mountain or on the porch; why a forty-foot pole on the side of a mountain?"

"Well, it's not his mountain," I said, feeling unaccountably annoyed, "it's Sarah's ... but the pole belongs to him, and that's why he sits on it."

"But where did he get it," she persisted, "and what for, and ..."

I cut her off. "It's his!" I said, nearly shouting.

"He won it ..." I was getting this really fantastic scene in my head.

"What did he win it for?" Hirschman asked, carefully removing sharp objects from her desk top.

"Swimming!" I shouted with glee. "For swimming!"

"Remarkable," she said; "I hadn't known he was a swimmer."

"Not just any swimmer," I said, "but a great swimmer. And once he swam the Ohio River ... and there's a lake in the mountains ... and there's a tunnel!"

"A train tunnel?" she said.

"No, no ..." By then I was out of my chair grabbing my suitcase and, in my mind, already on the plane home.

"Don't forget to write," Hirschman called softly as I reached the door.

"Yeah, sure," I said, by way of farewell.

That was it. There would be no more of those talks between us for quite a spell.[1]

[1] Virginia Hamilton, "Newbery Award Acceptance," *Horn Book* (August 1975), pp. 341–342. Used with permission.

Virginia Hamilton was born in Yellow Springs, Ohio, on March 12, 1936. She grew up there in an environment quite similar to the one she uses as a backdrop for her books. On finishing high school, she was granted a full scholarship to Antioch College in Yellow Springs. She was a student at Antioch from 1952 to 1955. She later attended Ohio State University and the New School for Social Research.

For several years, Hamilton lived in New York City, where, she tells us, her career consisted of "every source of occupation imaginable, from singer to bookkeeper." During her stay there, she married Arnold Adoff, a young English teacher from the Bronx. Their two children, Leigh and Jaime, were born in New York. In describing the family's decision to leave, she writes: "I loved the City until I could no longer stand it, which happened one day between four and five in the afternoon."

Virginia and Arnold with their two children turned back toward Yellow Springs, the corner of Ohio where Hamilton's many relatives had lived since before Emancipation. It had been a station on the Underground Railroad and is still inhabited by the descendants of abolitionists and runaway slaves. Once again, Hamilton would be living in the midst of the kind of people she writes about.

Several reviewers and critics have attributed Virginia Hamilton's skill in characterization to her many relationships—both real and vicarious—with all kinds of people. When we meet Thomas and Pluto, the Smalls, the Darrows, and other characters from *The House of Dies Drear,* we have the feeling that the author must have known these people intimately, or at least she must have heard many vivid stories about them. Each character is used very skillfully and carefully to weave a fine mystery story. It won for Virginia Hamilton the Edgar Allan Poe Award for "best juvenile mystery" of 1968. With young readers, it remains one of her most popular books.

In speaking of the social message in her books, Virginia Hamilton maintains that she will never allow her fictional black people to become human sacrifices in the name of social accuracy:

> For people reading M.C., particularly the poor and the blacks, have got to realize that his effort with his bare hands to stay alive and save his way of life must be their effort as well. For too long, too many have suffered and died without cause. I prefer to write about those who survive—such as old Sarah McHiggon of the mountain, Banina Higgins, and the Killburns, who have good cause for living.[2]

Virginia Hamilton is black. She writes about other black people, and her books are extremely popular with black students; they are liked equally well by other racial groups. Her characters are real people, not stereotypes; they speak of struggle and accomplishment, life and survival, to all young people who read them. The letter Hamilton received from a young female student in Toronto is typical of letters she receives from young people of various racial groups. She said, "Miss Hamilton, I am white, but I just as well could be black. Either kind, I'd be okay. Your books taught me to say that."

BOOKS BY VIRGINIA HAMILTON

Zeely, 1967

[2]Ibid, p. 343.

The House of Dies Drear, 1968
The Time-Ago Tales of Jahdu, 1969
The Planet of Junior Brown, 1971
W. E. B. Dubois: A Biography, 1972
Time-Ago Lost: More Tales of Jahdu, 1973
Paul Robeson: The Life and Times of a Free Black Man, 1974
M. C. Higgins, the Great, 1974
Writings of W. E. B. Dubois (edited by Virginia Hamilton), 1975
Arilla Sun Down, 1976
Justice and Her Brothers, 1978

The Language-Experience Approach There is probably no better way to give students an understanding of the structure of the English language than by affording them many opportunities to observe the teacher carefully and deliberately transcribing oral language into written form. A teacher using the language-experience approach writes down the speech of children and uses it as their own reading material (For an explanation of how to make language-experience charts, see Chapter 9.) No matter how meager a child's English vocabulary happens to be, by building on those known words, by recording them on chart paper or on the chalkboard, by rereading and discussing them, the teacher will enlarge and enrich the child's storehouse of English words and concepts. An experience chart may begin as simply as "My name is Kim" and, over a period of months, progress to one that is elaborate and rich in colorful language.

Because the child who does not speak standard English is likely to have a background radically different from that of boys and girls portrayed in traditional textbooks, charts made by the teacher are essential because they provide reading material within the child's realm of experience and understanding. The language-experience method deserves the teacher's study and practice until it becomes a smooth, efficient, and routine part of the language arts program. It is an absolute necessity for students struggling to be-

come fluent in the use of English as their second language.

Teaching English as a Second Language The teaching of English as a second language (TESL) is practiced in unique school programs with varying degrees of success. The programs range from separate school curricula utilizing a bilingual teacher and bilingual teaching materials to curricula emphasizing the integration of the TESL student in the regular classroom. In the latter approach, the classroom teacher assumes the primary responsibility for language instruction.

In developing TESL teaching strategies, the language arts teacher should keep in mind three principles: First, the teacher must genuinely accept the child's culture, language, and dialect. This is accomplished by emphasizing the unique value of the child's native language (or dialect), not making pronouncements or value judgments about correctness. Second, the value of peer group influence should never be underestimated as a means to inspire improvement. Techniques such as cross-age tutoring and the use of "classroom buddies" may help all students understand language differences. The buddy system is the pairing of students to complete a school assignment. Most often, one of them speaks English without difficulty. Such a procedure helps both students develop trust and understanding. Third, all TESL programs should underscore the impor-

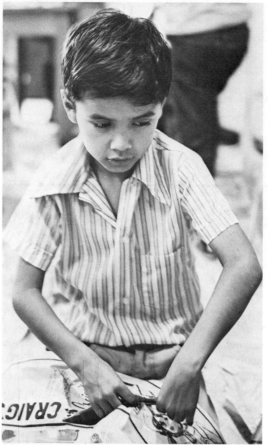

A TESL student uses everyday consumer materials in one activity aimed at enlarging his English vocabulary. (Courtesy of Beaumont Independent School District, Beaumont, Texas.)

tance of oral language. The TESL strategy emphasizes the value of listening and speaking for both information and understanding.[12] Guidelines for teaching English as a second language in the elementary language arts classroom are listed in Display 15.3.

Individualized Instruction Individualized instruction focuses on the development of the child rather than on materials or the content sequence. Although the term is widely used, there is no one specific program entitled "individualized instruction." For language arts teachers, individualized instruction consists of allowing students to select, from a variety of sources in the classroom, materials that they find interesting and challenging. Such materials are likely to motivate the child to listen, speak, read, and write. For the culturally or linguistically disadvantaged child, language is regarded not as a distinct subject area but rather as a tool to be used in all learning situations.

The objective of individualization is to promote the maximum development of the child's skills, abilities, and interests. As the child gains confidence in the use of language arts skills, the experiences of choosing learning materials, self-pacing, independent activities, and teacher-student conferences are likely to positively affect permanent language behavior.

According to Arthur Heilman there are two major advantages of the individualized approach: "one is flexibility and the other is open-endedness."[13] In our discussion of personalized instruction in Chapter 3, we outlined the philosophy and major practices most often associated with these two concepts.

Guidelines for individualizing instruction to meet the special needs of culturally and linguistically disadvantaged children are listed in Display 15.4. Persons advocating individualized instruction emphasize that these ideas and practices should be incorporated into the total language arts program. The adoption of such a plan will help teachers diagnose the needs of individual students, prepare and evaluate a wider variety of instructional materials, and promote a more personal student-teacher relationship.

[12]Walter T. Petty, Dorothy C. Petty, Marjorie F. Becking, *Experiences in Language,* 2d ed. (Boston: Allyn and Bacon, 1976), p. 492.

[13]Arthur Heilman, *Principles and Practices of Teaching Reading,* 4th ed. (Columbus: Charles E. Merrill, 1977), p. 388.

Display 15.3 Strategy for TESL

1. Language activities should emphasize the conversational aspects of standard English.
2. The child's language background should be carefully evaluated in order to determine his or her immediate needs in using standard English.*
3. The use of tape recorders and visual aids is particularly beneficial. Many fine materials are commercially available to teachers.
4. Manipulative experiences that provide immediate feedback and positive reinforcement should be frequently utilized in TESL programs. Such materials are commercially available or might be made by the teacher.
5. Premature or forced experiences with reading should be avoided; children must be given the opportunity to become gradually acquainted with printed material in their own "natural" language. The language-experience approach is most often employed to achieve this goal.
6. Drill and practice exercises based on the specific language needs of the child should be given priority in the developmental sequence of the formal language arts curriculum.
7. The pronunciation of individual speech sounds in standard English varies in difficulty. The child should receive instruction with speech sounds that are known before proceeding to those that are unfamiliar.
8. A resource person is often needed to assist a TESL child in the regular classroom. Such a person will help both the teacher and the student to resolve the inevitable language conflicts that arise in TESL instruction. The resource person can be a student, a teacher, or some other appropriate person.
9. Literature is a powerful tool to help children respect and appreciate the diversity of all cultures.

*Thomas L. Franke, "English as a Second Language: The Role of the Reading Teacher," *Journal of Reading* (December 1976), pp. 232–236.

Summary

Some children have emotional, physical, or mental handicaps or language deficiencies that require restricted learning environments or unique teaching procedures. Recent legislation and the desire to equalize learning opportunities for all children have brought about some badly needed changes that affect such children and their teachers. Teachers are now expected to meet the individual and diverse needs of most learners within the milieu of the regular classroom. This new approach to special education is termed "mainstreaming." In the case of boys and girls with severe emotional, physical, or mental problems, this new philosophy is a radical departure from the previous practice of segregating such children in isolated educational units.

The passage of Public Law 94-142 in 1975 brought some welcome uniformity and consistency to disparate state and local regulations affecting education. As a result, a more meaningful special education delivery service has been

1. Reading material should include the best children's books available rather than just a set of textbooks.
2. Instruction can begin with whatever materials are available regardless of the purpose for which they were intended.
3. Instruction should capitalize on the child's special interests and unique background.
4. The child should progress at a rate that is appropriate for him or her.
5. The teacher should adapt teaching techniques to fit the child's best mode of learning.
6. The skills program should be modified to fit the child's unique needs.
7. Constant modification of teaching methods and procedures should be made.
8. The child should not be asked to complete unneeded exercises while the teacher works with other children.
9. The teacher-pupil conference should be personalized and emphasize the development of humanistic traits rather than skills alone.
10. The teacher should base a detailed plan for skills training on the use of workbooks, manipulative materials, textbooks, and trade books.

created to support "high incidence," "low incidence," and "sensory-impaired/physically handicapped" children. Professional educators tend to agree that curricula for the handicapped should not differ in content from curricula for the nonhandicapped. Instead, teachers should be prepared to modify the way content is presented, modify the way the child is asked to respond to the content, and modify the child's position in the content sequence.

Some children requiring special assistance in the regular classroom have been broadly defined as culturally or linguistically disadvantaged. Culturally disadvantaged children speak nonstandard English. Linguistically disadvantaged children speak a language other than English as their first language. The language arts teacher needs to be familiar with practical strategies for meeting the language needs of these girls and boys. By using the language-experience approach, by teaching English as a second language, and by individualizing instruction, teachers will ensure that children with dissimilar backgrounds have an opportunity to achieve language competency.

Best Books for Children

Berries Goodman, written and illustrated by Emily Neville. New York: Harper & Row, 1965. When his family moves from New York to the suburbs, Berries meets another outsider, Sidney, a Jewish boy. The situation that develops when Sidney suffers a near-fatal accident by skating in a dangerous area forces Berries to recognize the power of prejudice. A book of this kind could be used to explore values and the basic causes of prejudice. (M,U)

Bright April, written by Marguerite de Angeli. New York: Doubleday, 1946. April Bright is the youngest member of a hard-working and closely knit black family. Acts of discrimination happen to her father, her brother, and her sister. Finally, several insults put April herself to the test. By identifying with April's emotional pains, readers in the middle grades are able to gain insight into the nature of prejudice. (M)

Bronzeville Boys and Girls, written by Gwendolyn Brooks and illustrated by Bonnie Solbert. New York: Harper & Row, 1956. Pulitzer Prize winner Gwendolyn Brooks has written a collection of thirty-four poems about black children who live in the inner city. There is Lyle, who envies a tree because he has to move away from home for the seventh time; Michael, who is afraid of the storm; and Eunice, who feels happiness when her whole family is in the dining room. Some of the poems are happy, some thoughtful; and some have elements of sadness. They all reflect the intense feelings of children in the inner city. (M,U)

Daughter of the Mountains, written by Louise Rankin and illustrated by Kurt Wiese. New York: Viking Press. 1948. Momo, a young Tibetan girl, makes a long journey alone from her mountain home in Tibet to the coast of India in search of her stolen dog, Pempa. Both the author and the illustrator have lived there and thus depict in graphic terms the mountain pass traveled by the girl. Their careful attention to detail helps to draw the reader into Momo's adventure: "Four bamboo poles were lashed together and slung from the steep hillsides across the stream with a rope handrail to comfort the laden or the timid." (M,U)

Don't Feel Sorry for Paul, written and photographed by Bernard Wolf. Philadelphia: Lippincott, 1974. This real-life account of Paul Jockimo shows the challenges faced every day by a child who is orthopedically handicapped. Sometimes his classmates make unkind remarks, and sometimes people treat him with pity. Such reactions hurt Paul, but he is able to triumph over them when his mother says, "Don't feel sorry for Paul. He doesn't need it." (M)

The Door in the Wall, written and illustrated by Marguerite de Angeli. New York: Doubleday, 1949. Presented against the background of fourteenth-century England, this Newbery Award book is the story of a nobleman's son who is lame. With his father off to fight in the Scottish wars and his mother in the service of the queen, Robin goes forth to serve as a page. He becomes ill with a strange malady and is taken to a monastery, where he learns to walk with the aid of crutches he makes with his own hands. More importantly, he acquires the patience and courage to live with a handicap. (U)

Goggles! written and illustrated by Ezra Jack Keats. New York: Macmillan, 1969. Peter and Archie find a pair of old motorcycle goggles. A group of older boys sees them and tries to take the goggles away. When one of the bullies pushes Peter and the goggles fall, Peter's dog Willie snatches them and runs off. A short, lively story that might provide encouragement to younger children troubled by older ones. (P)

The House of Dies Drear, written by Virginia Hamilton and illustrated by Eros Keith. New York: Macmillan, 1968. Dies Drear, an abolitionist who turned his house into a station on the Underground Railroad, was murdered by bounty hunters in the house, and his ghost was said to walk the rooms. Young Thomas searches for answers to the secrets held by the old house. (U)

Johnny Tremain, written by Esther Forbes and illustrated by Lynd Ward. Boston: Houghton Mifflin, 1943. A Newbery Award book that recounts the experiences of fourteen-year-old Johnny during the period of the Revolutionary War. A crucible of molten silver spills on his hand, leaving him with a severe handicap. This classic novel of a critical period in U.S. history gives a fascinating interpretation of Paul Revere, John Hancock, and other heroes. (U)

Juanita, written and illustrated by Leo Politi. New York: Scribner, 1948. Juanita celebrates her fourth birthday, according to the Mexican custom, with cake, candles, and *cascarones.* Her gift is a live dove. On the day before Easter Sunday, "The Blessing of the Animals" takes place, and Juanita's dove receives a blessing. The Politi style of illustration is reminiscent of the great mural painters of Mexico. (P)

Karen, written by Marie Killilea. Englewood Cliffs, N.J.: Prentice-Hall, 1966. Made up of three distinct narratives, this book is primarily the story of Karen, who has cerebral palsy. It is also the story of the remarkable Killilea family and their emotional support for Karen. Progress is slow and painstaking, but gradually Karen advanced from walking with the aid of parallel bars to hesitant steps with crutches. (M,U)

Me Day, written by Joan M. Lexau and illustrated by Robert Weaver. New York: Dial Press, 1971. Rafer wakes up and feels the excitement that children feel on their birthday. He gets out of doing chores and looks forward to a cake for supper and the delight of selecting his favorite TV shows. Even with such special privileges, Rafer feels a growing sense of disappointment. He has not seen his father for some time. His mother sends him on a mysterious errand, and Rafer's "Me Day" becomes a special opportunity to be with his father. (P,M)

The Planet of Junior Brown, written by Virginia Hamilton. New York: Macmillan, 1971. Junior Brown and Buddy Clark skip their eighth-grade class all semester and hide behind a false wall in the school boiler room where the janitor has built a model of the solar system. Companionship between them overcomes deep-seated problems. (M,U)

Roll of Thunder, Hear My Cry, written by Mildred Taylor. New York: Dial Press, 1976. Mildred Taylor, the second black woman to receive the Newbery Medal, helps older readers understand the struggle faced by black people during the Depression era. The story portrays one family's struggle to retain the land they have owned since Reconstruction. (U)

Sam, Bangs, and Moonshine, written and illustrated by Evaline Ness. New York: Holt, Rinehart and Winston, 1966. Samatha (everyone calls her Sam) is a fisherman's daughter who has the reckless habit of exaggerating rich and lovely dreams—"moonshine." When a sudden storm brings near-disaster to her friend Thomas and her cat Bangs, Sam repentantly draws a permanent line between "moonshine" and reality. The Caldecott Award book for 1967. (P,M)

The Summer of the Swans, written by Betsy Byars and illustrated by Ted CoConis. New York: Viking Press, 1970. Sara, a fourteen-year-old, is extremely devoted to her mentally retarded younger brother. Yet Sara's moods that summer were as unaccountable as the sudden appearance of the swans—the swans that so fascinated Charles as he watched them glide silently about the lake. Then, during the night, Charles disappears. Sara's own small miseries are left behind

as she searches for her lost, helpless brother. This book won the Newbery Medal in 1971. (M,U)

Up a Road Slowly, written by Irene Hunt. Chicago: Follett, 1966. An outstanding novel of conflict and resolution. Julia, after the death of her mother, is sent to live with an aunt. Two sequences deal with the problems of handicaps. One is the death of a schoolmate, Aggie, who is mentally retarded. The second involves a lovely woman gone mad. Julia is involved in and influenced by both experiences. This is a realistic treatment of the intricate emotional conflicts within a family. A Newbery Award book. (U)

Zeely, written by Virginia Hamilton and illustrated by Symeon Shimin. New York: Macmillan, 1967. Geeder Perry spends the summer on her uncle's farm and meets the hauntingly beautiful Zeely, whom she identifies with a Watusi queen. One of the best-loved books written by Virginia Hamilton. (U)

Bibliography

Baker, Augusta. *The Black Experience in Children's Books*. New York: New York Public Library, 1971.

Burling, Robbins. *English in Black and White*. New York: Holt, Rinehart and Winston, 1973.

Butler, Dorothy. *Cushla and Her Books*. Boston: Horn Books, Inc., 1980.

Cagney, Margaret A. "Children's Ability to Understand Standard English and Black Dialect." *The Reading Teacher*, March 1977.

Carlson, Ruth Kearney. *Emerging Humanity: Multi-Ethnic Literature for Children and Adolescents*. Dubuque, Iowa: Wm. C. Brown, 1972.

Cawley, J.; A. Fitzmaurice; M. Goodstein; A. Lepore; R. Sedlack; and V. Althaus. *Project MATH*. Tulsa: Educational Progress, 1976.

Chall, Jeanne S., Eugene Radwin, Valarie W. French, and Cynthia R. Hall. "Blacks in the World of Children's Books." *The Reading Teacher*, February 1979.

Cohen, Sandra B., and Stephen P. Plaskon. "Selecting a Reading Approach for the Mainstreamed Child." *Language Arts*, November–December 1976.

Croft, Doreen J. *Parents and Teachers: A Resource Book for Home, School, and Community Relations.* Belmont, Calif.: Wadsworth, 1979.

Fedder, Ruth, and Jacqueline Gabaldon. *No Longer Deprived.* New York: Teachers College Press, 1970.

Franke, Thomas L. "English as a Second Language: The Role of the Reading Teacher." *Journal of Reading,* December 1976.

Goodman, Yetta M., and Rudine Sims. "Whose Dialect for Beginning Readers?" *Elementary English,* September 1974.

Hamilton, Virginia. "Writing the Source: In Other Words." *Horn Book,* December 1978.

Heilman, Arthur. *Principles and Practices of Teaching Reading,* 4th ed. Columbus: Charles E. Merrill, 1977.

Horn, Thomas D. *Reading for the Disadvantaged.* New York: Harcourt Brace Jovanovich, 1970.

Johns, Jerry L., ed. *Literacy for Diverse Learners.* Newark, Del.: International Reading Association, 1973.

Johnson, Kenneth R. *Teaching the Culturally Disadvantaged.* Palo Alto, Calif.: Science Research Associates, 1970.

Johnson, Terry D. "Language Experience: We Can't All Write What We Can Say." *The Reading Teacher,* December 1977.

Krening Hansen, Nancy. *Competency and Creativity in Language Arts: A Multiethnic Focus.* Reading, Mass.: Addison-Wesley, 1979.

Lee, Dorris M., and Joseph B. Rubin. *Children and Language.* Belmont, Calif.: Wadsworth, 1979.

Long, Margo Alexander. "The Interracial Family in Children's Literature." *The Reading Teacher,* May 1978.

McCutcheon, Gail, Diana Kyle, and Robert Skovira. "Characters in Basal Readers: Does 'Equal' Now Mean 'Same'?" *The Reading Teacher,* January 1979.

Mallett, Graham. "Using Language Experience with Junior High Native Indian Students." *Journal of Reading,* October 1977.

Monson, Dianne, and Cynthia Shurtleff. "Altering Attitudes Toward the Physically Handicapped Through Print and Non-Print Media." *Language Arts,* February 1979.

Perez, Samuel A. "How to Effectively Teach Spanish-Speaking Children, Even If You're Not Bilingual." *Language Arts,* February 1979.

Petty, Walter T., Dorothy C. Petty, and Marjorie F. Becking. *Experiences in Language,* 2d ed. Boston: Allyn and Bacon, 1976.

Smith, Nila Banton. "Cultural Dialects: Current Problems and Solutions." *The Reading Teacher,* November 1975.

Sowell, Thomas. *Black Education—Myths and Tragedies.* New York: McKay, 1972.

Spache, George D. *Good Reading for Poor Readers.* Champaign, Ill.: Garrard, 1974.

Stensland, Anne Lee. *Literature by and About the American Indian.* Urbana, Ill.: National Council of Teachers of English, 1973.

Tiedt, Iris M., and Pamela L. Tiedt. *Multicultural Teaching: A Handbook of Activities, Information, and Resources.* Boston: Allyn and Bacon, 1979.

Van Allen, Roach. *Language Experiences in Communication.* Boston: Houghton Mifflin, 1976.

Chapter 16

Folklore Comes Early and Stays Late:
Traditional Literature in the Language Arts Program

FOLKLORE IS THE traditional beliefs, practices, legends, and tales of common people. It is a body of material that has been spoken or sung and passed by word of mouth from person to person and place to place. Oral folklore embodies the traditions and values of a culture. Its medium of communication, the speech of ordinary people, is often characterized by nonstandard grammar, syntax, pronunciation, and vocabulary.

Some folklore has been transcribed into writing, thus easing and quickening its dissemination throughout the world and preserving it for future generations. According to some folklorists, oral lore reduced to written form loses much of its true character because features such as dialect, emphasis, and body language cannot be captured in print. Be that as it may, of all the literature available for use in the language arts program, folk tales are the richest in content.

Folk tales contain all literary devices; they are rich in characterization, vocabulary, and concepts. Their themes are timeless and as modern as tomorrow. Their plots have been the inspiration for much of the world's great art, literature, and music that will enrich the lives of children as they grow older. Fortunately, for the language arts teacher, folk tales are so well loved that force feeding is never necessary. Children need only a curriculum that introduces them to folk tales of all types.

In *The Dynamics of Folklore*, Barre Toelken describes the different perceptions held by people who routinely study folk tales and other types of folklore:

The historian may see in folklore the common person's version of a sequence of grand events already charted; the anthropologist sees the oral expression of social systems, cultural meaning, and sacred relationships; the literary scholar looks for genres of oral literature, the psychologist for universal imprints, the art historian for primitive

art, the linguist for folk speech and world view, and so on.[1]

What Toelken does not say is that language arts teachers study folklore for yet another reason. They constantly search for folk tales that will help them teach reading and writing, listening and speaking, in more successful ways. They respect folklore as coming early and staying late in the lives of children. The folk tale in its many varieties—that tale of unknown origin that is part of the oral tradition of peoples all over the world—captivates children.

The Universality of Folk Tales

Folk tales from one part of the world are often tantalizingly similar to those told in other parts of the world. Why this is so has been a subject of debate and conjecture ever since folklore became a field of study.

Every major country of the world has its own version of the Cinderella "rags to riches" story, and with slight variations, each one is very much like the others. Most countries tell a familiar legend or folk tale about their basic regional soup—"Stone Soup" in France, "Nail Soup" in Sweden, and "Hatchet Gruel" in Russia. There is a sameness in all these tales whether referring to minestrone, stew, borscht, or sopa. There are three plausible explanations for the resemblances.

"Borrowing" may account for much of the similarity. The ancient Romans adopted the gods of the Greeks, for example, without changing them to any great extent. Such borrowing has occurred many times between countries that had frequent contact with each other.

---

[1]Barre Toelken, *The Dynamics of Folklore* (Boston: Houghton Mifflin, 1979), p. 3.

Some theorists believe that ancient ancestors of modern people transmitted cultural values to their descendants, who then carried them to different parts of the world and passed them on. Another explanation is the commonly held belief that peoples in different parts of the world and in different eras posed the same basic questions about life and came up with similar answers.

Modern folk stories also have a way of traveling with lightning speed from one part of the country to another. Tales about haunted houses, a ghostly hitchhiker, buried treasure, and the like are usually related as if they happened to local people. Some are told mainly by children to other children, others by teen-agers to their peers; still others seem to appeal mostly to adults.

"The Girl in the Lavender Dress," for example, is a ghost story that spread quickly from one college campus to another across the United States. Since it featured a fraternity dance, the story was disseminated mainly by members who told it as though it happened to two of their own fraternity brothers. Interestingly enough, the same story is told with equal sincerity on European college campuses.

Whether the story is true does not matter. The fact that the same tales crop up among the same age groups all over this and other countries shows that they hold some psychological significance.

According to Smith and Park, folk tales appeal to children for the following reasons:

- They stimulate the imagination of the child because they are good stories.

- They generally contain a subtle humor that children understand and enjoy.

- They provide escape for children and reassure them that there are forces at work that will reward compassionate behavior.

- They give children hope that all problems are solvable.

- They present and/or reinforce the basic values of a culture.

- They help meet the emotional needs of children in a vicarious, if not in a direct way.

- They present children with a style, form, and character portrayal that are different from the stories of modern-day writing, and that appeals to children.

- They emphasize plot over characterizations. The characters in all folk tales are stereotyped, although memorable for some unique feature; e.g., Paul Bunyan differs from the giant in *Jack and the Beanstalk*.

- There is a great variety among folk tales: A teacher can find a folk tale to suit almost any topic or mood.

- Folk tales always contain a great deal of action, which begins early in the story. Children are drawn into the story immediately.

- Because they were originally conceived by those who could not read or write, the language is direct and simple.[2]

Why Use Folk Tales in the Classroom?

In *The Uses of Enchantment*, Bruno Bettelheim, a renowned child psychologist, advocates using old folk tales with today's children:

Like all great art, fairy tales both delight and instruct; their special genius is that they do so in terms which speak directly to children. At the age when these stories are most meaningful to the child, his major problem is to bring some order into the inner chaos of his mind so that he can understand himself better—a necessary preliminary for achieving some congruence between his perceptions and the external world.[3]

[2]James A. Smith and Dorothy M. Park, *Word Music and Word Magic: Children's Literature Methods* (Boston: Allyn and Bacon, 1977), p. 41. Used with permission.
[3]Bruno Bettelheim, *The Uses of Enchantment: The Meaning and Importance of Fairy Tales* (New York: Knopf, 1976), p. 53.

Bettelheim advocates that parents tell fairy tales to their children from infancy on; furthermore, he urges teachers to use them as a regular feature of the instructional program in the elementary school. He believes that because such stories meet basic psychological needs, they hold a universal appeal for children everywhere.

Folk tales used in the elementary classroom will acquaint children with world cultures, help them appreciate the interests, values, and dignity of people in all parts of the world, and ultimately make them concerned about the welfare of people they may never meet. In the words of Glazer and Williams:

"Costumes and dwellings vary from tale to tale depending on the nationality of the teller. In some folk tales, kings or queens reign; in others chiefs. Such details introduce children to different people, times and places as well as illuminate emotions and problems that are common to all people."[4]

Furthermore, folk tales from around the world have formed the basis of much great literature, art, music, and dance. It is therefore important for language arts teachers to become ever more knowledgeable about folk tales and more skilled in using them to enrich both the daily curriculum and the future lives of children.

Activities Based on Folk Tales

There has been a recent revival of interest in all things considered folkloric. The proliferation of recordings by professional folk singers, the popularity of television shows and movies based on folk themes, the mass production of toys from folk culture all attest to a renewed interest in folklore. It has always been a versatile tool for

language arts teachers; it is even more appropriate for today's students.

A brief survey of recent Caldecott Award winning books shows that children's literature reflects the current interest in folk tales of various types. Leo and Diane Dillon, the illustrators of *Why Mosquitoes Buzz in People's Ears,* recalled how they felt when they saw the manuscript for the first time; their reaction describes the features in folk tales that make them appealing to readers of all ages:

When we first read the manuscript, we were both amazed that in just a few pages there was such a wealth of material. Each paragraph was packed with action, each scene flowed into the next. The cast of characters was varied, and there was a wide range of emotion. There was humor, tragedy, seriousness, and silliness. Needless to say, we were delighted with the visual possibilities.[5]

The Dillons' full-color illustrations turned out to be as stunningly dramatic as the story itself.

Opportunities for using folklore in the language arts classroom to enhance reading, writing, listening, and speaking are practically endless; activities are as numerous as the teacher's imagination and ingenuity will allow. Some of the more obvious uses of folklore are given below:

1. Convert folk tales into readers' theatre scripts for classroom performances and school assemblies.
2. Use puppetry to dramatize a variety of folk tales, fables, myths, proverbs, and legends.
3. Prepare folk tales for storytelling by both the teacher and students. Illustrate the tales for feltboard productions.
4. Conduct art activities such as murals, friezes, collages, easel paintings, and sculpture based on folk literature.

[4]Joan I. Glazer and Gurney Williams, III, *Introduction to Children's Literature* (New York: McGraw-Hill, 1979), p. 216.

[5]Leo and Diane Dillon, "Caldecott Award Acceptance," *Horn Book* (August 1976), p. 373.

A Profile of Leo and Diane Dillon

WHEN LEO AND DIANE Dillon were awarded the Caldecott Medal in 1976 for *Why Mosquitoes Buzz in People's Ears: A West African Tale,* the citation held special significance for them and for all American illustrators. Leo was the first black artist to win the award. In 1977, for an unprecedented second year in a row, the Dillons again received the Caldecott Medal, this time for their illustrations in *Ashanti to Zulu: African Traditions.*

In addition to being two-time winners of the Caldecott Medal, the Dillons have won many other awards for their art work. It is thus interesting to note that they were cautioned on more than one occasion not to make art a career:

One instructor told Leo that although he was an excellent artist he would not be able to find work in the field of art because of his race. Another instructor told Diane he hated talented females because they married, had babies, and let their talent and training go to waste. Despite such discouraging and negative attitudes, the young couple continued their training in art, learning everything they could. Constantly experimenting with materials and techniques, they carefully avoided specialization and the development of a particular and recognizable style, hoping to bring a fresh approach to each project undertaken.

Although each book they illustrate looks completely different from the others, one characteristic present in all their work is a polished and elegant style. In discussing their work on *Mosquitoes,* Diane recalled:

> Suddenly it seemed that neither of us could tolerate even a tiny flaw, a minute speck on the black night sky, and we strove for artistic perfection on the book more than any other except *Ashanti to Zulu.* In a way when *Mosquitoes* won the Caldecott Medal, it was as much a reward for us as an award. We had worked harder to achieve perfection—although of course, we didn't achieve it—than we ever had before, and people somehow knew it.[1]

Leo was born and brought up in Brooklyn, New York. His parents had come to the United States from Trinidad during the Depression. From early childhood, he seemed to have a talent for drawing, and he devoted himself to it wholeheartedly. It not only brought him pleasure and entertainment but became an effective outlet for his feelings and emotions. "I could always draw my way out of bad situations," he has said.

Leo Dillon spent his four high school years at the School of Industrial Arts in Manhattan. He loved it, and the four years he spent there were years of bliss. For the first time he belonged. Race was irrelevant in this school; art was important.

On finishing high school, Leo served a tour of duty in the Navy. When he returned to New York, he enrolled in Parsons School of Design, where he met Diane.

Leo and Diane Dillon photo is used by permission.
[1] Diane Dillon, "Leo Dillon," *Horn Book,* (August 1977), p. 424.

Diane was born in Glendale, California. Like Leo, she wanted to be an artist from the very beginning and spent many childhood hours drawing and painting. On finishing high school, she spent the first summer working at Lake Tahoe to earn tuition money for Los Angeles City College. From there she transferred to Skidmore College and finally to Parsons. At Parsons she entered a three-year period of intense rivalry and competition with Leo, but eventually they settled their differences, fell in love, and married. At this point, they began to collaborate on their art work. Diane said:

> Each illustration is passed back and forth between us several times before it is completed, and since we both work on every piece of art, the finished painting looks as if one artist has done it. Actually, with this method of working, we create a third artist. Together we are able to create art we would not be able to do individually.[2]

On February 28, 1965, the Dillons' son Lee was born. The family now lives in a brownstone house in Brooklyn, New York. Leo describes their life and work together as wonderful—"better than anything I ever dreamed of."

BOOKS ILLUSTRATED BY LEO AND DIANE DILLON

The Ring in the Prairie: A Shawnee Legend (edited by John Bierhorst and Henry Schoolcraft) 1970
Behind the Back of the Mountain: Black Folktales (written by Verna Aardema) 1973
Why Mosquitoes Buzz in People's Ears: A West African Tale (written by Verna Aardema) 1975
Ashanti to Zulu: African Tradition (written by Margaret W. Musgrove) 1976
Who's in Rabbit's House? A Masai Tale (written by Verna Aardema) 1977

[2]Ibid., p. 376.

5. Read aloud from folk literature on a routine basis. Follow up the reading with group discussion.
6. Schedule time for students to make oral reports on folk literature as they finish reading it.
7. Plan creative writing sessions in which students write their own tall tales, pourquoi stories, myths, and legends.
8. Make a folklore map of the United States showing the origins of popular tales and legends.
9. Use book jackets and masks to make a folklore bulletin board for the classroom or library. Arrange a collection of folklore books to accompany it.
10. Conduct choral speaking sessions in which ballads, folk rhymes, and narrative poems are featured.
11. Play recordings made by popular folksingers, sing folk songs, and research the history of folk music.
12. Dramatize familiar folk tales, having upper grade students perform for younger children.
13. Show films and filmstrips of popular folk tales.
14. Make a comparison of pourquoi folk tales from different parts of the world.

Display 16.1 How the Tea Plant Came to Be: A "Why" Story from China

Many years ago in China a young man committed a crime and was taken before the judge. To punish the young man severely, the judge sentenced him to have both his eyelids cut off, a measure that would lead to total blindness because of the drying out of the cornea.

As it turns out, the poor wretch was innocent of the crime. But, alas, the news of his innocence came after the executioner had already performed his cruel task. The young man's eyelids dropped on the ground.

At the very spot where the eyelids fell, two tea plants sprang up from the earth and began to grow.

The young man then taught all his people how to brew a delicious drink from the leaves of the amazing plants. The people found, however, that the drink often deprived them of their sleep.

To this very day, when tea keeps people awake, they feel as if their own eyelids have been cut off, and they think of the innocent young man who gave tea to the world.

(Drawing courtesy of Barbara Ellis.)

Display 16.2 How the Anemone Came to Be: A "Why" Story from Greece

When Venus beheld the youthful and handsome Adonis, she fell passionately in love with him. She began to follow him through the woods as he hunted hares, stags, and other game. But in her love she became alarmed for his safety and admonished him, "Attack not the beasts that Nature has armed with weapons." She was especially fearful of bears, lions, and bristly boars.

Having given Adonis this warning, Venus drove away through the heavens in a chariot drawn by white swans. No sooner had she withdrawn than Adonis attacked a wild boar that had been roused by his dogs. The beast buried its long fangs in Adonis' side and left him dying on the plain.

Venus, hearing the groans of her beloved, turned her chariot around and returned to earth, where she found the lifeless body of Adonis. As a memorial to her grief, she changed his blood into a lovely flower.

Each summer the flower of bloody hue appears around the countryside. But it is short-lived as was Adonis. It is said that the wind blows the blossoms open and afterward blows the petals away. The flower is called anemone or "windflower."

(Drawing courtesy of Barbara Ellis.)

Display 16.3 How the Crown-of-Thorns Came to Be: A "Why" Story from Madagascar

Once, long ago, there lived a man named Euphorbus. He was the court physician to Juba, king of Mauritania. While working in the king's household, Euphorbus fell in love with the young and beautiful Letitia, a favorite niece of the king. Letitia soon grew to love him in return. Since it was unlawful for a commoner to marry a member of the royal family, Princess Letty and Euphorbus decided to run away and become husband and wife.

They set out one day in a small boat and sailed down the western edge of Africa, around the Cape of Good Hope, and up to Madagascar. Here they decided to make their home. Intrigued by Letitia's long red hair, the friendly natives made them welcome.

The couple lived happily until Letty became very ill. Euphorbus worked day and night trying to save her life, but Letty died in spite of his valiant efforts. The grieving Euphorbus buried his lovely Letty on a high hill. To protect her grave, he planted a hedge of thorny bushes around it. Soon the bushes began to blossom with clusters of red flowers to remind Euphorbus of Letty's long red hair. Thus the flowers became *Euphorbia splendens*, the splendor of Euphorbus, also known as crown-of-thorns.

(Drawing courtesy of Barbara Ellis.)

Display 16.4 How the Waratah Came to Be: A "Why" Story from Australia

Long, long ago an old Aboriginal man killed a bright red kangaroo. From its skin he made a warm cloak for his daughter Condula. She loved the cloak, for it was the most beautiful one in all the tribe.

Every day, after finishing her task of food gathering, Condula would climb to the top of a high rock to watch for her lover Bak-bak's return from the hunt. It made him very happy to see the figure in the bright red cloak waving to him.

There came a time when Bak-bak, along with other young men of the village, were sent to war against a neighboring tribe. Again,

Condula climbed to the pillar of stone to watch for Bak-bak.

When the warriors returned, Bak-bak was not among them. Condula realized that he was dead, but she refused to leave her lonely post. Finally, in her grief, she died.

The body of Bak-bak was changed into a great rock, and Condula, in her red cloak, became a beautiful crimson waratah flower growing beside the rock. Even in death, the lovers were together.

(Drawing courtesy of Barbara Ellis.)

Display 16.5 How the Orchid Came to Be: A "Why" Story from Venezuela

Long ago and far away, a lovely young goddess appeared before the natives of a small village. The maiden was clothed in a precious cloak of the softest silk. It was a lovely purple color and hung from her shoulders in soft folds. The natives were at once entranced with the grace and beauty of the maiden.

The goddess had come to the village to inspire the people with lofty ideals—to think wise thoughts, to perform great deeds, and to live noble lives. But the people did not want to hear this kind of teaching. Soon they began to persecute the young maiden.

When she could bear the suffering no longer, the girl ran away to hide in a lonely mountain cave. Her cloak was left spread over the rocks near the mouth of the cave.

One day some of the villagers came upon the cloak and were reminded of the maiden's kindness. They were filled with sorrow and begged her to return to the village. But the young goddess was sad and tired. She told the people that it was time for her to return to the heavens.

As she gathered up the cloak from the jagged rocks, some pieces were torn from it and left in the cracks and crevices of the rocks. In time, each piece of cloth took root and sent up a beautiful silken flower of soft purple color.

Even today the colorful blossoms like ancient silk spring from the cracks and crevices of rocks to remind the people of the kind and lovely goddess who gave the orchid to the world.

(Drawing courtesy of Barbara Ellis.)

Long ago, a terrible flood came upon the land and brought much suffering to the people. A long dry season followed the flood. Most of the wild animals died, and the people were without food. Would their suffering never end?

Many times the people prayed for relief, and finally the Great Spirit answered their prayers. He promised to make them safe and happy again if they would offer a sacrifice. He told them that the burnt offering must be the tribe's most treasured possession; it should be burned completely and the ashes scattered to the four winds.

A little Indian girl stood near the council fire listening to the wise men. In her arms she held a doll made of white deerskin. The doll was wearing a bonnet made of bright blue feathers. The little girl knew at once that her doll must be the burnt offering. What else in the tribe was more treasured?

The little girl slipped quietly through the darkness to a rocky hillside, and there she built a small fire and placed the doll upon it. When the fire died down, the child scraped the ashes onto a piece of flat bark and scattered them to the four winds.

When morning came, she led her elders to the scene of the burnt offering. And there covering the hillside were flowers as bright blue as the feathers of a blue jay. Every flower was the shape of a tiny bonnet.

Each spring, the hillsides of Texas are blanketed again with bluebonnets to remind us all of a small girl's love for her people.

(Drawing courtesy of Barbara Ellis.)

Summary

Of all the children's literature available to the language arts teacher and students, folk tales offer the most advantages. They are rich in vocabulary and concepts, and they include all literary devices. Folk tales form the basis for much of the great literature, art, and music that students will encounter throughout life.

Folk tales introduce students to world cultures. They will find a tantalizing similarity among them. Through the stories, they become acquainted with the foods people eat, the clothing they wear, the governments they live under, and the religious beliefs that sustain them. Several years ago, in her classic book on storytelling, Carolyn Bailey wrote about the significance of folklore:

The eternal soul of a nation is expressed in its folklore. It is remembered when all else is forgotten. A people may lose fame or even disappear from the face of the earth because of the cruelty of other nations, but its tales remain and are cherished. And they should be cherished by those who tell stories to children, for in them are the ingredients that make for a perfect story. They have all the elements of adventure, entertainment, and education.[6]

Many psychologists and child development specialists are convinced that folk tales hold deep psychological value for children as well as adults. They help people better understand themselves and others.

Best Books for Children

Asia

Baboushka and the Three Kings, retold by Ruth Robbins and illustrated by Nicholas Sidjakov. Emeryville, Calif.: Parnassus Press, 1960. A Russian Christmas story adapted from an old folk tale. A Caldecott Award book. (P)

[6]Carolyn S. Bailey, *The Story-Telling Hour* (New York: Dodd, Mead, 1935), p. 49.

Favorite Fairy Tales Told in India, retold by Virginia Haviland and illustrated by Blair Lent. Boston: Little, Brown, 1973. A collection of eight popular tales told in India for centuries. Large print and attractive illustrations. (P,M)

Favorite Fairy Tales Told in Japan, retold by Virginia Haviland and illustrated by George Suyeika. Boston: Little, Brown, 1967. A picture book containing five fairy tales told in Japan. It is one of a series of fifteen folklore books for younger readers. (P,M)

Favorite Fairy Tales Told in Russia, retold by Virginia Haviland and illustrated by Herbert Danska. Boston: Little, Brown, 1961. Stories told by Russian storytellers: "To Your Good Health," "Vasilisa, the Beautiful," "The Snow Maiden," "The Straw Ox," and "The Flying Ship." (P,M)

The Flying Carpet, retold and illustrated by Marcia Brown. New York: Scribner, 1956. A simplified read-aloud version of one of the Arabian Nights tales. (P,M)

The Funny Little Woman, retold by Arlene Mosel and illustrated by Blair Lent. New York: Dutton, 1972. The story of a little woman from Old Japan who liked to make rice dumplings. A Caldecott Award book. (P)

Lazy Stories, retold by Diane Wulkstein and illustrated by James Marshall. New York: Seabury Press, 1976. Three folk tales designed for retelling and recommended for ages "four through eighty-four." Japan and Laos. (P)

Once a Mouse, retold and illustrated by Marcia Brown. New York: Scribner, 1961. An ancient fable from India that contrasts arrogance and humility. A Caldecott Award book. (P)

Persian Fairy Tales, retold by Jane Carruth and illustrated by Margot Zemach. New York: Hamlyn, 1971. Eighteen tales of shahs and muleteers, poverty and wealth, and wise and foolish people. (M,U)

Russian Stories and Legends, retold by Leo Tolstoy and illustrated by Alexander Alexeiff. New York: Pantheon Books, undated. Eight tales collected by Tolstoy when he turned from writing novels to rewriting folk tales. (M,U)

Shen of the Sea, retold by Arthur Bowie Chrisman and illustrated by Else Hasselriis. New York: Dutton, 1968. Sixteen short Chinese tales for children. A Newbery Award book. (U)

Stories from India, retold by Edward A. Dolch and Marguerite P. Dolch. Illustrated by Gordon Laite. Champaign, Ill.: Garrard, 1961. Eighteen ancient folk tales of magic and lore from India. An easy-to-read book. (P)

Stories from Japan, retold by Edward W. Dolch and Marguerite P. Dolch and illustrated by Lucy and John Hawkinson. Champaign, Ill.: Garrard, 1960. Folk tales from small Japanese villages along the sea and from the hamlets in the mountains. An easy-to-read book. (P)

Stories from Old China, retold by Edward W. Dolch and Marguerite P. Dolch. Illustrated by Lucy and John Hawkinson. Champaign, Ill.: Garrard, 1964. Stories that reflect the differing ways of life in various parts of China. An easy-to-read book. (P)

Stories from Old Russia, retold by Edward W. Dolch and Marguerite P. Dolch and illustrated by James Lewicki. Champaign, Ill.: Garrard, 1964. Stories once told to help pass the hours during the cold, dark Russian winters. An easy-to-read book. (P)

Tales of a Chinese Grandmother, retold by Frances Carpenter and illustrated by Malthe Hasselriis. New York: Doubleday, 1937. Tales from Chinese folklore told against a background of one Chinese household. The grandmother is the storyteller. (P,M)

Tales the People Tell in Russia, retold by Lee Wyndham and illustrated by Andrew Antal. New York: Julian Messner, 1970. Thirteen favorite folk tales from Russia that are still enjoyed there today. (P,M)

The Talkative Beasts, Myths, Fables, and Poems of India, retold by Gwendolyn Reed. New York: Lothrop, Lee, and Shepard, 1969. In India there is a reverence for animal life that springs from the belief in reincarnation. The myths, fables, and poems to come out of this belief are made visible by sculptors who have carved the animals with much feeling and affection. This book is built around black and white photographs of those pieces of sculpture. (P,M,U)

Tikki Tikki Tembo, retold by Arlene Mosel and illustrated by Blair Lent. New York: Holt, Rinehart and Winston, 1968. A favorite story of elementary students to dramatize why the Chinese use only short names for their children. (P,M)

The Wave, retold by Margaret Hodges and illustrated by Blair Lent. Boston: Houghton Mifflin, 1964. An ancient folk tale about life and nature, translated from Japanese. (P)

Europe

The Alhambra, written by Washington Irving and illustrated by Warwick Goble. New York: Macmillan, 1926. In 1829 Irving went to Spain and lived for some time in an old Moorish palace in the heart of Granada. There he recorded these tales of the Alhambra. (M,U)

Favorite Fairy Tales Told in France, retold from Charles Perrault by Virginia Haviland and illustrated by Roger Duvoisin. Boston: Little, Brown, 1959. Stories include "The Twelve Dancing Princesses," "Puss in Boots," "Beauty and the Beast," "Sleeping Beauty," and "Drakestail." (P,M)

Favorite Fairy Tales Told in Germany, retold from the Brothers Grimm by Virginia Haviland and illustrated by Susanne Suba. Boston: Little, Brown, 1959. Stories include "The Frog Prince," "The Elves and the Shoemaker," "Rapunzel," "The Cat and the Mouse in Partnership," "Rumpelstiltskin," "Hansel and Gretel," and "The Bremen Town Musicians." (P,M)

Favorite Fairy Tales Told in Greece, retold by Virginia Haviland and illustrated by Nonny Hogrogian. Boston: Little, Brown, 1970. A book of eight favorite fairy tales from Greece written for younger readers. (P,M)

Favorite Fairy Tales Told in Ireland, retold by Virginia Haviland and illustrated by Arthur Marokvia. Boston: Little, Brown, 1961. Some of the most popular stories from Ireland's rich folklore. (P,M)

Favorite Fairy Tales Told in Norway, retold by Virginia Haviland and illustrated by Leonard Weisgard. Boston: Little, Brown, 1961. Some of the favorite tales of children everywhere are retold here—"The Three Billy Goats Gruff," "Why the Sea Is Salt," and others. (P,M)

Favorite Fairy Tales Told in Poland, retold by Virginia Haviland and illustrated by Felix Hoffman. Boston: Little, Brown, 1963. Polish stories written in a style suitable for reading aloud and for retelling. (P,M)

Favorite Fairy Tales Told in Scotland, retold by Virginia Haviland and illustrated by Adrienne Adams. Boston: Little, Brown, 1963. Six popular stories from Scotland including the Scottish version of "The Gingerbread Man"—"The Wee Bannock." (P,M)

Favorite Fairy Tales Told in Sweden, retold by Virginia Haviland and illustrated by Loni Solbert. Boston: Little, Brown, 1966. Contains six folk tales typically Swedish in nature. Written for younger readers. (P,M)

The Gingerbread Boy, retold by William Curtis Holdsworth and illustrated by William Curtis. New York: Farrar, Straus & Giroux, 1973. The English version of an old story told in many parts of the world. (P)

Gormless Tom and Other Tales from the British Isles, retold by John Greenway. Dallas: Silver Burdett, 1968. Nine stories, thousands of years old, from England and Ireland. (P,M)

Once upon a Dinkelsbuhl, retold by Patricia Lee Gauch and illustrated by Tomie De Paola. New York: Putnam, 1977. A legend, still told in Germany, about the faith and optimism of children. (P)

The Other World Myths of the Celts, retold by Margaret Hodges. New York: Farrar, Straus & Giroux, 1973. Stories of gods and goddesses, heroes, and commoners, brought to Ireland by the Celts. (M,U)

Stone Soup, retold and illustrated by Marcia Brown. New York: Scribner, 1947. The French version of an ancient tale about making soup from an unlikely object. (*Nail Soup* in Sweden and *Hatchet Gruel* in Russia.) (P)

Stories from France, retold by Edward W. Dolch and Marguerite P. Dolch and illustrated by Gordon Laite. Champaign, Ill.: Garrard, 1963. Nineteen French stories of clever animals, magic and witchcraft, and brave knights and ladies. An easy-to-read book. (P)

Stories from Italy, retold by Edward W. Dolch and Marguerite P. Dolch and illustrated by Colleen Browning. Champaign, Ill.: Garrard, 1962. Tales about nobles and common people. An easy-to-read book. (P)

Stories from Spain, retold by Edward W. Dolch and Marguerite P. Dolch and illustrated by Don Bolognese. Champaign, Ill.: Garrard, 1962. Old stories that date back to the time when Spain was divided into many small kingdoms, each different from the other. An easy-to-read book. (P)

Tales from a Finnish Tupa, retold by James Cloyd Bowman and Margery Bianco and illustrated by Laura Bannon. Chicago: Albert Whitman, 1950. Stories in this volume have been translated and retold from Finnish. Contains tales of magic, droll stories, and fables. (M,U)

Africa

The Adventures of Spider, retold by Joyce Cooper Arkhurst and illustrated by Jerry Pinkney. Boston: Little, Brown, 1964. "Why" stories that tell how spider got a thin waist, why it lives in dark corners, and why it has a bald head. (M,U)

Animal Stories from Africa, retold by Marguerite P. Dolch and illustrated by Vincent D. Smith. Champaign, Ill.: Garrard, 1975. Gathered from many tribes and translated from their languages are these "why" stories explaining the ways of animals. An easy-to-read book. (P)

Ashanti to Zulu, written by Margaret Musgrove and illustrated by Leo and Diane Dillon. New York: Dial Press, 1976. Twenty-six African tribes are featured in text and illustrations. A Caldecott Award book. (P,M)

Black Fairy Tales, retold by Terry Berger and illustrated by David Omar White. New York: Atheneum, 1969. Ten typically African folk tales revealing the land, the people, and the mood of South Africa as it was long ago. (M,U)

The Ox of the Wonderful Horns and Other African Folktales, retold and illustrated by Ashley Bryan. New York: Atheneum, 1971. Five stories from Africa, each beautifully illustrated with woodblock prints. (M,U)

Stories from Africa, retold by Marguerite P. Dolch and illustrated by Vincent D. Smith. Champaign, Ill.: Garrard, 1975. A collection of folk tales representa-

tive of the jungles, deserts, and forests of Africa. An easy-to-read book. (P)

Stories from Old Egypt, retold by Edward W. Dolch and Marguerite P. Dolch and illustrated by Gordon Laite. Champaign, Ill.: Garrard, 1964. Rich folk tales from one of earth's oldest civilizations. An easy-to-read book. (P)

The Voyage of OSIRIS, retold and illustrated by Gerald McDermott. New York: Windmill Books and E. P. Dutton, 1977. A famous myth of ancient Egypt illustrated by the Caldecott Award winning artist. A legendary story of planting and harvesting. (M,U)

Oceania

Backbone of the King, written and illustrated by Marcia Brown. New York: Scribner, 1966. The story of a young Hawaiian boy's ingenuity in helping his father regain his rightful place as "backbone of the king." (U)

New Zealand: Land of the Mighty Maori, retold by Eleanor Z. Baker. Austin: Steck-Vaughn Company, 1971. Romantic legends and myths that surrounded the Maoris who settled in New Zealand in the fourteenth century. (P,M)

Stories from Hawaii, retold by Edward W. Dolch and Marguerite P. Dolch. Champaign, Ill.: Garrard, 1960. Folk tales explaining the rising and setting of the sun and other mysteries of nature. An easy-to-read book. (P)

South America

Folktales of Spain and Latin America, selected by Lila Green. Dallas: Silver Burdett, 1967. Folk tales from Puerto Rico, Spain, Mexico, Nicaragua, and Uruguay. (M,U)

Stories from Mexico, retold by Edward W. Dolch and Marguerite P. Dolch. Champaign, Ill.: Garrard, 1960. Stories about the animals of Mexico and the people—both rich and poor—who managed the great haciendas. An easy-to-read book. (P)

Tales from Silver Lands, retold by Charles J. Finger and woodcuts by Paul Honoré. New York: Doubleday, 1924. The author learned these stories from the Indians in South America as he traveled from one village to another. (M,U)

North America

American Folklore, collected by the Editors of Life. New York: Time, Inc., 1961. A hundred pages of old-timers' ballads, exaggerations, traditions, jokes, and home remedies. (P,M,U)

Arrow to the Sun, written and illustrated by Gerald McDermott. New York: Viking Press, 1974. A Pueblo Indian myth that illustrates the universal quest for the source of life. A Caldecott Award book. (P)

The Fire Bringer, retold by Margaret Hodges and illustrated by Peter Parnall. Boston: Little, Brown,

1972. A private Indian legend that tells how fire came to help keep people warm and cook their food. (M,U)

The Girl Who Loved Wild Horses, written and illustrated by Paul Goble. New York: Bradbury Press, 1978. Based on the loyal affection that Indian people felt for their beautiful horses. The book features two Indian songs about horses. (P,M)

The Hodgepodge Book, collected by Duncan Emrich and illustrated by I. B. Ohlsson. New York: Four Winds Press, 1972. A book of American folk medicine, superstitions, and incantations—an almanac of information "not to be found anywhere else in the world." (M,U)

How the People Sang the Mountains Up, written by Maria Leach and illustrated by Glen Rounds. New York: Viking Press, 1967. This collection of more than eighty "why" stories from all parts of the world is based on the idea that people have always wondered and told tales about the origin of everything—the earth, living plants and animals, and the human race itself. (M,U)

Hush Little Baby, retold and illustrated by Margot Zemach. New York: Dutton, 1976. An early American lullaby and folk song. (P)

Indian Tales, written by Joseph Raskin and Edith Raskin and illustrated by Helen Siegl. New York: Random House, 1969. "How" and "why" stories handed down by Indian storytellers from various tribes. The stories reveal how the Indians loved and respected nature: "They knew the ways of animals, from the tiniest bird to the fiercest mountain lion. To them everything was alive, not only the deer and the wild flowers, but the mountains and lakes as well." (M,U)

The Rooster Crows, edited and illustrated by Maud and Miska Petersham. New York: Macmillan, 1945. A book of American rhymes, jingles, finger plays, jump-rope rhymes, and counting games—plus "Yankee Doodle." (P)

Stories from Alaska, retold by Edward W. Dolch and Marguerite P. Dolch and illustrated by Carl Heldt. Champaign, Ill.: Garrard, 1961. Twenty tales told by the Indians and Eskimos about their traditions before white settlers came. An easy-to-read book. (P)

Stories from Canada, retold by Edward W. Dolch and Marguerite P. Dolch and illustrated by Gil Miret. Champaign, Ill.: Garrard, 1964. Folk tales from the cultures represented in Canada—Eskimo, Indian, French, and English. An easy-to-read book. (P)

Upstate Downstate, Folk Stories of the Middle Atlantic States, retold by M. Jagendorf and illustrated by Howard Simon. New York: Vanguard Press, 1949. Fifty-seven authentic folk stories that have their origins in the cultures represented in the Middle Atlantic states. (P,M,U)

When Clay Sings, written by Byrd Baylor and illustrated by Tom Bahti. New York: Scribner, 1972. Inspired by pieces of broken pottery. The Indians believe that each piece of pottery is a piece of someone's life and is able to "sing in its own way." (M,U)

The White Archer, written and illustrated by James Houston. New York: Harcourt Brace Jovanovich, 1967. A burning hatred and desire for revenge make the young Eskimo Kungo determined to become a great archer. His teacher, however, helps him to have other values. (M,U)

Bibliography

Allen, Louis A. *Time Before Morning: Art and Myth of the Australian Aborigines*. New York: Thomas Y. Crowell, 1975.

Bailey, Carolyn S. *The Story-Telling Hour*. New York: Dodd, Mead, 1935.

Beatty, Bill. *A Treasury of Australian Folk Tales and Traditions*. London: Ure Smith Pty, 1968.

Bettelheim, Bruno. *The Uses of Enchantment: The Meaning and Importance of Fairy Tales*. New York: Knopf, 1976.

Butler, Francelia. *Sharing Literature with Children: A Thematic Anthology*. New York: McKay, 1977.

Dorson, Richard M. *Folk Legends of Japan*. Rutland, Vt.: Charles E. Tuttle, 1962.

Eberhard, Worlfram. *Folktales of China*. Chicago: University of Chicago Press, 1965.

Glazer, Joan I., and Gurney Williams, III. *Introduction to Children's Literature*. New York: McGraw-Hill, 1979.

Robinson, Herbert Spencer, and Knox Wilson. *Myths and Legends of All Nations*. New York: Doubleday, 1950.

Rudman, Masha Kabakow. *Children's Literature: An Issues Approach*. Lexington, Mass.: D. C. Heath, 1976.

Seki, Keigo. *Folktales of Japan*. Chicago: University of Chicago Press, 1963.

Smith, James A., and Dorothy M. Park. *Word Music and Word Magic: Children's Literature Methods*. Boston: Allyn and Bacon, 1977.

Thompson, Stith. *One Hundred Favorite Folktales*. Bloomington: Indiana University Press, 1974.

Toelken, Barre. *The Dynamics of Folklore*. Boston: Houghton Mifflin, 1979.

Appendix A

Newbery Award Books

1922 *The Story of Mankind* by Hendrik Van Loon (Liveright)

1923 *The Voyages of Doctor Dolittle* by Hugh Lofting (Lippincott)

1924 *The Dark Frigate* by Charles Boardman Hawes (Little, Brown)

1925 *Tales from Silver Lands* by Charles J. Finger (Doubleday)

1926 *Shen of the Sea* by Arthur Bowie Chrisman (Dutton)

1927 *Smoky, the Cowhorse* by Will James (Scribner)

1928 *Gayneck, the Story of a Pigeon* by Dhan Gopal Mukerji (Dutton)

1929 *The Trumpeter of Krakow* by Eric P. Kelly (Macmillan)

1930 *Hitty, Her First Hundred Years* by Rachel Field (Macmillan)

1931 *The Cat Who Went to Heaven* by Elizabeth Coatsworth (Macmillan)

1932 *Waterless Mountain* by Laura Adams Armer (Longmans)

1933 *Young Fu of the Upper Yangtze* by Elizabeth Foreman Lewis (Holt, Rinehart and Winston)

1934 *Invincible Louisa* by Cornelia Meigs (Little, Brown)

1935 *Dobry* by Monica Shannon (Viking Press)

1936 *Caddie Woodlawn* by Carol Ryrie Brink (Macmillan)

1937 *Roller Skates* by Ruth Sawyer (Viking Press)

1938 *The White Stag* by Kate Seredy (Viking Press)

1939 *Thimble Summer* by Elizabeth Enright (Holt, Rinehart and Winston)

1940 *Daniel Boone* by James H. Daugherty (Viking Press)

1941 *Call It Courage* by Armstrong Sperry (Macmillan)

1942 *The Matchlock Gun* by Walter D. Edmonds (Dodd, Mead)

1943 *Adam of the Road* by Elizabeth Janet Gray (Viking Press)

1944 *Johnny Tremain* by Esther Forbes (Houghton Mifflin)

1945 *Rabbit Hill* by Robert Lawson (Viking Press)

1946 *Strawberry Girl* by Lois Lenski (Lippincott)

1947 *Miss Hickory* by Carolyn Sherwin Bailey (Viking Press)

1948 *The Twenty-One Balloons* by William Pene du Bois (Viking Press)

1949 *King of the Wind* by Marguerite Henry (Rand McNally)

1950 *The Door in the Wall* by Marguerite de Angeli (Doubleday)

1951 *Amos Fortune, Free Man* by Elizabeth Yates (Dutton)

1952 *Ginger Pye* by Eleanor Estes (Harcourt Brace Jovanovich)

1953 *Secret of the Andes* by Ann Nolan Clark (Viking Press)

1954 *. . . and now Miguel* by Joseph Krumgold (Crowell)

1955 *The Wheel on the School* by Meindert DeJong (Harper & Row)

1956 *Carry On, Mr. Bowditch* by Jean Lee Latham (Houghton Mifflin)

1957 *Miracles on Maple Hill* by Virginia Sorensen (Harcourt Brace Jovanovich)

1958 *Rifles for Waite* by Harold Keith (Crowell)

1959 *The Witch of Blackbird Pond* by Elizabeth George Speare (Houghton Mifflin)

1960 *Onion John* by Joseph Krumgold (Crowell)

1961 *Island of the Blue Dolphins* by Scott O'Dell (Houghton Mifflin)

1962 *The Bronze Bow* by Elizabeth George Speare (Houghton Mifflin)

1963 *A Wrinkle in Time* by Madeleine L'Engle (Farrar, Straus & Giroux)

1964 *It's like This, Cat* by Emily Neville (Harper & Row)

1965 *Shadow of a Bull* by Maia Wojciechowska (Atheneum)

1966 *I, Juan de Pareja* by Elizabeth Borten de Trevino (Farrar, Straus & Giroux)

1967 *Up a Road Slowly* by Irene Hunt (Follett)

1968 *From the Mixed-Up Files of Mrs. Basil E. Frankweiler* by E. L. Konigsburg (Atheneum)

1969 *The High King* by Lloyd Alexander (Holt, Rinehart and Winston)

1970 *Sounder* by William H. Armstrong (Harper & Row)

1971 *Summer of the Swans* by Betsy Byars (Viking Press)

1972 *Mrs. Frisby and the Rats of NIMH* by Robert C. O'Brien (Atheneum)

1973 *Julie of the Wolves* by Jean Craighead George (Harper & Row)

1974 *The Slave Dancer* by Paula Fox (Bradbury Press)

1975 *M. C. Higgins, the Great* by Virginia Hamilton (Macmillan)

1976 *The Grey King* by Susan Cooper (Atheneum)

1977 *Roll of Thunder, Hear My Cry* by Mildred D. Taylor (Dial Press)

1978 *Bridge to Terabithia* by Katherine Paterson (Crowell)

1979 *The Westing Game* by Ellen Raskin (Dutton)

1980 *A Gathering of Days* by Joan W. Blos (Scribner)

1981 *Jacob Have I Loved* by Katherine Paterson (Crowell)

1982 *A Visit to William Blake's Inn: Poems for Innocent and Experienced Travelers* by Nancy Willard (Harcourt)

1983 *Dicey's Song* by Cynthia Voight (Atheneum)

1984 *Dear Mr. Henshaw* by Beverly Cleary (Morrow)

Appendix B

Caldecott Award Books

1938 *Animals of the Bible*, illustrated by Dorothy O. Lathrop (Lippincott)

1939 *Mei Li* by Thomas Handforth (Doubleday)

1940 *Abraham Lincoln* by Ingri d'Aulaire and Edgar Parin d'Aulaire (Doubleday)

1941 *They Were Strong and Good* by Robert Lawson (Viking Press)

1942 *Make Way for Ducklings* by Robert McCloskey (Viking Press)

1943 *The Little House* by Virginia Lee Burton (Houghton Mifflin)

1944 *Many Moons* by James Thurber, illustrated by Louis Slobodkin (Harcourt Brace Jovanovich)

1945 *Prayer for a Child* by Rachel Field, illustrated by Elizabeth Orton Jones (Macmillan)

1946 *The Rooster Crows* by Maud Petersham and Miska Petersham (Macmillan)

1947 *The Little Island* by Golden MacDonald, illustrated by Leonard Weisgard (Doubleday)

1948 *White Snow, Bright Snow* by Alvin Tresselt, illustrated by Roger Duvoisin (Lothrop)

1949 *The Big Snow* by Berta Hader and Elmer Hader (Macmillan)

1950 *Song of the Swallows* by Leo Politi (Scribner)

1951 *The Egg Tree* by Katherine Milhous (Scribner)

1952 *Finders Keepers* by Will (William Lipkind), illustrated by Nicolas (Nicolas Mordvinoff) (Harcourt Brace Jovanovich)

1953 *The Biggest Bear* by Lynd Ward (Houghton Mifflin)

1954 *Madeline's Rescue* by Ludwig Bemelmans (Viking Press)

1955 *Cinderella* by Charles Perrault, illustrated by Marcia Brown (Scribner)

1956 *Frog Went A-Courtin'* by John Langstaff, illustrated by Feodor Rojankovsky (Harcourt Brace Jovanovich)

1957 *A Tree Is Nice* by Janice May Udry, illustrated by Marc Simont (Harper & Row)

1958 *Time of Wonder* by Robert McCloskey (Viking Press)

1959 *Chanticleer and the Fox*, written and illustrated by Barbara Cooney (Crowell)

1960 *Nine Days to Christmas* by Marie Hall Ets and Aurora Labastida (Viking Press)

1961 *Baboushka and the Three Kings* by Ruth Robbins, illustrated by Nicholas Sidjakov (Parnassus)

1962 *Once a Mouse* by Marcia Brown (Scribner)

1963 *The Snowy Day* by Ezra Jack Keats (Viking Press)

1964 *Where the Wild Things Are* by Maurice Sendak (Harper & Row)

1965 *May I Bring a Friend?* by Beatrice Schenk de Regniers, illustrated by Beni Montresor (Atheneum)

1966 *Always Room for One More* by Sorche Nic Leodhas, illustrated by Nonny Hogrogian (Holt, Rinehart and Winston)

1967 *Sam, Bangs, and Moonshine* by Evaline Ness (Holt, Rinehart and Winston)

1968 *Drummer Hoff* by Barbara Emberley, illustrated by Ed Emberley (Prentice-Hall)

1969 *The Fool of the World and the Flying Ship* by Arthur Ransome, illustrated by Uri Shulevitz (Farrar, Straus & Giroux)

1970 *Sylvester and the Magic Pebble* by William Steig (Windmill Books)

1971 *A Story—A Story* by Gail E. Haley (Atheneum)

1972 *One Fine Day* by Nonny Hogrogian (Macmillan)

1973 *The Funny Little Woman* by Arlene Mosel, illustrated by Blair Lent (Dutton)

1974 *Duffy and the Devil* by Harve Zemach, illustrated by Margot Zemach (Farrar, Straus & Giroux)

1975 *Arrow to the Sun*, adapted and illustrated by Gerald McDermott (Viking Press)

1976 *Why Mosquitoes Buzz in People's Ears* by Verna Aardema, illustrated by Leo and Diane Dillon (Dial Press)

1977 *Ashanti to Zulu: African Traditions* by Margaret Musgrove, illustrated by Leo and Diane Dillon (Dial Press)

1978 *Noah's Ark* by Peter Spier (Doubleday)

1979 *The Girl Who Loved Wild Horses* by Paul Goble (Bradbury Press)

1980 *Ox-Cart Man* by Donald Hall, illustrated by Barbara Cooney (Viking Press)

1981 *Fables* by Arnold Lobel (Harper & Row)

1982 *Jumanji* by Chris Van Allsburg (Houghton Mifflin)

1983 *Shadow* by Marcia Brown (Scribner)

1984 *The Glorious Flight Across the Channel with Louis Bleriot* by Alice and Martin Provensen (Viking)

Appendix C

Individualization of Instruction Inventory

This inventory is intended for use by teachers and others as they consider the amount and type of individualization of instruction actually occurring in a given classroom. Descriptive ratings on the twenty lettered items below permit the user to make an objective analysis of teaching *as observed*. A teacher may describe himself or have another observer describe him using this inventory.

Circle the number on each five-point scale below that *best* describes the teaching under consideration.

a. Pupils do advanced level or enrichment work.

5	4	3	2	1
Nearly half of the pupils do obviously advanced level or enrichment work.		Several pupils do advanced level or enrichment work.		No pupil does advanced level or enrichment work.

b. The arrangement of furniture promotes flexible groupings.

5	4	3	2	1
Desks and chairs are arranged in varying patterns for a variety of types of work.		At least one special arrangement is provided for group work.		All desks and chairs are arranged in rank-and-file or other uniform pattern.

c. Materials used are at different levels of difficulty.

5	4	3	2	1
All pupils work with materials that reflect different levels of difficulty.		Nearly half the pupils use materials reflecting several different levels of difficulty.		All pupils use the same material.

d. Pupils lead the class or groups within the class.

5	4	3	2	1
Teacher arranges for one or more pupils to lead the class or a group for a substantial period of time.		One or more pupils are permitted to lead the class or a group but only for brief moments.		No pupil is permitted to lead the class or a group.

e. A variety of assignments is made to individuals and small groups.

5	4	3	2	1
Identical assignments are given only to small groups.		Identical assignments are given to all of the class only occasionally.		All pupils are given identical assignments most of the time.

f. Pupils work independently in intra-class groups.

5	4	3	2	1
Pupils work in small groups with little direction for prolonged periods of time.		Most pupils work independently in small groups for short periods of time.		Pupils work in small or large groups under the direction of the teacher at all times.

g. A variety of reference material is in use by both the teacher and the pupil.

5	4	3	2	1
Encyclopedias, dictionaries, atlases, supplementary texts, and other materials that are available are being used extensively.		Encyclopedias, dictionaries, etc., are used but in limited ways.		Little or no reference material is being used.

h. Pupils help each other with their work.

5	4	3	2	1
Pupils frequently help each other in constructive ways.		Pupils help each other on occasion.		Pupils attend strictly to their own individual tasks at all times.

i. Routine duties are being shared by pupils in a planned fashion.

5	4	3	2	1
Systematic procedures are employed to assure each student an opportunity to assume his share of responsibility.		Students have opportunities to share in assuming routine responsibilities; this is not systematic but assured.		There is little or no pupil sharing of routine duties.

j. There is freedom of movement within the class.

5	4	3	2	1
Pupils are permitted to change work stations as needs arise.		Teacher suggests or approves all changes that are made in work stations.		Pupils remain at work stations for nearly all activities.

k. A wide variety of teacher-made materials such as work sheets, games, transparencies, charts, and other aids is in use.

5	4	3	2	1
These materials are used frequently and in great variety.		These materials are used periodically but only in limited variety.		These materials are used sparingly or not at all.

l. Pupils are permitted to help in planning learning activities.

5	4	3	2	1
All pupils are actively involved in short- and long-range planning.		Pupils are permitted to offer suggestions for teacher planning.		Pupils are permitted little or no opportunity to help with planning.

m. Pupil participation is differentiated so as to be active, challenging, and purposeful to each individual.

5	4	3	2	1
All pupils participate actively with purposes that challenge their different abilities.		Pupils participate actively with purposes that challenge most.		Pupils participate passively with purposes that challenge only a few.

n. Intra-class groups vary in size and number to reflect pupil needs.

5	4	3	2	1
Groups range from one person to as much as half the class.		Groups vary in size, but only two or three groups are employed.		No intra-class grouping is employed.

o. A variety of newspapers, pamphlets, and magazines is in use.

5	4	3	2	1
Pupils use a variety of magazines and newspapers as a regular part of their work.		Pupils use a few newspapers and magazines occasionally.		Pupils make little use of any newspapers or magazines.

p. Pupils find and correct their own errors.

5	4	3	2	1
Pupils are encouraged to find and correct their own mistakes and to look for reasons.		The teacher points out errors and asks pupils to correct them.		The teacher finds and corrects mistakes for pupils.

q. Pupils reflect an interest in the classwork.

5	4	3	2	1
Nearly every pupil reflects interest in the assigned work.		Most pupils reflect interest in the assigned work.		Most pupils appear to have little or no interest in assigned work.

r. Intra-class groupings are flexible and task-oriented.

5	4	3	2	1
Small groups are formed and changed frequently to serve a variety of instructional purposes.		Small groups are formed and changed occasionally for some special purpose.		Small groups, if formed, are fairly permanent arrangements retained for months.

s. A variety of library books is in use.

5	4	3	2	1
Pupils use a wide variety of library books both within and outside the classroom.		Pupils use a variety of library books as recreational reading but sparingly for class assignments.		Pupils make limited use of library books.

t. Pupils are held responsible for their own actions.

5	4	3	2	1
The teacher leaves pupils free to carry out assignments independently.		The teacher gives advice to pupils while assignments are being carried out.		The teacher closely directs, checks, and advises pupils while assignments are being carried out.

u. Regular teachers work with individual pupils.

5	4	3	2	1
Teacher works with individuals during each activity for extended periods of time.		Teacher works with individuals during some activities but mostly for brief periods of time.		Teacher does not work on individual basis except for fleeting moments or in emergencies.

v. Special teachers work with individual pupils.

5	4	3	2	1
Special teachers devote most of their time to working on a one-to-one basis.		Special teachers work predominately with small groups but give some time to individuals.		Special teachers work most of the time on a small- or large-group basis.

w. All pupils serve as tutors of others.

5	4	3	2	1
Nearly all pupils serve as tutors on a daily basis.		Most pupils serve as tutors, some on a daily basis, others less frequently.		Few pupils serve as tutors except on an occasional basis.

x. Resource persons are used to assist individual pupils.

5	4	3	2	1
A variety of resource people serve as tutors on a daily basis.		A few resource people serve as tutors on a fairly regular basis.		A few resource people serve as tutors on an occasional basis.

y. Tutorial arrangements are planned and coordinated.

5	4	3	2	1
Tutorial assignments of teachers, pupils, and resource people are planned and coordinated, so confusion or inappropriate activities are rare.		Most tutorial assignments are preplanned and coordinated, but some last-minute arrangements are observed.		Tutorial assignments are coordinated primarily by tutors themselves; preplanning is not clearly evident.

PROFILE FOR INDIVIDUALIZATION

Directions:

Analyze the ratings previously made. Transfer the numerical rating for each item to the corresponding blank below. Sum the ratings for each cluster of items, sum all ratings for the total.

Class_____ No. of Pupils_____ Date_____ Teacher_____

Ratings by_____ Time of Observation_____ to_____

Topic and Subject_____

I. *Intra-Class Grouping*
  Items: b. Furniture arrangement . . . . _____
         f. Independent work . . . . _____
         j. Free movement . . . . _____   I.
         n. Group size . . . . _____
         r. Group flexibility . . . . _____

II. *Variety of Materials*
  Items: c. Different levels . . . . _____
         g. Reference materials . . . . _____
         k. Teacher-made materials . . . . _____   II.
         o. Periodicals . . . . _____
         s. Library books . . . . _____

III. *Pupil Autonomy*
  Items: d. Pupil leadership . . . . _____
         h. Mutual assistance . . . . _____
         l. Pupil planning . . . . _____   III.
         p. Self-evaluation . . . . _____
         t. Pupil responsibility . . . . _____

IV. *Differentiated Assignments*
  Items: a. Advanced or enriched . . . . _____
         e. Variety . . . . _____
         i. Routine duties . . . . _____   IV.
         m. Active, challenging, and purposeful . . . . . _____
         q. Interesting . . . . _____

V. *Tutoring*
  Items: u. Regular teacher . . . . _____
         v. Special teachers . . . . _____
         w. Pupil tutors . . . . _____   V.
         x. Resource tutors . . . . _____
         y. Planned and coordinated . . . . _____

TOTAL INDIVIDUALIZATION . . . . _____

Reprinted from *Elementary English*, March 1973. Copyright © 1973 by the National Council of Teachers of English. Reprinted by permission of the publisher and the authors.

Appendix D

Publishers' Addresses

Abelard-Schuman Ltd.
10 E. 53rd St.
New York, N.Y. 10022

Abingdon Press
201 Eighth Ave. S.
Nashville, Tenn. 37202

Addison-Wesley Publishing
  Co., Inc.
Reading, Mass. 01867

Allyn & Bacon, Inc.
470 Atlantic Ave.
Boston, Mass. 02210

American Book Co.
135 W. 50th St.
New York, N.Y. 10020

American Education
  Publications
1250 Fairwood Ave.
Columbus, Ohio 43216

American Heritage Publishing
  Co., Inc.
10 Rockefeller Plaza
New York, N.Y. 10020

American Library Association
50 E. Huron St.
Chicago, Ill. 60611

Atheneum Publishers
122 East 42nd St.
New York, N.Y. 10017

Atherton Press
70 Fifth Avenue
New York, N.Y. 10011

Ballantine Books, Inc.
201 E. 50th St.
New York, N.Y. 10022

Bantam Books
School and College Division
666 Fifth Ave.
New York, N.Y. 10019

A. S. Barnes & Co., Inc.
Forsgate Dr.
Cranbury, N.J. 08512

Barnes and Noble Books
10 E. 53rd St.
New York, N.Y. 10022

Beacon Press
25 Beacon Street
Boston, Mass. 02108

Beckley-Cardy Co.
1900 N. Narragansett
Chicago, Ill. 60611

Bobbs-Merrill Co., Inc.
4300 West 62nd St.
Indianapolis, Ind. 46206

Bodley Head Ltd.
9 Bow Street
London, England WC2E7AL

R. R. Bowker Co.
1180 Avenue of the Americas
New York, N.Y. 10036

Bowmar, Noble
  Publishers, Inc.
4563 Colorado Blvd.
Los Angeles, Calif. 90039

Bradbury Press, Inc.
2 Overhill Rd.
Scarsdale, N.Y. 10583

George Braziller, Inc.
1 Park Ave.
New York, N.Y. 10016

Broadman Press
127 Ninth Ave. N.
Nashville, Tenn. 37234

Wm. C. Brown Co., Publishers
2460 Kerper Boulevard
Dubuque, Iowa 52001

Burgess Publishing Co.
7108 Ohms Lane
Minneapolis, Minn. 55435

Cambridge University Press
32 E. 57th St.
New York, N.Y. 10022

Center for Applied Research
  in Education
70 Fifth Ave.
New York, N.Y. 10011

Century House
  Publishing, Inc.
Watkins Glen, N.Y. 14891

Chandler & Sharp
  Publishers, Inc.
11A Commercial Blvd.
Novato, Calif. 94947

Children's Book Council
175 Fifth Ave.
New York, N.Y. 10010

Chilton Book Company
Chilton Way
Radnor, Pa. 19089

Citation Press
50 W. 44th St.
New York, N.Y. 10036

William Collins
    Publishers, Inc.
2080 West 117th St.
Cleveland, Ohio 44111

F. E. Compton Co.
425 N. Michigan Ave.
Chicago, Ill. 60611

Coward, McCann and
    Geoghegan, Inc.
200 Madison Ave.
New York, N.Y. 10016

Cowles Book Co.
488 Madison Ave.
New York, N.Y. 10022

Creative Education, Inc.
123 S. Broad St.
Mankato, Minn. 56001

Criterion Books
666 Fifth Ave.
New York, N.Y. 10019

Crowell-Collier
866 Third Ave.
New York, N.Y. 10022

Thomas Y. Crowell Co.,
    Publishers
666 Fifth Ave.
New York, N.Y. 10019

Crown Publishers, Inc.
1 Park Ave.
New York, N.Y. 10016

John Day Co.
257 Park Ave. South
New York, N.Y. 10010

Delacorte Press
Dell Publishing Co., Inc.
1 Dag Hammarskjold Plaza
New York, N.Y. 10017

Dial Press
1 Dag Hammarskjold Plaza
New York, N.Y. 10017

Dillon Press, Inc.
500 S. Third St.
Minneapolis, Minn. 55415

Dodd, Mead & Co.
79 Madison Ave.
New York, N.Y. 10016

Doubleday and Co., Inc.
245 Park Ave.
New York, N.Y. 10017

Dover Publications, Inc.
180 Varick St.
New York, N.Y. 10014

Gerald Duckworth & Co. Ltd.
436 Glouster Crescent
London, England NW170V

Dufour Editions, Inc.
Chester Springs, Pa. 19425

E. P. Dutton & Co.
2 Park Ave.
New York, N.Y. 10016

Educational Technology
    Publications
140 Sylvan Ave.
Englewood Cliffs, N.J. 07632

Encyclopaedia Britannica, Inc.
425 N. Michigan Ave.
Chicago, Ill. 60611

M. Evans and Co., Inc.
216 E. 49th St.
New York, N.Y. 10017

Eye Gate House
146-01 Archer Ave.
Jamaica, N.Y. 10017

Faber and Faber Ltd.
3 Queen Square
London, England WCIN3AV

Farrar, Straus & Giroux, Inc.
19 Union Sq. W.
New York, N.Y. 10003

F. W. Faxon Co., Inc.
15 Southwest Park
Westwood, Mass. 02090

Fearon Pitman Publishers, Inc.
6 Davis Drive
Belmont, Calif. 94002

Field Enterprises
    Educational Corp.
510 Merchandise Mart Plaza
Chicago, Ill. 60654

Follett Publishing Co.
1010 W. Washington Blvd.
Chicago, Ill. 60607

Four Winds Press
50 W. 44th St.
New York, N.Y. 10021

Franklin Publishing Co.
2047 Locust St.
Philadelphia, Pa. 19103

Free Press
866 Third Ave.
New York, N.Y. 10022

Funk & Wagnalls Inc.
55 E. 77th St.
New York, N.Y. 10021

Garrard Publishing Co.
1607 N. Market St.
Champaign, Ill. 61820

Ginn and Co.
191 Spring St.
Lexington, Mass. 02173

Golden Gate Junior Books
1224 W. Van Buren St.
Chicago, Ill. 60607

Golden Press
1220 Mound Ave.
Racine, Wis. 53404

Grade Teacher
P. O. Box 225
Cortland, N.Y. 13045

Greenwillow Books
105 Madison Ave.
New York, N.Y. 10016

Grosset and Dunlap, Inc.
51 Madison Ave.
New York, N.Y. 10010

Grossman Publishers
44 W. 56th St.
New York, N.Y. 10019

Hammond, Inc.
515 Valley St.
Maplewood, N.J. 07040

Harcourt Brace
　Jovanovich, Inc.
757 Third Ave.
New York, N.Y. 10017

Harper & Row,
　Publishers, Inc.
10 E. 53rd St.
New York, N.Y. 10022

Harvey House, Publishers
20 Waterside Plaza
New York, N.Y. 10010

Hastings House
　Publishers, Inc.
10 E. 40th St.
New York, N.Y. 10016

Hawthorn Books, Inc.
260 Madison Ave.
New York, N.Y. 10016

D. C. Heath and Co.
125 Spring St.
Lexington, Mass. 02173

Hill & Wang
19 Union Sq. W.
New York, N.Y. 10003

Holbrook Press
470 Atlantic Ave.
Boston, Mass. 02210

Holiday House, Inc.
18 E. 53rd St.
New York, N.Y. 10022

Holt, Rinehart and Winston
383 Madison Ave.
New York, N.Y. 10017

Horn Book, Inc.
Park Square Bldg.
31 St. James Ave.
Boston, Mass. 02116

Houghton Mifflin Co., Inc.
2 Park St.
Boston, Mass. 02107

International Reading Assoc.
P. O. Box 695
Newark, Del. 19711

Island Heritage Ltd.
828 Fort St. Mall
Suite 400
Honolulu, Hawaii 96813

Alfred A. Knopf, Inc.
201 E. 50th St.
New York, N.Y. 10022

Lerner Publications Co.
241 First Ave. N.
Minneapolis, Minn. 55401

Library Association
7 Ridgemount St.
London, England WCIE7AE

Library of Congress
Washington, D.C. 20540

Lion Books
111 E. 39th St.
New York, N.Y. 10016

J. B. Lippincott Co.
521 Fifth Ave.
New York, N.Y. 10017

Little, Brown and Co.
34 Beacon St.
Boston, Mass 02106

Longmans, Green & Co.
55 Fifth Ave.
New York, N.Y. 10003

Lothrop, Lee & Shepard
　Books
105 Madison Ave.
New York, N.Y. 10016

McCutchan Publishing Corp.
2526 Grove St.
Berkeley, Calif. 94704

McGraw-Hill Book Co.
1221 Avenue of the Americas
New York, N.Y. 10020

David McKay Co., Inc.
2 Park Ave.
New York, N.Y. 10016

McKinley Publishing Co.
P. O. Box 77
Ocean City, N.J. 08226

Macmillan, Inc.
866 Third Ave.
New York, N.Y. 10022

Mentor Press
New American Library, Inc.
1633 Broadway
New York, N.Y. 10019

Meredith Corp.
1716 Locust St.
Des Moines, Iowa 50336

G. & C. Merriam Co.
47 Federal St.
Springfield, Mass. 01101

Charles E. Merrill
　Publishing Co.
1300 Alum Creek Dr.
Columbus, Ohio 43216

Julian Messner
1230 Avenue of the Americas
New York, N.Y. 10020

William Morrow & Co., Inc.
105 Madison Ave.
New York, N.Y. 10016

National Council of Teachers
　of English
1111 Kenyon Road
Urbana, Ill. 61801

National Education
　Association Publishing
1201 16th St. N.W.
Washington, D.C. 20036

Natural History Press
277 Park Ave.
New York, N.Y. 10017

Thomas Nelson, Inc.
407 Seventh Ave. S.
Nashville, Tenn. 37203

New American Library, Inc.
1633 Broadway
New York, N.Y. 10019

New York Graphic Society
  Books
41 Mt. Vernon St.
Boston, Mass. 02106

W. W. Norton & Co., Inc.
500 Fifth Ave.
New York, N.Y. 10036

Oddo Publishing, Inc.
Storybook Acres
Beauregard Blvd.
Fayetteville, Ga. 30214

F. A. Owen Publishing Co.
Dansville, N.Y. 14437

Oxford University Press, Inc.
200 Madison Ave.
New York, N.Y. 10016

Paddington Press Ltd.
95 Madison Ave.
New York, N.Y. 10016

Palo Verde Publishing Co.
609 N. Fourth Ave.
Tucson, Ariz. 85716

Pantheon Books, Inc.
201 E. 50th St.
New York, N.Y. 10022

Parnassus Press
P. O. Box 8443
Emeryville, Calif. 94608

Parents' Magazine Press
52 Vanderbilt Ave.
New York, N.Y. 10017

Penguin Books, Inc.
625 Madison Ave.
New York, N.Y. 10022

Pergamon Press, Inc.
Maxwell House
Fairview Park
Elmsford, N.Y. 10523

Personalized Reading Center
Xerox Education Center
Columbus, Ohio 43216

Personnel Press
191 Spring Street
Lexington, Mass. 02173

Peter Pauper Press
135 W. 50th St.
New York, N.Y. 10020

S. G. Phillips, Inc.
305 W. 86th St.
New York, N.Y. 10024

Pitman Publishing Co.
6 Davis Dr.
Belmont, Calif. 94002

Platt and Munk Co.
1055 Bronx River Ave.
Bronx, N.Y. 10472

Pocket Books
1230 Avenue of the Americas
New York, N.Y. 10020

Praeger Publishers
521 Fifth Ave.
New York, N.Y. 10007

Prentice-Hall, Inc.
Englewood Cliffs, N.J. 07632

G. P. Putnam's Sons
200 Madison Ave.
New York, N.Y. 10016

Harlin Quist Books
1 Dag Hammarskjold Plaza
New York, N.Y. 10017

Rand McNally & Co.
8255 Central Park Ave.
Skokie, Ill. 60076

Random House
201 E. 50th St.
New York, N.Y. 10022

Regnery/Gateway, Inc.
Box 207
South Bend, Ind. 46624

St. Martin's Press, Inc.
175 Fifth Ave.
New York, N.Y. 10010

W. B. Saunders Co.
West Washington Square
Philadelphia, Pa. 19105

Scarecrow Press
52 Liberty St.
Metuchen, N.J. 08840

Schocken Books, Inc.
200 Madison Ave.
New York, N.Y. 10016

Scholastic Books, Inc.
200 Madison Ave.
New York, N.Y. 10036

Scholastic Book Services
Scholastic Magazines, Inc.
50 W. 44th St.
New York, N.Y. 10036

Scholastic Productions
Pleasantville, N.Y. 10570

Science Research Associates
155 N. Wacker Dr.
Chicago, Ill. 60606

Scott, Foresman & Co.
1900 E. Lake Ave.
Glenview, Ill. 60025

Charles Scribner's Sons
597 Fifth Ave.
New York, N.Y. 10017

Scroll Press, Inc.
559 W. 26th St.
New York, N.Y. 10001

Seabury Press, Inc.
815 Second Ave.
New York, N.Y. 10017

Silver Burdett Co.
250 James St.
Morristown, N.J. 07960

Signet Books
New American Library, Inc.
1633 Broadway
New York, N.Y. 10019

Simon and Schuster, Inc.
1230 Avenue of the Americas
New York, N.Y. 10020

Stackpole Books
Cameron and Kelker Sts.
Harrisburg, Pa. 17105

Sterling Publishing Co., Inc.
2 Park Ave.
New York, N.Y. 10016

Taplinger Publishing Co.
200 Park Ave. South
New York, N.Y. 10003

Teachers College Press
Columbia University
1234 Amsterdam Ave.
New York, N.Y. 10027

Time-Life Books, Inc.
Alexandria, Va. 22314

Tudor Publishing Co.
31 W. 46th St.
New York, N.Y. 10036

Charles E. Tuttle Co., Inc.
28 S. Main St.
Rutland, Vt. 05701

U.S. Government
  Printing Office
Washington, D.C. 20401

Van Nostrand Reinhold Co.
135 W. 50th St.
New York, N.Y. 10020

Vanguard Press, Inc.
424 Madison Ave.
New York, N.Y. 10017

Viking Press
625 Madison Ave.
New York, N.Y. 10022

Henry Z. Walck, Inc.
2 Park Ave.
New York, N.Y. 10016

Walker and Co.
720 Fifth Ave.
New York, N.Y. 10019

Frederick Warne & Co., Inc.
2 Park Ave.
New York, N.Y. 10016

Washington Square Press
1230 Avenue of the Americas
New York, N.Y. 10020

Watson-Guptill Publications
1515 Broadway
New York, N.Y. 10036

Franklin Watts, Inc.
730 Fifth Ave.
New York, N.Y. 10019

Western Publishing Co., Inc.
1220 Mound Ave.
Racine, Wis. 53404

Westminster Press
925 Chestnut St.
Philadelphia, Pa. 19107

David White, Inc.
14 Vanderventer Ave.
Port Washington, N.Y. 11050

Albert Whitman & Co.
560 West Lake St.
Chicago, Ill. 60606

John Wiley & Sons, Inc.
605 Third Ave.
New York, N.Y. 10016

Windmill Books, Inc.
1230 Avenue of the Americas
New York, N.Y. 10020

Xerox Education Publications
245 Long Hill Rd.
Middletown, Conn. 06457

Yale University Press
302 Temple St.
New Haven, Conn. 06511

Young Scott Books
Addison-Wesley Publishing
  Co., Inc.
Reading, Mass. 01867

Index

Reading readiness, *continued*
  disparity in, 180
  what it is, 181
Reading vocabulary, 213
Real Mother Goose, The (Wright), 228
Receptive skills in language arts, 2
Recipes, 93–95
Record keeping
  of reading, 48–50, 56, 57
  of spelling progress, 124, 125
Records, for libraries, 293
Reed, Gwendolyn, 361
References, in language arts unit plan, 21,
  23, 25
Reflections on a Gift of Watermelon Pickle
  (Dunning, Lueders, and Smith), 248
Registers of language, 145–148, 153
Repetition in propaganda, 217
Reports
  book, 49–50
  informational, 90
  oral, 12, 90
Resource centers, items in, 43
Resource persons for creative writing, 164
Respect, need for, 313–314
Rey, Hans A., 176
Rhyme in classroom poems, 234
Rhyme time, 71
Rhythm in classroom poems, 233
Richards, Laura E., 230, 238, 240
Riddle Pot, The (Wiesner), 104
Riddle Walk (Moore), 97
Riddles, telling, 96–97
Rimanelli, Giose, 242, 248
Robbins, Ruth, 360
Robbut: A Tale of Tails (Lawson), 76, 81
Robinson, Richard D., 206n
Roche, A. K., 247
Rod puppets, 258
Roll of Thunder, Hear My Cry (Taylor),
  346
Rooster Crows, The (Petersham and
  Petersham), 104, 365
Root, Shelton L., Jr., 249
Rorshach projections, creative writing
  about, 165–166
Roser, Nancy, 206n
Ross, Laura, 275
Rosten, Leo, 202, 203
Rounds, Glen, 103, 364
Runaway Bunny, The (Brown), 175
Ruskin, John, 50
Russian Stories and Legends (Tolstoy), 361

Safety needs, as basic, 312–313
Salt (Zemach), 276
"Salute to Trees, A" (van Dyke), 272–273
Sam, Bangs, and Moonshine (Ness), 346
Sandburg, Carl, 50, 230, 235
Sanders, David C., 43n
Savage, John F., 87, 97n, 310
Sawyer, Ruth, 5, 93
Schechter, Ben, 301
Scherr, Julian, 93
Schillinger, Julius F., 244
Schindelman, Joseph, 100

Schultz, Charles, 97
Schwartz, Alvin, 104
Scope and sequence in phonics, 209
Scrapbooks, 174
Scripts for puppet shows, 261–265
  adapted from children's literature,
  262–263
  published, 261–262
  pupil written, 262
Scripts for readers theatre, 266–268
Sculpture, for libraries, 293
Sea Star, Orphan of Chincoteague (Henry),
  62
Seashore Story (Yashima), 327
Seasonal words, spelling, 120, 121
Sebesta, Sam L., 318–319
Secret Garden, The (Burnett), 327
See My Lovely Poison Ivy (Moore), 248
Selden, George, 301
Self, Maslow concepts about, 315–317
Self-actualization, characteristics of, 317
Self-actualization needs, 315–318
  of Abraham Lincoln, 316
  of Albert Einstein, 316
  of Albert Schweitzer, 316
  of Aldous Huxley, 316
  of Baruch Spinoza, 316
  of Eleanor Roosevelt, 316
  of Jane Addams, 316
  of Thomas Jefferson, 316
  of William James, 316
Sendak, Maurice, 12, 104, 124, 154, 175,
  191, 198, 247, 262, 276, 301,
  319, 320
  books by, 127, 128–129
  profile of, 126–127
Sense appeal, in classroom poetry,
  237–238
Sentence activities, 204
Sentence diagrams
  in structural grammar, 141
  in traditional grammar, 138, 139, 141
Sentence holder, 204
Sentence patterns in structural grammar,
  140
Sentence strips, 204
Sentences
  arrangement of, 138, 152–153
  generating, 142
Service, Robert W., 240
Service words, 118, 186
  in spelling, 118–119
Seven Stories by Hans Christian Andersen
  (Carle), 276
Sewell, Helen, 176
Sex-appeal propaganda, 217
Shakespeare, William, 73–74
Shape, letter legibility and, 12, 109–110
Shape words, 167–168
Shelley, Percy Bysshe, 227
Shen of the Sea (Chrisman), 361
Shepard, Ernest, 248
Shepherd, Tony, 304n
Sherman, Harriet, 248
Shulevitz, Uri, 81
Shurtleff, Cynthia, 334

"Sick" (Silverstein), 236
Sidjakov, Nicholas, 360
Siegl, Helen, 364
Sight vocabulary, 185, 213
Sight words, 185–187, 202, 204–205
Silverstein, Alvin, 128
Silverstein, Shel, 230, 236, 249
Silverstein, Virginia B., 128
Simmen, René, 256n, 257n
Simon, Howard, 365
Simont, Marc, 199, 200
Sing Down the Moon (O'Dell), 223
Size, letter legibility and, 12, 110
Slang, 146–148
Slant, letter legibility and, 12, 111–113
Sledd, James, 139
Slides
  for libraries, 16, 293
  making, 299
  teaching with, 298–299
Slobin, Dan, 135
Slobodkin, Louis, 327
Slobodkina, Esphyr, 199
Slogans, in propaganda, 217
Slovenly Peter, 306, 308–309
Small Plays for Special Days (Alexander),
  276
Smeller Martin (Lawson), 81
Smith, Hugh, 248
Smith, James A., 237, 350
Smith, Susan Carlton, 247
Smith, Vincent D., 363
"Snail" (Hughes), 240
Sneetches and Other Stories, The (Geisel),
  104
"Snow in the City" (Field), 226
Social content of reading textbooks, 306
Sock puppets, 258, 259
Solbert, Bonnie, 345
Solbert, Loni, 362
Solbert, Ronni, 242
Some Swell Pup (Sendak and Margolis),
  128–129
Something Special (De Regniers), 248
Songs, for language arts unit, 30, 31
Sound barrels/boxes, 70
Sounder (Armstrong), 314–315, 327
Sounds, of animals, 74
South America, folk tales from, 363
Spache, Evelyn B., 213n
Spache, George D., 213
Spacing, letter legibility and, 12, 110–111
Spanish-speaking students, 338
Speaking, 2–3
Speaking skills, 84
  activities to improve, 87–97
  checklist for evaluating, 99, 100
  evaluating, 97–100
  setting for learning, 84–85
Speaking vocabulary, 213
Special education, for the handicapped,
  331
Special needs, in language arts learning,
  17, 329–347
Special-needs children, kinds of, 330, 331
Specialization, self-direction and, 45